THE SOUTHERN AGRARIANS
AND THE NEW DEAL

Essays after I'll Take My Stand

THE PUBLICATIONS OF THE
SOUTHERN TEXTS SOCIETY

Michael O'Brien, Editor

THE SOUTHERN AGRARIANS AND THE NEW DEAL

Essays after I'll Take My Stand

EDITED BY EMILY S. BINGHAM
AND THOMAS A. UNDERWOOD

Published for the Southern Texts Society
by the University Press of Virginia
Charlottesville and London

THE UNIVERSITY PRESS OF VIRGINIA

© 2001 by the Southern Texts Society

All rights reserved

Printed in the United States of America

First published 2001

♾ The paper used in this publication meets the minimum requirements
of the American National Standard for Information Sciences—Permanence
of Paper for Printed Library Materials, ANSI Z39.48-1984.

Library of Congress Cataloging-in-Publication Data

The southern Agrarians and the New Deal : essays after I'll take my stand /
edited by Emily S. Bingham, Thomas A. Underwood.

    p. cm. — (The publications of the Southern Texts Society)

    Includes bibliographical references and index.

    ISBN 0-8139-1995-9 (cloth : alk. paper)

    1. Southern States—Politics and government—1865–1950.
2. Agrarians (Group of writers) 3. Southern States—Intellectual
life—1865– 4. Authors, American—Southern States—Political and
social views. 5. Conservatism—Southern States—History—20th
century. 6. Southern States—Social conditions—1865–1945.
7. Industrialization—Social aspects—Southern States—History—
20th century. 8. Land reform—Southern States—History—20th
century. 9. New Deal, 1933–1939—Southern States. I. Bingham,
Emily. II. Underwood, Thomas A. III. Series.

F215 .S686 2001

975'.04—dc21   00-051256

Contents

Illustrations

Abbreviations

BOOKS

IAS   Michael O'Brien, *The Idea of the American South, 1920–1941* (Baltimore, 1979)

ITMS   Twelve Southerners, *I'll Take My Stand: The South and the Agrarian Tradition* (1930; rept., with an introduction by Louis D. Rubin Jr. and biographical essays by Virginia Rock [Baton Rouge, 1977])

LC   *The Literary Correspondence of Donald Davidson and Allen Tate,* ed. John Tyree Fain and Thomas Daniel Young (Athens, Ga., 1974)

SA   Paul K. Conkin, *The Southern Agrarians* (Knoxville, 1988)

WOA   Herbert Agar and Allen Tate, eds., *Who Owns America? A New Declaration of Independence* (Boston, 1936)

JOURNALS

AHR   *American Historical Review*
AR   *American Review*
JAH   *Journal of American History*
MQ   *Mississippi Quarterly*
NR   *New Republic*
SAQ   *South Atlantic Quarterly*
SR   *Southern Review*
VQR   *Virginia Quarterly Review*

Acknowledgments

The editors wish to thank a number of people for their assistance with this project, which took shape in 1990. For permission to reprint articles, we are grateful to Helen Ransom Forman, the late Andrew Lytle, Mrs. H. Clarence Nixon, the late Harriet C. Owsley, and Helen Tate. Michael O'Brien secured funding to cover word-processing costs and made available his own research assistant. A faculty development grant came thanks to Ann Muth of Nassau Community College (SUNY), who secured funds from the NCC Foundation. Joseph Palmore typed articles onto disks. For stimulating discussions about the Agrarians, we thank our students and colleagues at the various institutions where we have taught. (Thomas A. Underwood delivered a portion of the introduction in different form as "Allen Tate and the Bifurcated Historiography of Southern Agrarianism: Thoughts on the Limits of the 'New Historicism'" at Harvard University in February 1992.)

The reference works we consulted are too numerous to cite here, but a few deserve special mention: *Who Was Who in America,* the *Encyclopedia of Southern Culture,* 4 vols. (ed. Charles Reagan Wilson and William Ferris), and James D. Hart's *Oxford Companion to American Literature,* 5th ed.

A number of scholars helped with citations or offered criticism: Alan Brinkley, Fred Hobson, Peter F. Walker, James Ralph, Ben Johnson, Caldwell Titcomb, W. Fitzhugh Brundage, and an anonymous reader for the Southern Texts Society. Reference librarians at Harvard College, especially Steve Love, generously helped track down obscure allusions. The thoroughness of Michael O'Brien's editing sharpened the final product, for which we thank him. We are grateful to Gary Kessler and the staff at the University Press of Virginia for their work in bringing the manuscript to completion.

Last but by no means least, we express great gratitude to our spouses for living patiently with us in the present during our extended excursion into the past.

Editorial Method

This volume is one in a series commissioned by the Southern Texts Society, founded in 1988 to publish book-length volumes of primary documents or rare printed texts, and to advance understanding of "the culture of the American South and its expressive life." That there have been competing and often conflicting voices in the formation of that culture is implicit to the group's mission. The Agrarian movement, which generated as much controversy among intellectuals during the half century following its demise as it did in the half-dozen years of its life span, touched upon the issues that set the terms of the twentieth-century debate over Southern distinctiveness and continuity. Yet while there are shelves full of secondary works and monographs on Agrarians, the publication of primary documents—essential to a full evaluation of the movement—has lagged behind.

The volume is fully annotated. We have identified writers, events, and politicians when we believed that doing so would assist readers not conversant in the various political and literary discourses of the 1920s and 1930s. Because we are historians, and because we hope to clarify the way the Agrarians absorbed, interpreted, and manipulated narratives of American history, we have also written notes identifying and elaborating on the historical works and schools of thought they drew upon. Whenever an Agrarian text drew its evidence from severely dated or racist historical interpretations, we provided citations of later works (or current secondary literature) that offer corrective evidence. Both in our notes and in our prefaces, we have given biographical information on the essayists when it seemed to illuminate the personal circumstances under which particular essays were written. However, we refrained from adding extensive biographical background, since this volume is foremost a primary source that will facilitate secondary synthesis. Each selection opens with a preface that places the essay within the context of the Agrarian movement, provides a brief summary of its essential argument, and identifies specific events that were, for some articles, their direct inspiration.

We reprinted the articles in full, silently correcting small errors of fact, quotation, or attribution made when the authors transcribed material. In most cases, brackets within the text of the essays denote our editorial additions. The Agrarians and some of the editors they wrote for anglicized spellings and punctuation, both of which we have normalized according to current standards in the United States. Since the essayists often cited dates in ways that might be unfamiliar to modern readers, we converted them to standard style.

The table of contents, in which the essays are grouped chronologically by author, results from our view that the movement is most accurately reconstructed as an evolving debate among distinct individual intellectuals. Readers will detect considerable variation, some tension, and occasional contradiction among the essayists. The angle of Agrarianism shifts, depending upon which writer one reads. In choosing essays, we were guided by the desire to present such inconsistencies in the Agrarians' thought without losing sight of the many ideas about which they agreed. When we reprint articles published before the New Deal era, which we are defining as the years 1933 to 1939, it is to provide essential background information on the Agrarian movement.

Several times, we found that authors made minor revisions to an essay and republished it under a new title. In such cases, and when two different articles by the same writer seemed to overlap to a great degree, we chose the stronger and usually the longer piece. A few of the essays have already appeared in *Who Owns America?*, which is out of print and not often read. None of *I'll Take My Stand*, which remains in print by Louisiana State University Press, is included here.

THE SOUTHERN AGRARIANS
AND THE NEW DEAL

Essays after I'll Take My Stand

Introduction

On 14 November 1930, sixty-five years after the battle of Appomattox, thirty-five hundred people squeezed into the Richmond City Auditorium to consider their future. The *Richmond Times-Dispatch* was promising a vigorous debate between two men on the fate of the Southern United States. Would the South continue to embrace the industrialism, modernization, and finance capitalism Northerners accepted as a matter of course? Or would twentieth-century Southerners rededicate themselves to the culture, politics, and world views associated with their agrarian origins? Following the lead of the powerful editor H. L. Mencken, who attended that evening with the mayor of Richmond and Virginia's governor, many Americans believed that the agrarian South was no more than a brainless backwater, a "Sahara of the Bozart." With the Great Depression worsening daily, the Southern economy in tatters, and an illiteracy rate nearly double the nation's, more than a few Southerners were beginning to wonder whether the South was even worth saving as a distinctive region and culture.[1]

Virginians who knew something of the Southerners about to debate might have wondered how one came to be more committed to traditionalism than the other. John Crowe Ransom and his opponent, Stringfellow Barr, were both professors at conservative Southern universities. The two men, however, were notably cosmopolitan. After tasting European culture as Rhodes scholars and gaining prominence in the world of letters (Ransom as a poet and Barr as a historian), neither man could be characterized as provincial in his intellectual interests. Yet like the moderator of their debate, Sherwood

Anderson—who spent years writing short stories exposing the grotesque features of small-town America but wound up retreating to rural Virginia to edit country newspapers—they retained intense native loyalties.

Where the two debaters differed was in their attitude toward the rise of industry in the South. In this regard, Ransom made himself known that night as a clear defender of traditionalism. Representing the Agrarians, a group of Southern conservatives who had recently emerged from Nashville's Vanderbilt University to enter the national limelight, Ransom made bold to claim that a world without "progress" was superior to the economy so cherished by urban Northerners. The same argument appeared in *I'll Take My Stand: The South and the Agrarian Tradition,* a book of essays the Agrarians published that year. In the book, Ransom and eleven other Southerners advocated "a Southern way of life against what may be called the American or prevailing way," a difference they described as "Agrarian *versus* Industrial." The Agrarians had not yet worked out an economic program in support of their beliefs, but they were certain that farming, "the best and most sensitive of vocations," ought to "have the economic preference and enlist the maximum number of workers." The Agrarians warned other Southerners against continuing to embrace a soul-destroying world of cities dominated by hideous factories, dehumanizing labor conditions, and cheap commercialism. The South, they urged, must reconsider its roots and take hold of its destiny.[2]

Stringfellow Barr, Ransom's antagonist that evening, conceded that industrialism was no unqualified boon to the South. Half a dozen years earlier, Barr had traveled to the Royal Archives in Belgium to undertake some research, only to find himself absorbed—and horrified—by an account he read of the effects of industrialization in the province of Namur during the early nineteenth century. After studying the labor system in their factories, officials in Namur had voted to stop hiring children at starvation wages—but only because of the costs associated with extricating dead children from the machinery. Still reeling from the account, Barr wrote an indictment of such capitalist practices and submitted it to the Agrarians, who had enthusiastically asked for an article for *I'll Take My Stand.* But the Vanderbilt men were disappointed to discover that Barr was advocating liberal regulation of industry instead of promoting Southern Agrarianism, and they rejected the article. Barr, who was just then assuming the editorship of the *Virginia Quarterly Review,* revised and published the piece anyway. The essay, "Shall Slavery Come South?," took the Agrarians to task for failing to coexist peacefully with industrialists, precipitating the Richmond debate.[3]

Neither man seemed to win that night in Richmond. Ransom, who warned that Barr's "regulated industrialism" would result in "Russian communism," claimed that his opponent admired traditionalism only "as a gardenia to stick in his buttonhole when he goes traveling to New York."[4] After the debate, another Agrarian claimed, "Ransom won because Barr got angry. Barr's a good fellow, a clever debater, but he has no position. He was arguing for industrialism, but he doesn't believe his own argument."[5] Yet Barr remembered things differently. Ransom, he recalled years later, "spoke less well than he wrote," and his speech was marred by "too much professorial solemnity." Seeing an opportunity for mockery, Barr "turned ironical and ribald," bringing the house down with his concluding line: "When problems are complex, you ought never to cry 'I'll Take My Stand' but 'Sit Down and Think.'" Although Barr was later embarrassed by the way he manipulated the audience, he was still able to conclude: "I think many of my listeners shared my desire not to go to Namur while singing Dixie!"[6]

The debate over Agrarianism would continue, not merely in public forums throughout the South, but in the pages of national periodicals. Many critics of the Agrarians were less interested in defending industrialism than they were in publicizing the disastrous state of agriculture in the South. Reviewing *I'll Take My Stand,* they portrayed the Agrarians as frustrated farmers who romanticized living by the land. Gerald W. Johnson, for instance, asked of the twelve Southerners: "Are they unaware of pellagra and hookworm, two flowers of Southern agrarianism? Have they never been told that the obscenities and depravities of the most degenerate hole of a cotton-mill town are but pale reflections of the lurid obscenities and depravities of Southern backwoods communities?" Southern liberals such as Johnson, who called the Agrarians "the latest cult in Dixie," refused to rally behind a Southern economy that ensnared millions in economically desperate lives of tenancy and sharecropping.[7]

Were it not for the Agrarians' angry reaction to such criticism—and for a dramatic transformation in the American political landscape—Agrarianism would likely have begun and ended with *I'll Take My Stand.* But the failure of the administration of Herbert Hoover and the worsening of the Great Depression helped keep the movement alive well after the book appeared. In 1932, when Franklin D. Roosevelt was elected president of the United States, the Agrarian group found their greatest opportunity to bring their ideas to the public. Fearing that the New Deal would pass them by, half of the original Agrarian group joined the latest national debate over the American economy and began publishing articles defining, refining, and defending a more concrete version of Agrarianism. Well into Roosevelt's second term, when both Agrarianism and the New Deal itself had begun disintegrating, six Agrarians continued to write essays in which they presented themselves as social thinkers whose ideas could and should be translated into public policy. While they never stopped believing that Agrarianism demanded as much of a spiritual conversion among Americans as a political one, they now sought to explain exactly how the South (and the United States as a whole) would benefit from a rejection of monopoly capitalism and its ethos—and from a promotion of small-scale, subsistence agricultural economies.[8]

Students have rarely had access to Agrarian writings of the New Deal era and have consequently assumed that the movement was limited to the philosophy laid out in *I'll Take My Stand*.[9] Conceived in the late 1920s, that book was not explicitly political; it consisted mainly of a philosophical critique of a nation that valued "progress" above spirituality. Indeed, the two principal events that elicited *I'll Take My Stand*—the Scopes anti-evolution trial in 1925 (in which Southern fundamentalists were skewered for backwardness and ignorance) and the humanist movement of Paul Elmer More and Irving Babbitt (which Allen Tate condemned as an effort to secularize religious faith)[10]—were only loosely connected to the redefined Agrarianism that emerged during the New Deal. As the historian Paul K. Conkin has observed, it is "a mistake" to think *I'll Take My Stand* embodies Agrarianism. "The book was, at best," he said, "only a prelude to an organized agrarian movement."[11]

The Southern Agrarians and the New Deal collects not only the Agrarians' policy pronouncements during the 1930s, but also those essays in which the group attempted to define an activist version of Southern conservatism. After the Richmond debate, the inner circle of the Agrarian group began holding planning meetings. They met at Southern writers' conferences, on farms owned by members of the group, and in academic and editorial offices at Southern universities. More than one scholar has observed that during these gatherings, in which already intense bonds of friendship were strengthened over lavish Southern meals, flowing libations, and freewheeling discussion, the Agrarians behaved almost as if they were generals planning a battle.[12] Intoxicated by the notion that they might transform their abstraction of the South into a design for the nation, they conceived and orchestrated a series of political and intellectual skirmishes. They vowed to fight Northeastern historians over any narrative of American history that cast the industrial North as a moral exemplar, to denounce social scientists who claimed to understand Southern social relations, and to battle liberal policymakers who wanted to collectivize—or to corporatize—agriculture in the South. This new interest in politics did not mean they abandoned cultural battles; on the contrary, in order to defend conservative principles, Agrarians continued their more abstract debates with the liberal intellectuals who edited and published in periodicals such as the *New Republic*. Annoyed by the absence of conservative news organs, the Agrarians even discussed founding a weekly newspaper to promote their policies, both agricultural and moral.

By shifting the focus of Agrarianism to the years following *I'll Take My Stand,* this volume hopes to provide readers with a more balanced representation of the movement and to offer a new answer to the critical question: Which of the twelve Southern Agrarians ought to be studied as its architects? The Agrarians most often identified as the movement's true representatives are those who were associated with the Fugitive poetry movement that emerged at Vanderbilt in 1922: John Crowe Ransom (1888–1974), Donald Davidson (1893–1968), Allen Tate (1899–1979), and Robert Penn Warren (1905–89). These so-called Fugitive-Agrarians (the conflated term that still appears in the database of the Modern Language Association) made lasting impressions on the world of literature.[13]

John Crowe Ransom made his mark early with critically acclaimed poetry; after departing Vanderbilt, he founded the *Kenyon Review* in 1939 and became one of the most powerful journal editors in America.[14] Donald Davidson, who remained in Tennessee, was not as successful, but continued to write verse after the Fugitive poetry movement ended in 1925. He served as book review editor for the *Nashville Tennessean* until 1930, eventually achieving modest fame as a poet, essayist, and folklorist. Volumes such as *The Tall Men* (1927) and *Lee in the Mountains and Other Poems* (1938) and essay collections such as *The Attack on Leviathan* (1938) contributed to his reputation as a diehard regionalist.[15] Throughout his life, he made numerous pilgrimages to the Breadloaf School of English in Vermont, sojourns that tended to strengthen his belief that agrarian cultures produced the best writers. Were it not for his unchanging social views (he supported segregationism even during the Civil Rights movement), he might have enjoyed wider literary acclaim.[16]

Allen Tate, once Ransom's protégé, made a name for himself as the modernist Southerner who wrote "Ode to the Confederate Dead," two biographies of Confederate heroes, and an acclaimed Southern novel, *The Fathers* (1938). He went on to serve as editor of the *Sewanee Review,* as Chair of Poetry at the Library of Congress, and, in his later years, as president of the American Academy of Arts and Letters. His friendships with and influences on some of the most prominent American literary figures—and his piercing criticism of their work—kept him in the public eye for much of his life.[17]

Robert Penn Warren, of course, was the most famous of the group. After founding the influential *Southern Review,* he went on to receive Pulitzer Prizes not only for fiction but for poetry. While novels such as *All the King's Men* (1946) won him a large readership, he retained his reputation as a literary and social critic. In 1950, he was appointed professor at Yale University, and almost four decades later he became the first poet laureate of the United States. Yet Warren, who had all but abandoned Agrarianism by the time

Franklin Roosevelt assumed office, wrote not a single political statement defining Agrarianism during the New Deal and ought not to be considered an influence on the Agrarian program. Warren scholars are familiar with "The Briar Patch," the paternalistic endorsement of segregation he wrote for *I'll Take My Stand*. That essay helped prompt him, during the early Civil Rights era, to a guilt-ridden reexamination of race relations in the South. In the years immediately following the publication of *I'll Take My Stand,* however, he neither amended nor added to his Agrarianism.[18]

Warren's Vanderbilt associates—Ransom, Tate, and Davidson—deserve their reputation as the most important Agrarians, but few people have actually read their 1930s periodical articles. Critical fascination with the Agrarians' achievements as poets and literary critics before and after the New Deal has served to obscure the essays. Indeed, the near willful lack of interest in the Agrarians' political commentary may extend from the critical theory modern scholars learned from the Agrarians themselves. In the 1930s, Ransom, Tate, and Davidson were already formulating (with Warren and Cleanth Brooks, who cofounded the *Southern Review*) the New Criticism, a text-centered approach to literature the academy absorbed in the decades after World War II. Having learned from the Agrarians that texts should be evaluated by formal aesthetic criteria, younger critics showed little interest in evaluating the Agrarians' work through their biographies and social views.

The overlap among Fugitive poets, Agrarians, and New Critics has also deflected critical attention from those Vanderbilt Agrarians who did not have such prominent careers, literary or otherwise. Accordingly, this volume endeavors to direct scholarly attention to three additional Southerners who joined the Fugitive-Agrarians in disseminating a collectively formed political ideology during the New Deal: Andrew Nelson Lytle (1902–95), Herman Clarence Nixon (1886–1967), and Frank Lawrence Owsley (1890–1956).

Lytle, a native of Murfreesboro, Tennessee, attended Vanderbilt and fell under the influence of the Fugitives. Although he went to New England to study at the Yale School of Drama and tried to make a career as a playwright, his experience researching a life of Bedford Forrest while hovering in Menckenesque New York City literary circles made him eager to collaborate on *I'll Take My Stand* with his Vanderbilt classmates.[19] Because he devoted most of his later career to novel writing, scholars have come to think of Lytle as a fiction writer more interested in the human condition than in farm policy.[20] Yet Lytle, whose vision of the South was more experiential than analytical, had a powerful influence on the Agrarians during the New Deal. His time spent managing (and attempting to save) his family's farm in Guntersville, Alabama, left him with an abiding commitment to subsistence agriculture. He developed a particular talent for portraying the small farm owner in the South as the true American.

Another figure usually seen as peripheral to the Agrarian movement is Herman Nixon. Never close to the Agrarians who founded the *Fugitive,* Nixon was a social scientist and not a man of letters. In his *I'll Take My Stand* essay on the Southern economy and in his subsequent writings, he articulated a less mythical, more materially based assessment of Southern culture—the antithesis of Lytle's pastoralism. Nixon's numerous articles about the condition of agriculture, industrialization, and rural life in the South frequently made him sound more like a cohort of the liberals at the University of North Carolina, Chapel Hill. Yet he shared the Agrarians' belief that industrial expansion was not a panacea for the South and joined wholeheartedly their efforts to protect Southern farmers. In fact, a strong case can be made that Nixon, who was essentially a New Deal liberal in the company of classical conservatives, held much more political clout than the others; his chairing in 1935 of the Southern Policy Commission made him the Agrarian who came closest to influencing Franklin Roosevelt's brain trust.[21]

Finally, Frank Owsley is frequently seen not as an Agrarian activist, but as a fire-eating, Alabama-born historian whose neo-Confederate loyalties motivated him to write a series of important, but ultimately tendentious, works in Southern history. Yet Owsley, a professor at Vanderbilt, mined from his own scholarship a powerful sympathy for the "common folk" of the South, whom he defined as small, usually white landholders—and whose impact on the region he believed was grossly undervalued.[22] His 1935 article "The Pillars of Agrarianism" received near unanimous support from the Agrarians, and stands as the movement's clearest political statement. The article was said to have influenced directly New Deal farm policy.

Owsley's essay suggests the change that had occurred since 1930, when the twelve contributors to *I'll Take My Stand* were more interested in defending Southern culture than in shaping public policy. By the 1936 publication of *Who Owns America?,* a follow-up collection, an evolved group of Agrarian contributors wanted nothing more than to influence lawmakers—so much so that they pushed Southern culture into the background in order to foster alliances with English intellectuals arguing for radical, land-based economic reform. Only a year later, the Agrarians would be moving in such different directions that it would no longer be possible for them to speak as a group.[23] For the better part of the New Deal, however, a coalition of six men—Ransom, Tate, Davidson, Lytle, Nixon, and Owsley—were responsible for promoting the Southern agricultural economy as a practicable political and economic model for America. Embedded in a moment, their movement responded to the call for political change and sought to win the nation's respect.[24]

To understand fully the revised paradigm of Agrarianism that emerges with the publication of the primary documents collected in this volume, one must consider the manner in which Agrarianism has been represented in the secondary literature over the years. Because the Agrarians outlived their own movement, they exercised considerable influence over its interpretation by later critics. Arguing that their movement was never intended to advance a practicable political program, the Agrarians were aided by a group of sympathetic scholars, some of whom were their friends or protégés. These neo-Agrarian scholars, who pointed to the Agrarians' alluring pastoralism, to their prophetic environmentalism, and to their appealing animadversions against mass culture, accepted at face value Allen Tate's postmortem definition of their movement as "a reaffirmation of the humane tradition."[25] Neo-Agrarians shared the Agrarians' belief that the entire United States was fast falling victim to a grossly materialistic, fraudulent culture, and that its deracinated citizens were experiencing a devastating psychic disintegration. As alienated by these trends as their mentors, the neo-Agrarians joined them in calling for a return to an integrated life in which land, community, and spirit were inextricable and were experienced immediate and whole, almost without thought.

Not knowing about, downplaying, or ignoring many of the essays in this volume, the neo-Agrarians, who were by and large tradition-minded professors of Southern literature, kept their scholarship focused on the Agrarians' modernist poetics and abstract ideas rather than on their political statements.[26] Agrarianism, the neo-Agrarians held, ought to be studied as a timeless philosophy rather than as a political movement. As Richard Weaver (1910–63), one of the earliest and most influential neo-Agrarian critics, put it, "What the Agrarians, along with people of their philosophic conviction everywhere, were saying is that there are some things which do not have their subsistence in time, and that certain virtues should be cultivated regardless of the era in which one finds oneself born." Calling Agrarianism "a vital religious-aesthetic movement," Weaver—who wrote his master's thesis under Ransom at Vanderbilt and his Ph.D. dissertation at Louisiana State University under Cleanth Brooks—argued that the group had, if anything, a consciously apolitical strategy. "Political claims," he wrote, "alter with circumstances. But claims based upon ethical and aesthetic considerations are a different matter; they cannot be ignored at any time, and it was these which furnished the[ir] principal means of attack."[27]

A variety of conservative English professors followed Weaver's neo-Agrarian interpretation. When critics speak of Weaver, it is most often in the company of M. E. Bradford (1934–93), an academic trained at Vanderbilt by Donald Davidson and for many years on the faculty at the University of Dallas. According to one scholar, while Bradford was not as focused on religion as Weaver was, the two shared an Agrarian "distrust of the 'political,'" both in the form of a hostility to state centralization and an indifference to political participation by people, whatever their race." Bradford also shared Weaver's alarm over "the unrestrained workings of the market economy, the gimcrack nature of the consumer culture and the onset of mass society dominated by the mass media."[28]

A far less partisan neo-Agrarian critic better known to students of Agrarianism is Louis D. Rubin (1923–), University Distinguished Professor emeritus of English at the University of North Carolina, Chapel Hill. The edition of *I'll Take My Stand* that remains in print includes two sympathetic introductions by Rubin, one published in 1962 (after being approved by Allen Tate) and another in 1977. In the second introduction, Rubin wrote that it had been somewhat "misleading" in the first one to define Agrarianism merely as "the vision of poets." Yet he continued to overlook the Agrarians' overtly political essays and reaffirmed his original premise, namely that Agrarianism could be understood best on the basis of a "metaphoric" reading of *I'll Take My Stand* as an "assertion of the values of humanism."[29]

Continuing to focus on *I'll Take My Stand,* Rubin further developed this rather apolitical reading of Agrarianism in his paradigmatic book *The Wary Fugitives* (1978). Although the book grew out of a seminar paper submitted to historian C. Vann Woodward during the 1950s, Rubin switched disciplines soon thereafter. Since then, Rubin has written prolifically and gained a reputation as the dean of Southern literary studies.[30] Dedicating *The Wary Fugitives* to Tate, Warren, Davidson, and Ransom, he portrayed the Agrarians as a gravely misunderstood "band of prophets" whose spiritual protest ought not to be examined as a political program. "What the Agrarians had to offer," Rubin argued, "both individually and as a group, was . . . a reasoned, intelligent, planned defense of religious values and humane community attitudes." Arguing that *I'll Take My Stand* was never intended to be "a book about farming," Rubin held that the Agrarians were merely trying "to make people aware that plumbing and electrical appliances were not the be-all and end-all of existence."[31]

Much deserves to be preserved from the accounts of such neo-Agrarians, who argue that, despite their weaknesses, the twelve Southerners offered a forceful critique of modern American culture. What is more, the personal acquaintance of neo-Agrarian critics with their mentors frequently translated into a kind of familial insight unmatchable by revisionist historians.[32] Yet the neo-Agrarians, many of whom wrote their work while still in contact with the Agrarians, sometimes remained reticent on the unpleasant aspects of Agrarianism. Their interpretations focused on the good in the movement, passing over its social failings; as a result, their abstracted version of Agrarianism was often ahistorical in its disassociation from the political, economic, and social context of the South during the New Deal.

Not all English professors who have written about the Agrarians were neo-Agrarians. From time to time, liberal literary scholars such as John L. Stewart (1917–) and the late Alexander Karanikas (1916–?) rankled neo-Agrarians by publishing critical studies of the group. While Stewart and Karanikas accepted the neo-Agrarians' conflation of Fugitives and Agrarians, both scholars made large dents in the reigning interpretation of the Agrarian movement. The Agrarians were at first pleased with Stewart, but the relationship soured when he published *The Burden of Time: The Fugitives and Agrarians* (1965). Praising improvements in the economy, in race relations, and in labor conditions throughout the South, Stewart concluded, "The New South has come to pass and it has turned out to be much better than the Agrarians had prophesied."[33] So annoyed were the neo-Agrarians by Stewart's liberalism and his aesthetic judgments (he dared to rank the poetry of Warren, Ransom, and Tate) that they enlisted friends and students to attack the book in a variety of periodicals.[34] One neo-Agrarian wrote, "The truth is that Stewart doesn't like Agrarian ideas and is uncomfortable, sometimes angrily so, in their presence."[35]

Both the Agrarians and the neo-Agrarians were further agitated when Karanikas's *Tillers of a Myth* appeared in 1966. An independent Democrat who once ran for Congress in New Hampshire, Karanikas was born and raised on an eighty-acre, rural New England estate complete with apple orchards. After studying under the left-leaning F. O. Matthiessen at Harvard, he received his doctorate in English at Northwestern. A Northern liberal, he could barely contain his dislike for the Agrarians. Adopting a disdainful tone, he extended his analysis of the group well beyond the 1930s into their subsequent promulgation of aesthetic formalism. He especially took them to task for their apologetic views of the South's racial caste system and for their romanticized advocacy of farming. The title of the book revealed its thesis; to Karanikas, the Agrarians were, literally, "tillers of a myth"—and that myth was the viability of a self-supporting agricultural society populated by an independent, culturally sophisticated Jeffersonian yeomanry. The Agrarians to him were propelled by a litany of reactionary ideologies put forth by right-wing Frenchmen such as Joseph de Maistre and Charles Maurras, by British medievalists such as William Morris and John Ruskin, by the arch-conservative T. E. Hulme, by distributists such as Hilaire Belloc, and by the anglophile T. S. Eliot.[36]

Karanikas's book was the first full-scale study of Agrarian thought to appear, and its suggestion that the Agrarians belonged to a reactionary conspiracy permeated the secondary literature and elicited strong reactions. One of Karanikas's chief detractors was not a neo-Agrarian English professor, but Edward S. Shapiro, evidently the first historian to take an interest in the Agrarians. In a scathing review, Shapiro wrote that *Tillers of a Myth* was "probably destined to go down as the worst" book about the Agrarians. Shapiro lambasted Karanikas for demonstrating "a complete lack of sympathy for his subjects" and for portraying them "as aristocratic reactionaries pining for the good old days when cotton was king and Negroes knew their place." Indicting Karanikas for having only "a superficial knowledge of the secondary material," Shapiro called *Tillers of a Myth* "a shoddy piece of scholarship" that misrepresented the Agrarians as "medievalists, whereas actually they were Jeffersonian liberals." The Agrarians, Shapiro wrote, "criticized the New Deal not for being too liberal, but for being too conservative." Defending their race attitudes as progressive in comparison to those of their Southern contemporaries, Shapiro complained that "it has become a scholarly cliché" to insist "that the Agrarians were racists." All told, Shapiro concluded, Karanikas had failed to "understand the subtleties and shadings of Agrarian thought."[37]

Shapiro's own work on Agrarianism, an extensively researched dissertation followed by a series of five journal articles published in the 1970s, offered a trained historian's perspective on the movement. Shapiro, who became interested in the Agrarians after reading *I'll Take My Stand* in graduate school, prepared his thesis at Harvard under the direction of Frank B. Freidel, the historian of the New Deal. A conservative who subscribed personally to the distributist-decentralist political philosophy, Shapiro situated the Agrarians within the context of competing and allied movements during the 1930s. Like the neo-Agrarians, his interpretation underplayed ideological differences among the men and avoided the problem of their ideas about race. He also blurred the specifically Southern context of the movement by grouping the Agrarians with other "American Distributists." Yet in a significant departure from the neo-Agrarian paradigm, Shapiro made it clear that Agrarianism was far from apolitical.[38]

Shapiro's skills in political and legislative history (and his careful attention to manuscript sources) enabled him to show that the Agrarians articulated "a coherent reform program" responding to "collectivist" policies inaugurated during the Roosevelt administration. With other American distributists,

Shapiro explained, the Agrarians "opposed the National Industrial Recovery Act which suspended the anti-trust laws, were dubious of the Agricultural Adjustment Act's commercial view of the farmer, and distrusted the social welfare tendencies and the growth of bureaucracy of the New Deal." Yet, he continued, "they were enthusiastic over the Bankhead Farm Tenant Act, approved of Thurman Arnold's trust-busting, and endorsed (with the exception of Donald Davidson) the Tennessee Valley Authority. They suggested a more extensive farm tenant program and a stronger attack on economic centralization through such things as heavily graduated corporate income taxes and a more vigorous anti-trust policy."[39] The Agrarians, held Shapiro, were anti-monopolists who wanted to place property in the hands of all Americans.

In the articles that emerged from his dissertation, Shapiro, who joined the faculty at Seton Hall University, continued to advance a sympathetic interpretation of the group that challenged the general assumption of Agrarianism as a conservative movement. The decentralists, as he also called the Agrarians, had been misrepresented by liberal historians. He explained:

> When collectivistic and urban-oriented historians read that the Agrarians favored the widespread distribution of property, aid for rural America and the destruction of economic, political and demographic centralization, they immediately conclude that Agrarianism was, at best, "conservative," or at worst an American version of lower-middle-class fascism. In truth, the Agrarians were anti-fascist as well as radical critics of the New Deal. When they criticized the New Deal it was for failing to move more vigorously against high finance and big business, and for neglecting the small businessman and the small farmer.[40]

Liberal historians soon joined the battle over the interpretation of Agrarianism. Almost simultaneously, three intellectual historians, Richard King (1942–), Michael O'Brien (1948–), and Daniel Joseph Singal (1944–), launched an attack against the neo-Agrarian interpretation. This triumvirate lacked the intimate understanding of Agrarianism the neo-Agrarians gained as a result of their personal contact with the group. Substituting the history of ideas and Southern intellectual history for poetics, aesthetic theory, and Anglo-American literary history, they read the novels and poems produced by the Agrarians as reservoirs of information rather than as aesthetic objects. Yet they were the first historians to construct a fully revisionist model of Agrarianism.

King's book *A Southern Renaissance* appeared in 1980. A Tennessean by birth, he attended Chapel Hill, where his experiences during the turbulent 1960s, as well as his subsequent training at Yale and the University of Virginia, confirmed him as a Southern liberal. In the introduction to his book, he stated flat-out that he had "little use for Southern conservatism of the Agrarian or aristocratic or any other sort." A devoted Freudian, he used ideas from psychoanalytic theory to diagnose the ills of Southern culture and its oedipally inclined, guilt-ridden intellectuals. He attached the prefix "Southern" to Freud's concept of the "family romance," depicting Southern conservatives such as the Agrarians as adolescents unwilling to let go of the racial fantasies of their culture's childhood. Burdened by "what Neitzsche called 'monumental' historical consciousness," the Agrarians, King wrote, were caught between their neurotic need to repeat history and their self-conscious desire to exorcise it. Moreover, he argued, the typical Agrarian bore uncanny resemblance to "Barrington Moore's 'Catonist,'" a land-worshipping reactionary identifiable by his xenophobia, his fear of cultural disintegration, and his rejection of materialism. Any merits to the indictment of modernity in the Agrarians' "hysterical" anthology *I'll Take My Stand* were mitigated by their fascistic Catonism.[41]

A less severe indictment appeared at about the same time in O'Brien's *The Idea of the American South*. O'Brien, an Englishman who did not set foot in the South until 1968, could claim an outsider's objectivity toward the Agrarians, many of whom were still teaching in the 1970s. Although he picked up his master's degree in history at Vanderbilt, he earned a doctorate at Cambridge University and has since described himself as a "Fabian socialist."[42] "To him," O'Brien explained in the third person, "it does not matter personally whether Southerners are racist baboons or the true heirs of Aristotle." O'Brien, in fact, was less interested in evaluating the Agrarian movement than in explaining the way in which Southern intellectuals of the era had internalized and refashioned the symbolic construct or "intellectual perception" they called "the South."

According to O'Brien, early-twentieth-century Southerners such as the Agrarians faced a unique psychic conflict. Assaulted by the fragmentary forces of modernization, their modernism allowed them to recast but not to banish their romantic obsession with wholeness and the idea of nationhood. O'Brien's Agrarians, who worshipped Europe but who were not conscious of the nineteenth-century romanticism that shaped their thought, saw the South as "an organism." Striving for psychic integration, intellectuals such as Tate "tried to fashion the Southern tradition into a solvent for the dilemma of belief." Tate, O'Brien explained, "was between two cultures: he was provincial and metropolitan" and responded to his Eliot-like "dissociation of sensibility" by generating a symbolic construct of the South.[43]

Singal's prize-winning *The War Within* appeared in 1982. Substituting Victorianism for romanticism, Singal (trained at Columbia by Richard Hofstadter and Eric McKitrick) also identified the Agrarians as "transitional figures," but he located them in the middle of a three-stage transformation of Southern culture between the first and second world wars. The first stage in this revolution was most apparent in the *weltanschauungen* of prominent Southern intellectuals of World War I such as U. B. Phillips, Broadus Mitchell, and Ellen Glasgow. These post-Victorian thinkers, Singal said, were debilitated by their lingering belief in a rigid dichotomy between a morally alert, civilized culture and the ever threatening forces of primitivism, barbarism, and savagery. While such post-Victorians found it increasingly difficult to sustain such a dualistic system of thought in the face of the pervasive ideas of Darwin, Freud, and Marx, they remained conservative Southerners clinging tenaciously to the Cavalier myth.

By contrast, Singal argued, Tate and his Agrarian colleagues Ransom and Davidson, along with William Faulkner and the North Carolina sociologist Howard Odum, managed to become modernists "by the skin of their teeth." Rejecting the oft repeated theory that it was the South-baiting rhetoric of Mencken or the 1925 Scopes trial that elicited the Agrarian movement, Singal argued that Agrarianism was an "attempt to overcome the anguish of cultural transition by *fiat*." He wrote insightfully of the Agrarians' intellectual "pain" and "agony," of their need to compensate for the tensions of chronically divided psyches. Tate, especially, according to Singal, suffered a "tormenting inner dualism." It was not the Agrarians' Southern "chauvinism as such, but the effort to escape this deadlock of ambivalence arising from the clash of their nineteenth century heritage with their equally powerful Modernist values" that made them "construct their own special myth of the South." Myth or no myth, however, they remained trapped in a premodernist limbo.[44] (While praising *The War Within* as an important and thought-provoking work, O'Brien, a neo-Hegelian uncomfortable with the neat periodization of history and skeptical about the possibility of politically neutral definitions, asked, "What *is* Singal's modernism? Does it not look remarkably like reform liberalism, with a little psychology and anthropology thrown in for good measure?")[45]

Defining their terms differently, King, O'Brien, and Singal had each advanced interpretations stressing modernism. Yet all three might have paid much more attention than they did to the complex aesthetic movement overseen by Ezra Pound, T. S. Eliot, Gertrude Stein, and James Joyce; they too often defined modernism as a sociocultural phenomenon rather than as an event in literary history. Moreover, they tended to speak of the Southern literary renaissance in sociological terms, slighting, if not ignoring, the tangled webs of artistic and linguistic influences among the writers. Finally, they skirted the complicated relationship between the Agrarians and the communist literary critics of the 1930s.[46]

Although apparently not conscious of doing so, the three historians had explained the Agrarian movement using what is essentially a cultural extension of the theory of cognitive dissonance, a model that has served so many Southern historians (especially those examining race) from W. J. Cash to Joel Williamson.[47] To King, O'Brien, and Singal, the Agrarians were emotionally needy intellectuals rather than proponents of a tangible social program. Yet these three revisionists had still succeeded in producing the first critical historical model of Agrarianism—and in reshaping the debate over the movement's origins and meaning.

By the 1980s, the literature examining Agrarianism had grown into two labyrinths: one negotiated by English professors and the other by historians.[48] The gulf between scholars in the two disciplines, which continues to prevent a meaningful synthesis of the literature, widened with the appearance of the 1988 textbook *The Southern Agrarians*[49] by political historian Paul Conkin. Conkin's previous work on land movements in the New Deal had promised a different type of study.[50] Taking Agrarian political activism seriously, Conkin (1929–) depicted the Agrarians as devoted anti-federalists opposed to monopoly capitalism. While ideologically diverse, they were unified by "support for the proprietary ideal," the belief "that each head of a household could aspire to individual ownership of, and control over, productive property."[51] Yet the group's preoccupation with subsistence farming, he argued, was unrealistic. Moreover, there was a contradiction between their goals and their philosophy; while they wanted to stand at the helm of the New Deal, their Jeffersonian distrust of centralized government told them that it was wrong to do so.[52] Conkin also offered a more thorough examination of the Agrarians' race attitudes. Yet for all of his criticism, he did not abandon entirely the sympathetic paradigm established by the neo-Agrarians. After all, he was a Tennessean raised on a farm, and the book began as a chapter in his history of Vanderbilt University, where he studied under Herman Clarence Nixon and where he eventually became a professor of history. In his preface, Conkin confessed that he considered the group "almost a part of [his] family."[53] While such sympathy in some ways brought the scholarship full circle, the combination of Conkin's liberalism and his failure to discuss aesthetic matters annoyed the neo-Agrarians. M. E. Bradford, who had called Karanikas and Stewart "malicious 'mythographers,'" aimed similar criticism at Conkin, whose book he found "petulant and condescending."[54]

If Agrarian ideas found a more secure home in Bradford's canon, the exact nature of their appeal to other contemporary conservatives has not been fully explored.[55] Indeed, conservative movements in general have gotten short shrift from academic historians, becoming, as Alan Brinkley has written, "something of an orphan in historical scholarship."[56] Agrarianism, an eight-year movement with a shifting membership and at least six major spokesmen, may not submit to synthesis by historians, yet the group's writings offer an opportunity to examine closely one permutation of the American right. Richard King may be correct in his judgment that "the Vanderbilt Agrarians offered the closest thing to an authentic conservative vision which America has seen."[57]

What kind of conservatives were the Agrarians? All manner of conservative styles are to be found among the group. There were hierarchical European traditionalists and medievalists and populist-sounding American proponents of "forty acres and a mule." One hears not only simple haters of liberal self-righteousness but also hysterical racists and wavers of the bloody shirt. Even the elitist strain of anti-modern conservatism that emerged in America at the turn of the century is represented.[58] Such an eclectic blend suggests a conservatism both reactionary and radical.

The eclecticism may explain the attraction of Agrarianism to a contemporary historian such as Eugene Genovese, a former leftist who is now a neoconservative. Genovese treated the group at some length in *The Southern Tradition* (1994), a sympathetic explication of conservative thought among white Southerners throughout history. Southern conservatives such as the Agrarians, Genovese argued, deserve "a respectful hearing" because "their critique of modernism—and, by extension, of postmodernism—contains much of intrinsic value that will have to be incorporated in the world view of any political movement, inside or outside the principal political parties, that expects to arrest our plunge into moral decadence and national decline." The Agrarians to Genovese were the conduit through which Southern conservative ideas conceived in the early republic and antebellum eras were channeled to more recent writers such as Weaver and Bradford. Common to all Southern conservatives, Genovese maintained, is a Christian worldview, resolute ideas about property ownership, rejection of abstract definitions of equality, and an unremitting criticism of monopoly capitalism. One of their most distinguishing traits is their "belief in a transcendent order or natural law in society as well as nature, so that political problems are revealed as essentially religious and moral."[59]

The advocacy of a political order in which moral and religious values take precedence over ever changing governmental policies has been explicit in the thought of many prominent conservative intellectuals in America. It appears, for instance, in the writings of Russell Kirk—perhaps the major postwar intellectual on the right. Outlining a philosophical agenda for American conservatism at midcentury, Kirk predicted further "resistance to the idea of a planned society, through restoration of an order which will make the planned society unnecessary and impracticable." Moreover, he cited the

continuing need to grapple with "the problem of spiritual and moral regen-
eration" and to work toward "the restoration of the ethical system and the
religious sanction upon which any life worth living is founded." Such a restoration, he warned, may be "conservatism at its highest; but it cannot be
accomplished as a deliberate program of social reform."[60] Perhaps Kirk
would further agree that the paradox of American conservative thought of
his era—and of Southern Agrarianism during the New Deal—was an unwillingness to heed its own advice.

The essays in this volume demonstrate that the Agrarians did, during the era
of the New Deal, put aside issues of the spirit in order to alter government
policies and to plan a society. At the very least, they were determined to
point out the flaws in the political planning of others. The World War II economic boom that stopped America's Great Depression—and the international economic recession that precipitated the collapse of the Soviet Union
fifty years later—makes it difficult to keep in mind that when these essays
were written, many Americans doubted the future of capitalism and even
of democracy. In the early 1930s, conservative Agrarians and leftist radicals
alike fervently believed that the entire system was in its death throes. Among
socialistic intellectuals, hopes rose for wholesale political change that might
regulate capitalism, redistribute wealth, and aid the oppressed. The Agrarians' New Deal essays confirm the now familiar scholarly view that there was
much common ground between the Southerners' ideas and those of the
1930s radicals, for both groups nursed a hatred of the corporate domination
of the United States.[61] So great was the Agrarians' hatred of the industrial-
izing forces of monopoly capitalism that by the mid-1930s they advocated
federal intervention to ensure massive rural resettlement. Land redistribution such as that proposed by Owsley in "The Pillars of Agrarianism"—
government-sponsored migration back to the countryside to land either purchased or confiscated by the state—was radical not only by Agrarian anti-
statist standards but also by the standard of cautious New Deal "liberals,"
who, in spite of being reform-minded, were already beginning to forge "an
accommodation with modern capitalism."[62]
    Yet the Agrarians abhorred the prospect of mass political movement and
the notion of class-based struggle that infused socialist thought in the 1930s.
In the socialists' response to the worsening economic hardship endured by
millions, the Agrarians thought they heard an opportunistic urging of dic-
tatorships and revolutions that would speed the day of full-scale communism. Then, after Roosevelt's reelection in 1936, as Alan Brinkley has observed, many in the South "feared that [the president] would attempt to use
his landslide to promote 'dictatorship' and 'radicalism.'" To make matters

worse, events overseas suggested frightening political options for the United States: fascism represented by Hitler on the right and communism represented by Stalin on the left. Given this context, the Agrarians believed they were establishing a middle ground between two equally repressive political systems.[63]

The group, as their essays suggest, worried that American Communists were wielding too much influence over the New Deal in general—and especially in the area of Southern agricultural policy. Anti-communism was not a new feature to Agrarianism; Warren had lobbied the group to title their first manifesto "Tracts against Communism" over "I'll Take My Stand," a line from the Southern anthem "Dixie." When they were planning the book in 1929 and 1930, most of the group believed that a communist solution to the Great Depression would mean the expiration of art, truth, religion, and humanity. Inspecting some of the leftists who appeared at various stages of the New Deal promising to solve the nation's social ills, they were further convinced that a group of positivistic scientists and Marxist policymakers were bent on abstracting Americans into economic categories bearing little or no relation to their inner lives.[64]

Even worse, the Agrarians believed, were leftists who questioned the self-contained "organic" nature of Southern society and culture. Davidson, Tate, and Owsley, in particular, denounced liberal social scientists whom they believed used the South as a laboratory to study poverty, backwardness, and social injustice. The Agrarians were especially annoyed when these experiments were undertaken by other Southerners such as those affiliated with the Chapel Hill school of sociology led by Howard Odum.[65] For a time, it seemed as if the Agrarians might ally themselves with the regionalist movement of Odum and Rupert P. Vance.[66] Deeply suspicious of centralized power in Washington, D.C. (Ransom wanted to move the nation's capital "deep in the interior," away from the East), the Agrarians were allured by Odum's pluralistic national model, in which regions would attempt to solve their own social problems without federal oversight. But in the end, the program put forth by the regionalists, who were also known as the Chapel Hill Planners, was not Southern enough for the Agrarians.[67] Writing about Odum's research, Tate complained: "[T]o have money [to complete it] he went to the foundations, and going to the foundations in the East one must leave politics outside, and leaving politics outside, for Odum, meant substituting regionalism for sectionalism."[68]

The Agrarians were irked by the frequency with which the Chapel Hill group and other liberals—Southern or otherwise—used sociological models to explore Southern race problems.[69] Taking exception to the methodology of studying individuals statistically, the Agrarians argued that "tradition," and all that it brought to a community, could not and should not be weighed and measured by external standards. While the Chapel Hill sociologists were not themselves free of racism, as more than one scholar has observed, they saw "many Souths"—including a white South and a black South that were unfortunately at odds.[70] The Agrarians, however, could only see the region as a unitary idea, a organism that must live by the principles of agriculture and an unspoken, but certain, social hierarchy or else be lost. If the Agrarians intended their South to be "humane," they did not believe all Southerners were equals. The Agrarians, one of the Chapel Hill critics elaborated, "assert that virtue is derived from the soil, but see no virtue in the Negro and the poor white who are closest to the soil."[71] Indeed, the Agrarians' Arcadian world of small subsistence farms assumed not only a culture accepting of economic disparities but one based upon white supremacy and racial segregation.

It is not only one of the greatest ironies of the Agrarian movement but undoubtedly its tragic flaw that its proponents failed to include, and were often hostile to, African Americans. The Agrarians' New Deal essays suggest that most in the group not only refused to consider blacks as full-fledged citizens of the republic, but barely thought of them as sentient beings. The Agrarians' view of the South as a land victimized from the nineteenth century onward by outsiders meant that, when they considered blacks at all, it was more often than not to make them the obsession of Northerners who wanted to meddle in the South's internal affairs. Subscribing to the prevailing myth of Southern history, in which blacks elected to office during Reconstruction were thought to have colluded with the North in the destruction of a once great civilization, the Agrarians depicted black Americans not as an autonomous, politically conscious people who could and did make their own choices, but as minstrel "darkies" or as childlike freed slaves.[72] Never themselves subject to the terrorism of lynch mobs, the Agrarians ignored the physical danger and emotional pain blacks endured—and they downplayed the rigid economic, educational, political, and social discrimination that persisted in the South throughout the 1930s (and which the New Deal did little to eliminate).[73] As Lillian Smith observed, the Agrarians were blind to "the massive dehumanization which had resulted from slavery and its progeny, sharecropping and segregation, and the values that permitted these brutalities of spirit."[74] Even when they made suggestions for improving the lot of black tenant farmers, they did so with the goal of preserving a segregated society. With the exception of Nixon, whose increasing race liberalism eventually alienated him from the group, most of the Agrarians were not only patronizing to the extreme, but unable to contain their fears of racial intermixing.[75]

Racist essays such as Frank Owsley's on Scottsboro and Davidson's "A Sociologist in Eden" represent Agrarianism in its most offensive form. Yet by confronting these essays head on, one is reminded of the human damage that intellectuals such as the Agrarians were capable of legitimizing. Exposing the extent of the Agrarians' racism also serves to deconstruct the still common myth that the movement was nearly silent on the most destructive issue in American history. More than a few historians, some of whom believe that one can study Southern conservatives without discussing their race attitudes, have made the argument that the Agrarians really had little interest in (and few ideas about) race relations.

On the contrary, the Agrarians' frequent essays on such matters during the New Deal chart the devolution of the movement from a promising critique of modern American industrialism to a jeremiad about preserving the "organic" structure of the South. From the earliest days of the Roosevelt presidency, the group began disseminating their proposals in the *American Review* (where many of the essays reprinted in this volume first appeared) and, in so doing, became associated with a right-wing editor named Seward Collins and the often reactionary European intellectuals he liked to publish. With Collins's deep pockets and his commitment to promoting groups such as the British distributists—who advocated a property and land redistribution followed by government supervision of small business—the Agrarians hoped that at last they had found a dependable vehicle for their ideas. But the affiliation with Collins, more than anything else, would befoul their image, for when the editor admitted in 1936 to being a fascist, many of the Agrarians' critics believed they had found further proof that the group also harbored reactionary views.[76] Although the Agrarians continued publishing social essays through the decade, the episode severely tainted them. Further compounding their problems, factions that had been latent for almost a decade emerged with the publication of *Who Owns America?* in 1936.

Splintered by disagreement over the movement's ultimate purpose, the Agrarians grew distracted by their own careers, which seemed at times to follow diverging trajectories. While Ransom was losing all interest in the South, Davidson was becoming obsessively neo-Confederate. As Tate's literary ambitions began to exceed any interest he had in public policy, Nixon's bureaucratic talents brought him into the engine of the New Deal. While Lytle began moving away from the teaching of Southern history to the writing of historical fiction, Owsley was further transferring his conservative Agrarianism to his academic work in Southern history. Traveling such different paths—and perhaps recognizing that America had changed irrevocably—the Agrarians abandoned their own movement.

The belief held by some Agrarians that only a spiritual awakening would alter the American political system sheds further light on the failure of their New Deal political phase. At no time during those years would the Agrarians have wanted their political writings dismissed as mere poetry, yet some of the Agrarians reprinted in this volume were so committed to the "religious humanism" of *I'll Take My Stand* that they came to believe that their political and social essays in the 1930s were an exercise in futility. This self-defeating contradiction in the movement is most visible in the essays of Allen Tate, who years later explained that he was more interested in "the moral and religious outlook of western man" than he was "in any immediate political program or reform." "What I had in mind twenty years ago," he wrote of Agrarianism in 1952, was that "the possibility of the humane life presupposes, with us, a prior order, the order of a unified Christendom."[77]

Whether or not one accepts Tate's claim, the Agrarians cannot be accurately assessed unless their entire body of writing, not just *I'll Take My Stand,* is available for study. *The Southern Agrarians and the New Deal* aims not only to encourage critical study of the group's lesser known essays, but to facilitate the debate that has emerged between liberals and conservatives over the ultimate significance of Agrarianism. While neo-Agrarians have applauded the movement as a forward-looking criticism of the dehumanizing tendencies of American culture—as a communal intellectual event akin to the transcendentalist movement of the American renaissance—revisionist historians have seen the Agrarians as victims of their own faulty logic, as politically alienated intellectuals tainted by undemocratic social views. The editors of this volume share with the revisionists a belief that Southern Agrarianism, in spite of its many merits, cannot—and ought not to—be evaluated as a phenomenon freed of responsibility for such views.[78]

Yet the sense that something is amiss in the life of all modern Americans continues to attract revisionists, and even neorevisionists, to the study of a complex movement in the intellectual history of the United States. The Kentucky poet and farmer Wendell Berry has salvaged an important element of Agrarian thought when he charges that individuals removed from the land wither, that the land itself gets spoiled, and that all Americans lose their spirituality in the wake of excessive materialism and rampant individualism. Resurrecting the spirit of Southern Agrarianism, Berry has called for a renewed national and social political commitment to the cultivation of small farms and the proper care and protection of the planet. With such a commitment, Berry believes, even the most distressed agrarian "communities . . . might still become the seeds of a better civilization than we now have—better economy, better faith, better knowledge and affection."[79] Whether this commitment is more easily secured by the outwardly political or by the inwardly spiritual remains—as it was in the Richmond City Auditorium in November 1930—a matter of vigorous debate.

NOTES

1. Mencken, "The Sahara of the Bozart," in *Prejudices: Second Series* (New York, 1920), 136–54. Out of the many conflicting accounts of the debate, we draw from Donald Davidson, *Southern Writers in the Modern World* (Athens, Ga., 1958), 48–49; Paul K. Conkin, *SA*, 90; Thomas Daniel Young, *Gentleman in a Dustcoat: A Biography of John Crowe Ransom* (Baton Rouge, 1976), 217–23; and M. Thomas Inge, "Richmond's Great Debate: Agrarians Sought a Simpler Life," *Richmond Times-Dispatch*, 6 Dec. 1970. Conkin puts the size of the audience at three thousand, while Davidson, Young, and Inge say thirty-five hundred.

2. "Introduction: A Statement of Principles," *ITMS*, xxxvii–xlviii; xxxvii, xlvii.

3. Barr (1897–1982), a University of Virginia history professor, edited the *VQR* from 1930 to 1934. See Tate to Davidson, 11 Dec. 1929, *LC*, 242; Conkin reports that Barr "wanted such modifications in the statement of principles that Davidson decided to drop him" (*SA*, 62); Barr, "Shall Slavery Come South?," *VQR* 6 (1930): 482–94.

4. Ransom quoted in Davidson, *Southern Writers*, 49.

5. Tate to Malcolm Cowley, 19 Dec. 1930, Cowley Papers, Newberry Library, Chicago.

6. Here and above, we draw from Stringfellow Barr to Michael Plunkett, 10 March 1975, Accession no. 292-i, University of Virginia Library, and Young, *Gentleman in a Dustcoat*, 222.

7. Gerald W. Johnson, "The South Faces Itself," *VQR* 7 (1931): 152–57 (157); Johnson, "No More Excuses: A Southerner to Southerners," *Harper's* 162 (1931): 331–37; 332.

8. The conservative Agrarians were fervent in their opposition to monopoly capitalism (as Edward S. Shapiro and others have argued—see below), but they were ultimately no more successful in keeping the issue at the top of the domestic agenda in America than were the so-called "New Dealers" of the late 1930s, the liberal, if fleeting, anti-monopolists Alan Brinkley described in *The End of Reform: New Deal Liberalism in Recession and War* (New York, 1995). Although Brinkley does not treat Agrarianism, his book has aided our understanding of the complex and at times remarkably conservative "liberalism" of the New Deal. Brinkley concludes that American liberals abandoned their attack on monopoly capitalism in favor of a romance with Keynesian economics and that "the reform liberalism of the New Deal years gave way to the consumer-oriented liberalism of the postwar era" (*End of Reform*, 12, 269).

9. By "New Deal era" we mean the years 1933 to 1939 and thereby include several distinct stages in the New Deal's evolution. An excellent, brief account by Robert Dallek of the history of domestic policy during these years appears in Bernard Bailyn et al., *The Great Republic: A History of the American People*, 3d ed. (Lexington, Mass., 1985), 732–47.

10. A number of critics, including John L. Stewart in *The Burden of Time: The Fugitives and Agrarians* (Princeton, 1965), 327–30, and Michael O'Brien in *IAS*, 19, 127,

144−47, have explored the antagonistic, if complementary, relationship between the early Agrarian movement and the coeval movement known as humanism. The anti-romantic humanist movement was shaped by three academics: Paul Elmer More (1864–1937), a Princeton University classicist; Irving Babbitt (1865–1933), a Harvard University French professor; and Norman Foerster (1887–1972), a University of North Carolina Americanist who left for the University of Iowa in 1930 and edited *Humanism and America: Essays on the Outlook of Modern Civilisation* (New York, 1930). "Humanism," according to Foerster, "conceives that the power of restraint is peculiarly human, and that those who throw down the reins are simply abandoning their humanity to the course of animal life" (*Humanism and America,* xiii). Tate attacked the humanists in "The Fallacy of Humanism," *Criterion* 8 (1929): 661−81 (revised for *The Critique of Humanism: A Symposium,* ed. G. Hartley Grattan [New York, 1930], 131−66). See also Leonard Greenbaum, "Humanism," in his *The Hound and Horn: The History of a Literary Quarterly* (The Hague, 1966), 77−95.

11. In *SA* Conkin added, "Even in volume its twelve essays made up no more than a sixth of the important agrarian essays eventually composed by its twelve contributors." Davidson, Ransom, and Tate, Conkin observed, considered the initial book "to be only the opening salvo in a much larger crusade" (57, 89).

12. For a behind-the-scenes view of the social bonds that governed the Agrarian movement, see Ann Waldron, *Close Connections: Caroline Gordon and the Southern Renaissance* (New York, 1987); Virginia Rock, "The Fugitive-Agrarians in Response to Social Change," *Southern Humanities Review* 1 (1967): 170−81 (176).

13. Reminding critics of the "historic and factual difference between the Fugitives and the Agrarians," Inge called these four "the only writers who can accurately be called 'Fugitive-Agrarian' for at least a part of their careers, and to collapse the two phases otherwise is to be historically inaccurate and to do an injustice to these powerful forces in Southern literature and culture" ("The Fugitives and the Agrarians: A Clarification," *American Literature* 62 [1990]: 486−93 [488, 492, 493]).

14. On Ransom, see Young, *Gentleman in a Dustcoat;* Young and George Core, eds., *Selected Letters of John Crowe Ransom* (Baton Rouge, 1985); and Marian Janssen, *The Kenyon Review, 1939–1970: A Critical History* (Baton Rouge, 1990). Ransom's works include *The World's Body* (1938), *The New Criticism* (1941), *Beating the Bushes: Selected Essays 1941–1970* (1972), and *Selected Poems* (1945).

15. Davidson's works are cited in Young and Inge, *Donald Davidson: An Essay and a Bibliography* (Nashville, 1965); see also Davidson's *Still Rebels, Still Yankees and Other Essays* (Baton Rouge, 1957).

16. Here and throughout, we are indebted to the useful "Biographical Essays by Virginia Rock" appended to *ITMS*. Rock (1923−) wrote "The Making and Meaning of *I'll Take My Stand: A Study in Utopian Conservatism*" (Ph.D. diss., University of Minnesota, 1961) and published a condensed version of her work as "They Took Their Stand: The Emergence of the Southern Agrarians," *Prospects* 1 (1975): 205−95. See also Rock, "Fugitive-Agrarians," cited above.

17. See Tate, *Essays of Four Decades* (Chicago, 1968) and *Memoirs and Opinions, 1926–1974* (Chicago, 1975); Radcliffe Squires, *Allen Tate: A Literary Biography* (New York, 1971); Squires, ed., *Allen Tate and His Work: Critical Evaluations* (Minneapolis, 1972); Marshall Falwell, *Allen Tate: A Bibliography* (New York, 1969); and Thomas A. Underwood, *Allen Tate: Orphan of the South* (Princeton, 2000).

18. See Inge's remarks on "The Briar Patch" in "The Continuing Relevance of *I'll*

Take My Stand," *MQ* 33 (1980): 445–60 (447). Warren, *Segregation: The Inner Conflict in the South* (New York, 1956) and *Who Speaks for the Negro?* (New York, 1965). Only two of Warren's essays from the New Deal era, both published in 1936, are Agrarian in tenor: "Some Don'ts for Literary Regionalists," *AR* 8 (1936): 142–50, and "Literature as a Symptom," in *WOA,* 264–79.

19. The biography Lytle produced, *Bedford Forrest and His Critter Company* (New York, 1931), is neo-Confederate.

20. M. E. Bradford, ed., *The Form Discovered: Essays on the Achievement of Andrew Lytle* (Jackson, Miss., 1973). Bradford did, however, also edit *From Eden to Babylon: The Social and Political Essays of Andrew Nelson Lytle* (Washington, D.C., 1990). Yet another collection is Andrew Lytle, *Southerners and Europeans: Essays in a Time of Disorder* (Baton Rouge, 1988), with a foreword by Lewis P. Simpson.

21. An invaluable source for revisionists of the Agrarian movement is Sarah Newman Shouse's *Hillbilly Realist: Herman Clarence Nixon of Possum Trot* (University, Ala., 1986).

22. See Owsley's *State Rights in the Confederacy* (Chicago, 1925) and *Plain Folk of the Old South* (Baton Rouge, 1949). See also O'Brien's chapter, "Frank Owsley: 'The Immoderate Past,'" in *IAS,* 162–84. For sympathetic interpretations, see M. E. Bradford, "What We Can Know for Certain: Frank Owsley and the Recovery of Southern History," in *The Reactionary Imperative: Essays Literary and Political* (Peru, Ill., 1990), 177–82; Harriet Chappell Owsley, ed., *The South, Old and New Frontiers: Selected Essays of Frank Lawrence Owsley* (Athens, Ga., 1969); and, also by Harriet Owsley, *Frank Lawrence Owsley: Historian of the Old South* (Nashville, 1990).

23. In an attempt to explain why most of the Agrarians eventually began living and writing in the North, Richard Weaver has written, "What has been represented as the flight of the Agrarians may appear on closer examination to be a strategic withdrawal to positions where the contest can be better carried on." See *The Southern Essays of Richard M. Weaver,* ed. George M. Curtis III and James J. Thompson Jr. (Indianapolis, 1987), 44.

24. In identifying these six essayists as the ones who best represent Agrarianism of the New Deal era, we have deliberately excised from the canon the other half of the original twelve contributors to *ITMS.* Warren and five other Agrarians not included in this volume (John Donald Wade, John Gould Fletcher, Henry Blue Kline, Stark Young, Lyle Lanier) either wrote no, or almost no, social essays during the New Deal, did not exhibit the same group loyalty as the other six men, or placed their professional and intellectual priorities elsewhere.

In 1936's *WOA* the list of contributors had grown to twenty-one in number. Except for Nixon, rejected by Tate and others because he was beginning to sound too much like a collectivist, the key New Deal–era Agrarians (Davidson, Lytle, Owsley, Ransom, and Tate) reappeared, along with three members of the original group (Lanier, Wade, and Warren) and thirteen newcomers.

25. Tate to Davidson, 4 Dec. 1942, *LC,* 328–29. Mary Ann Wimsatt is compelling when she observes that the various instances in which the Agrarians made the "religious humanism" argument "may be after-the-fact-rationalization" ("Political and Economic Recommendations of *I'll Take My Stand,*" *MQ* 33 [1980]: 433–43 [434, 434n]).

Beginning with "*I'll Take My Stand:* A History" (1935), reprinted here, Davidson made it his mission to publish official accounts of the Agrarian movement. See his "The 'Mystery' of the Agrarians: Facts and Illusions About Some Southern Writers," *Saturday*

Review of Literature 26 (1943): 6–7. Davidson's fullest and most representative account is contained in *Southern Writers in the Modern World,* the first Lamar Lectures. In the second lecture, Davidson identified Agrarianism (the impetus for which he located in the Fugitives' reaction to the 1925 Scopes anti-evolution trial) with "the cause of Western civilization itself" (45).

Lytle, Nixon, Owsley, Ransom, Wade, and Tate joined Davidson in "A Symposium: The Agrarians Today," *Shenandoah* 3 (1952): 14–33. In 1956, the principal members of the Vanderbilt group reconvened in Nashville, where they were joined by critics such as Louis Rubin; see *Fugitives' Reunion: Conversations at Vanderbilt, May 3–5, 1956,* ed. Rob Roy Purdy and Louis D. Rubin Jr. (Nashville, 1959). Defending themselves against the usual charges, Tate, Davidson, Lytle, Owsley, Ransom, and Warren tended to act as a bloc. They called *ITMS* "a defense of poetry," a "reaffirmation of religious humanism," "a set of values," and a celebration of Jeffersonian individualism and decentralization (*Fugitives' Reunion,* 181, 183, 204). See also Bruce Williams, "Fugitives 'In Harmony, Yet Complete Disagreement,'" *Nashville Banner,* 7 May 1956, 12.

26. The first book-length histories of the Vanderbilt group focused almost exclusively on the Fugitive period. While John M. Bradbury's *The Fugitives: A Critical Account* (Chapel Hill, 1958) had little to say about Agrarianism, the book's ranking of their poetry, fiction, and criticism annoyed some of the Vanderbilt men. After Tate, whose work Bradbury criticized roundly, called the book "awful," Davidson reminded Tate of Bradbury's Yankee affiliation (Tate to Davidson, 8 March 1958, Davidson Papers, Vanderbilt; Davidson to Tate, 22 March 1958, *LC,* 374). The group was therefore excited about the appearance, in the following year, of a book the research and publication of which they had encouraged. Its author, Louise Cowan (1916–), was a Texan who received her doctorate in English from Vanderbilt in 1953; several years later, she was one of the few critics admitted into the Fugitive reunion. Still an indispensable work of scholarship, Cowan's *The Fugitive Group: A Literary History* (Baton Rouge, 1959) focuses on the group's poetic achievements and closes just as Agrarianism is germinating. The year of the book's publication, Cowan (and her husband, Don, a Vanderbilt-trained physicist) began teaching at the University of Dallas. On the Cowans, see Waldron, *Close Connections,* 363–67, and Ashley Brown, "The Criticism of Louise Cowan," *SR* 12 (1976): 277–86.

27. Richard M. Weaver, "The Tennessee Agrarians," *Shenandoah* 3 (1952): 3–10 (8, 9, 5). This essay and two equally filiopietistic accounts of Agrarianism, "The Southern Phoenix" (1963) and "Agrarianism in Exile" (1950), were collected in *Southern Essays of Richard M. Weaver.*

Weaver's revised dissertation was published posthumously as *The Southern Tradition at Bay: A History of Postbellum Thought,* ed. George Core and M. E. Bradford (Washington, D.C., 1989 [a 1969 edition includes an introduction by Davidson, another of Weaver's Vanderbilt teachers]). In the book's Agrarian-sounding introduction, Weaver wrote that the South's "claim to attention lies not in its success in impressing its ideals upon the nation or the world, but in something I shall insist is higher—an ethical claim which can be described only in terms of the mandate of civilization." Perhaps not realizing the extent to which he was confessing the principal failing in his argument, Weaver added, "It will seem to many anomalous that a slaveholding society like the South should be presented as ethically superior" (13, 19).

28. Richard H. King, "Anti-Modernists All!," *MQ* 44 (1991): 193–201 (197, 198). Using Bradford's "typology" for differentiating Southern conservatives, King, one of the

revisionist scholars we describe below, calls Weaver a "Tory" and Bradford a "Whig" (194–95). For Bradford's homage to Weaver, as well as his "altogether personal" inter-pretation of Agrarianism, see "The Agrarianism of Richard Weaver" (1970) and "The Agrarian Tradition: An Affirmation" (1972), both reprinted in Bradford's *Remembering Who We Are: Observations of a Southern Conservative* (Athens, Ga., 1985), 73–90, n. 164–170, 83. Although Bradford was familiar with (and praised) some of the essays in this volume, he insisted, "The point of reference for all study of the Agrarian teaching must be the 'Statement of Principles' with which *I'll Take My Stand* was prefaced and to which all twelve of its authors subscribed" (85).

29. *ITMS*, xvi–xvii. The 1962 reissue of *ITMS* brought the book back into the hands of college students. For a critical, neo-Agrarian review of that edition, see Edward M. Moore, "The Nineteen-Thirty Agrarians," *Sewanee Review* 71 (1963): 133–42. Another effort to rehabilitate the Agrarians while criticizing them is Thomas Lawrence Connelly, "The Vanderbilt Agrarians: Time and Place in Southern Tradition," *Tennessee Historical Quarterly* 22 (1963): 22–37.

30. Rubin stands at the center of a parallel controversy over the definition of the Southern literary canon. In a review of *The History of Southern Literature,* edited by Rubin et al. (Baton Rouge, 1985), Michael Kreyling, a newly prominent revisionist, criticized scholars whom he believed had rejected interdisciplinary, pluralistic models of the ren-aissance in favor of a "conservative consensus" in which "the study of Southern literature shall be reserved for the community of the faithful who believe in the South as icon above and beyond history and intellect" ("Southern Literature: Consensus and Dis-sensus," *American Literature* 60 [1988]: 83–95 [94, 95]). Trained at Cornell University, Kreyling has become an outspoken critic of the monopoly of literary criticism by Fugi-tive-Agrarian-New Critics. Another revisionist work of Kreyling's that came to our at-tention after this introduction was written but that deserves citation is *Inventing South-ern Literature* (Jackson, Miss., 1998), esp. 3–18. Twenty years earlier, Michael O'Brien charged that critics such as those who edited *History of Southern Literature* suffer from a "theological approach to literature" ("The Last Theologians: Recent Southern Literary Criticism," *Michigan Quarterly Review* 17 [1978]: 404–13 [408]). O'Brien expanded his critique of the Agrarian/neo-Agrarian interpretation of Southern literary history in "A Heterodox Note on the Southern Renaissance," in *Rethinking the South: Essays in Intellec-tual History* (Baltimore, 1988), 157–78.

31. Rubin, *The Wary Fugitives: Four Poets and the South* (Baton Rouge, 1978), 246, 228, 207; see also Rubin's *The Writer in the South: Studies in a Literary Community* (Athens, Ga., 1972), esp. 94–95.

32. Two early critics who have been especially successful in making such insights are Lewis P. Simpson (1916–) and Thomas Daniel Young (1919–). Simpson, editor emeritus of the *SR,* is notable for gaining the attention of neo-Agrarian and revisionist critics alike. While continuing to use *ITMS* as the representative Agrarian document, his work makes illuminating comparisons between the Southern and New England "mind." See "The Southern Republic of Letters and *I'll Take My Stand*," in *A Band of Prophets: The Vanderbilt Agrarians After Fifty Years,* ed. William C. Havard and Walter Sullivan (Baton Rouge, 1982), 65–91, and "The Fable of the Agrarians and the Failure of the American Republic," in Simpson's *The Fable of the Southern Writer* (Baton Rouge, 1994), 13–23.

Thomas Daniel Young is also more scholarly than Weaver or Bradford, and he de-serves recognition for his tireless editing of the collections of Agrarian correspondence, editions that have fostered critical work by scholars of all stripes. Though he displayed little of Bradford's unrelenting partisanship, Young has written and supported work that sets Agrarianism in its best light. In 1980, for instance, he edited "*I'll Take My Stand:* Fifty Years Later" (*MQ* 33 [1980]: 420–60), in which his essay "From Fugitives to Agrarians" joined those by Martha E. Cook, Mary Ann Wimsatt, and M. Thomas Inge. Adopting somewhat the same tone as Louis Rubin, Young stressed "the prophetic nature of the central argument of *I'll Take My Stand*" (424). Cook, by means of a careful explication of the literary techniques employed by Andrew Lytle and John Donald Wade, offered the needed reminder that some of the arguments advanced in *ITMS* were also crafted as if works of literature ("The Artistry of *I'll Take My Stand,*" 425–32). Wimsatt explored the Agrarians' economic ideas and adopted a centrist view, arguing that "it is within the framework of humanistic philosophy that the economic and political recommendations of *I'll Take My Stand* may best be understood." Wimsatt further maintained, accurately, that the agricultural views the group defined in their book, and in their subsequent New Deal articles published by the *AR,* failed—that their recommendations were ignored or backfired and the long-term effect of New Deal farm policy "was to commercialize farming and turn it into a major American business run by business methods" ("Political and Economic Recommendations of *I'll Take My Stand,*" 434, 440). Inge made the novel argument that the Agrarians' development of a group identity based upon locale prefigured "the recent emphases on the importance of ethnicity and regionalism in the arts." He concluded that the book "remains perhaps American literature's strongest challenge of the humanistic spirit to the paradoxical forces of conformity and chaos in the twentieth century" ("The Continuing Relevance of *I'll Take My Stand,*" 449, 452). Delivered at the Modern Language Association convention in December 1979, these poignant essays cite "the energy shortage" (424), the emergence of the Volkswagen Rabbit (432), "the accident at Three Mile Island" (442), and "dirty air and water" (450) as persuasive evidence of the accuracy of Agrarian assessments of industrialism. Inge also appended to his essay a series of nine evaluations of "the book's continued durability" (452) by critics including Cleanth Brooks, Shapiro, Simpson, and Young. Not long afterward, in *Waking Their Neighbors Up: The Nashville Agrarians Rediscovered* (Athens, Ga., 1982), Young focused again on *ITMS* and concluded that the Agrarians were Thoreau-like prophets. (A condensed version of this argument appears as "The Agrarians" in *History of Southern Literature,* 429–35.) For a record of Young's far-ranging influence on Southern literary studies, see *The Vanderbilt Tradition: Essays in Honor of Thomas Daniel Young,* ed. Mark Royden Winchell (Baton Rouge, 1991).

33. Stewart, *Burden of Time,* 197. Stewart also observed, correctly, that "[t]he proposals for socio-economic action over which the Agrarians were so busy during the next half-dozen years [after *ITMS*] have been forgotten by all but readers and students seeking a better understanding of the works of Ransom, Tate, and Warren" (172).

34. Bradford was undoubtedly not exaggerating the number of neo-Agrarians when he called "the visible inheritance of the Southern Agrarians" the "body of students who have scattered all across the South and the country, carrying with them all or part of the vision of their masters. I know of above one hundred men and women who are part of the scholarly community in the South and who self-consciously represent the Agrarian position" ("Agrarian Tradition," 89).

35. Marion Montgomery, "Bells for John Stewart's Burden: A Sermon upon the Desirable Death of the 'New Provincialism' Here Typified," *Georgia Review* 20 (1966): 145–81 (152–53). Louis Rubin reviewed the book and concluded, "As Mr. Stewart's favorite writer Robert Penn Warren says . . . in a phrase that might serve nicely as a summation of Mr. Stewart's 552 pages (including index) of labor, 'much is told that is scarcely to be believed'" ("Tracking Down the Fugitives," *VQR* 41 [1965]: 451–59

[459]). Clearly irked by the way his mentor had been treated, Bradford wrote of Stewart: "He repeatedly insists that Donald Davidson, one of the most fully engaged, outspoken, and philosophically consistent of American men of letters, is an 'escapist' who has 'in place of a comprehensive moral scheme . . . only a set of prejudices'" ("Leviathan's Predictable Servants," *University Bookman* 6 [1965]: 3—7 [6]). Citing "Stewart's faulty procedure," Brewster Ghiselin called the study "unreliable as a work of scholarship and of criticism" ("The Burden of Proof," *Sewanee Review* 74 [1966]: 527—40 [536, 534]).

36. *Contemporary Authors,* ed. Ann Evory, vols. 33—36 (Detroit, 1978), 459—60; Alexander Karanikas, *Tillers of a Myth: Southern Agrarians as Social and Literary Critics* (Madison, Wis., 1966), esp. 30, 55—56, 81. Distributism both shaped and tainted Agrarian ideology. As explained by Conkin, "The small Distributist movement originated in the work of Hilaire Belloc, who published his opening manifesto, *The Servile State,* in [1912]. . . . In England, Belloc had long advocated the restoration of a rooted and stable English peasantry as an antidote to an otherwise inevitable socialist or fascist form of totalitarianism" (*SA,* 111—12). The distributists' eventual ties to fascism have been discussed by Jay P. Corrin. On the Agrarian and distributist involvement with the reactionary *American Review,* and on the fascism of Seward Collins, the review's editor, see Corrin's *G. K. Chesterton and Hilaire Belloc: The Battle Against Modernity* (Athens, Ohio, 1981), esp. 163, 180.

37. Only "Virginia Rock's soon to be published book," Shapiro added, would set the record straight (review of *Tillers of a Myth* in *Southern Humanities Review* 1 [1967]: 199—202). Bradford praised the work of Shapiro, "who, along with Miss Rock, may be expected to give us a fine book on the Agrarians" (*Remembering Who We Are,* 168). Intellectual historians and others continue to make use of Karanikas's work; see, for instance, Richard Nelson, *Aesthetic Frontiers: The Machiavellian Tradition and the Southern Imagination* (Jackson, Miss., 1990).

38. Shapiro, "The American Distributists and the New Deal" (Ph.D. diss., Harvard University, 1968). We disagree with Shapiro on a number of points, but his work aided greatly our interpretation of the Agrarians' attitude toward the New Deal. See "The Southern Agrarians and the Tennessee Valley Authority," *American Quarterly* 22 (1970): 791—806; "Decentralist Intellectuals and the New Deal," *JAH* 58 (1972): 938—57 (a distillation of Shapiro's dissertation); "The Southern Agrarians, H. L. Mencken, and the Quest for Southern Identity," *American Studies* 13 (1972): 75—92; "American Conservative Intellectuals, the 1930's, and the Crisis of Ideology," *Modern Age: A Quarterly Review* 23 (1979): 370—80; and "Catholic Agrarian Thought and the New Deal," *Catholic Historical Review* 65 (1979): 583—99. This last article is further evidence of Shapiro's command of the legislative history of the New Deal. Interpreting Catholic ruralists in much the same vein as he does the Southern Agrarians, he concluded, "The basic problem with the New Deal, the Catholic agrarians asserted, was that it was seemingly more interested in economic recovery than with fundamental economic and social reform along agrarian and decentralist lines." Their "disillusionment . . . with the halfway measures of the New Deal was inevitable," Shapiro added, in light of their obsession with pure Jeffersonianism in an era of nationwide "compromise and improvisation" (597). By 1980, Shapiro was somewhat more critical of the Agrarians' race attitudes than he had been in his 1967 review of Karanikas; see Shapiro, untitled remarks appended to Inge, "Continuing Relevance of *I'll Take My Stand,*" 458.

39. Shapiro, "American Distributists and the New Deal," four-page summary appendix, 3.

40. Shapiro, "Southern Agrarians and the Tennessee Valley Authority," 805. An ex-

cellent overview of the historiography of American conservatism is by another historian trained by Freidel, Alan Brinkley: "The Problem of American Conservatism," *AHR* 99 (1994): 409–29.

41. Richard H. King, *A Southern Renaissance: The Cultural Awakening of the American South, 1930–1955* (New York, 1980), x, 7, 51, 53. More recently, King wrote that the conservatism of neo-Agrarian Richard Weaver "was congenial with certain aspects of fascism. What Weaver shared with fascism was what Walter Benjamin referred to as the desire to 'aestheticize' and to spiritualize politics" ("Anti-Modernists All!," 200).

42. *Contemporary Authors* (Detroit, 1987), 121:324–25; 324.

43. O'Brien, *IAS,* xi, xiv, 222, xvi, 136, 138.

44. Daniel Joseph Singal, *The War Within: From Victorian to Modernist Thought in the South, 1919–1945* (Chapel Hill, 1982), 111, 35, 10, 201, 219, 206, 223, 249, 201. The true, end-stage modernists Singal defined as moral relativists who accepted a chaotic world, considered conflict to be functional, and were willing to explore evil in humanity, almost with voyeuristic enthusiasm. Firmly entrenched in Southern culture by the end of World War II, anxious to examine their region openly and critically, they were best represented by the editor William Terry Couch, by so-called "New Sociologists" such as Rupert Vance, Guy B. Johnson, and Arthur F. Raper, and by Robert Penn Warren, whom Singal conspicuously resurrected from the pre-modernist purgatory of Tate and the other Agrarians.

45. O'Brien, *Rethinking the South,* 175.

46. On this relationship, see Richard H. Pells's discussion of Tate and the communist writers: *Radical Visions and American Dreams: Culture and Social Thought in the Depression Years* (New York, 1973), 184–86. Annotating this collection, we have also profited from Daniel Aaron's *Writers on the Left: Episodes in American Literary History* (New York, 1961). Aaron described the ideological conflicts, the liberal, leftist, and Marxist publications, and many of the individuals whom the Agrarians debated—and sometimes befriended. Although he enjoyed a friendship with Tate, Aaron's subsequent critique of the Agrarians' writings on the Civil War is notably free of neo-Agrarianism; the Agrarians, he concluded, "slanted history in order to make the usable past more usable" (*The Unwritten War* [New York, 1975], 290–309 [295]).

Professor Jacquelyn Dowd Hall of the University of North Carolina, Chapel Hill, has made a further, important criticism of revisionists such as King, O'Brien, and Singal: "In the intellectual histories of the 1980s, virtually all the Southerners who 'tell about the South' are white men" ("Katherine Du Pre Lumpkin and the Minds of the Modern South," Walter Lynwood Fleming Lectures in Southern History, Louisiana State University, Baton Rouge, 20–21 April 1994, 28, unpublished ms. in possession of editors). For the critical exclusion of gender in Southern literary and intellectual history, see *Haunted Bodies: Gender and Southern Texts,* ed. Anne Goodwyn Jones and Susan V. Donaldson (Charlottesville, Va., 1999), 4–5.

The failure of the Agrarians to include women in their movement has been taken up by Virginia Rock in "Revising the Southern Agrarians: Negotiating a Feminist Critique" and by Susan V. Donaldson in "*Penhally* and Caroline Gordon's Rewriting of *I'll Take My Stand,*" both delivered at the annual MLA meeting in a session titled "*I'll Take My Stand* at Fin de Siècle: The Southern Agrarians Reconsidered," 27 Dec. 1998, San Francisco.

47. See Leon Festinger, *A Theory of Cognitive Dissonance* (Stanford, 1957); W. J. Cash, *Mind of the South* (New York, 1941); Joel Williamson, *The Crucible of Race: Black-White Relations in the American South Since Emancipation* (New York, 1984).

48. Elizabeth McKinsey's intelligent review essay, "Back with the Agrarians," *New Boston Review* (1978): 17–20, has proven useful to us in a number of ways.

49. Conkin's *SA*, a balanced account of the movement, serves as background to readers of this volume. See also Thomas A. Underwood's review of the book in *American Literature* 61 (1989): 115–17.

50. Conkin has written numerous works on the New Deal, beginning with *Tomorrow a New World: The New Deal Community Program* (Ithaca, 1959), a useful work that explores the many agrarian experiments that sought or received governmental sponsorship during the New Deal.

51. *SA*, 171.

52. As Thomas Lawrence Connelly has observed, the Agrarians "once had advocated cheap electric power, government subsidies, accelerated programs of rural education, and government sponsorship of soil erosion control. When these very principles were activated by Roosevelt, however, the Agrarians retreated back into their principles" ("The Vanderbilt Agrarians," 33).

53. *SA*, x.

54. Bradford, *Remembering Who We Are*, 168n, and Bradford, "The Agrarians: A Partial Account," *Sewanee Review* 97 (1989): cii–cvi; cvi.

55. When Andrew Lytle, the last remaining Agrarian, died in 1995, he inspired a column by pundit George F. Will on the permutations of Southern conservatism ("Save Your Confederate Money, Boys . . . ," *Washington Post*, 28 Dec. 1995, A23).

56. "Problem of American Conservatism," 409.

57. *Southern Renaissance*, 51.

58. See Brinkley, "Problem of American Conservatism," 419–20, and T. J. Jackson Lears, *No Place of Grace: Antimodernism and the Transformation of American Culture, 1880–1920* (New York, 1981). In "Anti-Modernists All!" King wrote, "Whether one begins with what Louis Hartz names the 'reactionary Enlightenment' of the antebellum period or with the publication of *I'll Take My Stand* in 1930, American conservatism, when one discounts nineteenth-century liberalism, aka libertarian conservatism and anti-Communist conservatism, has been largely Southern and/or European in provenance" (194).

59. Eugene D. Genovese, *The Southern Tradition: The Achievement and Limitations of an American Conservatism* (Cambridge, Mass., 1994), 102, 7, 22. Genovese, like most scholars, derived his understanding of Agrarianism principally from two texts, *ITMS* and *WOA*. He has commended, in addition to Weaver and Bradford, the neo-Agrarian-tending John Shelton Reed. Reed, a sociologist at the University of North Carolina, Chapel Hill, has studied Agrarianism as a "nationalist movement" in "For Dixieland: The Sectionalism of *ITMS*," in *Band of Prophets*, 41–64; 51. In "The Same Old Stand?" (published in the largely neo-Agrarian golden-anniversary version of *ITMS*) and Fifteen Southerners, *Why the South Will Survive* (Athens, Ga., 1981), 13–34, Reed recounted his own joy, as a Southern college student at MIT, in discovering *ITMS;* see also Reed's "Taking my stand," *Raleigh News and Observer*, 19 Sept. 1993, G1, G5.

Mark G. Malvasi, a student of Genovese's, has written a book about Agrarianism based upon Tate, Ransom, Davidson, Weaver, and Bradford. Malvasi endorsed much of the neo-Agrarian argument by stressing the Agrarian preoccupation with spirituality over politics, although he is more critical of the Agrarians' views on race. In addition, his comparative analysis of Marxist and Agrarian ideas about capitalism is impressive. See *The Unregenerate South: The Agrarian Thought of John Crowe Ransom, Allen Tate, and Don-*

ald Davidson (Baton Rouge, 1997) and Thomas A. Underwood's review in *American Literature* 7 (1998): 911–12.

60. Brinkley, "Problem of American Conservatism," 420; Kirk, *The Conservative Mind: From Burke to Santayana* (Chicago, 1953), 414. Kirk also noted Tate's "deep conservatism of spirit and intellect" (420). In 1957, Davidson identified Richard Weaver and Kirk as "leaders in the conservative movement now strongly resurgent throughout the United States" (*Southern Writers in the Modern World*, 60).

Conkin has cataloged the almost protean appeal of *ITMS: SA*, 87–88, and Genovese, *Southern Tradition*, 13.

61. Pells, *Radical Visions*, esp. 102–5, 111; Singal, *War Within*, 250–51. Shapiro has observed that "[t]he Agrarians, by and large, are Democrats, and if they had one complaint regarding the New Deal it was that it did not fundamentally attack the power of big-business finance but preferred a pragmatic tinkering with the economy. If Arthur M. Schlesinger, Jr., is correct in his *Age of Jackson* that opposition to the world of big business is the central thread of American liberalism, then the Nashville Agrarians are more 'liberal' than the late Franklin D. Roosevelt" ("Liberal Agrarians," *Reporter* 32 [28 Jan. 1965]: 10, 12).

62. Brinkley, *End of Reform*, 176, 5–6, 269. Owsley and the Agrarians dismissed the plan's reliance on the government. See Robert L. Dorman, *Revolt of the Provinces: The Regionalist Movement in America, 1920–1945* (Chapel Hill, 1993), 280–81. Bradford observed that the Agrarians were "not hostile to any New Deal measure in which they sensed a potential for undoing some of the damage to the South wrought by conquest, reconstruction, and economic colonialism: that is, where they sensed a 'restorative' potential in such measures" ("Agrarian Tradition," 87).

63. The Agrarians' ally, Herbert Agar, perhaps expressed this idea most clearly. "[A] third choice is possible for America," he claimed, in the form of a "return to an ideal which was an important part of the plan on which this nation was founded: the ideal of the widest possible distribution of property" ("The Task for Conservatism," *AR* 3 [1934]: 1–22 [13]). Also see Brinkley, *End of Reform*, 155; 17. Despite their concerns about Roosevelt, Agrarians such as Tate had supported his reelection. See Tate, "How They Are Voting: IV," *NR* 88 (21 Oct. 1936): 304–5.

64. See Rubin, "Introduction," *ITMS*, xxxiv, and appendix B to *LC*, 406–8, for details of the conflict. Warren, Tate, and Lytle opposed the title but were defeated by Davidson and Ransom. On the relationship between Marxist and Agrarian thought, see Malvasi, *Unregenerate South*.

65. Odum founded the sociology department at the University of North Carolina and established the influential Institute for Research in Social Science. With Rockefeller money, the institute funded countless examinations of Southern problems. Singal, *War Within*, 115–16, 119–22.

66. See John Crowe Ransom, "Regionalism in the South," *New Mexico Quarterly* 4 (1934): 108–19.

67. An article identifying the commonality and tensions between the Agrarians and the regionalists is Marion D. Irish's "Proposed Roads to the New South, 1941: Chapel Hill Planners vs. Nashville Agrarians," *Sewanee Review* 49 (1941): 1–27. Ransom, "A Capital for the New Deal," *AR* 2 (1933): 129–42; 136. See also Ransom, "The Aesthetic of Regionalism," *AR* 2 (1934): 290–310. King observed, "Where the Regionalists supported economic integration and national cooperation with aid from the New Deal, the Agrarians were much more wary of help from the national government. In contrast they

felt that the South's fate depended on control of its own affairs" (*Southern Renaissance*, 62). Stewart pointed out that, in reaction to *WOA*, "critics noted the inconsistency of demanding massive government intervention and reorganization of society on behalf of a system which, it was believed, would greatly reduce size and power of institutions, including the government itself" (*Burden of Time*, 186). O'Brien, "Regionalism," in *Encyclopedia of Southern Culture*, ed. Charles Reagan Wilson and William Ferris (New York, 1989), 3:487. On the regionalists, see also Dorman, *Revolt of the Provinces*.

68. Tate to Davidson, 5 April 1937, Davidson Papers, Vanderbilt University. In "Regionalism as Social Science," *SR* 3 (1937): 209–24 (revised and reprinted as "Social Science Discovers Regionalism" in *The Attack on Leviathan: Regionalism and Nationalism in the United States* [Chapel Hill, 1938], 39–64), Davidson expressed guarded optimism about the regionalists but remained skeptical that the U.S. government would decentralize.

69. On liberal Southerners, see Singal, *War Within*, chap. 5, 9, and 10; John Egerton, *Speak Now Against the Day: The Generation Before the Civil Rights Movement in the South* (New York, 1994), 64–70; and Morton Sosna, *In Search of the Silent South* (New York, 1977).

70. Dorman, *Revolt of the Provinces*, 136–37.

71. W. T. Couch, "The Agrarian Romance," *SAQ* 36 (1937): 419–30, esp. 429. Couch first delivered this critique in response to a talk by Donald Davidson; see R. H. Woody, "The Second Annual Meeting of the Southern Historical Association," *Journal of Southern History* 3 (1937): 76–90; 83–84.

72. The Agrarians were much influenced by the Dunning school, named for William Archibald Dunning (1857–1922), whose histories vilified those who sought to remedy inequities in the Southern racial and social system during Reconstruction. Similarly, Thomas Dixon Jr. (1864–1946), the sensational and racially incendiary novelist, misportrayed Reconstruction as a brutal threat to civilization itself—a notion broadly popularized in *Birth of a Nation*, D. W. Griffith's 1915 film version of Dixon's novel *The Clansman* (1905).

73. On the New Deal and African Americans, see Brinkley, *End of Reform*, 165–67. Anyone unfamiliar with African Americans' fight against the dehumanizing treatment and extreme violence they suffered during the New Deal era ought to read (from Richard Wright's *Uncle Tom's Children* [1938]) "The Ethics of Living Jim Crow" (reprinted in *Black Writers of America: A Comprehensive Anthology* [New York, 1972], ed. Richard Barksdale and Keneth Kinnamon, 542–48); Nell Irvin Painter, ed., *The Narrative of Hosea Hudson: The Life and Times of a Black Radical* (New York, 1979); George C. Wright, *Racial Violence in Kentucky, 1865–1940: Lynchings, Mob Rule, and 'Legal Lynchings'* (Baton Rouge, 1990); and W. Fitzhugh Brundage, *Lynching in the New South: Georgia and Virginia, 1880–1930* (Urbana, 1993). As Lem Coley has written, "The South that Richard Wright described in *Black Boy* or that Alice Walker reveals in her essay 'But Yet and Still the Cotton Gin Kept on Working' was not unknown to the Agrarians. But they turned their faces away from it. . . . When they discuss race, or when race is missing from its logical place in their discussions, there is often a sense of evasion or sophistry" ("Memories and Opinions of Allen Tate," *SR* 28 (1992): 944–64 [956]).

74. *Killers of the Dream* (New York, 1949), 225.

75. Tate felt humiliated by the 1966 publication of Greenbaum's history of *Hound and Horn*, which quoted from a 1933 letter in which he called "the negro race . . . an inferior race," admitted he favored white "rule," and denounced racial intermixing. "The

Agrarians," Greenbaum concluded, "emerge as a relatively unappealing group" (*Hound and Horn,* 145–48, 125–59, 259). On Tate, Agrarianism, and racism, see also Egerton, *Speak Now Against the Day,* 68–69.

76. On the debacle of Collins and the *AR,* see Albert E. Stone Jr., "Seward Collins and the *AR:* Experiment in Pro-Fascism, 1933–37," *American Quarterly* 12 (1960): 3–19, and Shapiro, "American Conservative Intellectuals." See also the exchange between Tate and Grace Lumpkin in "Fascism and the Southern Agrarians," *NR* 87 (27 May 1936): 75–76. Karanikas argued that the Roosevelt administration preferred the Chapel Hill liberals to the Agrarians in *Tillers of the Myth,* 40–41, 177. For speculation on why Agrarianism or the Southern conservatism it helped to define never embraced fascism, see King's "Anti-Modernists All!," 200–201.

After the *AR* catastrophe, Herbert Agar joined "back-to-the-land" promoters such as Ralph Borsodi in a new magazine, *Free America* (in which Davidson published "An Agrarian Looks at the New Deal," reprinted in this volume). Borsodi, whose ideas the Agrarians did not endorse fully, also attempted less than successfully to interest the New Dealers in a subsistence/distributist program. See William E. Leverette Jr. and David E. Shi, "Agrarianism for Commuters," *SAQ* 79 (1980): 204–18; Davidson, "Agrarianism for Commuters" (a review of the 1933 reissue of Borsodi's *This Ugly Civilization* [1929]), *AR* 1 (1933): 238–42; and Conkin, *Tomorrow a New World,* esp. 24–27, 294–95.

77. "Symposium: The Agrarians Today," 14–33; 28–29; Wimsatt, "Political and Economic Recommendations," 434.

78. An example of a more balanced revisionist criticism may be found in Paul V. Murphy's essay "The Sacrament of Remembrance: Southern Agrarian Poet Donald Davidson and His Past," *Southern Cultures* 2 (1995): 83–102 (84, 96).

79. See Berry's *The Unsettling of America: Culture and Agriculture* (San Francisco, 1977) and *Another Turn of the Crank* (Washington, D.C., 1995), 47.

The Agrarians, caricatured here in a 1933 issue of the Vanderbilt *Masquerader,* attempted to enter the New Deal as legitimate policymakers. (Courtesy of Special Collections, Vanderbilt University)

Andrew Lytle, who attempted to save his family's farm in Guntersville, Alabama, developed an abiding commitment to subsistence agriculture. (Courtesy of Special Collections, Vanderbilt University)

Donald Davidson, shown here in
1928 before the Agrarians became
politically active, later took on the
role of official historian of their
movement. (Courtesy of Special
Collections, Vanderbilt University)

The historian Frank Lawrence Owsley proposed government-sponsored migration to
land purchased or confiscated by the state.
(Courtesy of Special Collections, Vanderbilt
University)

Herman Clarence Nixon's chairing in 1935
of the Southern Policy Commission made
him the Agrarian who came closest to
influencing Franklin Roosevelt's brain trust.
(Courtesy of Special Collections, Vanderbilt
University; photograph by Walden Fabry)

In 1956, Allen Tate, Merrill Moore, Robert Penn Warren, John Crowe Ransom, and Donald Davidson gathered for a reunion of Fugitive poets. Of the five pictured here, only Tate, Ransom, and Davidson were active in the New Deal phase of the Agrarian movement. Moore was never an Agrarian, and Warren had all but abandoned Agrarianism by the time Franklin Roosevelt assumed office. (Courtesy of Special Collections, Vanderbilt University; photograph by Joe Rudis)

Donald Davidson

First Fruits of Dayton:
The Intellectual Evolution in Dixie

In 1925, John T. Scopes was arrested and charged with teaching Darwin's theory of evolution to a high school class in Tennessee. When the case went to trial in Dayton, Tennessee, in July of the same year, the renowned Clarence Darrow came to town to defend Scopes. William Jennings Bryan, the former Populist presidential candidate, by that time both physically and intellectually weakened, represented the state. Although Darrow's brilliant performance did not persuade the jury to acquit Scopes, the evolutionists achieved a victory when H. L. Mencken and dozens of other journalists disseminated vituperative articles about Bryan and fundamentalism. By the time Donald Davidson wrote "First Fruits of Dayton" several years later, he and the other Vanderbilt poets were anxious to prove to the rest of America that the South was not the cultural, artistic, and intellectual vacuum Mencken depicted in his writings.[1]

Reprinted from *Forum* 79 (1928): 896–907.

---

1. Scholars have disagreed whether coverage of the proceedings in Dayton was the principal impetus for Agrarianism. "The first cause, without doubt," Fred Hobson has argued, "was the impact of the Dayton trial—and its exploitation by Mencken and the Menckenites" (*Serpent in Eden: H. L. Mencken and the South* [Baton Rouge, 1974], 150). See also Edward S. Shapiro, "The Southern Agrarians, H. L. Mencken, and the Quest for Southern Identity," *American Studies* 13 (1972): 75–92, esp. 79. Daniel Singal, however, held that "this explanation does not begin to account for the sudden emergence of their Southern consciousness" (*The War Within: From Victorian to Modernist Thought in the South, 1919–1945* [Chapel Hill, 1982], 200–201; 200).

When Austin Peay died not long ago during his third successive term as Governor of Tennessee, editorial writers were inclined to base his epitaph upon a single item of his career. He had signed the anti-evolution law, and therefore he surely must have been an enemy of what many well-intentioned gentlemen are pleased to call progress.[2] They did not stop to remember that Peay had promulgated vast schemes of public education which will prepare the way for the heresies that Fundamentalism thought to check. They knew nothing of his great program of improvements in state administration. They could not think of him as he really was—a grave, hard-working man with a dogged conscientiousness that chilled politicians to the bone.

Such an instance is but one of many that might be cited to show the risk of generalizing on intellectual progress in the South. But a great many writers have taken the risk during the past few years, with an innocent abandon which has produced bewilderingly various results. Their discussions range all the way from denunciation and satire to boastful symposia which detail the surprising phenomena of the New South in terms of such physical and cashable matters as water power, climate, mineral resources, and cheap labor. They are bitter, or they are enthusiastic. And all are right, yet all are wrong, for all have fallen into the easy mistake of simplification.

People do not like to think, of course, that the truth may be more sober and complex than a story in the *New York Times* or an editorial in the *Nation* would encourage them to believe. They prefer a simple myth to a complicated truth. Let Mr. Mencken announce that Tennesseans worship a God with whiskers, and his statement becomes gospel because it offers a dogma with the catchiness and news value dear to the American heart. In the 1860s, the Abolitionists did not find it hard to convince people that Southern gentlemen habitually flogged a Negro or two before breakfast. In 1918 it was equally simple to persuade Americans that Germans were baby eaters. We are always ready to entertain exciting notions when they require no mental labor more than believing the worst of our neighbors. And today a Southerner, emboldened to make the retort courteous, might ask whether he is invited to judge the East by the activities of the Watch and Ward Society

---

2. Austin Peay (1876–1927), governor of Tennessee 1923–27, was a Democrat and a Baptist. Although Peay thought the anti-evolution bill had no chance of becoming "an active statute," he called it "a distinct protest against an irreligious tendency to exalt so-called science, and deny the Bible in some schools and quarters—a tendency fundamentally wrong and fatally mischievous in its effects on our children, our institutions, and our country" (quoted in Ray Ginger, *Six Days or Forever? Tennessee v. John T. Scopes* [New York, 1974], 7).

of Boston, the Middle West by the zealotry of Mayor Thompson, or the Far West by the delicate maneuvers of Aimee Semple McPherson.[3] But this process of charge and countercharge is ungracious and sterile. It obscures the real issues.

The difficulty of understanding the South is increased by the very variety of conditions in this section. Here, by and large, are the mingled phenomena of a period of transition. The earlier reconstruction, which was literally concerned with building up what had been torn down, has not ended; it has only passed into an advanced stage in which powerful economic forces, destined strongly to affect Southern life and thought, have freer play than ever. Hence the South is thickly sown with contradictions.

Gaudy filling stations edge their way among ancestral mansions. The DuPonts build a rayon factory a few miles from the ancient residence of Andrew Jackson. North Carolina harbors (or has harbored) journalists as different as Gerald Johnson and Josephus Daniels. Atlanta produces Coca Cola and Frances Newman. The churches of Nashville unite for revival services under Billy Sunday or Gypsy Smith;[4] and later Nashville entertains the annual convention of the American Association for the Advancement of Science. Tennessee contains both Vanderbilt University, with its modern laboratories and independent spirit of culture, and the newly founded Bryan Memorial University.[5] Think of Cole Blease and Carter Glass, Jim Heflin and Oscar Un-

---

3. Founded by a group of moralistic Bostonians as the New England Society for the Suppression of Vice, the Watch and Ward Society (incorporated in 1884) fought corruption and censored the arts. In 1926, the society banned Mencken's *American Mercury.* William Hale ("Big Bill") Thompson (1869–1944) was a machine politician who served as mayor of Chicago 1915–23 and 1927–31. Popular radio evangelist Aimee Semple McPherson (1890–1944) vanished at a California beach in 1926 and was presumed dead until she turned up in Mexico. Although the district attorney of Los Angeles accused her of perjury after she told a story about being abducted, he abandoned his case in 1927. See Edith L. Blumhofer, *Aimee Semple McPherson* (Grand Rapids, 1993), 232–300.

4. Gerald White Johnson (1890–1980), a liberal North Carolina journalist and editorialist who wrote for the *NR* and the Greensboro *Daily News,* was also an associate of Mencken's and became a major critic of the South. Josephus Daniels (1862–1948), secretary of the navy under Woodrow Wilson and editor of the Raleigh *News and Observer* for more than half a century, held more conservative views. Georgia-born Frances Newman (1883–1928) sparked a scandal with her sexually aware writing, beginning with *The Hard-Boiled Virgin* (1926). William Ashley Sunday (1862–1935) was an immensely popular evangelist who advocated prohibition. British revivalist Rodney Smith (1860–1947) began touring the U.S. in 1889.

5. The American Association for the Advancement of Science convened in Nashville both in 1877 and in 1927. Fundamentalists began endowing (William Jennings) Bryan

derwood, Pastor Norris and Dr. Poteat,[6] magnolias and billboards, colonial mansions and real estate developments, paved roads and pig tracks, horse races and Methodist conferences—and you have symbols that are a rebuke to quick conclusions.

Furthermore, the South is geographically and socially diverse. Grant that there is a distinct Southern tradition and a solidarity among the states; there are also marked differences. Southern tradition itself includes historically not only the genial, aristocratic ideal of leisure that belonged to the Old South, but also the more restless, democratic tradition of the frontier, embodied in "Old Hickory," and still far from moribund. Alabama is not like Kentucky, Tennessee not like South Carolina. The spirit of Charleston or Richmond is not the spirit of Birmingham and Atlanta. The mountain people of North Carolina and East Tennessee are not the same as the folk of the Delta country; the tidewater Virginians are but distant cousins of the bluff Texans.

THE VALUE OF FUNDAMENTALISM

If we remember these facts, and if we admit, too, the healthy Jeffersonian conception that anything *can* happen and probably *ought* to happen in a democratic state, we shall not use up all our grave concern for anti-evolution laws and Ku Klux outrages as having major meanings in themselves. What mean-

---

University in Dayton, Tennessee, during the Scopes trial. Davidson conflated its name with that of the Bryan Memorial Association, which funded the institution after Bryan's death (Ginger, *Six Days or Forever?*, 140−41, 196).

6. Cole L. Blease (1868−1942), who served as governor of South Carolina 1911− 15 and U.S. senator 1925−31, was popular with many poor whites and hostile to African-American causes. Carter Glass (1858−1946) served as congressman from Virginia 1902−19, secretary of the treasury 1918−20, and U.S. senator 1920−46, and helped elect Wilson to the presidency. James Thomas Heflin (1869−1951) was an anti-Catholic Alabama congressman who belonged to the Ku Klux Klan and served in the U.S. senate 1920−31. Oscar W. Underwood (1862−1929), another Alabama congressman 1895−1915 and U.S. senator 1915−27, sought the Democratic presidential nomination in 1912, battled the Ku Klux Klan, and opposed Prohibition. John Frank Norris (1877−1952), a prohibitionist Baptist clergyman, was born in Alabama. An opponent of gambling, Norris headed First Church of Fort Worth, Texas, and edited the *Fundamentalist*. William Louis ("Dr. Billy") Poteat (1856−1938), liberal president of North Carolina's Wake Forest College, voiced public support for the theory of evolution. On his battles with the fundamentalists, see Willard B. Gatewood Jr., *Preachers, Pedagogues and Politicians: The Evolution Controversy in North Carolina, 1920−1927* (Chapel Hill, 1966).

ing they have is more relevant to the general state of society and government in America than to the special condition of the South alone. Anti-evolution legislation may even be taken as a kind of progress; for it signifies that Fundamentalism has appealed an issue of battle—already lost elsewhere—to law-making bodies, and that sort of appeal is characteristic of the American idea that law can effect what society in its inner workings cannot.

Or consider, too, that Fundamentalism, whatever its wild extravagances, is at least morally serious in a day when morals are treated with levity; and that it offers a sincere, though a narrow, solution to a major problem of our age: namely, how far science, which is determining our physical ways of life, shall be permitted also to determine our philosophy of life. No matter what the degree of pessimism in which we indulge our souls, we shall not do well to neglect considerations like these; and the longer we look, the more reasons we find for distrusting those scornful ones who cry, "Out damned spot!"[7] without knowing very much about the seat of infection.

The Fundamentalists, for example, argued with genuine moral fervor that they were out to save the younger generation, but they did not inquire whether the younger generation wanted to be saved. The younger generation, in fact, seems to be tending away from the kind of salvation that Fundamentalism proposes, and such matters as the Dayton flurry hastened rather than checked their apostasy. It is not merely that students in colleges and universities—where one naturally expects to find the forward fringes of intellectual progress—are being systematically exposed to the heresies of scientific and literary courses. The mental temper of the young gentlemen (and the young ladies, by all means!) is alert and quite sensitive, almost too joyously responsive, indeed, to what might be called alien influences. They are familiar with the pages and the preaching of liberal Northern journals. They are, for better or worse, much inveigled by the jeremiads of Mr. Mencken, and are often led to imitate him. They have read Mr. Cabell and Mr. Sinclair Lewis. They have fished in strange waters of sociology and economics. Many of them have brushed against the philosophers from Plato to Dewey.[8]

The evidence will be found in their magazines, even the ostensibly comic sheets. These practice a sophisticated, thoroughly modern tone. They have a dashing, sometimes a recklessly critical spirit. They are likely to sandwich

---

7. William Shakespeare, *Macbeth*, 5.1.31.

8. Both James Branch Cabell (1879–1958), the Virginia author who won fame with his neo-medievalistic, allegorical novels, and Sinclair Lewis (1885–1951), who won a Nobel Prize for literature in 1930, won high praise from Mencken. John Dewey (1859–1952) was a philosopher and educator.

well-seasoned book reviews among college jokes and prepare state and local versions of the [*American*] *Mercury*'s "Americana."[9] And there are also the debating teams, which go up and down the country, arguing with fine tolerance any side of dubious questions like prohibition and war—sometimes viewed with suspicion, but generally finding an audience. These, of course, are leaders and minorities. The great mass of college students doubtless remain intent on football now and good jobs eventually; but in these respects they are like college students everywhere.

The whole matter of education comes into the reckoning. The physical growth of institutions is important, though it is unspectacular and therefore not greatly advertised. We may take comfort in the creation—or recreation—of Duke University, with its endowment of millions. We may recall that Chancellor Kirkland's answer to the Dayton episode was to build new laboratories on the Vanderbilt campus. We may rejoice in the press, the *Journal of Social Sciences,* the notable activities of the University of North Carolina. We may observe with interest the amazing growth of George Peabody College for Teachers, realizing its greatness among institutions of its kind and knowing the vast influence it is having on common school education in the South.[10] Whatever education can do, it will presently have an opportunity to do in the South. Anti-evolution statutes are straw barriers against a great wind.

But we go astray if we dwell merely on the facts of mass education, which, after all, may be questioned on principle anywhere. It is far more important to realize that Southern educational institutions are the nuclei from which ideas work outward, impregnating the commonwealth of social thought. From them come editors, preachers, statesmen, and especially writers, for the student of the literary revival of the South must be keenly aware that Southern colleges and universities have been a great source of creative activity. Remember that Paul Green is a professor of philosophy at the Uni-

---

9. The *American Mercury* was cofounded in 1924 by Mencken and George Jean Nathan. A section of the literary magazine called "Americana" reprinted newspaper pieces that reported on unflattering aspects of American life.

10. Trinity College, a Methodist institution founded in 1859, was renamed Duke University in 1924 after James B. Duke endowed the college with $19 million to rebuild and expand its campus in Durham, N.C. James H. Kirkland (1859–1939), chancellor of Vanderbilt University 1893–1937, severed the institution's relationship with the Methodist Episcopal Church in the South. In referring to the *Journal of Social Sciences,* Davidson apparently meant Howard Odum's *Journal of Social Forces,* founded at Chapel Hill in 1922. Peabody College for Teachers was endowed in Nashville, Tennessee, in 1909 from the reorganized Peabody Normal College and the University of Nashville.

versity of North Carolina, that Edwin Mims[11] and John Crowe Ransom are professors of English at Vanderbilt University; and you have an indication of resident spiritual forces that outweigh all the statistics of literary or illiteracy that you may wish to compile.

It is the quality of intellectual progress, however, not formidable arrays of figures, that we should consider most attentively. Go into almost any department of Southern life, and you can make out a case for progress as easily as for backwardness, although you must do so with considerable assumptions as to the kind of progress that is being illustrated. I might discourse at length on liberal religious leaders like Bishop Mouzon, Dr. Wilmer, Bishop Maxon. I might list the progressive editors—Julian Harris, Grover C. Hall, Louis Jaffe, George Fort Milton, Douglas Freeman, James I. Finney,[12] and others; or "point with pride" to the campaign of the *Birmingham News* against the Alabama floggers;[13] or exhibit the work of T. H. Alexander of the *Nashville Tennessean,* whose widely syndicated column, "I Reckon So," gets in a bantering, humorous criticism of Southern life far more valuable than astrin-

---

11. Paul Green (1894–1981), a prolific playwright who espoused liberal causes, won a Pulitzer Prize for *In Abraham's Bosom* in 1927. Edwin Mims (1872–1959), a liberal Southerner and literary critic, headed the Vanderbilt University English department 1912–42.

12. Edwin DuBose Mouzon (1869–1937) was a Methodist bishop and a founder of Southern Methodist University in Dallas, Texas. Cary Breckenridge Wilmer (1859–1958), a Virginia-born priest who served as superintendent of the Colored Orphan Asylum in Lynchburg, Virginia, later became a theology professor at the University of the South in Sewanee, Tennessee. James Matthew Maxon (1875–1948) was an Episcopal bishop in Tennessee. Julian LaRose Harris (1874–1963), a civil rights advocate and editor, received a Pulitzer Prize for his anti-creationist, anti-Klan stands in the *Enquirer-Sun* of Columbus, Georgia, during 1925. Grover Cleveland Hall (1888–1941) edited the *Montgomery Advertiser* (Alabama) and won a Pulitzer Prize for his 1928 editorials on religious freedom and civil rights. Louis Isaac Jaffe (1888–1950) edited the Democratic *Norfolk Virginia-Pilot.* Tennessean George Fort Milton (1894–1955) was a historian and editor of the *Chattanooga News* who in 1930 became chairman of the Southern Commission on the Study of Lynching. Douglas Southall Freeman (1886–1953) edited the *Richmond News Leader* 1915–49 and won the Pulitzer Prize for his biographies of Robert E. Lee and George Washington. James I. Finney (1877–1931) was the Louisiana-born editor in chief of the *Nashville Tennessean.*

13. The *Birmingham News* was established in 1888. In 1927, Victor Hanson, the paper's editor, joined Grover C. Hall in condemning the Ku Klux Klan for its growing practice of abducting for flogging any Alabamian of whose actions they disapproved. The newspaper campaign helped erode dramatically the Klan as a political force in Alabama. David M. Chalmers, ·*Hooded Americanism: The First Century of the Ku Klux Klan, 1865–1965* (Garden City, N.Y., 1965), 81–84. On Hall, see Caleb Jaffe, "All

gent gentlemen could effect.[14] (In the South, said Alexander recently, there are Four Horsemen who rove the land with evil tread—the clergyman, the lawyer, the newspaper, the banker.)

I might write a whole essay on the progress of Southern literature, dealing with the activity of literary centers—Charleston with its Poetry Society of South Carolina,[15] Nashville with its *Fugitive* group, Richmond with its *Reviewer*[16] coterie, New Orleans, Dallas, and so on. There would be a vast list of Southern authors to catalogue who have gone into the ranks of the literary elect—Cabell, Heyward, Ransom, Stribling, Roberts,[17] and many more. I could dwell on the movement toward de-sentimentalization among these writers, the prevalence of a "modern" tone, the gingerly step with which they approach the Southern scene. Finally, I could survey Southern opinion itself, showing that it is more self-critical and approachable than it used to be, and give as one illustration the popularity of Edwin Mims's book,

---

Alabamians, Come Fight For Your Land! An Analysis of Grover C. Hall's Fight against the Klan with His Unique Brand of Liberalism" (unpublished seminar paper, Yale College, CSES 443, May 1994, in possession of the editors).

14. Truman Hudson Alexander (1891–1941) was a Vanderbilt-educated journalist and free-lance writer affiliated with the *Nashville Tennessean*. "I Reckon So" began appearing throughout the South on a daily basis in 1922. Davidson, who was the *Tennessean's* book review editor for more than six years, wrote the column under Alexander's byline on a number of occasions. See *The Spyglass: Views and Reviews, 1924–1930 by Donald Davidson,* ed. John Tyree Fain (Nashville, 1963), v–vi.

15. "Because we were utterly weary," wrote its founders, "of the reiterated pronouncements from commercial publishing centers in the North and West that America is vocal only in that territory, in October, 1920, we gathered together a few daring, perhaps foolhardy, but at least enthusiastic spirits, and organized the *Poetry Society of South Carolina*" (*Year Book of the Poetry Society of South Carolina for 1921* [Charleston, S.C., 1921], 5). Members included poets Hervey Allen, DuBose Heyward, and Josephine Pinckney. Upon its founding in 1920, "weekly meetings were held, a yearbook published, prizes offered, and 'missionary' work undertaken to encourage the organization of similar bands throughout the region. But before long the upper-crust background and amateur inclinations shared by most of the society's members began to show through, causing one associate to term the gatherings 'one-tenth poetry and nine-tenths society'" (Singal, *War Within,* 84). See also O'Brien, "'The South considers her most peculiar': Charleston and Modern Southern Thought," *South Carolina Historical Magazine* 94 (1993): 119–33, and Frank Durham, "South Carolina's Poetry Society," *SAQ* 52 (1953): 277–85.

16. The literary magazine *The Reviewer* (1921–25) was edited by Emily Clark, James Branch Cabell, and later Paul Green.

17. The poet, novelist, and playwright DuBose Heyward (1885–1940) cofounded the Poetry Society of South Carolina and peopled his writings, which included *Porgy* (1925), with African-American characters. The oeuvre of Tennessee novelist T. S. Stribling (1881–1965) included depressing depictions of life in the Southern mountains; he

The Advancing South,[18] which ran through several editions, was syndicated in various Southern newspapers, and reached—to judge from vehement expressions of praise and disagreement—a host of people whom outside criticism never touches.

WHITHER PROGRESS?

But all such exhibits are mere preliminaries to the real question, which is: Grant that the South is making progress, is apparently going to have progress forced on it, whether it will or no, what is the essential nature of that progress? Whose ideal of progress is the South to follow? The ideal of Mr. Mencken, if he has one? Of Oswald Garrison Villard? Of Mr. Walter Lippmann? Of the late Judge Gary?[19] Of the Merchants and Manufacturers Association? With so much advice offered gratis, the South can take its time and pick and choose. It has long been conservative. It has kept its old ways of life intact. It has clung stubbornly to traditions which have given it definite character. In this time of change it can and ought to be deliberate. Whatever the South may find to emulate in the example of other sections of the United States, it may also find mistakes to avoid. But deliberate selectiveness is impossible without proper leaders. And the two principles that are the core of the whole matter are these: first, the great intellectual problem of the South today is to find leaders and to follow them; and second, only that ideal of progress is justified which affirms and does not destroy the local individuality and true characteristics of the South.

The leaders must come from the South itself, and not from the "outside." I greatly fear that Northern criticism, which has in the main done little more

---

won a Pulitzer Prize in 1926 for *Teefallow,* set in a painfully small-minded Tennessee town. Kentucky poet and novelist Elizabeth Madox Roberts (1881–1941) often explored agrarian and folk themes.

18. Mims, *The Advancing South: Stories of Progress and Reaction* (Garden City, N.Y., 1926). Calling Davidson's "First Fruits of Dayton" "a mixed bag of emerging agrarianism and fading New South liberalism," O'Brien observed that the article nevertheless contained "sentiments almost straight from *The Advancing South*" (*IAS,* 188).

19. Oswald Garrison Villard (1872–1949) was an NAACP cofounder, New York *Evening Post* owner, and World War I peace activist who criticized the Wilson administration for endorsing segregation. Harvard-educated writer and editor Walter Lippmann (1889–1974) produced more than a dozen books on American public policy and foreign relations. U.S. Steel Corporation board chairman Judge Elbert Henry Gary (1846–1927) helped the corporation acquire the Tennessee Coal and Iron Company in 1907 and opposed the American Federation of Labor during the steel strike of 1919.

than shout about ignorance and foolishness, has overshot itself and is of doubtful value in the present situation. The critic who begins his analysis with a flogging or a lynching may be on the side of the right, but he often misses his mark because he reasons from insufficient data or misplaces his emphasis. Southerners who try the same role accomplish more, but they are likely to fall into a purely critical attitude which is as dangerous as the old habit of belligerent apologetics. The South has had enough criticism to give it a healthy distrust of itself. But if distrust goes far enough, it becomes unhealthy. It is not good for any nation or part of a nation to lose its self-respect. Just now the South needs the declarative, interpreting eye of the sympathetic student, not the lashing tongue of the scold.

The task of the leaders of Southern thought is as much to interpret the South to itself as it is to distribute the various doctrines of sweetness and light that are being offered by excited spectators. Once we had in the South—and still have, to a large extent—a tradition of repose and *noblesse oblige,* ways of quiet, cultured life not surpassed anywhere. But what will happen to that tradition before the modern doctrine which insists that progress is novelty, is energy, is quantity? Once we had romantic notions about the beauty and goodness of woman, and we even believed in God and good manners. Now we are offered biology, behaviorism, a handful of fossils, a tabloid newspaper, Mencken's essay on the liver as the seat of artistic inspiration, the opinions of Arthur Brisbane,[20] the vague, elusive thing called liberalism. Why should we not be slow to change? Why should we not search for certain accommodations? Surely it is the business of Southern leaders not merely to be progressive, but to study how to adapt the ways of progress to certain peculiarities of the Southern people which do not yet deserve to perish from the earth.

It is strange that the critics of the South have rarely if ever noted where the strategic key to the situation lies. We may as well be realists. The key is in the hands of the businessmen. They are the lords and masters of the industrial expansion which is the chief fact about the modern South, and they wield the balance of power here as elsewhere. Even the rural population, long unmanageable, yields to the sway of dividends when Kraft cheese factories and water power syndicates invade the countryside. Reconstruction made it respectable for a man to earn money by trade, and now the blood of the Cavaliers (as well as the canny Scots) promotes real estate subdivisions

---

20. Mencken, "The Divine Afflatus" in *Prejudices: Second Series* (New York, 1920), 155–71. Arthur Brisbane (1864–1936), the sensationalizing editor of Joseph Pulitzer's *Sunday World,* was hired at an enormous salary by William Randolph Hearst to edit the *Evening Journal.* Brisbane was the author of a syndicated column called "Today."

or manufactures a product with a fancy name—sometimes, perhaps, a little ashamed, secretly, of the vulgarities required.

The situation is not as new as it seems. Colonial Virginia was mercantile before it adopted the genteel tradition of its Cavaliers—a minority who set the tone for the majority of the population. The South has never blushed to acknowledge that the good life has its foundation in economic matters. But the plantation masters of old days and even the factory builders of the late nineteenth century mixed a considerable amount of civic responsibility and generous paternalism with their business affairs. The Southern business men of today seem to be out of touch with this tradition. Their public activities tend to be limited to the familiar process of boosting the home town, or to minor civic enterprises like widening a street or supporting the community chest. Privately they look after their own interests. They will talk to the government, if it needs any talking to, and, through their agencies such as the Merchants and Manufacturers Association, they will exert a strong negative and repressive power on persons who come out with dangerous or heretical doctrines. Above all, behind their genial front is a determined, though not consciously formulated, policy of aggrandizement. They are ready to egg on their industrial revolution enthusiastically without ever counting the evils they may be dragging in with it, and without considering whether they are hurrying the South into an artificial prosperity.

It is in their power to cast the deciding vote in the matter of intellectual progress. They can, if they wish, inhibit free expression. They can be the bogey looking over the shoulder of the editor, who wonders if what he is writing will offend the Chamber of Commerce and the local advertisers. They can agitate for the repression of unorthodox journalistic views, as they did in Atlanta when a "colyumist" talked freely about the Sacco-Vanzetti affair,[21] and as they have done in other and similar cases when somebody spoke out frankly. When burning issues arise, as in the Dayton unpleasantness, they can stand aside, with a don't-mix-in-politics attitude, although when child-labor legislation comes along, they do mix in politics with quiet, thorough-going cooperation. In short, they can make the efforts of all other leaders ineffective, by simply taking no interest in ideas or by being suspicious of them. In their behalf it must be said that the whole code of modern business in Amer-

21. Newspaper readers of Davidson's era referred to the increasing number of feature columns (often devoted to humor or social commentary) as "colyums." Nicola Sacco and Bartolomeo Vanzetti were accused in 1920 of having murdered two Massachusetts shoe-factory employees. In July 1927, after six years of litigation and worldwide protest, the two Italian-born anarchists, whom many Americans believed to be political scapegoats, were executed.

ica does not encourage them to consider a definition of progress or to be very social-minded.

On the other hand, the mere presence of a few business men will make any cause respectable, whether it be an imitation of Gridiron Club[22] frolics or a campaign for a stadium or an art museum. Whenever they have chosen to act in positive ways (and they often have), the results have been an impressive forecast of what can be accomplished when power and ideas work together. Under their touch art takes courage and independent opinion thrives. In Atlanta, there is grand opera. In Nashville a symphony orchestra enters its eighth season, and a beautiful replica of the Parthenon arises, to serve no use but beauty. In other cities libraries are built, or a progressive minister is sustained. A Birmingham newspaper victoriously assails the Ku Klux Klan. The "colyumist's" writings are retained in his home city, day in and day out, despite criticism, and are syndicated in many cities. A vocal genius is given a musical education and goes to the Metropolitan. A poetry magazine is supported by retail merchants.[23] A university endowment is increased. These things have happened when business men give aid; and they should happen more often, for this is the way of salvation, and it is sad to see the business men and the intellectuals often in apparently hostile camps, where each side suspects the other of deviltries unmentionable.

INTELLECTUAL DRY ROT

But there are certain reasons for not blaming the business men and others who have not been attracted by intellectual issues. The weakness of the liberal cause is its lack of flavor, which is the result of its dry insistence on purely intellectual things. Look where you will—in politics, religion, literature— liberals fear emotion, as much as Satan himself, without realizing that they cannot make reason and the will of God prevail until they instill a little emotion into the process. The souls of men refuse to be stirred by logarithmic arrangements of ideas, and even the admirable editorials of a liberal like Herbert Croly[24] leave a poor sinner a little cold. The leaders of intellectual

---

22. This Washington, D.C., dining club, founded by journalists in 1885, frequently hosted the politically powerful.

23. Davidson here alluded to the financial assistance *The Fugitive* received from the Nashville Associated Retailers (Louise Cowan, *The Fugitive Group: A Literary History* [Baton Rouge, 1959], 105, 137, 138n, 173).

24. Herbert Croly (1869–1930) wrote *The Promise of American Life* (1909) and was the *NR*'s first editor.

progress in the South—whether they be novelists, teachers, dramatists—may use all the reason they want in reaching their conclusions, but they overlook the possibilities of their audience if they can make no emotional appeal.

And that appeal, for the Southerner as for others, begins with his homeland, to which he may well turn with a lump in his throat and yet not put logic and truth aside. The South has been damned for its provincialism, but there never was a time when the South needed its provincialism more—if by provincialism is meant its heritage of individual character, the whole bundle of ways that make the South Southern. The South needs to keep its provincialism (it can be both detached and generous) if only as a balance against the feverish cosmopolitanism affected in some other sections. Some little spirit of disunity and retirement might be a boon, as a refuge against the cruel conformity ordered by our always accelerating, standardizing civilization.

The South is asked to remold itself! In whose image, then, and after what heart's desire? What problems are to be visited upon the South, what strikes, agitations, nervous retchings of society, wage slavery, graft, mountebankery, idiocies of merchant princes? No, give the South leave first to discover its virtues as other sections have discovered theirs. For the progress that comes through disruption and haste is not always a civilized thing.

A Southerner visits New York, let us say, as Southerners do. He boards the train at Charleston, leaving behind the marshes with wild birds and deer, the trees heavy with moss, the close, white-fronted houses—a quiet land, gracious and full of ancient peace. He passes the sandy flats, the pines and turpentine camps, the cotton fields, presently the greener country with its different soil, and then the rolling fields and variegated hills of Virginia, where are houses placid, old in generous traditions. Not even yet is it a thickly settled country. There is ugliness around the railroad stations, but not much elsewhere until Washington is passed, and then come the miles of slums, factories, railroads, a hopeless wreck of the soil, a triumph of ugliness until one plunges into the bowels of the earth and, issuing breathless, feels on his temples the roar of New York.

THE NEW SOUTH AND THE OLD

To contend that there are different ways of progress is not to be a foe to progress. The Southerner who takes such a journey may well ask himself what sort of progress he is going in for. To make Charleston over into the precise image of Pittsburgh would be a crime worse than the Dayton crime. Those who advocate progress without any positive regard for the genius of the South may presently find themselves in the unenviable company of the carpet-baggers and scalawags of the first reconstruction. They shall be as persons without a country—barren and importunate exiles—dwelling in a land that loves them not, that they have helped to kill.

Does such a view of the situation imply that there is a special kind of progress, different from other kinds, which the South ought to make its own? The answer is yes—it must be yes, so long as the individuality of the South is a living thing, affirmed by the very vehemence of the critics who make its case a special case; so long as its character and heritage have anything valuable to contribute to the term American. The doctrine of States Rights has long been politically submerged, and shows little prospect of being raised to life. Spiritually, it is more important than ever; for while we live under the blessings of national unity, we must take care that unity does not become uniformity. In the day of standardization we have the moral obligation to discover the uses of variety, which is an aid to the good life in New England, the South, or anywhere you will. There is more than political truth in the Wilsonian word, *self-determination;* it is a fair mixture of differences that makes a tolerable harmony.

Thus provincialism means, not sectionalism, not insularity and bigotry of mind, but differentiation, which is a thoroughly ancient and honorable and American idea. And as Matthew Arnold was unable to define the grand style much further than to say it was the style used by grand poets,[25] I should hesitate to say more than that the progress recommended to Southerners ought to be a Southern progress. It would be with danger hastily superimposed, but it ought to arrive naturally—and, in accordance with Southern character, slowly—from within. General and universal items of progress, such as modern education, religious tolerance, political liberalism, should be sought as a matter of course, like improved sanitation and good farm machinery; and in these things the South would be foolish not to accept intelligent guidance wherever it can be found.

But in the more particular items of progress, a man would be bold indeed

---

25. In a well-known passage, the British critic and poet Matthew Arnold (1822–88) praised Homer for writing "in the grand style," adding, "People complain that I do not define these words sufficiently. . . . Alas! the grand style is the last matter in the world for verbal definition to deal with adequately. One may say of it as is said of faith: 'One must feel it in order to know what it is.' . . . [T]he grand style arises in poetry, *when a noble nature, poetically gifted, treats with simplicity or with severity a serious subject*" ("On Translating Homer," in *On the Classical Tradition, The Complete Prose Works of Matthew Arnold,* ed. R. H. Super [Ann Arbor, 1960], 1 : 187–88). For further discussion of Arnold's use of the term, see David G. Riede, *Matthew Arnold and the Betrayal of Language* (Charlottesville, Va., 1988), esp. 22–23.

who would offer, as for Southerners only, an exact and systematic prescrip-
tion. One can readily see, however, that the social heritage of the South
ought naturally and unconsciously to modify the course of progress—intellectual and material—if only the mind of the South can develop a wise self-
reliance. Thus we can imagine a Southern industrialism, somewhat affected
by elder ideals, that would be not wholly utilitarian in its philosophy and
conduct. Or a clergy who could be liberal and yet command the fire and earnestness that the Modernists have left to be monopolized by their narrower-
minded brethren. Or writers who could be in touch with all that is new in
art and letters without ever allowing their own native character, idiom, consciousness of place to be obscured in their interpretations of the South—
writers with positive Southern warmth and good humor rather than the
painful acidity that passes for sophistication.

In short, the progress of the South deserves to be organic. It can be genuine progress only when, in the best sense of the word, it is growth. And as
growth means improvement of what you have, not mere addition or change,
the first step toward progress is for the South to turn back upon itself, to re-
discover itself, to examine its ideals, to evaluate the past with reference to
the present, and the present with reference to the past. We need to reaffirm
the principle which Mr. Stark Young so happily ascribed to the University of
Virginia—"a habit of allowing men to ripen of themselves and the vitality
natural to their characters to achieve the growth implicit in it." For only thus
can we retain "the old fragrance of civilization, which arose from public
graces and a desire for those forms of moral beauty in which men may live
best, not to themselves but in some sort of society together."[26]

---

26. Stark Young (1881–1963) was a Mississippi novelist, *NR* theater critic, and contributor to *ITMS*. Davidson quoted from Young's "Virginia Reflections," *NR* 51, (1927),
100–101.

Donald Davidson

Sectionalism in the United States

This essay, in which Davidson celebrated sectionalism as a check against "character-less and synthetic Americanism," appeared in the Hound and Horn *in the summer of 1933 — but only after being criticized by Allen Tate, who was then Southern editor of the magazine. Long beforehand, Tate had warned Bernard Bandler, coeditor of the* Hound and Horn, *about soliciting the essay from Davidson: "Don, I should say, is the least clear-headed person in Tennessee. . . . He would not do you a good article on Sectionalism in general, but he would surely write a paper in which the philosophy of Southern sectionalism received a stirring defense. Of all our people, Don is the great Literalist in doctrine, and probably our finest character, but sheer, realistic intelligence—no." Davidson, who was hurt by the lukewarm response to the essay by the* Hound and Horn *editors,[1] nevertheless remained enthusiastic about his subject; indeed, the essay led to his 1938 book,* The Attack on Leviathan: Regionalism and Nationalism in the United States.

Reprinted from *Hound and Horn* 6 (1933): 561–89.

---

    1. Tate to Bandler, 24 Feb. 1932, quoted in O'Brien, *IAS,* 191. Critic Yvor Winters complained to the editors that "nearly every one of the agrarians has written and published at least twice, and has used 30 pages to spread out five pages of matter. The agrarian question should be definitely shelved as far as the Hound and Horn is concerned unless (1) the critic in question works out a detailed economic and political program for the realization of his desire, or (2) unless he utilizes his position as a basis for a definite and detailed criticism of a specific and limited subject, literary historical, or what have you." This criticism not only infuriated Tate but precipitated the break between the

"Men in the past were often parochial in space, but the dominant men of our age are parochial in time. They feel for the past a contempt that it does not deserve, and for the present a respect that it deserves still less."[2]

The words are Bertrand Russell's. The sentiment is latent wherever men have begun to doubt their ability to make a new order of life in utter disregard of the old order. It is a new heresy which threatens the very center of orthodox progressivism and modernism. In its general form the new heresy means that science can no longer offer itself as the one reliable substitute for the civilizing agents which it once tempted men to destroy. In connection with my special subject it means that those who wish to remedy the confusion of American life can no longer ignore the existence of sectionalism. The vision of a uniformly progressive America, which once cloaked the irregularities of our sectional history, has begun to wear thin.

It never, in fact, quite fitted the reality of national life. From time to time the recurrence of sectionalism has embarrassed the plans of the orthodox progressives who call themselves liberals. Thus sectionalism got a bad name, not because it was bad, but because it did not suit the plans that were drawn up. It will again mar the plans of any who propose to save America by policies based upon too simplified notions of the history and real structure of the United States.

Yet most of our saviors do not bother to include sectionalism in their programs. They are under the delusion that the United States are a compact and well unified body, neat and coherent as a European state. They assume that some strong-handed process of reorganization may be applied, either through the Federal government or some central revolutionary organism. Some of these thinkers are Easterners who know Europe better than the Mississippi Valley or the Upland South; all are misled by the semblance of unity which the industrial apparatus has set up. They do not realize that many of our troubles derive from a misguided industrial effort to achieve the wrong kind of unity. They do not suspect that their programs, in outline pretentiously national, are really sectional programs in masquerade. Except through a conquest by force, like that which once subdued the South, no such program can win more than a temporary victory, and a permanent victory may recoil upon the victor. Even now, at long last, the North reaps the bitter harvest of Appomattox.

Sectionalism is no mere vestige from an older time, archaic and negli-

---

Hound and Horn editors and the Agrarians (Leonard Greenbaum, *The Hound and Horn: The History of a Literary Quarterly* [The Hague, 1966], 150, 149–53, 182).

2. Bertrand Russell, *The Scientific Outlook* (Glencoe, Ill., 1931), 267.

gible. It is a function of the national life. The sections are real entities, not sentimental fictions; they have a place in the making of events, along with the Federal system and the state governments, although their place and power are not yet formally recognized.

Today sectionalism displays two characters, or two countenances, according as politics and economics, or culture and the arts, are in the front of the issue. The first kind of sectionalism is organic in the American establishment. It has grown out of the accidents and purposes that have attended the adaptation of a people, democratically inclined and originally of diverse but not unrelated European stocks and traditions, to life on the North American continent. The history of the sections as sections is unwritten, and as yet almost unexplored, because historians have fixed attention too exclusively on the growth of the Federal organism, which they picture as dwarfing gradually the power of the states as it draws power unto itself. But if the historical bias is altered, if we study the people themselves, as they follow the extensions of the frontier and gather into geographic provinces whose interests over-run political boundaries, then the realities of sectional influence appear; the sections share with the Federal organism in the dwarfing of states. Taking this view, the late Frederick Jackson Turner passed naturally from a study of the frontier[3] to a study of the sections. He has at last altered the old false perspective and drawn the outline of a thesis which must inevitably raise the sections to a new level of importance.*

In the new view, sectionalism derives partly from geography and climate,

---

3. In 1893, at the annual meeting of the American Historical Association, Turner delivered his paradigm-creating lecture, "The Significance of the Frontier in American History," in which he argued, "The existence of an area of free land, its continuous recession, and the advance of American settlement westward, explain American development" (*The Significance of the Frontier in American History,* ed. Harold P. Simonson [New York, 1963]). For other Agrarian responses to Turner, see Fletcher's review of Turner's *The Significance of Sections in American History* ("Section Versus State," *AR* 1 [1933]: 483–89), and Frank Lawrence Owsley, "The Historical Philosophy of Frederick Jackson Turner," *AR* 5 (1935): 368–75.

*D.D. note: This essay was written in substantially its present form and submitted before the appearance of Frederick Jackson Turner's *The Significance of Sections in American History* (New York, 1932). I have since had the opportunity to make a few revisions which take cognizance, though necessarily of too meager a character, of Professor Turner's views of the importance of the sections. An earlier knowledge of the book, which brings together scattered articles and addresses not available to me at the time of writing, would have made it somewhat easier to take for granted what I have here taken much space to argue; but I would not, for that reason, have altered the approach I have preferred to make to the subject.

and from the economic bias that these invited or enforced; but partly also from purposes and traditions which colonists, frontiersmen, and immigrants brought with them. It is implied, too, in the fabric of democratic government itself, with its eternal problem of the reconcilement of liberty and union; and in the distant motivation of democratic theory, which forever encourages citizens to think more of rights than of duties. But sectionalism means nothing finally except in terms of geographic masses, separately differentiated and fairly homogeneous within themselves. The United States are unique among western nations in having developed this kind of differentiation. No matter what label Europeans may give the American type, for us there are only Americans of New England or the South or West—the familiar and inevitable divisions that "make sense" where American does not. Politically, this sectionalism is the tendency of groups of states, bound in physical contiguity and joined by social and economic ties, to think in common and, upon occasion, to act in common. It is the basic tendency which leads Turner to characterize the United States as "a nation comparable to all Europe in area, with settled geographic provinces which equal great European nations . . . a federation of sections, a union of potential nations."[4]

But there is another aspect of sectionalism which Turner does not suggest. In our time, sectionalism is a reactionary temper that gives a new emotional meaning and a fresh intellectual validity to tendencies that once sought political expression. Partly, it is a movement of artists, uncovering what politicians and economists ignore; it is a revolt against the excessive centralism of the machine age. Men are exhilarated to realize that the dilemmas of industrial civilization may be downed or escaped by reaffirming the ties, local and native, which once were only shackles to be cast off. Yet in its undeniable nostalgia this sectionalism contains a realistic answer to the question: Whom shall my soul believe? Worn out with abstraction and novelty, plagued with divided counsels, some Americans are saying: After all, I will believe the old folks at home who have kept alive, through many treacherous outmodings, some good secret of life. Such moderns prefer to grasp the particular. They want what is near to home and capable of understanding, for it engages both reason and loyalty. They distrust the advice of John Dewey to "use the foresight of the future to refine and expand present activities."[5]

---

4. Turner, *Significance of Sections,* 37.

5. Davidson misquoted Dewey, who wrote: "Human desire and ability cooperates with this or that natural force according as this or that eventuality is judged better. We do not use the present to control the future. We use the foresight of the future to refine and expand present activity. In this use of desire, deliberation and choice, freedom is actualized" (*Human Nature and Conduct* [New York, 1930], 313).

The future is not yet; it is unknowable, intangible. But the past was, the present is; of that much they can be sure. So they attach themselves—or re-attach themselves—to a home-section, one of the sections, great or small, defined in the long conquest of our continental area. They seek spiritual and cultural autonomy.

This temper, or this movement, has somehow acquired the name of regionalism. It is really sectionalism under another name. One does not obtain spiritual and cultural autonomy simply by moving into grandfather's house. Inevitably one is driven into social and economic questions. Soon "regionalism" becomes a criticism of a false conception of American life and treads the ground of sectional issues.

The urban thinker, engrossed in the seemingly uniform patterns of the civilization that makes loud noises around him, is nevertheless sure to question the pertinency of any talk of sectionalism. This is more an echo than a living voice, he will say.

If he dislikes Turner's notions of United States history, this urban thinker can be given his proof from the pages of the economic history which the urban dispensation seems to prefer. Consider, for example, what Mr. Charles A. Beard[6] says of the most pronounced sectional conflict in our history, the one of many conflicts that came finally to war. Mr. Beard examines and dismisses the causes usually cited for the war between North and South. Was slavery the cause? No, there was never, even in the North, a majority opinion favoring the abolition of slavery. Was it state sovereignty? No. "If the Southern planters had been content to grant tariffs, bounties, subsidies, and preferences to Northern commerce and industry, it is not probable that they would have been molested in their most imperious proclamations of sovereignty." Was it a matter of interpreting the Constitution? No. "The modern student . . . can hardly do otherwise than conclude that the linguistic devices used first on one side and then on the other were not derived from inherently necessary concepts concerning the intimate essence of the Federal system." What, then, was the cause? "The roots of the controversy lay

---

6. Charles Austin Beard (1874–1948) was a progressive (and prolific) historian whose economic interpretation of the Civil War appealed to Davidson and the other Agrarians. In *The Rise of American Civilization,* 2 vols. (New York, 1927), Beard and his wife, Mary Ritter Beard (1876–1958), explained the Civil War as the conquest of Southern agricultural interests by commercial-industrial capitalists in the Northeast. Davidson contrasted Turner and Beard in *The Attack on Leviathan: Regionalism and Nationalism in the United States* (Chapel Hill, 1938), esp. chap. 2.

elsewhere—in social [groupings founded on] differences, in climate, soil, industries, and labor systems, in divergent social forces."[7]

The implications of this view are the more significant for the conclusion that Mr. Beard omits to draw. He speaks definitely enough of the three great sections of the 1860s which, for all their common language, religion, law, and basic culture, had evolved real distinctions "woven out of the tough facts of daily existence."[8] He emphasizes the fact that the distinctions followed geographic lines; they were not the familiar distinctions generally diffused through the body of any civilized community. Such a situation, he says, had never arisen before "in the history of human societies." "No European country had ever had a highly developed group of capitalists [the East], a large body of independent farmers [the West], and a powerful landed aristocracy [the South] each to a marked degree segregated into a fairly definite geographical area."[9]

If this rather simplified description be accepted as correct, then why does Mr. Beard not go on to say that the causes of strife included all the causes he mentions, and still one great cause more? This, the final reason for the impasse of war, was that the quarreling sections had to live under a political instrument which did not provide for the rise of sectionalism. Obviously, Mr. Beard does not name this cause for the reason that his bias as a historian inclines him to glorify Federalism, or at least its industrial, socialistic development into what I will call Leviathanism.[10] Nevertheless the defect existed in 1860, and still exists. The Constitution, a remarkably adaptable device, had looked out for many things. But the one feature, sectionalism, that was unique and unheard of in the governments of the earth, was the very one for which no provision was made. Although the Constitution served admirably as long as parties were roughly national and the division of voters cut across sections, it failed when the majority vote concentrated in two sections and the minority vote in a third. Thus, in 1860, the Republic broke down so far as the Southern states were concerned, and they withdrew.

---

7. Beard, *Rise of American Civilization,* 2 : 38, 37, 51. The words in brackets were omitted in Davidson's article.

8. Beard, *Rise of American Civilization,* 2 : 663.

9. Beard, *Rise of American Civilization,* 1 : 663, 664.

10. It is unclear whether Davidson had read Beard's *The American Leviathan: The Republic in the Machine Age* (New York, 1930), which Beard and his coauthor, William Beard, described as "an effort to unite politics, government, and technology as reflected in the federal system of the United States, with emphasis on the newer functions created under the pressures of the machine age" (vii).

People are accustomed to look back on the War Between the States with the feeling that it ought to have been averted, but no one can say exactly how. The answer to this old question seems plainer now than it once did. The war could have been averted only by giving sectionalism the political recognition which was denied it in 1860. It was the dogmatic insistence on a Federal union of states, and the refusal to recognize a Federal union of sections that actually precipitated secession. As a matter of fact, from the Missouri Compromise to the Compromise of 1850, such a recognition was implicit in the conciliatory arrangements of [Henry] Clay and [Daniel] Webster. Like their successors of the Twentieth Century, the politicians of the 1860s breathed no word of heresy as to such a revised view of the union, but practically they worked toward it by the familiar method of give-and-take. Arguments and protestations about state sovereignty were, as Turner points out, simply the screen for sectionalism, or its defensive weapon, and state sovereignty, as Calhoun knew, amounted to nothing unless states combined and bargained like nations with other combinations of states.[11] In 1860, when the Whigs had lost power, there was no longer a channel through which bargains could be negotiated. Lincoln's preachment against a "house-divided" policy meant to the South that the revised union, which had recognized sectional reciprocity, was to be abrogated in favor of a presumptive national union which would be dominated uncompromisingly in the sectional interest of the North.

The event has confirmed Southern apprehensions. The union achieved after Lincoln, although outwardly conforming to the ideal of the Fathers, has been shaped to favor the commercial East, which has been able, not without difficulty and occasional yielding, to keep the West as its turbulent ally. The agrarian South, a reluctant appendage to this union, was confirmed by the long horror of Reconstruction in a far more intense sectionalism than existed even in 1860. The union under which we live today thus represents the crystallized injustice of a sectional victory. Time has mitigated its rigors to the modest extent of indulging the South in its practical nullification of the Negro suffrage amendments. But every Southerner knows that the American Leviathan is not of his making and was not constructed to serve his interests. And what every Southerner knows, the angry farmers of the West have just found out anew. Now the irrepressible conflict is between an internationally minded East, intent on money-lending and industrialism, and an agrarian west, or Middle West, which sees itself ruined by Eastern policies. This is the embarrassing result of voting under a government that recognizes only states as units and living under a dispensation which tells another tale.

---

11. See Ann Ward Amacher, "Myths and Consequences: Calhoun and Some Nashville Agrarians," *SAQ* 59 (1960): 251–64.

Nevertheless it will be argued that sectional differentiations are bound to die out, for the industrial system levels all differences, even individual ones.

People who think thus are misled by appearances—by the uniformities of manners and machinery which may be seen in our urban conglomerations. Actually, I believe, the Americans of the 1860s were far more alike everywhere than we are now. Then, too, North and South dressed alike, rode in carriages à la mode, worshipped the same God (with no division between Modernist and Fundamentalist such as we have now); they read newspapers of the same pattern, though of different political opinions; the cities had modest skylines of much the same model everywhere. Above all there was a more genuine attachment to the Republic, even in the aggrieved South, than we have for our Federal Leviathan today. A seasoned New Yorker of 1933, or a distant Californian, can discover nothing in his bosom to parallel the devotion to the idea of union which the Virginians of 1861 sacrificed at the trying moment of secession. All the superficial conclusions that could be drawn as to the famous uniformity of American life held as good then as now. Nevertheless the sections quarreled; still worse, they fought. They did so not because of the clothes they wore or the kind of cities they lived in, but because they thought differently about important matters.

We are more impressed with our uniformity because it makes a bigger noise. Besides, we have fed well, until lately, at the trough of Mammon, and sectional issues have lain quiescent—bribed into repose. When we are less well bribed, the sectional issues will quickly revive. In any time of pressure they may again appear, and in such case the lines of cleavage will again follow the delimitations of geographic masses—the sections to which nature and custom have bound us. That is the sort of country we are.

The organic sectionalism of the past has been well studied, although no one but Turner has grouped its phenomena to demonstrate a historical thesis. We know very well what the three great sections were like in the Nineteenth Century. But now, when we have a greater number of sections, large and small, our historical students make little attempt to establish their differentiations. They are looking for social democracy; they are fascinated by the wallowings of the American Leviathan. Yet, although the outlines of our contemporary sections still await the drawing of the historical expert, it seems feasible to indicate some of the elements that produce a sectional differentiation like that of an earlier time, or perhaps even more pronounced.

Population changes have brought about a sectional differentiation far more marked than at the time of Lee's surrender. The South alone has undergone no important population changes except a considerable exodus of Negroes to the industrial centers of the North. The Old East, once dominated by New England, has been whelmed with a tidal wave of immigrant stocks—

Irish Catholics, Jews from Central and Eastern Europe, and peoples from the Mediterranean basin. At the same time the East has received "native immigrants" from the United States at large—careerists who have cut loose from their native soil. The old New Englanders are still as much New Englanders as ever; but they cannot any longer determine the thought of the New East, and their old working alliance with New York is less effective than it was. The new stocks are ignorant of the American past. Their rise to power accelerates the detachment from the thought of other sections into which the urban East is falling. The "Our America" of Waldo Frank is decidedly not the America of Henry Cabot Lodge or Will Rogers.[12]

In the Old West, the states of the North Central group (now the "border states" of the Middle West) have undergone population changes like those of the East but on a less disruptive scale. The Yankees, the Scotch-Irish who came from the South, the long since assimilated Germans hold their own fairly well, although, as in the East, the new racial stocks have an increasing influence in the cities to which they have come in great numbers. But Chicago and Cleveland are much less detached than New York or Boston. They express a good deal of the spirit of their locale. They are lusty, and dislike Eastern softness—or at least Eastern interference, which they alternately deplore as too radical or too conservative. Further on, in the Middle West proper, the immigrant stock is more specialized. Areas that were empty a little more than a generation ago are filled with Scandinavians and Germans. These have recapitulated much of the old pioneer experience, but their agrarian temper is not quite of the Jeffersonian order that pervaded an earlier West, and, by a strange twist of events, produced the Lincolnian tradition.

In the Far West the racial infusion has been Oriental; in the Southwest,

---

12. The Yale-educated novelist Waldo Frank (1889–1967) wrote a nonfiction work for the French titled *Our America* (New York, 1919) in which he described America as "a sprawling continent—mountains and gardenland and desert—swarmed by a sprawling congeries of people. To bound it, is to stifle it" (8). Henry Cabot Lodge (1850–1924) was a Harvard-educated Republican congressman 1886–93 and senator 1893–1924 from Massachusetts whose 1890 "Force Bill" angered white Southern Democrats by advocating the federal oversight of black voting in the South. Lodge, who became an outspoken proponent of immigration restriction, also blocked American involvement in Woodrow Wilson's cherished League of Nations. Cowboy, performer, and author Will Rogers (1879–1935) published biting spoofs, including *The Cowboy Philosopher on Prohibition* (1919) and *Letters of a Self-Made Diplomat to His President* (1927). According to one historian, "By 1925 Will Rogers, the greatly beloved cracker-barrel philosopher of the decade, was beginning to hoot and jibe at people who called themselves 100 per cent American" (John Higham, *Strangers in the Land: Patterns of American Nativism, 1860–1925* [New York, 1969], 325–26).

Mexican. In these sections, too, there are large numbers of Indians. The result is a race problem which affects these sections alone.

New population groups have thus tended to concentrate in well-defined areas. Although they take on "Americanism" quickly enough, their concentration gives a new coloring to the sectional traditions they encounter.

The differentiation is strengthened by economic bias, which also follows sectional lines. The East is still plutocratic; its mainstays are manufacturing and banking. But its plutocratic spirit is now a little fatigued and skeptical where it was once bold. The boldness has migrated to sections where plutocracy is newer: to the North Central states, which have plunged heavily into manufacturing and still have much of the self-confidence and gusto that once made producers into conquistadors; or even to parts of the South, where profits in cotton stockings and cigarettes seduce the heirs of Jefferson. The East is less swayed by manufacturing interests than of old. Its financial mind has an international twist; its bankers are suspected of imperial ambitions. The other sections are not internationally minded at all; they embarrass the East by resisting the cancellation of European debts. Internationalism fits the detachment of the East as "American first" suits the lusty particularism of the West in general. But the westward and southward shift of manufactures has brought other changes. Eastern bankers begin to doubt Republican high tariff policies at the time when other sections are converted to high tariffs, and so an old bond of union begins to crack.

Such changes, however, need to be balanced by other observations. In the East, the admirable farming regions are thoroughly subdued and adjusted to the temper of the cities, whose sway is undisputed. Beyond the farms lies a gentled wilderness, the summer playground of urban multitudes. In Middle West or South it is not so. Country rules city or bitterly obstructs city leadership. This jostling contact forbids cities to assume the nonchalance of a New York, and the farther one goes into the so-called hinterland, the more this is true. An exception must be made for pleasure resorts, or for cities like Los Angeles that spring up into the Greatest Common Denominator of American averages. Climate and soil, too, enforce wide differences in agriculture. Mechanized farming has been taken up in the Middle West, but is rarely adapted to Southern conditions, where labor is cheap and irregular ground does not invite the tractor. In the still agrarian South, where industrial conquest is as yet more an advertisement than a reality, the farmer loves his acres, which are often enough his ancestral acres. They are his home. In the Middle West they may be only his investment. And the wilderness, in South and West, is hardly gentled, is not a playground. In the mountain cove or swamp land, rude folk keep their ancient ways, heedless that extinction is predicted for them. They belong to the backwoods and have not yet consented to be tamed. In the western country of desert and mountain, where the population is scattered, the wilderness is everything and man is nothing, and the concerns of industrial America seem hardly work talking about.

In every case the distinctions require sectional categories. One cannot write sensibly of the United States in any other terms. It is possible to pursue the distinctions much further, and trace the undeniable differences between states, or between parts of sections or parts of states—what Turner calls "sectionalism of minority areas." [13] But it is generalization enough to say that the United States at large are decidedly heterogeneous; and yet within well-marked sectional lines there is a real organic homogeneity which has been remarkably persistent. The wonder is, not that we have had one great sectional clash, but only one. In Turner's opinion we have been saved from utter Balkanization by two circumstances: first, the undeveloped West offered a "safety valve"; and second, our national, or inter-sectional, parties have been agents of practical compromise between the extreme particularism of the sections and the extreme centralism of the Federal instrument. Now the safety valve is gone. We approach, everywhere, a clash of interests between establishments, and should remember that the old quarrel of the 1860s occurred between the two sections that were most settled. Furthermore, the Federal instrument has been made more insistently national than ever. The situation by no means discourages sectionalism, but rather the contrary. The revolt of the Western farmers today is a sectional disturbance. It is easy to see where sectional issues might again gather head around special questions: the Negro problem in the South; border troubles in the Southwest; or anti-Japanese feeling in the Far West.

These are illustrations, not prophecies. Our contemporary sectional differences are for the most part but mildly contentious. The cities of the Great Lakes and the cities of the East differ about the St. Lawrence waterway. The New England states call for teamwork in protecting their political and commercial interests, and other groups of states are not backward in protecting theirs. There are farm blocs, and other kinds of blocs not quite so famous. Trade associations and professional societies have "regional" meetings. Occasionally, too, sectionalism gets open legal recognition: as in the Federal Reserve System; or the plans formulated for controlling hydro-electric power over sectional areas; or in the consolidation of railroad systems. These are

---

13. "There is, then," wrote Turner, "a sectionalism of the regions within the larger divisions, a sectionalism of minority areas, sometimes protesting against the policies of the larger section in which they lie and finding more in common with similar regions outside of this section" (*Significance of Sections,* 49).

sectional trends which will do to illustrate the anti-national tendency, but they do not indicate sectional belligerence. We are already approaching the condition Turner foresaw many years ago, when he wrote: "As the nation reaches a more stable equilibrium . . . the influence of the diverse physio-graphic provinces which make up the nation will become more marked. . . . The real federal aspect of our government will lie, not in the relation of state and nation, but in the relation of section and nation."[14]

Sectionalism itself need not be dangerous, but sectionalism masquerading as nationalism, or sectionalism unacknowledged, is always dangerous, or at least irritating and confusing. For example, the East provokes discord to-day by being a little too self-righteous; too confidently it undertakes to edu-cate the "hinterland"; too readily it encourages Scottsboro cases and Harlan County invasions and forgets the adage of live and let live.[15] This, the sec-tionalism of John Brown, is dangerous and bad in any quarter. But otherwise, if sectionalism is not a positive good in the ideal state of socialistic piety, at least in imperfect America it has its value. The economic historians after all fail to give a due place to loyalty, without which a government theoretically perfect in many respects might yet collapse. Sectionalism fosters loyalty, and a kind of loyalty not incompatible with affection for the Republic. It is re-markable how little affection the American Leviathan, which disregards sec-tionalism, attracts at present. It has been fashionable to hold Senators in con-tempt and speak sardonically of the government at Washington as if it were some wholly external pest. The trouble is that the Republic has become too abstract; it does not adequately express the things to which loyalty can attach.

The so-called regional movement, which is artistic and cultural section-alism, is on the side of loyalty. It is like an outbreak of the patriotic instinct which the monstrous circumstances of our age have thwarted. On its literary side it may be viewed as a correction of too much Leviathanism in the arts.

The nationalist party of Americans have never been content to let *E Pluri-bus Unum* signify political convenience only. From Emerson on down, critics

---

14. Turner, "Is Sectionalism in America Dying Away?," paper delivered by Turner at the American Sociological Society in 1907 and reprinted in *Significance of Sections,* 287–314 (313–14).

15. See Owsley, "Scottsboro, The Third Crusade," reprinted here. For a scholarly account, see Dan T. Carter, *Scottsboro: A Tragedy of the American South,* rev. ed. (Baton Rouge, 1979). By "Harlan County invasions," Davidson was referring to Communist Party efforts to unionize coal miners in Harlan County, Kentucky, in the early 1930s. In late 1931, Davidson refused to join Tate in protesting when the Commonwealth of Ken-tucky filed charges against writers who defended the miners.

have added: not only one nation, but one art; and our writers have sweated nervously under the self-imposed obligation to produce a distinctively American literature. In practice, no such literature has taken shape. We are never able to decide what American traits Hawthorne and Mark Twain have in common, but their sectional differentiations are readily discovered. And so with others.

Again, as in politics, what has been taken as nationalism turns out to be sectionalism in disguise. A sectional culture may develop and ambitiously propose itself as a national culture; but its partiality is sure to be detected and its leadership denied in the end. Consider, for instance, the history of Boston and New York, our two literary capitals, neither of which has ever succeeded in being the Paris of the United States.

Boston early became the seat of a highly developed New England culture, and naturally became a literary center. Its leadership was at first accepted— not always with perfect resignation—because neither South nor West could match New England in literary coherence or offer a rival capital. The New England stamp was long an apparently national stamp. So great was New England's prestige, so secure its command over channels of publication and critical judgments that the sectional bias of New England literature went unchallenged for many years. But in time Boston had to yield its pre-eminence. For all the splendor of its literary achievement, the mind of New England was far from being the national mind.

When Boston declined, New York took over the role of capital with an enthusiasm that ought to have deserved better than fate has allowed. Unfortunately New York assumed leadership at the time when its own development tended to dissociate it from the country at large. New York waxed great out of the commercial exploitation of America, but never, as a cultural capital, understood that its exploitation was also a dependency. It labors under the illusion—not altogether unjustified by years of recent memory— that what it thinks the country must think. But now it meets a growing resistance to the distribution of its ideas. Its ideas arise from its aspirations and malaises—bigness, tolerance of mixed populations, its blend of scientific idealism and urban fatigue; and its preoccupation with these reinforces its ignorance of the country beyond the Hudson and confirms it in dissociation. Through sheer power and masterful persuasion New York may rule fashions and win national support, up to a certain point, for its megalopolitan version of what the American arts and life ought to be. Then the outlying sections perceive that the megalopolitan image does them an injustice; it is not an acceptable national image, but a sectional one, against whose mastery they must protest.

Worst of all, New York becomes a center of confusion even to those who ask guidance of it. Literary innovations have their day of excitement; but it comforts nobody to discover that refinement is merely being heaped upon refinement, and beneath the fripperies there is nothing to believe in. Yet the artist must believe somehow; and soon there comes a Babel of arguing programs, which, for all their fine intentions, do not fit the diverse American scene. They are detached or irrelevant, and they suggest, not so much that American civilization is collapsing, as people keep saying, but that the East is sick.

It is not surprising that artists retire from a confusion that does not win them. Scattered individuals retired long ago, and now the numbers greatly increase. Unlike the expatriates of past years, the retiring artists are no longer Pilgrims of Eternity, hissing at American civilization from a safe refuge in Europe. They are discovering America. They are going back home—back to the South,[16] the West, New England. New York is still the bazaar where literary works must be vended. But loyalty knows bazaar talk for what it is and makes attachments that do not follow the rules of economic determinism.

In one phase "regionalism" is this retreat from the Leviathanism of New York. It is a process going on, not the slogan of some new group of innovators. But the flight of the artists is only the negative side of the process. The positive side is that the sections themselves are becoming more conscious of the validity of their own way of life. The frontier, long since passed by, has left them to grow up, and they have grown up. Now they seek to conserve and understand their own sectional traditions. Their self-conscious differentiation (which of course runs the risk of being too self-conscious) is no sudden phenomenon, whipped up by romantic agitators. Basically, it is an expression of the human desire for the particular as the complement of the universal, which in the murk of modernism has become too foggily abstract.

We have groaned too much over the leveling influences of our time. We over-estimate their power to change human nature; we under-estimate the counter-tendencies that hold them in check. What reporter of the progress of the Great American Bandwagon has adequately noted our passionate interest in genealogy, the increasing prestige of historical societies and memorial associations, the solicitude to preserve old shrines and landmarks—all

---

16. Davidson alluded perhaps to Tate and his wife, novelist Caroline Gordon (1895–1981), both of whom had been to Europe on Guggenheim grants twice in the previous several years and had both times made their way back to the South to live and write. In 1933, after years of European exile, Arkansas Agrarian Fletcher also repatriated himself. See also Malcolm Cowley, *Exile's Return: A Literary Odyssey of the 1920s* (New York, 1934).

the devices that turn Americans toward particularist, sectional attitudes? Family mansions are restored (not always, of course, by the blood that built them), antiques are sought out, handicrafts are revived, residence architecture again becomes "colonial" at the very moment when urban designers talk fantastically of communal burrows of glass, combining "dynamics" and "maximum service." It will not do to take all this as simply another fad. It comes too significantly in the midst of the new self-consciousness to which historians and biographers have been schooling us. It happens at the time when electric power, motor transportation, and regional economics make decentralization a practical issue. A powerful research into the past is paralleled by a new sense of place, the result of a centrifugal diffusion which is a natural recoil from over-concentration.[17]

The movement is part of a ground-swell which has long been making its way. The Local Color school of the 1870s was not an isolated phenomenon but an anticipation of a later tendency.[18] Since the World War, American literature has again been refreshed from sectional quarters, first from the Middle West and later from the South. The renaissance began, however, at the time when metropolitan criticism was being strongly colored by modern aestheticism, and so its sectional meaning got no intelligent attention. People who were quarreling over Imagism could give the new literature little consideration in terms of its background. Critics could see that [Robert] Frost's poetry was about New England, or that Willa Cather wrote about a West not composed of cowboys and Indians. But they speculated no further. They talked about realism, and failed to observe that the realism of *The Spoon River Anthology*[19] hardly concealed a powerful nostalgia for the tradition that the urbanization of Illinois was violating. At the same time the prestige of metropolitan opinion, which held provincial backwardness in contempt, often forced writers into condescension toward their materials, so that their work sometimes embodied a borrowed, not a native judgment. Criticism was in the realm of pure aesthetics or social reform; it occurred to nobody to talk of the integration of the artist with his environment. Al-

---

17. In "What Is a Traditional Society?" (*American Review* 7 [1936]: 376–87), Tate described much the same phenomena, but saw people chasing after superficial symbols of the past bearing no relation to the Agrarian tradition.

18. The local color school is usually dated to "The Luck of Roaring Camp," an 1868 short story about California miners by Bret Harte (1836–1902). Davidson, who may have had in mind Southern local colorists such as Thomas Nelson Page (1853–1922), Joel Chandler Harris (1848–1908), and George Washington Cable (1844–1925), saw all such writers as prefigurations of the literary regionalists of the 1920s.

19. *Spoon River Anthology* (1915), a collection of poetic vignettes by Edgar Lee Masters (1869–1950), related the fictional life stories of a village of Midwesterners.

though Chicago was a center of literary agitation, and Harriet Monroe's *Poetry,* and John Frederick's *The Midlander*[20] bid for leadership as periodicals, there was of course no real concert among Middle Western artists themselves. They worked as individuals—though hardly individuals who felt the deference for the East that Mark Twain once showed. They showed no signs of making a common cause.

The "regionalists"—at least the self-confessed ones—seem aware of a common cause. They openly profess allegiance to a place and its tradition. They distrust borrowed attitudes. Although they certainly abdicate no right of social criticism, they are prone to write of Gopher Prairie in terms of itself, not of what New York may think of Gopher Prairie.[21] They disdain mere "local color" and feel free to use whatever seems good in modern techniques, but they are more likely to explore the idiom of Gopher Prairie than simply to copy New York's copy of the idiom of James Joyce.

Yet it is not quite so simple as all that. In their most serious moments, the rebels against centralism conceive their problem in terms of a whole culture—at least of a whole sectional culture which has its invaluable peculiarities. Often they argue that the arts must rest ultimately upon folkways; always they look for a tradition. They collect and revive ballads and folk-tales; they restore the crafts of Southern highland and western plains. They amass an overwhelming body of evidence to disprove the quaint urban notion that America has no folk-art except Negro spirituals. While they admit the authority of the general European-American tradition, they want the arts to be organic with other kinds of activity, and not separated into "pure art"— above all, not to be incubated and wet-nursed into a pampered existence. But talk of a whole culture brings in politics and economics and so takes them to a sectionalism deeper than mere literary romanticism.

The tendency is much older and covers a wider field than one might think from glancing at arguments of special groups. In contemporary American

---

20. Monroe (1860–1936) founded Chicago's modernist serial *Poetry: A Magazine of Verse* in 1912 and edited it until 1936. By *The Midlander,* Davidson meant *Midland: A Magazine of the Middlewest,* founded in 1915 by Iowan John Towner Frederick (1893–?). "In establishing the magazine," Stephen Wilbers has written, "he sought to promote regional literature and a sense of regional culture. Frederick approached his task, which he saw as a challenge to the dominance of the New York based magazines and publishing houses, with all the zeal of a crusader. The magazine became a focal point for the growing regionalist movement and remained throughout the course of its eighteen-year existence a reflection of Frederick's personal hopes and convictions" (*The Iowa Writers' Workshop: Origins, Emergence, and Growth* [Iowa City, 1980], 13).

21. Gopher Prairie was the imaginary Minnesota village in which Sinclair Lewis set his novel *Main Street* (1920).

literature all the writers who have taken an affirmative hold of "American" materials base their work on a sectional and not a national image. Only those who assume a negative and critical view, like John dos Passos or Theodore Dreiser, by implication present a national image; they are idealists of a sort, whose works confess that the real America falls tragically short of the fine image they conceive. This broad view can only be suggested here. But the arguments of sectional groups must be considered, for in them alone do we find representative statements of their purposes.

In the Southwest—Texas, Oklahoma, Arizona, New Mexico—a sectional agitation, so far restricted to literary and cultural issues, has been carried on by a bold group of writers and students of folklore, all of whom are intensely loyal to Southwestern traditions and much concerned about the possibilities of a sectional art. They have their own magazines, *The Southwest Review* and *The Texas Weekly*,[22] which are frankly sectional in content; their own theaters, notably the Dallas Little Theater, which are hospitable to Southwestern drama; and at least one very active publishing house, the Southwestern Press. Above all, they feel that they have a stalwart land just coming into full consciousness of its strength. If the languid East objects that the Southwest has not yet produced one writer of unquestioned greatness, the Southwest laughs tolerantly and returns to its legends of Sam Houston and its study of Spanish-American culture.

Among themselves, however, in the columns of *The Southwest Review,* they have debated the question of whether the Southwest "can (or should) develop a culture recognizable as unique, and more satisfying and profound than our present imported culture and art."[23] The drift of their opinion is clearly toward an affirmative answer. They believe in the separate role of the Southwest. Henry Smith would even set off the Southwest from the South: "I despair of conveying to an Easterner or even to a Virginian the sense of strangeness with which a Southwesterner visits New Orleans, say, or reads the books coming out of the Deep South. . . ." And Mr. Smith, like most of the others, makes a bow to the European traditions but argues that "at the bottom must be a tradition built up bit by bit from heritages of the land

---

22. In 1924, Southern Methodist University in Dallas acquired the *Texas Review,* a University of Texas publication founded in 1915 (and edited that year by Stark Young), and renamed it the *Southwest Review.* Published and edited by Peter Molyneaux (1882–1953), *Texas Weekly* was an outgrowth of *Bunker's Monthly,* founded in 1928 in Fort Worth and renamed *Texas Monthly* the same year.

23. Here Davidson quoted from the unsigned editorial introduction to "Southwestern Culture: A Symposium," or "Points of View," *Southwest Review* 14 (1929): 474.

where it is to endure."[24] J. Frank Dobie goes farthest of all in calling for "cattlebrands and not signs of the zodiac" to decorate the façades of Southwestern buildings. Stanley Vestal holds that the Southwestern culture is fully alive and needs only to be disseminated through the schools. B. A. Botkin thinks that the Southwest enjoys enormous advantages in comparison with "the immigrant melting-pot of the East" and "the sterile provincialism that decadent isolation or imitation has given to New England and the South." Perhaps only the minority, like Mary Austin, would consent to cloud their hope for a sectional culture with an acknowledgment that Southwesterners are sometimes "more interested in possessing the assets of other cultures than in producing anything of their own."[25]

In such a discussion, the perils of becoming too self-conscious and partisan are plain enough. But it is enormously significant—and perhaps it is clear gain—that the Southwestern writers are restless under the Eastern yoke and are determined to find a means of independence. Yet the skyscrapers of Dallas, the price of cotton and oil, the Fords and Chryslers, the political wars between the Fergusons[26] and the progressive urban interests remain disturbing elements which are not directly faced by the talk about culture. How do the Southwestern artists propose to head off Southwestern

---

24. Henry [Nash] Smith, "A Note on the Southwest," *Southwest Review* 14 (1929): 267–78 (268, 277). Smith (1906–86), a Harvard-trained Americanist, served on the staff of the *Southwest Review* 1927–41; later, his landmark work in American Studies, *Virgin Land: The American West as Symbol and Myth* (Cambridge, Mass., 1950), helped introduce new methodologies to the field.

25. James Frank Dobie (1888–1964), an author and historian of Texas, wrote "True Culture Is Eclectic, But Provincial," *Southwest Review* 14 (1929): 482–83 (483). Stanley Vestal was a pen name used by the Southwestern writer Walter Stanley Campbell (1887–1957); Davidson referred to Vestal's "The Culture Is Here," *Southwest Review* 14 (1929): 478–80. Benjamin Albert Botkin (1901–75) was an author and folklorist; the quotation is from "Serenity and Light," *Southwest Review* 14 (1929): 492–93 (492). Mary Austin (1868–1934) was an Illinois-born novelist, playwright, and Western chronicler; the quotation is from "Regional Culture in the Southwest," *Southwest Review* 14 (1929): 474–77 (475).

26. According to Francis Butler Simkins, "Gaiety was added to the pageant of Southern politics by James E. Ferguson and his wife Miriam. When 'Jim' was removed from the governorship of Texas in 1917 after the state legislature found him guilty of malfeasance, 'Ma' Ferguson became a candidate for that office in order to vindicate her husband. She was elected in 1924 and again in 1932. The support of the 'one-gallus' farmers and of elements opposed to the revived Ku Klux Klan was responsible for her success. During her administration, scandals occurred in the state highway department and pardons were issued by the thousands (*The South Old and New: A History, 1820–1947* [New York, 1947], 442).

society if it decides to stampede into the skyscrapers? How can the artist become a cultural leader, anyway, if American society, for all its Guggenheim fellowships and art museums, secretly thinks him an ass, or at best an eccentric? Emerson and the New England transcendentalists answered this hard question by getting on the winning side and motivating it rather than by adopting a difficult nonconformity. The liberals of our day make a similar answer, though with weakened assurance as to which is the winning side. For a different answer I turn to the South.

Like the Middle Western writers of the post-war period, the new Southern writers of the 1920's were influenced by the prevalent spirit of critical realism. To share in a modern outlook, however, meant for them a very acute division of loyalties. The drift of the times influenced them to accept a progressive view of Southern life. Under this view, what was most historic and deeply characteristic had to be taken as merely picturesque, or as something backward which needed reprimand and disavowal. If they surrendered to the progressive view, either they specialized in the picturesque and wrote charmingly of Negroes and mountaineers, like Mr. DuBose Heyward; or they wrote Southern *Main Streets* like Mr. Stribling. If they had doubts and did not wholly surrender, they might take refuge in evasive ironies like Mr. Cabell or condemn with affection like Miss Glasgow.[27] The result is a remarkable array of writers in whom the Southern tradition speaks, but speaks under a repression that twists it out of character. The struggle of loyalties subdued this writer too far or made that one too loud. But meanwhile the progressive view itself got no critical examination at all.

Finally in 1930 a group of Nashville writers, enlisting the aid of other Southerners, united in disavowing the progressive view, as unfit for Southern needs and as, in some respects, a betrayal of what was most worthy of preservation. They gave their views in a symposium, *I'll Take My Stand: The South and the Agrarian Tradition.* The times had changed, they said with emphasis. It was folly for Southerners to twist themselves into awkward conformity to an ideal which, besides being false to Southern principles, was in itself inadequate and had in fact broken down.

These writers proposed, not a literal reestablishment of the old Southern tradition, but a new application of its meaning to the current situation.

---

27. Ellen Glasgow (1874–1945), who was James Branch Cabell's contemporary and friend, wrote several best-selling and critically acclaimed novels that illuminated the South's social history and gender relations and highlighted the perpetual tension between tradition and change.

The past, they granted, was irrecoverable in its old terms.[28] Nevertheless the Southern way of life, which they defined as agrarian, conservative, and stable, had survived its historic reverses so persistently that it seemed to have new merit for a country that had got itself hideously entangled in the progressive and fluctuating ways of the industrial order. Brushing aside the loose assumptions of nineteenth-century liberalism, they declared industrialism inadequate on the economic side and deceptive in its humanitarian motivation. They devoted their positive exposition to framing a philosophy of life which would be based upon the agrarian economy to which the South as a section seemed adapted. In this scheme art would have its place, but not a dissociated place. There could be no pure philosophy of aesthetics any more than there could be a pure science of economics, because human considerations were always getting in the way. They did not talk much about culture; they did not mention "regionalism." But like the regionalists of the Southwest and the Humanists of the East (whose ethical earnestness was perhaps New England's contemporary sectional contribution to the argument about modern life) they wanted no artificial culture. Unlike the Southwesterners, they did not wink at the intrusive sky-scrapers, but criticized them. Unlike the Humanists, who could not tell where to apply their doctrines, the twelve Southerners offered in the South a concrete example of a humanistic way of life.

The publication of *I'll Take My Stand* caused an outburst of controversy in the South, and the end is not yet in sight. As one who shared in the book and in the controversy, I entertain no delusions as to the extent to which "public opinion" was formally and immediately converted to the ideas of *I'll Take My Stand.* The publication of a book has never yet changed overnight the minds of newspaper editors and institutional leaders who have a vested interest in interpreting the mind of the people as favoring the delusions that they themselves have profited by advocating. "Public opinion" of the latter sort in the South has long rationalized its lack of ideas and disguised its exploitatory intentions by promulgating an Eastern brand of progressivism. The long strain of the depression has now fully revealed how far-fetched and costly was the attempt to apply progressivism where it did not fit, and how far the Southern progressives had detached themselves from basic Southern interests.

The same years of economic strain have strengthened the position of the

---

28. Davidson and Tate debated the recoverability of the past. Tate, criticizing Davidson's manuscript of *The Tall Men* (Boston, 1927), reminded Davidson that "our past is buried so deep that it is all but irrecoverable" (Tate to Davidson, 5 Jan. 1927, *LC,* 183).

twelve authors of *I'll Take My Stand*. Without discussing here the merit of their doctrines, I will simply say that they have pointed out a road away from Leviathanism. If one may judge by native temperament and past experience, that is a road which the South is naturally inclined to take. Furthermore they have removed obstacles from the paths of timid souls who winced under the charge of "professional Southerner" and dropped their sectional loyalty because they did not know how to make it consistent with self-interest and respectability. And they alone of professed sectionalists have made it clear that sectionalism—or "regionalism"—has a firmer substance than critics allow who have thought of it only as a decorative and fleeting literary mood. They have shown that "regionalism" is in fact sectionalism. That issue has not yet been squarely faced in gatherings of sectional groups, like the Iowa Writers conference, or the pleasant meetings of Southern writers at Charlottesville and Charleston,[29] where literary fellowship took precedence over serious discussion.

Hardly anywhere, in fact, outside of the South and Southwest, have writers made vows of sectional allegiance as definite as those I have recorded. It may be a matter of some dispute, too, as to how thorough-going the process of decentralization is. There can be do doubt that the tendency exists and will continue. It is better for sectional programs to be openly acknowledged than to have them appear in the disguise of national programs, such as the long dominant East has often assumed the special privilege of promulgating. That is a game at which more than one or two can now play. A testing of power, if provocation brought it about, might force the East to give up some of its pretensions and confess to being simply another section. New York might have to make itself over into a different sort of capital.

The results of sectional contentiousness would certainly be evil if they led again to scission and conflict, and so to a new unbalancing. A wise philosophy

---

29. Wilbers has traced the birth of the Iowa Writers' Workshop: "[University of Iowa] President [Walter] Jessup called [Norman] Foerster to his office and urged him to organize a national Conference on Creative Writing for the purpose of making known the program to the general public. Taking place on October . . . 1931, the conference was the first of several during the 1930s to draw national attention to Iowa's innovational writing program" ("New Humanism, Regionalism, and the Imagination" in *Iowa Writers' Workshop*, 43–59 [44, 46]). Foerster helped lead the humanists with whom the Agrarians had quarreled. On the October 1931 Southern Writer's Conference organized by James Southall Wilson at the University of Virginia, see Joseph Blotner, *Faulkner: A Biography*, 2 vols. (New York, 1974), 1 : 705–16. Davidson attended the Conference of Southern Writers that DuBose Heyward helped to organize in Charleston, South Carolina, in October 1932; see Davidson to Tate, 29 Oct. 1932, *LC*, 271–75.

of give-and-take would avoid such dangers by striving for balance and by re-moving provocations for sectional strife. It is strange that some of our think-ers have persisted in a contradiction: in one breath they scold the hither-land for not getting in step with the national army; and in the next breath they complain that the army is becoming an uncontrollable machine. Sec-tionalism is a natural check on the perils of regimentation; and a decent self-determination may prove to be a good means of restraining or sublimating sectional cantankerousness. In the sections rather than the states may be dis-covered the true counter-balance to extreme Federalism, whether political or cultural. Sectionalism fits democracy, as a further extension of Federalism does not. But to define its practical functions requires a less abstract view of American society than our most reputable mentors have been willing to take.

In the eternally difficult process of fitting the ideal to the real, it is fool-hardy to ignore the persistence of sectional traits or to condemn them as sheer inertia which must be battered down. That they do persist, despite ex-ternal changes, is plain. To think that inertia has no worth whatever is the sheerest conceit; the fish, in the evolutionary fable, did not cease to be a ver-tebrate when he became a bird. The responsibility and loyalty necessary to the good health of a decent society cannot be secured by "disembodied as-sertions of value"—to use a phrase applied by Helen Hill, in *The Sewanee Re-view,* to the propositions of Mr. Walter Lippmann and similar apostles of so-cial abstraction.[30] They require instead "an assertion of value which has very definitely a local habitation and a name." It is better to utilize an original character than to wipe it out. It is more sensible and natural to get along with Southern Americans and other kinds of sectional Americans than to try to make Americans in the laboratory of abstraction.

All of our centralists, whether plutocratic "individualists," old-style lib-erals, or new-style radicals, falsely assume a rigidly unified America as al-ready made or in the making. No matter what they devise, no matter what social mechanisms or dictatorship they may strive to set up, they will always face the problem of making their measures seem intelligible and just to the diverse folk who inhabit our "physiographic provinces." How diverse these folks are, it would need a Whitmanian catalogue to make clear. Their united consent is obtainable in an emergency, or in normal times when the national instrument remains within its sphere as the moderator of differences and

---

30. Helen Hill, "A Local Habitation," *Sewanee Review* 39 (1931): 460–65 (462). Hill's article, in which she contrasts the contributors to *ITMS* to the humanists, appeared with three others in that issue as "Regionalism: A Symposium."

the indispensable agent of general and continental need. Their consent will be withdrawn, or not given in the first place, if a program, born from a false notion of the United States as a unit, cuts too drastically into sectional interests.

The physicians of our disease have not faced the question of whether the patients have the will to take the universal remedies they offer. They need to ponder the vision of the complete scientific society, as Bertrand Russell has set it forth in *The Scientific Outlook*. Grant that science gives us a technique of power by which we can theoretically exercise any conceivable degree of control over nature. Would we consent to such power, if it meant placing control in the hands of a scientifically trained oligarchy while the rest of us were drugged into hedonistic slavery? Would we really want to have production adjusted to consumption, government purged of graft, and a complete quota of good citizens (bred in scientifically regulated studs) if the price were a tyranny such as even the crudest savage would be spirited enough to reject?

Mr. Russell doubts whether any human society would tolerate such a scheme. People love the world and its irregularities; and "it is only in so far as we renounce the world as its lovers that we can conquer it as its technicians."[31] American society is just as human as any other, and no more inhuman. Besides, it is sectionally organized. I do not think that any scheme of general renunciation can overcome the resistance of the existing sectional diversities; the perfect system would win about as many votes as the Prohibition candidate in the election of 1930.[32]

We do not really want a scientific society, even if we could get it. We do not want a perfected national society on an industrial plan. Its regime would be intolerable, because we do not want to live as it would require us to live, and because we are already losing the almost religious faith in science which it demands of its devotees. We are in disorder because of our unwillingness, while still dominated by fragmentary industrial patterns, to take the steps necessary to make the patterns complete. But we are too weary of regimentation ever to take those steps. Although historians like Mr. Beard would define our present agony as the struggle of a people, long ago committed to democratic institutions, to adapt those institutions to industrial patterns for which no allowance was made in the beginning, we might now, with just as much point, turn the observation the other way. We may require the

31. Russell, *Scientific Outlook*, 264.

32. Davidson apparently referred not to any particular candidate but to the 1930 congressional elections, in which Prohibitionists lost support.

industrial patterns to do the adapting. The democratic institutions may after all be capable of more absorption than our centralists imagine.

Sectionalism is inherent in the democratic institutions that have been established and developed in the United States. When it is omitted from consideration, the noblest speculations are diluted with ignorance and nonsense. The Old Adam, firmly entrenched in sectional America, can be counted on to put up a stubborn resistance against the civilization described by Spengler as a "standardized massing of humanity void of social structure, and uninspired by any common interest."[33] Long bewildered and betrayed in our search for perfect nationalism, we have just begun to realize that we have no adequate term even to designate a citizen of the United States—"American" is still a vague word. Our most characteristic national songs are those that record sectional experience. Our literature, architecture, folklore, history, accent dissolve the national complex into sectional entities. Rivers, mountain ranges, deserts, degrees of latitude, differences of soil and climate divide us. The concentration of racial strains, the prevalence of local traditions, the variance of laws, legends, histories—all this emphasizes the parts which are joined but not fused into a whole. The industrial revolution, which once threatened to bind us into a forced unity, now loses its hold as its gains turn into losses. Decentralization sets in: railroads lose their monopoly of transportation, factories shift away from urban concentrations, people return to the farms, power is diffused everywhere, the arts seek a domestic abode. Once we had two or three sections; now we have many. The official map of the United States does not acknowledge their presence, but they belong there, and in time will be charted.

The national unity of the United States is far less endangered by recognizing this sectional division than by disregarding it. Within limits, the national organism is a necessity to the sections and a natural check upon any chauvinism that may appear; other natural checks exist in the character of the sections themselves: there are no sectional languages or religions; people are habituated to the same political mechanisms everywhere; and within

---

33. Tate, Lytle, and Ransom were also intrigued by the work of German historical philosopher Oswald Spengler (1880–1936). Like the Agrarians, Spengler saw in modernism and industrialization the harbingers of cultural decay. Tate reviewed vol. 1 of *The Decline of the West* (New York, 1926) for the *Nation* 122 (12 May 1926): 532, 534. Later, however, Tate criticized parts of Spengler's *The Hour of Decision* (New York, 1934), calling it "so much Teutonic jingoism" ("Spengler's Tract against Liberalism," *AR* 3 [1934]: 41–47 [44]). For more on Spengler's intellectual connections with the Agrarian group, see Alexander Karanikas, *Tillers of a Myth: Southern Agrarians as Social and Literary Critics* (Madison, Wis., 1966), 124, 149.

themselves the sections have minority groups—the sections of sections—which restrain them from extreme measures and always facilitate the technique of compromise. But the real disturber of the peace is the characterless and synthetic Americanism, which has threatened to oppress them, and its prestige will lessen until it is absorbed and acclimated. In their somewhat different, yet related traditions the sections have a common interest to maintain what is organically American against what is synthetically imposed. Their national unity consists in the avowal which any section should rejoice for the others to make: that we are Rebels, Yankees, Westerners, New Englanders or what you will, bound by ties more generous than abstract institutions can express, rather than citizens of an Americanized nowhere, without family, kin, or home.

Donald Davidson

Dilemma of the Southern Liberals

With Virginius Dabney's 1932 study Liberalism in the South *as a point of departure,*[1] *Donald Davidson used this review essay to formulate an alternate history of
Southern political ideas. Progressive, pro-business New South ideology was in Davidson's view a patent failure; the Great Depression was sufficient proof of that. As for
more traditional Southern liberalism, the touchstone of the region's political thinking
might be found in Thomas Jefferson's agrarianism—his support of the yeoman—but
not, as Dabney proposed, in his declaration that "all men are created equal." Davidson found John Calhoun's pro-slavery ideology the more fitting expression of Southern
political thought. As for Franklin Roosevelt's federalist liberalism, Davidson was quick
to see it as a threat to key elements of the South's distinctiveness—Jim Crow segregation and what Davidson called the "time-honored differential between white and black
labor." Liberalism had reached a dead end, he declared. Its Southern adherents would
be forced to choose between the radical left—an ideology entirely alien and unsuited
to the region, and which, Davidson insinuated, might incite a racial war—and traditionalism as the Agrarians represented it. Davidson prescribed a remedy straight out
of* I'll Take My Stand: *to save themselves and the South, liberals had best become*

---

1. Dabney, *Liberalism in the South* (Chapel Hill, 1934). The journalist and historian
Virginius Dabney (1901–96) was at this time an editorial writer for the *Richmond Times-
Dispatch*. As Morton Sosna has observed, "*Liberalism in the South* demonstrated the young
man's yearning to find a liberal tradition in his region's tumultuous past. At times he
strained to prove his thesis" (*In Search of the Silent South* [New York, 1977], 125).

"more Southern." To discover what Davidson meant by "Southern" in this context is to
understand the shrinking appeal of his increasingly reactionary, embattled writings.

Reprinted from *American Mercury* 31 (1934): 227–35
(also included in Davidson's *Attack on Leviathan*, 261–84).

Years ago, when the Southern liberals were a new party and the millennium
seemed just ahead, Walter Hines Page, the bustling editor of the *World's Work*,
kept calling on the South "to fling off the dead hand of the past." In the bright
tomorrow of his liberal vision there must be no "Ghosts" from yesterday, and
above all there must be no "Mummies"—no unregenerate traditionalists
who did not know they were dead.[2]

The tomorrow that Page looked for has come. But it is not bright; and it
is not the millennium. Modern civilization has been stricken with profound
convulsions at the very moment when the South seemed ready to make a
belated choice in its favor. The South has in some plenitude, the schools, colleges, roads, and industries that the liberals advocated; but now it looks
doubtfully at these great acquisitions. Modern civilization is not living up to
the promises that were made in its name. The liberals are prophets whose
miracle has not worked. The stage was set, the people were waiting, but Je-
hovah perversely favored the priesthood of Baal.[3]

The crisis enforces hard decisions that the upswing of prosperity allowed
Southern liberals to postpone. No longer can they avoid the labor of thinking by claiming to be on the side of the angels. The money with which they
could once persuade Southern Mummies to become Southern Babbitts has
vanished. The times are hard for middle-of-the-road men who, by affecting
to be disinterested, can escape the necessity of choosing between radical and

---

2. The North Carolina–born journalist Walter Hines Page (1855–1918) spent
most of his career in New York after briefly editing a Raleigh newspaper in the 1880s.
His critical remarks about the region's poverty, racial injustice, and destructive habit of
clinging to the past made him a villain in the eyes of many Southerners. Dabney quoted
Page in *Liberalism in the South* (235). Page invoked the image of the mummies in his
"Mummy Letters" of 1886 and addressed Southern ghosts in his 1909 novel, *The Southerner*. See Burton J. Hendrick, *The Earlier Life and Letters of Walter H. Page* (Boston, 1928),
175–92, and *The Life and Letters of Walter H. Page*, 3 vols. (New York, 1925), 1:91. For
a full study of Page, see John Milton Cooper Jr., *Walter Hines Page: The Southerner as American, 1855–1918* (Chapel Hill, 1977).

3. Davidson referred to the Old Testament story in which the prophet Elijah challenged all the priests of Baal—a competing faith which focused on agricultural fertility—to a test in which the true God would be revealed. On the top of Mount Carmel,
God answered when Elijah called upon him, but made no sign to the priests of Baal
(1 Kings 18:17–40).

conservative programs. But such is the choice that liberals now have before them.

What commitments they will finally make, I do not attempt to predict. Certainly they are less ready than of old to talk of throwing off the dead hand of the past. Everywhere the sociological liberals are turning away from the formulas derived from the university laboratories of Chicago or New York, and are studying, in its natural habitat, the cultural tradition and human geography that their predecessors sought blindly to uplift. The journalistic and literary liberals are beginning to read history over again. They are discovering that even liberalism has a past, and they are attempting to rationalize Twentieth Century liberalism by getting up a pedigree for it. The powerful biographies that have come from men like George Fort Milton, Robert Winston, Broadus Mitchell, and Gerald Johnson[4] have a homesick flavor that is new in liberal writing. That the biographies deal with Southern dissenters or industrial pioneers does not hide the fact that they are historical fortifications. They are works of defense, not of offense.

The fullest statement of the new liberal position is to be found in Virginius Dabney's *Liberalism in the South,* a historical study which essays to give the complete anatomy of liberalism from Revolutionary times down to date. Although it appears rather oddly as a success story in a day when liberalism is well-nigh bankrupt, it is nevertheless a genuine "Summa Theologica" of liberal thought. Its general thesis is that the Southern liberalism of today is continuous with the liberalism of the past; or, to put it in concrete terms, that Thomas Jefferson is the spiritual grandfather of the swashbuckling idealists who want the government to guarantee everything from bank deposits to

---

4. George Fort Milton wrote *The Age of Hate: Andrew Johnson and the Radicals* (New York, 1930) and *The Eve of Conflict: Stephen A. Douglas and the Needless War* (Boston, 1934). Robert Winston (1860–1944), a prominent North Carolina lawyer, published several biographies, including *Robert E. Lee: A Biography* (New York, 1934), after retiring from his Raleigh practice. After coming of age in Richmond, Broadus Mitchell (1892–1988) published *The Rise of Cotton Mills in the South* (Baltimore, 1921) and a biography of a pioneer cotton mill owner, *William Gregg: Factory Master of the Old South* (Chapel Hill, 1928). Though himself a socialist, Mitchell embraced Southern industrialism. Davidson's compliment of his work may be disingenuous. The month before this article appeared, he called Mitchell "the perfect example of the Scalawag." Tate claimed that "[t]he reduction to absurdity of the whole liberal-industrial outlook is in Broadus Mitchell's article: the South is still three-fourths agricultural, but in order to catch up with the world and have enlightened labor problems to solve, we must have more industrialism in order to solve them. Good God! That is actually his reasoning!" (Davidson to Tate, 12 Jan. 1934, and Tate to Davidson, 9 Jan. 1934, *LC,* 288, 287). Gerald Johnson wrote *Andrew Jackson: An Epic in Homespun* (New York, 1927).

tonsillectomy for mountain children. The difficulties of this thesis are the difficulties that always plague enthusiasts who want to disguise vague principles with noble reasons. For all his labor, Mr. Dabney is never able to contrive a definition of liberalism that will fit all its historic manifestations. It is a cloudy something, floating airily between the old libertarianism and the new state socialism. Never is Mr. Dabney able to formulate a test by which one can recognize the genuine and absolute liberal.

The truth is that no definition will stretch far enough to cover all the inherent contradictions. Long ago liberalism ceased to have any real consistency, and it has less consistency now than it ever did. If liberalism means tolerance, for example, why should we decline to hear the complaint of Fundamentalists that only the teaching of science, and not the teaching of religion, is tolerated in progressive Southern institutions of learning? Why is it illiberal to favor laws that forbid the sale of liquor, and liberal to favor those that forbid child labor? Continually one discovers the liberals in the act of abolishing the evils of chain-gangs by proposing to put everybody in chains. In the end it becomes a question of whose ox is gored. The liberals are obviously ready to sacrifice a good deal of freedom to secure their pet reforms, and do not want complete tolerance, but only the tolerance, or rather the preference, of social mechanisms that interest them.

Beyond such obvious inconsistencies lies the historical question that the liberals themselves have raised. But the history of the South in general, and of Southern liberalism in particular, by no means affords the sanctions that Mr. Dabney and his colleagues would like to discover.

If the appeal is to Jefferson, out of whom in fact the South's ante-bellum liberalism proceeded, it will never do for liberals to emphasize his fight on the established church and his anti-slavery principles, and at the same time to ignore the theory of government and the practical economics which were fundamental in his thinking.[5] The modern liberals are guilty of opportunism; they are in trouble because they really do not know what kind of society they prefer. But Jefferson's notion of a free and tolerant society rested on a firm presumption that government should be decentralized and that, for the sake of its good health, it would need to favor an agrarian economy.

It is impossible to conceive a Jefferson who would argue abstractly for freedom and tolerance against the background of a highly centralized government and the industrial economics which the Southern liberals half

---

5. For a discussion of the Agrarians' portrayal of Jefferson, see Merrill Peterson, *The Jefferson Image in the American Mind* (New York, 1960), 363–66.

accept and half reject. The essential Jefferson of political and economic theory is not the paternal ancestor of men who seek consolidation in government and at the same time despise the farmer. Their intellectual pedigree must be traced on the Northern side of the Potomac. Their family portraits are among the Hamiltonians and the New England humanitarians; their contemporary relatives are the Marxians and the now somewhat faded progressives.

The South early adopted a liberalism of the older variety, and it has remained far more Jeffersonian in temper than the liberals themselves. It has long distrusted consolidation; it is still largely agrarian. The famous "backwardness," a "lag" in the face of encroaching modernity, is a Jeffersonian relic, for basically it is a deep-rooted lack of faith in governmental mechanisms.

During the period of war and Reconstruction, which the modern liberals always tiptoe gingerly around, Jeffersonian liberalism underwent important revisions. Southern leaders of the Calhoun school saw before 1850 that the old equalitarian features of Jeffersonian liberalism would not meet all new contingencies. The democratic principle, to them, had no meaning apart from a society which could make it work. They agreed with Jefferson in thinking that such a society must be agrarian in foundation, and they had no faith that democracy could survive in the industrial regime that was developing in the North.

But the North, using all of the old equalitarian arguments, was attacking slavery, which, to be sure, was one feature, though not the only one, of the South's agrarian economy. Thus what ought to have remained a minor issue was pushed to the front. Calhoun's defense of agrarian democracy became under stress a rationalization of the South's "peculiar institution." The difficulty, Calhoun pointed out, was with the doctrine of equalitarianism, which must now be abandoned. Although liberty and equality were in a sense united, it was wrong to think them "so intimately united that liberty cannot be perfect without perfect equality." And he added, as if foreseeing the economic equalitarianism of our own day: "To make equality of *condition* essential to liberty would destroy both liberty and progress." It would lead to "the tyranny of majorities," or mob rule.[6]

Unfortunately for realistic Southerners, their northern brethren insisted on a thoroughly romantic application of equalitarianism, and bolstered it with their own concept of a glorified Federal Union which (they somehow neglected to state) was rather partial to the "peculiar institutions" of the

---

6. John Calhoun, "Disquisition on Government," in John M. Anderson, ed., *Calhoun: Basic Documents,* 64. Also see Ann Ward Amacher, "Myths and Consequences: Calhoun and Some Nashville Agrarians," *SAQ* 59 (1960), 251–64.

North. The war that followed was a struggle between romantic and realistic brands of liberalism. When the battles were over and the liberal extremists of the Thad Stevens school had done their worst, the romantic Northerners found themselves after all helpless to administer the results.[7] The realistic Southerners were at last left in charge. Although the Confederacy had failed, the mutual interests of the Southern States were more strongly marked than ever, and the South quickly became the Solid South.

When the carpet-bag governments had been expelled, the Southern people turned again to their old leaders. For about twenty years the governments of the Southern States were in the hands of ex-Confederates, who occupied themselves with straightening up the mess as best as they could. Historians agree that few State governments have ever been more economical and honest.[8] But the time came when human possessiveness began to assert itself a little overbearingly. The Confederate "brigadiers" became a clique. They paraded their war records and neglected their political fences.

This was a lamentable error. War and Reconstruction had brought all classes into a close working sympathy. But the "Bourbons" (to give them their later name) let slip the old community of interest between planter and yeoman farmer and at the same time allied themselves with the new commercial interests which were promoting railroads and factories. In their new-found pursuits they were solaced by the utopian vision of Henry Grady, who was busily urging Southerners to sow "towns and cities instead of theories and put business above politics."[9] They had forgotten about the farmers and small folk. But the farmers and small folk, destructively swept aside by the new commercialism, were in no mood to be forgotten. The Populist

---

7. Davidson's argument for Southern redemption after Reconstruction follows closely that made by Claude Bowers in *The Tragic Era: The Revolution after Lincoln* (New York, 1929). According to this historical perspective, Pennsylvania radical Republican Thaddeus Stevens (1792–1868) exemplified the naiveté of liberals' attempts to impose racial justice.

8. A common element in early-twentieth-century historical narratives of Reconstruction was the heroism and honesty of the politicians who "rescued" the South from "Black rule." For example, see Holland Thompson, *The New South* (New Haven, 1921), 25. C. Vann Woodward, in his classic work, *Origins of the New South, 1877–1913* (Baton Rouge, 1951), 73–74, countered the myth. For a thorough revision of the role African Americans played in the Reconstruction era, see August Meier, "Afterword: New Perspectives on the Nature of Black Political Leadership during Reconstruction," in Howard Rabinowitz, ed., *Southern Black Leaders of the Reconstruction Era* (Urbana, 1982), 393–409.

9. Henry Woodfin Grady (1850–1889), celebrated publisher of the *Atlanta Constitution,* popularized the term "New South." His "New South Creed" soft-pedaled sectional conflict, called for forgiveness on both sides, and actively solicited Northern busi-

agitation began to flame. The old leaders were rudely dispossessed, and, except for their subsequent role as lobbyists and manipulators, they have remained, as a class, in political exile.

In their place the new-style Jeffersonians vaulted into power. South Carolina banished the "Charleston snobs" and seated in the chair of Calhoun the blunt upcountryman, Ben Tillman, who denounced the money power as "more insolent than the slave power." The revolt went on apace everywhere, but it was not a mere elevation of "poor whites" to power, as it has often been represented. The movement had gradations, typified in such diverse leaders as Ben Tillman in South Carolina, Bob Taylor in Tennessee, and Tom Watson in Georgia.[10] Fundamentally it was an agrarian protest against the leadership of planters who had transferred interests to industrial interests, and so broken the continuity of the Southern political tradition. The Bourbons were in fact making a surrender that had not been made at Appomattox. Even while they talked sentimentally about the Old South, they were betraying it by admitting that the way of the Yankee might be right after all.

But though the Bourbons had been kicked off the political stage, they still could, and did, speculate on the merits of a role behind the scenes. The Gilded Age had reigned in the North but hardly touched the impoverished South. Why stand on the virtues of poverty when an age of industrial prosperity was beckoning through the twilight of the dying Nineteenth Century? Let the new-style Jeffersonians have the political offices, if they insisted. The drama would have a catchy title, "Let the people rule"; but what would really matter was the box-office receipts. So, with the new-style Jeffersonians in political office and the old-style Jeffersonians, now industrial Bourbons, in the banks and factories, a new kind of team-work developed. It was not always as perfect as the Bourbons would have wished, but it was good enough while the money lasted, and the better as there was the more money.

---

ness and investment ("The New South," in *The New South: Writings and Speeches of Henry Grady* [Savannah, 1971], 8). Also see Harold E. Davis, *Henry Grady's New South: Atlanta, A Brave and Beautiful City* (Tuscaloosa, 1990). The Agrarian John Donald Wade published a mocking biographical sketch, "Henry W. Grady," *SR* 3 (1938): 479–509.

10. "Pitchfork Ben" Tillman (1847–1918), a Democratic governor and senator from South Carolina who helped organize farmers alliances in the movement's early stages, also exhibited a harshly racist streak. Robert Taylor (1850–1912) became governor and then senator from Tennessee; not himself a Populist, he moderated between the farmers movement and the Democratic Party. U.S. Representative Tom Watson (1856–1922), a Georgia Populist leader with a devoted national following, ran in 1896 for vice president on the William Jennings Bryan ticket. In time, Watson grew to be a demagogue. See C. Vann Woodward, *Tom Watson: Agrarian Rebel* (New York, 1938).

In the years that followed this tacit alliance, Southern politics became chaotic and vile. As in a series of spasms, Southern States ratified woman suffrage amendments but defeated child labor amendments; passed anti-evolution laws but supported huge educational projects; voted for Prohibition but fought anti-lynching laws. Such inconsistencies have been due above all to irresponsible leadership. Behind the scenes the industrial Bourbons have applied a simple but adequate technique for controlling legislatures that are nominally rural in composition. The essence of the system is to swap off humanitarian improvements for private concessions. Where the business interests are affected, they rule; where they are indifferent, they let their bought legislatures flounder. Of course, they welcome humanitarian improvements, for without these they could not so easily engage in swapping, and, more importantly still, they would not have a screen of respectability to cover their quiet operations.

The liberals of the New South school furnished this screen. They entered upon history at about the moment when the Bourbons decided to become industrialists. One can see how the Bourbons, bereft of their lands and ruined by war, were persuaded to see industrialism as a way out, a matter of self-preservation. The liberals, however, seemed more attracted to the cultural by-products that seemed to go along with the Northern model of civilization. The South looked shabby to them, and the North glittered. Apparently without a single critical glance to the Northward or a quiver of concern as to the virtue of the institutions they were abandoning, they, too, made their surrender. And thus, about the turn of the century, the real conquest of the South by the North finally began.

Generally the new Southern liberals were educators, like Edwin A. Alderman, or journalists, like Walter Hines Page. A few were political leaders like Aycock of North Carolina.[11] Their reforms developed at first on institutional lines. They sought to build public school systems and State universities or to establish agencies for fighting hookworm and pellagra. Some, like Clarence Poe and Seaman A. Knapp,[12] were interested in "progressive

---

11. Edwin A. Alderman (1861–1931) was president of the University of Virginia 1904–31. Along with his fellow North Carolinian, Page, Alderman battled to extend and reform public education in the South. Charles Aycock (1859–1912), the Democratic governor of North Carolina, advocated universal public education, child labor reform, anti-lynching legislation, and higher corporate taxes.

12. The North Carolinian agricultural reformer Clarence Poe (1881–1964) spent his career working for, editing, and eventually owning *Progressive Farmer* magazine. His image of the virtuous small farmer resembled that of the Agrarians. Poe, however, believed the agrarian life style could be preserved only with modern farming techniques, improved education, and cooperative organizations. Seaman A. Knapp (1833–1911), a

farming." Undoubtedly, many of their activities were philanthropic and useful. But their enthusiasm led them on from institutional reform to general social programs, and they were soon committed to the ambitious task of changing the whole character of Southern life.

What they attempted to do is best epitomized in the career of Walter Hines Page of North Carolina, who, after getting a substantial Southern education and roving adventurously East and West, returned to convert his native State to the progressivism that had intoxicated him. From the descriptions in *The Southerner,* a semi-autobiographical novel that he later wrote, one grasps what was on the young enthusiast's mind at this period.[13] The South to which his hero comes home, after going to college in the East, is a dirty, ramshackle land, governed by an aristocracy that dwells in the past, and heedless of the essentials of progress. It is a stifling atmosphere, to which the native son can make only a few affectionate concessions, and it is painted in disadvantageous contrast to the free and expansive culture, untinged with sectionalism, that is attributed to the North.

Like his fictional hero, Page failed in his early missionary attempts. He moved North, where in time he became editor of the *Atlantic Monthly* and, later, founder and editor of the *World's Work.* From these strategic positions he kept up a brilliant and strenuous agitation for Southern liberalism. In the South itself, the up-and-coming young men listened attentively to Page, and many were persuaded to turn their backs on the unvictorious past. In the North he had the ear of philanthropists who were interested in exterminating the hookworm or in giving money for education. He was eloquent, and the money of the philanthropists was even more eloquent. Presently it was modern and fashionable for young men to rage against the Mummies, or to pooh-pooh the three Ghosts that Page said were strangling the South: "The Ghost of the Confederate dead, the Ghost of religious orthodoxy, the Ghost of Negro domination."[14]

Although Page professed to follow Jefferson, he was at bottom a brilliant

---

native of New York, inspired the Farmer's Cooperative Demonstration Work Program, a federally funded initiative to improve agricultural practices. Page supported the work of both Poe and Knapp. Poe had joined Page's Watauga Club of young progressives in Raleigh in the 1880s (Hendrick, *Earlier Life and Letters of Walter H. Page,* 169–73).

13. Page, *The Southerner* (New York, 1909).

14. Page's "Ghost passage" is from his *Southerner,* quoted in Dabney, *Liberalism in the South,* 235. The foregoing paragraph apparently was drawn from the work of Hendrick (*Life and Letters of Walter H. Page,* 1 : 91). For more on Page's youthful followers, see Hendrick, *Earlier Life and Letters,* 169–73. For his philanthropical efforts to improve Southern education and health, in which he interested John D. Rockefeller to the tune of some $52 million, see *Earlier Life and Letters,* 370–73.

opportunist, incapable of original thought, devoid of principles other than the loose concepts of Nineteenth Century idealism, and most of all devoid of Southern principles. For the South he had but two magic prescriptions to offer: the South must industrialize in order to get money, and it must promote public education in order to get culture. Negatively, it must abandon all that it stood for in the years from 1850 to 1876. That period must be wiped out of remembrance utterly.

In the clarity of hindsight it would be wrong to condemn Page and his followers too severely. He was no philosopher-economist, but a journalist who was taken in by the half-baked idealisms of the [Theodore] Rooseveltian era. He was the kind of man who would inevitably be charmed by the same phenomena that harrowed Henry Adams.[15] If Page, like Adams, had been content merely to write books, little harm would have been done. But in blithe foolhardiness Page went powerfully into action, under the singular delusion that the Southern notions of life, good enough up to 1850, had only to be swapped off if the New Jerusalem were to be entered. He jeered at the three Ghosts without seriously asking himself whether the three factors that lay at the heart of Southern problems could be or ought to be simply hooted out of existence.

He failed to see, and he prevented his followers from seeing, that what America needed at the turn of the century was the strengthening rather than the weakening of the conservative economics and culture of the South. An opposition South, growing according to the rule of its own character, might have balanced or even checked the rush towards over-industrialization and social chaos. The tragedy of Page's career is that, with the best intentions in the world, he obstructed the growth of such a South.

Conservative Southerners fought hard against the liberal program, but their appeal to sectional loyalty, still couched in the vocabulary of war and Reconstruction, was not adequate for the new situation. The liberals had a fresh vocabulary, and the men of the old school, unable to think in terms that would offer sound opposition, were confounded by sheer glibness. They were made to appear hopeless diehards, standing out against the onward rush of history.

Besides, the new policies had a political meaning. Both the Populist-Democratic prophets (now machine bosses) and the business group were quick to see the possibilities of the liberal program. It called for large ex-

---

15. At the beginning of the twentieth century, Adams regarded modernization and "progress" as evidence of civilization's decline. See "The Dynamo and the Virgin," in *The Education of Henry Adams* (New York, 1983), 1066–76.

penditures by State treasuries. Why should it not also provide the sinews of war for the chests of political factions? And so it did provide. Under the new motivation, the industrialists were no longer greedy and predatory trusts, but the beneficent producers of wealth that would be the material basis of liberal culture. Offstage the liberals, the chambers of commerce, and the politicians shook hands over the prostrate body of the Old South; out in front the show went on to the old theme of "Let the People Rule."

In the middle 1920s a liberal could say with real assurance that the Dayton episode was unrepresentative of a South that was getting more progressive every day. The Dayton trial, in fact, played into liberal hands, for, with much public ado, the poorly led conservatives were put in the wrong and made to feel the brunt of a nationwide disapproval. Young Southerners who had been brought up under the new-fangled public education were now predisposed to accept the liberal interpretation of social issues. It was not only that they were uninstructed in the Southern past, or had been taught out of text-books edited in the North, as the U.D.C. Ladies claimed;[16] but they had been fully exposed to all the precepts of modernism without any real counter-balancing.

As a matter of course, they were inclined to believe that culture comes out of books; that success, especially financial success, is virtue; that religion is a silly fable, or at best a loose rationalization of Christianity in terms of sociology; that progress is real and depends on science; that politics is unimportant and agriculture debasing; and that education really educates. Everybody was shouting about the backwardness of the South. The bustle of the rising cities and the disadvantageous condition of the farmer confirmed them in disrespect for the old agrarian culture. If they needed further confirmation, they could find it in the novels of Mr. Stribling, or Miss Newman, or even Miss Glasgow, all of whom, in one way or another, were producing Southern versions of what New York thought was wrong with the South.

To outward appearance, the liberals had triumphed by 1930. But the economic crisis soon revealed the weakness of their position. The whole movement had come from without; it had from the beginning calamitously failed to associate itself with the real fabric and inner feeling of Southern society. The liberals had never gone before the people as a separate party, but had detached and channelized their activity into the institutions which they hoped to superimpose on Southern life. And they had depended most of all on money, from public and private sources.

Today, without money, the institutions languish, and the liberal situation

---

16. The United Daughters of the Confederacy, founded in 1894, included among its aims the dissemination of history more favorable to the South.

has become precarious. There are no more philanthropic subsidies for liberal projects. State treasuries are empty, or worse than empty. The unholy alliance between the liberals and the politico-business group has fallen apart with the cutting of appropriations. The brand-new system of public schools is everywhere in disorder. The theory of public education is itself being subjected to savage attacks. State universities are being gutted of funds. Normal and technical schools are being curtailed or abolished. In the popular eye, all these are no more than the fancy primping of boom days.

On the other hand, nothing has been more amazing than the refusal of State highway departments to be liquidated. Except in Georgia, where Governor Talmadge has called out the militia to rout them, they resist economy campaigns.[17] Evidently the liberal doctrine of education has penetrated only skin-deep, for roads everywhere take precedence over schools. The liberal axiom that intellectual culture accompanies industrialization has failed to work out.

More than this, Southerners are beginning to connect the liberal program with the tax burden under which they groan and to comprehend that it has been used as a mask for the political machinations of the various Bilboes and Huey Longs that have flourished in nearly every Southern State. Money collected for liberal purposes has been the source of power for demagogues and the means of debauching legislatures and voters. There is hardly a Southern State except Maryland and Virginia that has not been looted more effectively than in carpet-bagger times. The staggering figures of treasury deficits and bonded debts—my own State of Tennessee, for example, has $125,000,000 outstanding in bonded debts—tell the citizens that the years of liberal progress have also been years of financial madness. In the headachy morning-after, they know only too well that they have gambled beyond their means.

To make matters worse, the industrialists, the old friends of liberal promotion, are not in good odor. Some are bank presidents whose laurels are withered. Others are owners of mills or mines where the difficult contentions of capital and labor have brought unsavory notoriety. But the agricultural South, which liberals once despised, is again feeling its strength, and is asking the hard questions that should have been put long ago.

---

17. In the summer of 1933, the flamboyant Governor Eugene Talmadge (1884–1946) declared martial law and seized control of the state's highway department, famous for its corruption and massive pork barrel expenditures. Fifty-three percent of the state's budget was in highway department hands. Talmadge eventually had to back down under a court injunction. William Anderson, *The Political Career of Eugene Talmadge* (Baton Rouge, 1975), 87–89.

Under such pressure the liberals must make a difficult choice. It would have to be made, soon or late, anyway. But now the sudden advent of industrial codes which wipe out child labor and cheap labor, and threaten at one stroke to abolish the time-honored differential between white and black labor, rubs hard on all the old Southern sore places.[18] The Scottsboro case and other cases less celebrated have furnished a series of irritants that combine with the pressure of the uniform wage rules to make race relations more disordered, or at least more potentially dangerous politically, than in any other time since the 1870s. And towering over all is the new doctrine of national self-sufficiency, which, if carried out, may ruin the South's export trade in cotton and tobacco and reduce the Southern States to the condition of pensioners upon a socialized America.

Compromise is less easy than of old, the questions will not wait, the choice must be made. Clearly it lies between becoming more liberal or more conservative. If the liberals go with the radical party, they will have to advocate, or seem to advocate, ideas that in the past have been peculiarly abhorrent to the South as a section. For example, they must favor a Federal Union more gigantically centralized than ever and more forbidding in its attitude toward private initiative; and, along with this Union, a dispensation that will enforce tenets of a decidedly Socialist cast: science to the limit, antagonism to all but the most diluted forms of religion, and equality for the Negro—a full equality that ultimately will go far beyond suffrage reforms and the destruction of such discriminations as now appear in Jim Crow laws and biracial school arrangements.

Entirely aside from the merits or demerits of such a program, it is certain that liberals who make the extreme choice will face the possibility of an isolation much greater than they now labor under. Of course, they will be alienated still further from conservative groups of every persuasion, whether chamber of commerce boosters and industrialists, or rural folk, or varying degrees of traditionalists; but they will also lose the support of the more or less liberal groups who fear that their own moderate programs will be endangered by radical action.

These, whether white or black (and it should be remembered that Southern Negroes are in general without radical inclinations) will thus be driven

---

18. At the time Davidson wrote, African-American Southerners suffered (and white employers benefited) from the twin facts that black labor was remunerated at a discount and certain jobs were considered fit only for black workers. The National Recovery Act (1933) attempted to rectify the racist differential by stipulating minimum wages and maximum hours for participating businesses and industries.

into the conservative camp.[19] Furthermore, a radical program, even if it should gather strength, must inevitably have the effect of strongly renewing the South's old sectionalism. In any event the radical view can hardly achieve a peaceful victory. The three Ghosts that Page feared have never ceased to walk; they need but little encouragement to become the hard actualities of a period of violence.

If the liberals shrink from this extremity, they may choose to strengthen the inclination within their ranks to readjust their ideas in the light of the tradition they once sought to overthrow. The South can ill afford to lose whatever good things they may have to offer; it is not, after all, disposed to play the coward before its problems. But the South of the 1930s, stirred to a new self-consciousness by the turn of events and by the proddings of a new school of writers and social students who are free of the old sense of inferiority, is not the inert South of twenty or even ten years ago. It is beginning to ask its saviors to mix a little local originality with their statesmanship and, if they insist on being humanitarian, at least to base their humanitarianism on a foundation nearer home than the *New Republic*.

The liberals can serve this South if their intelligence achieves a natural association with the sources of feeling which, however blindly and confusedly, have kept alive in the South a sense of civilization, its own and not another's, which the decay of industrial capitalism makes it timely to encourage. The Southern liberals, in short, may escape their dilemma by becoming more Southern.

---

19. The "radical inclinations" of at least some black Southerners in the 1930s are the focus of two books. Nell Irvin Painter's *The Narrative of Hosea Hudson: The Life and Times of a Black Radical* (New York, 1994) is an oral history of a sharecropper and member of the Communist Party; Robin D. G. Kelley interpreted the movement in *Hammer and Hoe: Alabama Communists during the Great Depression* (Chapel Hill, 1990).

Donald Davidson

I'll Take My Stand: *A History*

More than his fellow Agrarians, Donald Davidson remained ready to respond to the critics of I'll Take My Stand; *indeed, he considered himself the official historian of the movement and often attempted to correct the record in periodicals. Yet Lambert Davis, editor of the* Virginia Quarterly Review, *recognized Davidson's motives in the following article and refused it — thereby alienating the Agrarians forever.*[1] *Eventually, the essay, in which Davidson makes a distinction between the idea of Agrarianism and the specific agricultural programs the group began formulating in the mid-1930s, found its way to the* American Review *(formerly the* Bookman*), a periodical published and underwritten by a wealthy, ultra-conservative Princeton graduate named Seward Collins. Collins allowed the Agrarians to commandeer his magazine, and they rejoiced in having an organ that would publish anything they wrote, no matter how partisan. Yet more than any other action, it was the Agrarians' misjudgment in affiliating themselves with Collins, who also published pro-fascists and who admitted publicly in 1936 that he was himself a fascist, that discredited Agrarianism both as a philosophical and an economic movement.*[2]

Reprinted from *American Review* 5 (1935): 301–21.

1. Edward S. Shapiro, "The Southern Agrarians, H. L. Mencken, and the Quest for Southern Identity," *American Studies* 13 (1972): esp. 81–87; O'Brien, *IAS,* 192–93.

2. See Albert E. Stone Jr., "Seward Collins and the *American Review:* Experiment in Pro-Fascism, 1933–37," *American Quarterly* 12 (1960): 3–19.

In the autumn of 1930 I was one of twelve Southerners who made an avowal of their concern for the destiny of the South. This avowal took the form of a book of essays, preceded by a statement of principles, the whole under the title: *I'll Take My Stand: The South and the Agrarian Tradition.* For certain obvious reasons it seems proper to review the origin and history of this adventure in social criticism. Among those reasons is the desire—I trust, a pardonable one—to have one true account of the book's history appear as a matter of record. It is with this purpose that I now write. But it should be understood that my expression is not the result of any new and systematic collaboration by the twelve original contributors. I am depending upon my own memory and am giving my own interpretation. When I use the first person plural, I do so for convenience only, and no presumption is intended.

In publishing *I'll Take My Stand* we were hardly so aspiring as to look for a great deal of support outside the South; but within our own section we took for granted that we might speak as Southerners. We thought that our fellow-Southerners would grasp without laborious explanation the terms of our approach to Southern problems; and that the argument, which was certain to follow, would proceed within a range of assumptions understood and accepted by all. We welcomed the argument, since we felt that all parties would benefit by a free public discussion, of a sort unknown in the South since antebellum days. Such a discussion has taken place.

Yet with due respect to the able critics, whether of South or North, who have praised or blamed, seriously or jokingly, I beg leave to point out that the discussion of *I'll Take My Stand,* although it has continued briskly over a period of nearly five years, has been somewhat less profitable than it might have been, because the contending parties have too often argued in different terms. So far as the South was concerned, we were not altogether right in assuming that we could speak as Southerners to Southerners. For all that some of our critics and we had in common in the way of premises, we might as well have been addressing Mr. Henry Ford or Mr. Granville Hicks.[3] No doubt we should have spared ourselves many surprises if we had corrected our manuscripts accordingly. But let that pass! Between these critics and ourselves is a gap of misunderstanding which in times like these ought not to be left yawning.

To our critics (if I may judge by their pronouncements), industrialism in 1930 was a foregone conclusion, an impregnable system moving inexorably on a principle of economic determinism and already dominating the United

---

3. Granville Hicks (1901–82) was a Marxist literary critic and author who edited the *New Masses.*

States and the South. It had evils, which might be softened by humanitarian devices; but its possibilities for good outbalanced the evil. Mr. Gerald Johnson, for one, spoke of "a glittering civilization" that ought to arise in an industrialized South.[4] It is easy to imagine the pictures in his mind of a wealthy, urbanized South, plentifully equipped with machines, hospitals, universities, and newspaper literates as alert as he is. The pictures of agrarianism were correspondingly bleak. To such critics, agrarianism suggested doomed farmers eaten up with hookworm, brutal labor from sunrise to sunset, or at best an idealized plantation life vanishing or utterly gone; or, so far as agrarianism meant agriculture in the strict sense, it signified a snappy commercialized occupation, making large-scale use of machines and scientific agronomy. When we championed agrarianism, they were amused and incredulous, if not disgusted, and therefore the tone of their discussion was often one of scornful levity.

It was easy enough, and sometimes exciting, to meet such levity with the retort called for under the circumstances. It would be easy now to inquire in all seriousness whether industrial civilization still glitters. But since we, no less than our critics, underestimated the speed and the thoroughness of the industrial collapse, I put this question, too, aside. Such uncomplimentary exchanges get nowhere, since they leave the premises of argument untouched. We did not and we do not think of industrialism and agrarianism in the terms that our critics have used. For their part, they have been unable to see the purposes of *I'll Take My Stand* in the proper context. It is that context which I wish to describe.

I'll Take My Stand was intended to be a book of principles and ideas, offering, with whatever implications it might have for America in general, a philosophy of Southern life rather than a detailed program. It was based upon historical analysis and contemporary observation. It was not a handbook of farming or economics. It was not a rhapsody on Pickett's Charge and the Old Plantation. It was first of all a book for mature Southerners of the late nineteen-twenties, in the so-called New South—Southerners who, we trusted, were not so far gone in modern education as to require, for the act of comprehension, colored charts, statistical tables, graphs, and journalistic monosyllables, but were prepared to use intelligence and memory.

In so far as it might benefit by an historical approach, the book needs to be considered against the background of 1929 and the years previous when

4. Johnson attacked *ITMS* in "The South Faces Itself," *VQR* 7 (1931): 152–57. Davidson quoted from a second critique of Agrarianism by Johnson: "No More Excuses: A Southerner to Southerners," *Harper's* 162 (1931): 331–37 (337).

it was being germinated and planned, and not, as it has been interpreted, against the background of Mr. Hoover's failure, the depression, and the New Deal. If we could have foreseen these events, we would have contrived to make the essays point clearly the moral that was even then implicit in them. But we were not, like the Prophet Moses, aware of any impending plagues to which we could refer for confirmation. In those years industrial commercialism was rampant. In no section were its activities more blatant than in the South, where old and historical communities were crawling on their bellies to persuade some petty manufacturer of pants or socks to take up his tax-exempt residence in their midst. This industrial invasion was the more disturbing because it was proceeding with an entire lack of consideration for its results on Southern life. The rural population, which included at least two-thirds of the total Southern population, was being allowed to drift into poverty and was being viewed with social disdain. Southern opinion, so far as it was articulate, paid little serious attention to such matters. The older liberals of the Walter Hines Page school still believed in the easy humanitarianism of pre-World-War days. The younger liberals were damning the Fundamentalists, and rejoicing in the efforts of the sociological missionaries who were arriving almost daily from the slum-laboratories of Chicago and New York. The business interests were taking full advantage of the general dallying with superficial issues.

I do not know at what precise moment the men who contributed to *I'll Take My Stand* arrived at the notion of making their views public. I do know that as individuals, observing and thinking separately, they arrived at the same general conclusions at about the same time. Although some of us were intimate friends, we had recently been scattered and had been writing in widely different fields. I remember that we were greatly and very pleasantly surprised, when we first approached the Southern topic, to find ourselves in hearty agreement. Each had been cherishing his notions in solitude, hardly expecting them to win the approval of the determined moderns who were his friends. But if we who had been so far separated and so differently occupied could so easily reach an understanding, were there not many other Southerners, fully as apprehensive and discontented as ourselves, who would welcome a forthright assertion of principles? These must be Southern principles, we felt, for the only true salvation of the South had to come from within—there had been already too much parasitic reliance on external counsel. But the principles must also be relevant to the new circumstances. What were the right Southern principles in the late nineteen-twenties?

Of course we never imagined that Southern principles, once defined, would apply just as benevolently in New York City as some wise men thought that Eastern metropolitan principles would apply in the South. We never dreamed of carrying across the line some kind of Southern crusade to offset the Northern push which at our own doors was making noises like a Holy War. In only one contingency (which at that time seemed remote enough) could we possibly conceive that Southern principles might have a national meaning. Whoever or whatever was to blame for the condition of American civilization in those days—and there were malcontents even in the North who were asking such embarrassing questions—certainly the South was not in any responsible sense the author of that condition. The characteristic American civilization of the nineteen-twenties had been produced under Northern auspices. It was the result of a practically undisturbed control over American affairs that the North had enjoyed since its victory at Appomattox, and of a fairly deliberate and consistent exclusion of Southern views. If ever it should occur to the people of the North that that exclusion was a defect— if ever Southern opinions should again be as hospitably entertained as were Mr. Jefferson's and Mr. Madison's in other days, then Southern principles would again have a meaning beyond the borders of the South.

The idea of publishing a book dealing with the Southern situation went back perhaps as far as 1925 and certainly had begun to take shape by 1928. For it was American industrialism of the boom period that disturbed us, no less than the later spectacles of industrial disorder. Before even a prospectus could be outlined, a great deal of discussion and correspondence was neces-sary. A sketch of what we had been doing just before the publication of *I'll Take My Stand* may be worth noting, since it indicates the diversity of inter-ests from which we were drawn to focus on a single project. Tate had been in France, finishing his biography of Jefferson Davis and writing poetry and literary criticism. Ransom had been at work upon *God Without Thunder,* a study of religion and science. Wade had been writing a biography of John Wesley. Owsley was continuing the historical research that grew out of his *State Rights in the Confederacy* and that was to lead to his *King Cotton Diplo-macy.*[5] Nixon, who had just left Vanderbilt for Tulane, had been studying the Populist movement and the problem of the tenant farmer.[6] Warren was at

---

5. Tate, *Jefferson Davis: His Rise and Fall* (New York, 1929). Ransom, *God Without Thunder: An Unorthodox Defense of Orthodoxy* (New York, 1930). John Donald Wade, *John Wesley* (New York, 1930). On Wade, see O'Brien, *IAS,* 97–113. Frank Lawrence Ows-ley, *State Rights in the Confederacy* (Chicago, 1925) and *King Cotton Diplomacy: Foreign Re-lations of the Confederate States of America* (Chicago, 1931).

6. Davidson's 5 Jan. 1930 letter to Nixon soliciting an essay for *ITMS* is, as Shouse pointed out, a concise statement of the Agrarians' initial view of the movement: "What we wish . . . is a group of closely associated articles and essays that will center on the South as the best historical and contemporary example in American society of a section

Oxford; he had published a biography of John Brown. Lytle had been in the East, writing plays and acting.[7] Lanier had been teaching at New York University and doing research in the psychology of race.[8] Kline had just received a Master of Arts degree in English at Vanderbilt University. I was attempting to edit a book page and to follow the curious tergiversations that modernism produced among the rising Southern writers. As for the other two contributors (who were not of the "Nashville group"), Stark Young, in addition to dramatic criticism, had written some excellent novels on Southern themes which at that time were none too well appreciated; and John Gould Fletcher, in England, had turned to social criticism in *The Two Frontiers,* a comparative study of Russia and America.[9]

---

that has continuously guarded its local and provincial ways of life against a too rapid modernization. We don't advocate a restoration of the 'Old South' scheme, and we are not going to give ourselves up to a purely sentimental and romantic recession to the past. But we are firmly convinced that the South needs to be redefined, understood, and, so far as possible, placed in a favorable and appealing light—and for two reasons: (1) to save the South, so far as it can be saved, from the 'New South' people who are ready to sacrifice local integrity for 'prosperity' and the vague sort of liberalism that talks of 'progress'; (2) for the country at large, which needs to have before it some strong example of, and if possible an active set of partisans for, agrarianism (country life and economy) as opposed to centralization. In other words, we don't simply want to make sensational 'studies' of the South or to come out as rabid pro-Southerners (though we may be such, in a way), but to make the ideas we believe in, which are and have long been in essence Southern, go deep and carry far, and have a philosophy behind them that we hope is important for the times" (quoted in Sarah Newman Shouse, *Hillbilly Realist: Herman Clarence Nixon of Possum Trot* [University, Ala., 1986], 52).

7. Warren, *John Brown: The Making of a Martyr* (New York, 1929); Warren received his B. Litt. from Oxford in 1930. Lytle studied in the 47 Workshop under George Pierce Baker at the Yale School of Drama from 1927 to 1928.

8. With his mentor, Joseph Peterson of the George Peabody College for Teachers, the Tennessee-born Lanier, who became an assistant professor of psychology at Vanderbilt, published *Studies in the Comparative Abilities of Whites and Negroes* (Baltimore, 1929), based in part on Lanier's study of twelve-year-olds during a two-year instructorship at New York University. While planning *ITMS,* Tate said of Lanier, "He is one of our most valuable men: he is a technically trained scientist who intends to acquire more scientific technique, largely to philosophical ends—i.e., in order to criticize the abuses of science" (Tate to Davidson, 11 Dec. 1929, *LC,* 242). In a 1930 letter to Tate, however, Lanier revealed that he possessed neither a scientific nor an unbiased approach to the race issue (Lanier to Tate, 1 Aug. 1930, Tate Papers, Princeton University Library, 27:8). For a happier view of Lanier, see M. Carr Payne Jr., "Lyle Hicks Lanier (1903–1988)," *American Psychologist* 45 (1990): 549.

9. Henry Blue Kline (1905–51) received his M.A. in 1929 and contributed "William Remington: A Study in Individualism" to *ITMS.* He became a strong proponent (and civil servant) of the New Deal's planned economy. Davidson edited the book page for the *Nashville Tennessean* 1924–30; see Davidson, *The Spyglass, Views and Reviews,*

Most of us had a good deal of cosmopolitanism in our systems, the result of travel or residence abroad or of prolonged absorption in literature, pedagogy, or technical research. Those of us who had written poetry and criticism were painfully aware of the harsh constriction that modern life imposes on the artist. We were rebellious that such constriction should operate upon Southern artists—or, for that matter, upon any artist; and some of us had written essays asking why this should be so. All of us, I think, were turning with considerable relief from the shallow social criticism and tortured art of the nineteen-twenties to the works of the new historians and biographers who were somehow avoiding both the complaisance of the old Southern liberals and the dissociated cynicism of the younger ones. In their perfectly objective restatement of Southern history and American history we found new cause for our growing distrust of the scorn that was being volleyed at the "backward" South. What the historians said was in all really important points at startling variance with the assumptions of social critics and the "social workers" whose procedure was based on big-city attitudes. Suddenly we realized to the full what we had long been dimly feeling, that the Lost Cause might not be wholly lost after all. In its very backwardness the South had clung to some secret which embodied, it seemed, the precise elements out of which its own reconstruction—and possibly even the reconstruction of America—might be achieved. With American civilization, ugly and visibly bent on ruin, before our eyes, why should we not explore this secret?

We were the more inclined to this course because of a natural loyalty to the South which the events of the nineteen-twenties had warmed and quickened. This was our first and most enduring point of agreement. That loyalty had both combative and sentimental aspects, I am sure. We were and are devoted to the South in spite of its defects, because it is our country, as our mother is our mother. But we have never been in the false and uncritical position attributed to us by some interpreters, of invariably preferring Southern things merely because they are Southern. For the record let it be noted that no more drastic criticisms of Southern life and affairs, past and present, can be found than in some of the books and essays of Owsley and Tate; and they, with Wade and others, have on occasion been denounced by Southern organizations for their "disloyalty." We never believed that one could be a good Southerner by simply drinking mint-juleps or by remarking sententiously on the admirable forbearance of Lee after Appomattox.

Such were our guiding motives. The search for Southern principles was a more deliberate affair, and doubtless had a good deal in it of that

---

1924–1930, ed. John Tyree Fain (Nashville, 1963). Fletcher, *The Two Frontiers: A Study in Historical Psychology* (New York, 1930).

rationalization which is so often condemned and so generally indulged in. I am sure that at first we did not do much thinking in strictly economic terms. Uppermost in our minds was our feeling of intense disgust with the spiritual disorder of modern life—its destruction of human integrity and its lack of purpose; and, with this, we had a decided sense of impending fatality. We wanted a life which through its own conditions and purposefulness would engender naturally (rather than by artificial stimulation), order, leisure, character, stability, and that would also, in the larger sense, be aesthetically enjoyable. What history told us of the South, what we knew of it by experience, now freshened by conscious analysis, and what we remembered of the dignity and strength of the generation that fought the Confederate War (for most of us were old enough to have received indelible impressions from survivors who never in anything but a military sense surrendered)—all this drove us straight to the South and its tradition. The good life we sought was once embodied here, and it lingered yet. Even in its seeming decline it contrasted sharply with the mode of life that we feared and disliked. The pertinent essays and reviews which we wrote before the appearance of *I'll Take My Stand* all had this central theme. Readers who wish to look for them will find them in *Harper's Magazine, The Forum,* the *Sewanee Review,* the *Nation,* the *New Republic,* the *Mississippi Valley Historical Review,* and elsewhere.[10]

As we thought and talked further, we realized that the good life of the Old South, in its best period, and the life of our own South so far as it was still characteristic, was not to be separated from the agrarian tradition which was and is its foundation. By this route we came at last to economics and so found ourselves at odds with the prevailing schools of economic thought. These held that economics determines life and set up an abstract economic existence as the governor of man's effort. We believed that life determines economics, or ought to do so, and that economics is no more than an instrument, around the use of which should gather many more motives than economic ones. The evil of industrial economics was that it squeezed all human motives into one narrow channel and then looked for humanitarian means to repair the injury. The virtue of the Southern agrarian tradition was that it mixed up a great many motives with the economic motive, thus enriching it and reducing it to a proper subordination.

---

10. See Ransom, "The South Defends Its Heritage," *Harper's* 159 (1929): 108–18; Davidson, "First Fruits of Dayton (1928, reprinted here); Ransom, "The South—Old or New?," *Sewanee Review* 36 (1928): 139–47; Tate, "Last Days of the Charming Lady," *Nation* 121 (1925): 485–86; Tate, "Life in the Old South," revision of *Life and Labor in the Old South* by Ulrich B. Phillips, *NR* 59 (1929): 211–12; Owsley, "Local Defense and the Downfall of the Confederacy," *Mississippi Valley Historical Review* 11 (1925): 492–525.

Therefore the agrarian tradition was necessarily defined as "a way of life" from which originated, among other things, an economy. In *I'll Take My Stand* we did not enlarge upon the technical features of the economy, which could wait for a later description, but we treated other features of the Southern tradition at elaborate length and in broad contrast with the hostile industrial conceptions. The times seemed to call for just this emphasis, but I can see now that it puzzled our critics, who had somehow learned to think of "agrarian" in the strictly occupational terms used by newspapers and professional economists. Though it undoubtedly took too much for granted in our readers, the definition was sufficient for our immediate purposes. To us it signified a complete order of society based ultimately upon the land. It presupposed several kinds of farmers and endless varieties of other occupations. The elements of such a society had always existed in the South. They must now be used and improved upon if people were to remain their own masters and avoid the consequences of an industrial order which we could already see was headed toward communism or fascism.

The large-scale plantation had been an important part of the older Southern life, but we were rather critical of the plantation, both because we felt its role had been over-emphasized and sentimentalized, and because we were interested in correcting, for the modern South, the abuses of the plantation system. We thought the role of the small farmer, or yeoman farmer, had been very much underestimated. We were concerned with the fate of the tenant farmer, with rural towns and communities, and with their importance in setting the tone of Southern life, even in the cities. We wished that the greatest possible number of people might enjoy the integrity and independence that would come with living upon their own land. Therefore we tended to push the large plantation into the background of consideration and to argue the case of the yeoman farmer. In this we followed Jefferson; but where the political role of the South was concerned we followed Calhoun,[11] for it was the obvious, if regrettable, duty of the South to continue to defend itself against an aggressive, exploiting North.

Yet undeniable as our nostalgia for old times may have been—and quite justified—we had no intention of drawing a mellow and pretty picture of an idealized past. We leaned rather far in the other direction. Certainly Lytle's essay, "The Hind Tit," was aimed to show the merits of an agrarian life even in its roughest and most backwoodsy state. We were determined, furthermore, to make the broadest possible application of the general theory, and therefore we planned and secured essays that discussed religion, education,

---

11. See Ann Ward Amacher, "Myths and Consequences: Calhoun and Some Nashville Agrarians," *SAQ* 59 (1960): 251–64.

manners, the theory of progress, the race problem, the historical background, the arts, the problem of the college graduate. Only one of the essays dealt with economics specifically. One essay outlined the general argument of the book, and like several of the other essays included a close negative analysis of industrialism, which we took pains to define rather carefully. We did not, of course, mean that the term industrialism should include any and every form of industry and every conceivable use of machines; we meant giant industrialism, as a force dominating every human activity: as the book says, "the decision of society to invest its economic resources in the applied sciences."

From the outset we had to deal with the problem of who the contributors ought to be. This finally resolved itself into the problem of who could be trusted to approach the issues as we saw them. A few of us, at Nashville, had enjoyed the benefits of long friendship and much discussion. We knew each other's minds, but we needed help. A memorandum in my file indicates that we planned the volume to be "deliberately partisan" to an extent which would exclude certain kinds of contributors: "sentimental conservatives whose sectionalism is of an extreme type" and "progressives whose liberalism is of an 'uplift' type." My note further says: "The volume will emphasize trans-Appalachian Southern thought and will therefore have a minority of contributors (if any at all) from the Atlantic states." But the names of possible contributors as recorded in this prospectus suggest how catholic our intention, or how great our innocence of mind, was in those days. Besides some names of the actual contributors, it includes the following: William E. Dodd, Broadus Mitchell, Newbell Niles Puckett, W. W. Alexander, Julia Peterkin, G. B. Winton, Grover Hall, Louis Jaffee, Julian Harris, Judge Finis Garrett, Chancellor James H. Kirkland. To these were later added the names of Gerald Johnson, Stringfellow Barr, John Peale Bishop.[12] But of the persons

---

12. William Edward Dodd (1869–1940), a North Carolina–born historian of the South, served as ambassador to Germany 1933–37. Both Nixon and Owsley trained under Dodd at the University of Chicago (Shouse, *Hillbilly Realist*, esp. 21–22, and O'Brien, *IAS*, 163). Newbell Niles Puckett (1897–1967) was born in Mississippi, taught sociology at Western Reserve University, and wrote *Folk-Beliefs of the Southern Negro* (Chapel Hill, 1926). The Pulitzer Prize–winning South Carolina author Julia Peterkin (1880–1961) explored the world of Gullah-speaking African Americans in her novels. George Beverly Winton (1861–1938), a Southern Methodist Episcopal clergyman and professor, served as dean of the Vanderbilt University School of Religion 1930–36. Finis James Garrett (1875–1956), a Tennessee attorney and congressman, in 1929 became a judge in the U.S. Court of Customs and Patent Appeals. The West Virginia–born, Princeton-educated poet and author John Peale Bishop (1892–1944) was a friend of F. Scott Fitzgerald's and of Tate's; see *The Republic of Letters in America: The Correspon-*

named only two were actually solicited—Gerald Johnson and Stringfellow Barr; and both declined, Mr. Johnson with a curt jocular quip, Mr. Barr after a friendly exchange of correspondence which seemed at first to indicate his adherence.[13]

Perhaps these rebuffs discouraged us from a wider solicitation. At any rate the contributors finally agreed upon came into the book largely because, by reason of close acquaintance, this or that person felt they could be counted on and could presume to approach them. Even then, for the sake of unity, we felt obliged to draw up the "Statement of Principles" printed as an introduction. Each contributor was asked to approve these principles and to offer suggestions of his own. The "statement" was revised several times. Nearly all of the contributors had something to suggest, and most of the suggestions were duly embodied. Finally, it represented composite opinion, arrived at after much trouble. The actual phrasing was the work of Ransom, except for some passages and sentences here and there. I remember one last-minute change of wording. The second paragraph originally began: "Nobody now proposes for the South, or for any other community in this country, an independent political destiny. That idea was finished in 1865." The latter sentence was changed to read, "That idea *is thought to have been* finished in 1865."

There was no editor in the usual sense; the book was a joint undertaking. However, some of us at Nashville acted as an informal steering committee and were obliged to hold many consultations more or less editorial. One hotly argued editorial difficulty arose not long before the book was scheduled to appear. Tate, Warren, and Lytle held that the title ought to be changed from "I'll Take My Stand" to "A Tract Against Communism." Over against this suggestion, which had good reason in it, was the embarrassing fact that the book was practically ready for issue. The following extract from a letter by Tate, written immediately after this incident, is prophetic of what was in store for us: "It is over now. Your title triumphs. And I observe that Alexander [of the *Nashville Tennessean*] today on the basis of the title defines our aims as an 'agrarian revival' and reduces our real aims to nonsense. These are, of course, an agrarian revival in the full sense, but by not making our appeal through the title to ideas, we are at the mercy of all the Alexanders—for

dence of John Peale Bishop and Allen Tate, ed. T. D. Young and John J. Hindle (Lexington, Ky., 1981).

13. Barr recalled, "When Allen Tate visited me and asked me to take part in *I'll Take My Stand,* I wrote a piece called 'Shall Slavery Come South?'—meaning of course, wage slavery. It was justly found unsuitable, whereupon James Wilson published it" (in *VQR* 6 [1930]: 481—94) (Barr to Michael Plunkett, 10 March 1975, Accession no. 292-i, Manuscript Department, University of Virginia Library).

they need only to draw portraits of us plowing or cleaning the spring to make hash of us before we get a hearing."[14]

Tate was exactly right as to what would happen, though he now says: "It would have happened anyway." In the contentious months that followed, when we argued with all objectors who were worth arguing with, such portraits or far worse ones were drawn. We had virtually dared our contemporaries to debate with us the question, then more or less tabooed, of whether the new industrialism was as good for the South as was claimed. With due allowance for various friendly receptions and a generous allotment of newspaper space which certainly gave us a hearing of a sort, it seems worth while to record a few samples of the raillery, not always good-humored, with which our contemporaries greeted us. They begged to remind us of ox-carts and outdoor privies, and inquired whether we ever used porcelain bathtubs. If we admired agrarianism, what were we doing in libraries, and why were we not out gee-hawing? Had we ever tried to "make money" on a farm? Did we want to "turn the clock back" and retreat into "a past that never was"?

The *Chattanooga News,* although it complimented us with a series of very lengthy editorials, dubbed us "the Young Confederates," smiled indulgently over our "delightful economic absurdities," and said: "This quixotic tilting of literary lances against industrialization smacks of the counsel of despair." The *Macon Telegraph,* famous liberal newspaper that carries on its masthead a quotation from Mill's "Essay on Liberty," tore into the book, even before it was published, with all the savagery of the *Chicago Tribune's* best South-baiting editorials. Under the sarcastic title, "Lee, We Are Here!" the *Telegraph* began its insinuations thus: "One of the strangest groups to flourish in the South is the Neo-Confederates. This socially reactionary band does not come out of Atlanta—hatch of the Ku Klux Klan and the Supreme Kingdom—but appears to have its headquarters in Nashville." Later, with the book in hand, the *Telegraph* represented it as "a nostalgic cult owning a basis no more serious than sentiment," "an amusing patter-song," "a high spot in the year's hilarity." The *New Orleans Tribune* quoted with avowed relish some phrases which the *New York Times* had editorially applied to the book: "a boy's Froissart of tales," "twelve Canutes," "worn-out romanticism."

A few critics, but only a very few, were more serious-minded and friendly. Some of these, oddly enough, were Eastern critics, who had lived at close quarters with industrialism and learned to dislike it; and in the end an Eastern magazine, *The American Review,* gave us both understanding and

---

14. Tate to Davidson, 7 Sept. 1930, *LC,* 255. Truman Hudson Alexander (1891–1941) was a Vanderbilt-educated journalist and free-lance writer affiliated with the *Nashville Tennessean.*

hospitality of a sort we have never received, for example, from the *Virginia Quarterly Review*.[15] And among Southern critics, it was a notable fact that our most consistent newspaper support came from Birmingham, the South's most highly industrialized city; from John Temple Graves II, of the *Birmingham News*.[16]

Since we are not thin-skinned, we have managed to survive a curious notoriety of the sort that tempts friends to smile askance and tap their foreheads significantly. But our publishers practically dropped the book, no sooner than it was issued.

To the more sober charge that the agrarian proposals were not accompanied by a specific program we have always been disposed to give heed. We had not attempted to frame any positive set-up for industry under an agrarian economy, and even our program for the farm was not much particularized in the book itself. To an eminent and friendly Tennessean, who deprecated our lack of a political program, one of us answered that we represented "a body of principles looking for a party," and he was thereupon invited to run for Governor on an agrarian ticket. The truth is that *I'll Take My Stand* was by necessity a general study, preliminary to a specific application which we hoped the times would permit us, with others, to work out slowly and critically. The emergencies of 1930 and later years made such deliberate procedure impossible. But even when the book was in press we should have been pleased to add the very specific proposals which were, in fact, made public during the debates sponsored by various newspapers and educational institutions. Ransom, for example, throughout 1930 and 1931 argued for a kind of subsistence farming (hardly of the later [Franklin D.] Rooseveltian model) and for government policies which would bring about a wide distribution of owned land. He has later developed these proposals in magazine articles and pamphlets. In fact most of the contributors, through whatever media have been open to them, in recent years have pushed the principles of agrarianism far beyond the point represented in *I'll Take My Stand* and have made proposals about as specific as could be expected from men who do not have the good fortune to be members of Congress or of the Brain Trust. These may be viewed as a substitute, however inadequate, for a second volume of *I'll Take My Stand,* which through causes beyond our control we have not been able to publish.

---

15. Shapiro observed that Davidson inserted this remark because he was angry at Lambert Davis ("Southern Agrarians," 85, 91n).

16. John Temple Graves II (1892–1961) was a Georgia-born attorney and author who in 1929 became an editor at the *Birmingham Age-Herald,* apparently misnamed by Davidson here as the *News*.

Since my purpose here is expository rather than argumentative, I will do no more than indicate the direction of agrarian proposals. Most of them have been fully stated by Frank Owsley in his recent article, "The Pillars of Agrarianism." We consider the rehabilitation of the farmer as of first importance to the South, the basis of all good remedial procedure; and we therefore favor a definite policy of land conservation, land distribution, land ownership. At the risk of appearing socialistic to the ignorant, we favor legislation that will deprive the giant corporation of its privilege of irresponsibility, and that will control or prevent the socially harmful use of labor-saving (or labor-evicting) machinery. We advocate the encouragement of handicrafts, or of modified handicrafts with machine tools. In this connection, we believe that the only kind of new industry the South can now afford to encourage is the small industry which produces fine goods involving craftsmanship and art. We oppose the introduction of "mass-producing" industries that turn out coarse goods and cheap gadgets. We favor the diversion of public and private moneys from productive to non-productive uses—as for example to the arts—that over-accumulation of invested capital may be forestalled. We hold very strongly for a revision of our political framework that will permit regional governments to function adequately; and that will enable the national government to deal sensibly with issues in which the interests of regions are irreconcilable, or prevent the kind of regional exploitation, disguised as paternalism, now being practiced on the South. That is to say, we favor a true Federalism and oppose Leviathanism, as ruinous to the South and eventually fatal to the nation.

It may be said of such proposals that they are not at all points peculiar to the Southern Agrarians, but are held by persons of various bias, some of whom may lean to an industrial point of view. I am sure this observation would be correct. The so-called Agrarians are not a neatly organized band of conspirators. They are individuals united in a common concern but differing among themselves as to ways and means. They hope that their concern for the South, and to some extent their approach to Southern problems, is shared by many persons. They are conscious that many other minds than theirs are busy with these problems. They would be glad, as the book states, to be counted as members of a national agrarian movement.

Nevertheless, it is fair to emphasize at least two points of fundamental difference between the agrarian approach and others. We are interested in a way of life that will restore economics, among other things, rather than in an economics that promises merely to restore bare security, on hazardous terms, while leaving untouched the deep corruptions that render the security hardly capable of being enjoyed or nobly used. For this reason we are obliged to regard the Roosevelt Administration with a mixture of approval and distrust, for its approach, to the Southern situation especially, is too much of the latter order. At times President Roosevelt and his advisers seem to be governed by only two motives: the economic and the humanitarian. They propose to repair our faltering economic system and to guarantee a modicum of comfort to the human casualties of our false way of life. But they are doing nothing to repair the false way of life. Rather they seem to want to crystallize it in all its falsity. We believe that no permanent solution of our troubles can be found in that way. Complication will be heaped upon complication, until we shall be destroyed in the end from sheer moral impotence. But that is hard to explain to people who insist in believing that labor can be benefited only by the invention of machinery and the promotion of labor unions, or who do not admit that the same human will which builds skyscrapers can also abandon them.

The second point of difference is one on which we would make few concessions, or none. Undoubtedly the South is a part of modern economy. Who could deny that? We should nevertheless insist that the South still has liberty to determine what its role will be with relation to that economy; and that the liberty ought not to be abrogated by the South or usurped by others. Unless the South can retain that power of decision, it can retain little of what may be, in any good sense, Southern. Above all, it cannot keep its self-respect or ever have the confidence in its own genius which is the greatest moral necessity of a living people.

Donald Davidson

A Sociologist in Eden

Arthur Raper's 1936 book Preface to Peasantry [1] *struck a particularly tender nerve for Donald Davidson. The "Eden" of Davidson's title was Macon County, one of two Georgia counties Raper chose for his study of community life and race relations. But Davidson also thought he knew Macon County. He spent the academic year of 1932– 33 as a guest on the plantation of fellow Agrarian Donald Wade, a sojourn that provided an escape from professional frustration and a chance to discover the texture of the rural South. [2] Now he learned that a sociologist had, like the serpent, invaded his "Eden," and had been gathering statistics there to build a case against the inequality and injustice of life in the Black Belt — against its dead-end agricultural economy and racial peonage, its painfully inadequate schools and poor health conditions. Yet Davidson's "Eden" was a paragon of Southern rural life and racial harmony. Most roiling of all to Davidson was Raper's critique of racial segregation. What Raper considered a caste and class system Davidson believed to be a biologically ordained race system. [3]*

1. Arthur F. Raper, *Preface to Peasantry: A Tale of Two Black Belt Counties* (Chapel Hill, 1936).

2. Davidson was intrigued by the popularity of shape note singing and produced an article on the practice in Macon County ("The Sacred Harp in the Land of Eden," *VQR* 10 [1934]: 203–17). Also see O'Brien, *IAS*, 194–95.

3. The following year, Davidson expanded upon his racist views in a review of John Dollard's *Caste and Class in a Southern Town* (1937) called "Gulliver with Hay Fever," *AR* 9 (1937): 152–72. Paul V. Murphy discusses the review in "The Sacrament of

It is well known that Davidson emerged in the 1950s as a vocal opponent of inte-
gration. He alienated most of the original Agrarians, who eventually moderated their
stands on segregation. "I fear his Southernism," Allen Tate confided to Robert Penn
Warren in 1960, "for all its cunning and learning, is now at the level of mere White
Supremacy."[4] *But Tate's concern came nearly a quarter of a century after the publica-*
tion by Davidson of essays that remain unknown to (or ignored by) those who have
sidestepped the virulent racism that tainted Agrarian thinking throughout the 1930s.
Indeed, after reading Davidson's review of Preface to Peasantry *and other Agrarian*
essays in the American Review, *the African-American poet Sterling Brown observed,*
"It is not only among the demagogues and their Gestapos — the frontier thugs, the
state constabularies, the goon squads and the lynchers — that violent aversion to
change is found."[5]

Reprinted from *American Review* 8 (1936): 177–204.

In Georgia, about a hundred miles south of Atlanta, is a plantation region to
which, in one or two fugitive sketches, I once made bold to apply the name
of Eden.[6] There were two reasons why this name suggested itself.

One was the nature of the country itself. The climate is mild and ingrati-
ating. Winter there is hardly more rigorous than the autumn of the upland
country which ends about at Atlanta. Field crops and flowers grow the year
long. With a little luck one can have fresh vegetables from his own garden
for a Christmas dinner in Eden, and without fail he can have narcissus and the
rich blooms of camellia japonica. Summers are hot, but the heat is moderated by airs from the coast, and droughts are rare. The land is fertile, and the
planters do not seem to abuse its great productivity. The crops are cotton, of
course, and much besides — the cereals, especially corn and wheat; peaches,
pecans, peanuts; vegetables in trucking quantities, asparagus, sweet and Irish
potatoes, cabbage and collards, turnips, peppers; sugar cane and sorghum
cane; and other things in abundance, though grass and hay do not flourish as
well as in the uplands. There is still good hunting. There is still good timber.
And it is a beautiful land, a land of long-leaf pines and water-oaks and red
earth beneath skies of ever-changing color. And the people are the best of all.

Remembrance: Southern Agrarian Poet Donald Davidson and His Past," *Southern Cul-*
tures 2 (1995): 83–102 (96). Dollard's theories about the role of sex in racial relations
prefigured Cash's *Mind of the South.*

4. Tate to Warren, 5 Oct. 1960, Warren Papers, Beinecke Library, Yale University.

5. Brown, "Count Us In," in Rayford W. Logan, ed., *What the Negro Wants* (Chapel
Hill, 1944), 323.

6. Davidson, "Sacred Harp."

Like Cousin Roderick and Sister Caroline (in whom I once attempted to epitomize their qualities) they have the graciousness and repose of the old Southern tradition without the pretentiousness that came to characterize some of its later stages.[7] They have nothing to do with the "moonlight and magnolias" tradition of cheap movies and anti-Southern propaganda. In short, they represent the better side, at once homely and fine, of the plantation South, miraculously preserved from the General Shermans of the 1860s and the 1930s. Last, in nothing do they seem more admirable than in their relations with the Negroes, who here outnumber white people nearly three to one. The old master-slave relation, in this land of Eden, seems to have developed here into nothing so alarming as, say, in Arkansas.[8] The old feeling of white responsibility and of black loyalty and devotion seems to have carried over, partially at least, into the modern regime, and one would think this the last place to which the agitator and reformer would ever have the impulse to penetrate.

Such were the impressions I gained from a residence of about ten months in this country just at the time when Hoover was going out and Roosevelt was coming in. I did not, of course, make a "survey." I passed out no questionnaire sheets. But I heard much with my own ears and saw much with my own eyes. It was what any normal person could not help hearing and seeing informally, upon being made almost a member of the family and invited to feel perfectly at home. It would have seemed a violation to "write up" this Eden as places get written up nowadays, and so, when in the course of certain attempts at regional comparisons I referred to it, I veiled its identity and location, for I wanted to save the region and the individuals in it from even

---

7. Sister Caroline and Cousin Roderick (the latter was probably based on John Donald Wade) stood as Southern ideal types in Davidson's article "Still Rebels, Still Yankees," *AR* 2 (1933): 58–72, 175–88, reprinted in Davidson, *Still Rebels, Still Yankees and Other Essays* (Baton Rouge, 1957), esp. 247–53. He owed the names and style of country address to Wade himself. See Wade, "The Life and Death of Cousin Lucius," *ITMS*, 265–301.

8. The racially integrated Southern Tenant Farmers' Union, organized in 1934 to protest the hardship New Deal policies caused the poorest farmers, was a threat to many powerful Arkansans. In 1935, after African-American sharecroppers in Marked Tree, Arkansas, were violently attacked by white landowners, Norman Thomas of the American Socialist Party lobbied for federal intervention. See Donald H. Grubbs, *Cry from the Cotton: The Southern Tenant Farmers' Union and the New Deal* (Chapel Hill, 1971), and the memoir by H. L. Mitchell, *Mean Things Happening in This Land: The Life and Times of H. L. Mitchell of the Southern Tenant Farmers' Union* (Montclair, N.J., 1979). The Arkansan John Gould Fletcher, a fellow Agrarian, later wrote about the union in "The Sharecropper's World," in *Arkansas* (Chapel Hill, 1947), 335–53.

the small portion of the curse of modern publicity that might—it was just possible—come from an obscure essay. That was the second reason for calling this country an Eden.

But how vain was my concern, how feeble my conception of the all-seeing eye of sociology! I now discover that the wise serpent, the Light-Bringer himself, was in that region before and after my visit, not for purposes of temptation so much as to focus upon Eden the central blaze of a high-powered social-scientific investigation.

The results—with statistical tables, photographic illustrations, maps, prefaces, foreword, introduction, text, conclusion, and index—are now available to the world in a four-hundred-page book, *Preface to Peasantry,* by Arthur Raper, Research and Field Secretary of the Commission on Interracial Cooperation.[9] From a complicated statement in the preface one gathers that the book grew out of a doctoral dissertation which was expanded to fit a larger scheme for study of the Negro in industry and agriculture. The committee in charge of this scheme were as follows: Will W. Alexander, who has just been appointed by President Roosevelt to replace Rexford G. Tugwell in the resettlement administration; Edwin R. Embree of the Rosenwald Foundation; Charles S. Johnson, professor of sociology at Fisk University. Although the preface does not say so, the book ties up, at least unofficially, with the line of research which has been followed out for some years under the auspices of the Social Research Council and under the immediate administration of a Southern Regional Committee. Howard Odum's *The Southern Regions of the United States,* Rupert Vance's *Human Geography of the South,* Kendrick and Arnett's *The South Looks at Its Past* are examples of how useful this general line of study has been.[10]

---

9. Formed in 1919, the Atlanta-based Commission on Interracial Cooperation (CIC) produced books, research, and school materials (with funding from national foundations) demonstrating the necessity of reform in Southern race relations.

10. Davidson here listed the forces of Southern liberalism in the 1930s—individuals, committees, councils, and scholars he and other Agrarians resented. Alexander helped found the CIC and served as its executive director until he joined the Roosevelt administration in 1936. At the Resettlement Administration and later as director of the Farm Security Administration, Alexander formed policies to assist small as well as large farmers. See Wilma Dykeman and James Stokely, *Seeds of Southern Change: The Life of Will Alexander* (Chicago, 1962). Rexford Guy Tugwell (1891–1979), Roosevelt's close first-term adviser, was replaced by Alexander when he left the administration under fire in 1937. See Bernard Sternsher, *Rexford Tugwell and the New Deal* (New Brunswick, N.J., 1964). Edwin Embree (1883–1950) grew up in Berea, Kentucky, where his family was associated with the progressive, integrated Berea College. He directed the Julius Rosenwald Fund from 1928 until its dissolution in 1948. The Rosenwald Fund, established by

This setting will serve to identify Mr. Raper as one of the younger group of Southern sociologists and economists whose leadership seems to be in the direction of the University of North Carolina. Upon an elaborate foundation of research these men are shaping up a heaven-towering superstructure of social reform. The indication, in *Southern Regions,* is that the reform is eventually to be carried out under two six-year plans, administered by a regional planning board modelled after the TVA.[11]

But Mr. Raper's part in such projects is rather special, and I am none too certain that, in a strict sense, he belongs in the array mentioned above. He is interested in the race problem above everything else. His first book, *The Tragedy of Lynching,* is a detailed case study of about a dozen lynchings.[12] In this book the case studies are as circumstantial and dispassionate as one could ask for social science to be, but they are preceded by a lengthy introduction which contains as much hysteria as science. One discovers by reading the introduction that Mr. Raper is not much interested, as sociologist, in the mores which he has been at such pains to record. All that he wants to do is to stop lynching by any means whatsoever. But with all this passionate concern, he seems to have no condemnation for the crimes which, in the South, are sometimes punished by the spectacular and brutal lynching process, and apparently he is not much worked up over what happens (though it is often terrible beyond description) to the victims of the criminal. It is the method

---

the president of Sears and Roebuck, focused on education, funding the construction and improvement of segregated black schools and granting higher education scholarships to African-American students. Charles S. Johnson (1893–1956) in this period chaired Fisk's Department of Social Science, from which he directed pioneering research on race relations and black life in the South. The Social Science Research Council, a national group of scholars in the social sciences, developed goals for research and awarded grants. Johnson, Embree, and Alexander were once labeled "the triumvirate that directed the liberal South during the thirties and forties" (Dykeman and Stokely, *Seeds of Southern Change,* 185). The Chapel Hill cabal was led by Georgia-born sociologist Howard W. Odum (1884–1954), who headed the Department of Sociology at Chapel Hill. Odum intensified the study of Southern class, race, and folk life through the Southern Regional Committee of the Social Science Research Council, the Institute for Research in Social Sciences at Chapel Hill, and the *Journal of Social Forces.* His magnum opus, *Southern Regions of the United States* (Chapel Hill, 1936), Rupert Vance's *Human Geography of the South* (Chapel Hill, 1932), and Benjamin B. Kendrick and Alex M. Arnett's *The South Looks at Its Past* (Chapel Hill, 1935) were all published by the University of North Carolina Press, directed by William T. Couch. Odum's career and his role in Southern intellectual history are examined in Daniel Singal, *The War Within: From Victorian to Modernist Thought in the South, 1919–1945* (Chapel Hill, 1982), 115–52, and O'Brien, *IAS,* 70–93. On Couch, see Singal, *War Within,* 265–301.

11. Odum's vision is articulated in *Southern Regions,* 204–5, 596.

12. Arthur F. Raper, *The Tragedy of Lynching* (Chapel Hill, 1933).

of punishment that engages his complete attention and converts him into an advocate. He is shocked at the mob who with reciprocal savagery burn the Negro rapist to death; he is perfectly calm if the reciprocal savagery takes place by judicial process, and the rapist is burned to death in an electric chair before a few quaking witnesses, physicians, and newspapermen.[13] Sociology is queer; it is moved by some things and unmoved by other things. But the point is, sociology is hardly entitled to use the literary word, tragedy, unless it is prepared to be catholic in its emotions. But it would be more correctly scientific, I am sure, if it were moved by nothing and could remain perfectly matter-of-fact. I find this partiality a little odd, but I can guess at one possible explanation. It has something to do with the fact that Mr. Raper turns his investigation in his new book upon two counties, in one of which there has not been a lynching for twenty-five years, in the other for fifteen years. (The figures are his own.)

But these introductory marks should be taken partly by way of contrast. Mr. Raper's new book is far, far pleasanter reading, even with some dark passages, than his earlier one. It suggests to me that some of the Southern sociologists who are interested in the Negro may have decided that their old approach is not valid or will not get results. They are now centering their attention on the economic position of the Negro, and, since that is not to be separated from the economic position of the South as a whole, they have become concerned with the tenant problem and, beyond that, with the general agrarian problem. This is a wise step, if by such means they can bring the special race problem into the perspective where it belongs. The method will get results unobtainable by force bills, interracial committees, and horatory propaganda.

The thesis of *Preface to Peasantry,* as stated in W. W. Alexander's foreword, is that the old cotton kingdom of the Southeast is well on the way to collapse. Its soil has been exhausted by misuse of the land—a misuse due, Mr. Raper claims, to the plantation system, as a system, and to no other cause. Even before the boll weevil came, we are told, the Southeast was losing in competition with newer cotton regions, since it had to spend too much money on fertilizer. Then the boll weevil put the final ruinous touches. In the "collapse" of the cotton culture, everybody has gone down, but the Negro and the landless white tenants have gone down farthest of all, because, where life was getting precarious for everybody, no special attention could be spared to the least fortunate. The solution, Mr. Alexander says (and Mr. Raper in greater

---

13. In the 1930s and for many years after, rape was a capital offense in all the Southern states along with Missouri, Oklahoma, and Nevada. Hugo Adam Bedau, *The Death Penalty in America,* rev. ed. (New York, 1967), 43.

detail affirms this), is a restoration of the land through diversified farming, and a rehabilitation of the people based upon a new land policy which will afford "an opportunity for ownership of the land by the man *who works it*."[14] (The italics are Mr. Alexander's.) The frontispiece of the book is a photograph of two cotton wagons on a Georgia road. Underneath it is the following caption: "The Black Belt's riddle—To whom does this cotton belong: to the tenant farmer who grew it, to the landlord who furnished the tenant, or to the banker who financed the landlord?"

In his presentation of this thesis, Mr. Raper confines himself to a survey of two Georgia counties. One of these, Greene County, lies slightly southeast of Atlanta, in the lower Piedmont region not far from the South Carolina line. Its history, as an older plantation region settled in Revolutionary times, is apparently one of progressive ruination ever since the 1860s, when it must have suffered somewhat as did the "Tara" region of Miss Mitchell's *Gone With the Wind*. I know nothing at firsthand of Greene County, and therefore shall not discuss it here. But Macon County, Mr. Raper's other example, is the county I know as a land of Eden. It is "younger" by some fifty years than Greene County, and to this fact alone Mr. Raper seems to ascribe its sociological misbehavior in failing to decay quite as rapidly as Greene County. The plantation system, he explains, has not yet had time to destroy itself in Macon County. But he has little doubt that it will do so, and that soon. A glance through his sociological microscope shows the decay germs already busily gnawing.

What differences are there between the (doubtless) inferior alchemical pottering of a humanistic, or literary, interpretation of Eden and the (surely) superior interpretative method of the trained social scientist? It will be most interesting, I tell myself as I begin this book, to see what the sociologist has to say about a region somewhat closer than the Fiji Islands.

It is all in the neatest possible order: geographic, historic, and social factors; annual cash income, per family; housing and sanitation; size of holdings in relation to fertility of soil; forms of tenancy; schoolhouses; lodges; Federal relief; and so on. Some of it is only an extension of what one can find in various other books; but some of it, particularly the detail, is new.

But as one goes from humanism to sociology, something happens that is like what happened to the unfortunate young man in Tennyson's "Locksley Hall"; "The individual withers, and the world is more and more."[15] Where

---

14. Arthur F. Raper, *Preface to Peasantry: A Tale of Two Black Belt Counties* (Chapel Hill, 1936), x.

15. Alfred Tennyson's "Locksley Hall" (1842) was a love lament couched in an anguished protest against modernization. Davidson quoted line 142.

are Cousin Roderick and Sister Caroline and all their kin and friends? Where
are the black individuals, surely also individuals: the grinning E. Pluribus,
well-named, one of many of Uncle Amos's numerous progeny; Emmett,
who could "read" the passion flower and show you, in a sprig of vine with a
single bloom, Christ, the Virgin Mary, and the Apostles on the road to Cal-
vary; "Preacher," who was trusted with curing the meat; Tom, the gifted of
tongue, who beguiled his landlord (who happened to be a landlady) into buying him a mule, and then into lumber to make a stall for the said mule, and
next into share-cropping a bit of land which had been intended for horticul-
ture or floriculture, not for cotton? All these notable people have gone down
in ruins with the cotton economy and become statistical items lumped in-
distinguishably with the notable and unnotable in tables and summaries. Macon County has become a type and stopped being a beloved place to which
men cling with more than rational attachment. And though everybody except the sociologist knows that X's plantation is not to be mentioned in the
same breath as Y's, there is nothing here to tell the difference. Negroes are
wage-hands, croppers, renters, or owners. Familiar landmarks have disappeared. One would never know that this is Macon County. It might as well
be Zero County, where a man needs a map to get about, and where anything
you say (I warn you, this is the law), no matter how carelessly dropped, will
be used against you.

This is of course the defect of sociology. It cannot examine human ways
without indulging in abstractions which to the lay reader seem to dehuman-
ize. But this paper is not an attack upon sociology in its rightful capacity.
There is no use in raising objections to a useful science as long as its practi-
tioners pursue science, not history, literature, or religion. At the same time
we may be grateful if at times the sociologist is not too stiffly scientific and
wanders off into bits of reporting which have some literary characteristics.
In his article, "Sociology and the Black Belt," in the *American Review* of December, 1934, Mr. John Crowe Ransom noted this tendency in connection
with a book by Professor Charles S. Johnson.[16] Mr. Raper also has such in-
advertent moments, or perhaps at times deliberately indulges himself, so
that we get a little of the flavor of life in Macon County. For example:

> A Negro wage hand bought a plug of Taylor's special tobacco and a plug of
> Brown Mule. He put the latter in his pocket with no wrapping on it. "There
> is always more chewers than buyers," he said, "so I always has some cheap
> backer loose in my pocket—it takes less when it's been sweated on." [28]

---

16. Ransom's review of Johnson's *Shadow of the Plantation* is reprinted here.

But these moments are few. For the most part Mr. Raper is engaged in plain, very solemn analysis and presentation. On that ground, then, it is necessary to meet him. Since he insists on ponderable measurements, what is his standard for measuring? How does he apply it to the matters which he groups under such headings as "Planes of Living," "Man-Land Relations," "Population Movements," "The New Deal," and so on?

A difficulty at once arises. It is hard to tell whether this sociologist has a uniform standard, since in one paragraph he may be a hard-headed pragmatist and in the next a soft-headed humanitarian idealist. Now he is a scientist, content merely to heap up, under classified headings, mountains of fact about population trends or housing conditions; but now he is an advocate, hurling thunderbolts of opinion over his mountains of fact. At one moment he deals with tangible matters like health and income; at another, he has gone adventuring among "attitudes."

In this respect Mr. Raper is like some other sociologists who explore things contemporary and near at hand. His anxiety to get quick results from his findings is greater than his discriminating desire to see just what he has found. The Macon County people are not away off yonder like Margaret Mead's Samoans. They are only two or three hours' ride from Mr. Raper's Atlanta office. The temptation to chide them and make social prescriptions for them is irresistible. It is obvious that Mr. Raper's attitude toward such temptation must at best be described as coyly yielding rather than sternly ascetic. But when one searches about to discover him in the act of pronouncing the gospel word of salvation, one finds him committed to nothing very precise. We must learn by implication what standard of life, material and nonmaterial, Mr. Raper wants the Macon Countians to measure up to.

There are hints of the standard in passages like the following:

> The city's working family has advantages unknown to the farm tenant, such as public hospitalization, public outdoor nurse service, public clinics, and public school facilities infinitely superior to those provided in the rural section where many of the white and practically all the Negro children attend one-teacher schools. [6]

And more hints in this passage:

> Though one Negro farmer in Macon has a windmill which pumps water into his yard and barn, not one in either county has a cotton gin, peanut picker, tractor, sawmill, Delco light plant, or stationary gasoline engine. Just as the work not done by power-driven machinery must be done by work animals, that not done by work animals must be done by members of the farm family. [82–83]

It is clear from such observations, as from much else in the book, that Mr. Raper looks at the Macon County scene through urban eyes. He has an urban standard, or, more than that, the standard of an urban center which has the means and inclination to go a long way towards "socializing" medicine, education, and perhaps more besides. He does not in his own mind concede that there are or ought to be any great differences, inherent in the two situations, between city life and country life today. At the utmost he will concede only a difference of *Machinery*. He thinks of a farm as a well-capitalized investment that uses tractors instead of steam cranes.

Where did he get such a standard and the "attitude" that goes with it? Not from Macon County, by any means. Not from the South, where by no means all the individual white cotton farmers can afford a great deal of power-driven machinery or find it, in all cases, necessary to success. Mr. Raper is not estimating a Southern situation in Southern terms. He is divesting himself of his southern bias, if he has any, and is substituting, not the pure objectivity that we should expect, but a different kind of bias.

What bias this is can be seen from the agitation to which Mr. Raper gives way whenever he comes up against the problem of race relations. It appears in his repeated insistence that the Negro, particularly the Negro cropper, renter, and wage hand, suffers from some causeless, totally irrational "exploitation" at the hands of the white planter and the plantation system. Witness the following passage:

> The Emancipation Proclamation by no means eradicated distinctions felt by both Negroes and whites, nor did it change the paradoxical feelings of affection and devotion which have always existed between many members of both races, as is shown in the following incidents.
>
> "Stand up! Stand up! Can't you see it's a white man?" stormed a stout Negro woman to her pupils when she answered a knock at the schoolhouse door and saw a white man there. Bewildered, the visitor asked the children to sit down—he had little expected such obsequiousness, even in Greene County. [26–27]

The clue to Mr. Raper's bias is in the word paradoxical. Why should the affection be paradoxical? Why should the unnamed white visitor be bewildered? The "feelings of affection" and the manners here called "obsequious" are commonplace in the plantation South, as Mr. Raper well knows. In consideration of the business that he is about, we could understand his trying to suppress his own Southern viewpoint, but why can he not state the facts without coloring them? A physicist does not say that the magnet paradoxically attracts the iron filings!

Sometimes Mr. Raper notes an isolated fact without comment, in such a way as might invite a false generalization, as, for example, when he says: "In another field there was a thirteen-year-old boy with a hoe; he had been hoeing seven years" [29]. The instance suggests some rather brutal and debilitating form of child labor, but a boy hoeing in Macon County should suggest no such generalization. Agricultural tasks are in many cases not too complicated or arduous to be undertaken, without harm, by children, and they change with the seasons. This boy did not hoe the year round, he did not hurt himself a-hoeing, he probably loafed more than he worked. If he had been a cotton-mill worker, Mr. Raper's concern might have been justified.

He is equally naive, or assumes naiveté, over methods of cultivation in Macon County. The methods are "primitive," for the farms are not "mechanized." Laborers chop cotton with a hoe and pick cotton by hand. The land is scarcely ever turned with two-horse plows. It is "a one-horse civilization" [84]. But Mr. Raper omits to note that the deft and special process of chopping cotton—in which thinning, weeding, cultivating, and replanting go on together—can only be done efficiently with a hoe. It is just as if Mr. Raper should say of Cousin Roderick: "Look, how primitive! The man chews with his teeth!" As for cotton picking by hand—the mechanical cotton picker, of which elsewhere Mr. Raper has a doubtful word to say, is justly viewed with scepticism in the Southeast. And possibly the very up-to-date farmers in Macon County do not more often use the two-horse plow simply because the two-horse plow is not needed except in special cases. Their soil is loose and sandy, where it has been frequently cultivated it can almost be turned with a stick.

Elsewhere is another kind of thing—a subtle suggestion, a slight alteration in emphasis. Mr. Raper does not say that relations between the two races are generally peaceful, partly because the white man, after long experience with the Negro, is indulgent toward him, thinking him to be a less responsible person than a white man. Mr. Raper, instead, says this:

> The general peaceful relations between the two races in these counties rest, to no small degree, *upon the Negro's acceptance* of a role in which he is neither moral nor immoral—just nonmoral; neither saint not sinner—just a rowdy; neither deceitful nor trustworthy, just lazy and easy-going; neither slave nor free man [—just an inferior man,] just a "nigger." [23] (Italics mine—D.D.)

The phrase italicized changes completely the usual emphasis—as John Brown of Ossawatomie once changed it. Possibly I may be reading into this and other passages a meaning not intended to be there. I should be glad to be proved wrong. But Mr. Raper's bias is inescapable. One finds it in still more astonishing outline in the bits of historical interpretation with which he garnishes his analyses—or in the items of historical interpretation that he neglects to put in.

The major theme of the book is the "decay" of the plantation system, and the consequent effect of this "decay" upon the land and the people. At the outset Mr. Raper speaks of the collapse of the plantation system and attributes this to "its exploitation of soil and labor" [3]. Later on, after a harangue in which he indicts the "landed oligarchy" for disfranchising the Negro, for opposing (he says) Negro education, and for holding the Negro "irredeemably inferior," he makes the following summary:

> Such are the rationalizations and defense mechanisms which the controllers of the plantation system have fabricated into a philosophy which justifies and maintains the politically sterile "Solid South," and its outmoded agricultural structure based upon the human relations of a disintegrating feudalism.
>
> The assumptions and sanctions of the plantation system have their price, and Greene and Macon counties have paid with one-crop farming, excessive erosion and depleted soil, low incomes for shifting landless workers, frequent bankruptcies for owners, emigration, and, most devastating of all, human relations built upon the idea that the vast majority of the population— the landless, whether white or Negro—are incapable of self-direction. [170–71]

But before considering this summary, we should consider a really extraordinary passage in which Mr. Raper, while omitting any substantial reference to what went on in Reconstruction times, attributes the post-bellum "exploitation" of the Negro and the slogan of "white supremacy" to some strange, insane desire to find a "scapegoat";

> They (the planters) were in need of each other's constant sympathy. For their loss of property and power at home and prestige abroad they compensated partially by much talking and theorizing among themselves about the superiority of the southern whites. They and their less refined successors—moneylenders and time merchants—have provided a white supremacy manifesto for the racial determinists of the South.
>
> The various grievances of the southern whites were heaped upon the inarticulate ex-slave; the white South's humiliation and poverty, its hatred of the Yankees and of the central government, along with its fears of the blacks, found a convenient scapegoat in the nominally free but defenseless Negro. And there, upon the back of the black man, most of the load has remained; for many politicians in government and business and religion have found the agitation of the race question the surest road to election. [96–97]

One ought, I suppose, to be charitable with the errors of a man of Mr. Raper's earnestness and ability. But how can charity hold out against such garblings and wild imaginings? It would be charitable to say that Mr. Raper must have derived his knowledge of history from that eminent mythologizer, V. F. Calverton, or from Carl Carmer's journalistic slush.[17] Such frenzied caricature takes us back to the days of the South-haters: Secretary Stanton, Ben Butler, and the oratorical Bob Ingersoll who thundered, in the election campaign of 1876: "Every man that shot down Union soldiers was a Democrat. . . . Every man that raised bloodhounds to pursue human beings was a Democrat. . . . Shall the solid South . . . unified by assassination and murder, a South solidified by the shotgun—shall the solid South with the aid of a divided North control this great and splendid country?"[18] Is it this kind of reckless anger that drives Mr. Raper to such distortions? Not even the most partisan of historians has ever made himself ridiculous by charging that Southern planters wreaked their baffled rage upon the Negro because there was nobody else feeble enough for them to be revenged upon.

It is hard to straighten out the general muddle and find the leading ideas and logical connections as they must exist in Mr. Raper's mind. There seem to be two main motifs, the economic and the social, and the chain of reasoning goes about like this. First, the plantation system has failed economically simply because it is a plantation system and for no other reason. Its faults have been inherent, all of them. No external causes have had anything to do with its decadence. And, second, the bad social conditions have something to do with a dervish-like trance to which Mr. Raper thinks the planters, out of motives of pure spite against the black man and the Yankee, have worked themselves up, and kept themselves worked up, unremittingly, for

---

17. V. F. Calverton (1900–40) of Baltimore founded *Modern Quarterly: A Journal of Radical Opinion,* a leftist literary magazine of the 1920s and 1930s that helped disseminate Marxist and Freudian critical interpretations. The New York poet and journalist Carl Carmer (1893–1976) published the best-selling *Stars Fell on Alabama* (1934), a book of folklore and description of Deep South culture.

18. The Ohioan Edwin M. Stanton (1814–69) served as Lincoln's secretary of war and, despite deep disagreements with Andrew Johnson, remained in office as a dedicated Radical Republican until 1868. The Union general Benjamin Butler (1818–93) was hated in the South for his leadership of the Federal occupation of New Orleans. After the war, Butler represented Massachusetts in Congress, where he led the attempt to impeach Johnson. Along with Thaddeus Stevens, Butler (known to Southerners as "Spoons" for his troops' alleged looting of flatware) piloted the radical wing of the Republican Party. The New York Republican Robert Ingersoll (1833–99), whose "bloody shirt" speech Davidson quoted, was much prized as a campaign speaker in the years following the Civil War (Claude Bowers, *The Tragic Era: The Revolution after Lincoln* [1929], 492).

about seventy years. In this uncouth trance induced by their assumptions, rationalizations, and sanctions, they slash out at all and sundry, and do not mind cutting themselves to pieces in the process if they can only give full expression to their religious mania and, above all, revenge themselves upon the Negro.

If Southern planters had ever had the sharp animus toward the Negro that Mr. Raper describes, the northward, cityward emigration of the Negro would have started seventy years ago, and Macon County would now be devoid of Negro inhabitants, as are many of the mountain counties of Georgia and other states. If Mr. Raper thinks that the planters "keep down" the Negro by some complicated exercise of Machiavellian cunning, he is badly off the track. It would be nearer the actual sociological truth to say that something like the old master-slave relation hangs on merely because both races are used to it and like it. That sort of truth in the Macon County situation really deserves some sociological study of the sort that Mr. Raper has not even attempted; it would make an interesting contrast with the situation, say, in Chicago, St. Louis, Harlem, Arkansas. As for white supremacy, that is another social truth (it may be sociological too) which merits some honest contemplation, of a sort to which Mr. Raper has evidently not devoted himself. White supremacy has been used as a bogus political issue by a few charlatans, whose importance is negligible. But it has also been at times a real political issue—a veritable matter of life and death, indeed, when the course of events forced Southerners to consider on what terms a white South could survive at all. It first became a political issue because of pressure external to the South. It has not been a serious political issue for a long time, but it will again become just that if external pressure again makes it an issue.

And what of Mr. Raper's tremendous simplifications with regard to the plantation system in the role of destroyer? Here Mr. Raper's errors are less vicious, if not to some degree excusable, for the system has bulked out prominently in many discussions, shallow and wise, and like all well-established institutions, it is always getting blamed for sins of which it is not necessarily guilty.

If erosion and soil depletion are to be attributed to the inherent faults of the plantation system, and if small ownership will stop it, what of the small owners' places in the upper Tennessee Valley, where there is no plantation system at all? According to the TVA, small ownership there has not checked erosion and soil depletion. Nor has it done so in many other regions. In Middle Tennessee I can point out many a ruined field, not a part of a plantation system. And if bankruptcy, low incomes, and so forth are bodily secretions of the plantation system, why have the same phenomena appeared in all non-plantation agricultural areas, almost without exceptions?

Mr. Raper fails to distinguish between good farming and bad farming. He also fails to see that the disabilities of the plantation are also in some degree the disabilities of agriculture at large. He not only gives us a faulty interpretation of his facts, but he fails to gather all the relevant facts.

In his tale of the two Georgia counties he should have told how the survival of the plantation system is a consequence of the repossession of the Deep South by Southerners after the attempt to treat it as a conquered province had ceased. The post-bellum form of the plantation system, with its various relations between owner and tenant, was and is nothing more than a practical adjustment, an attempt to "carry on" within the Union, a product of defeat and reconcilement, not of a conspiracy against the Negro. All this is clearly set forth in many books, notably in Rupert Vance's recent *Human Factors in Cotton Culture*.[19] But now, instead of Abolitionism, the plantation faces the subtler forces of Industrialism, which, while it holds out seemingly great rewards in the shape of markets, really sets the planter, as a producer of low-priced raw materials, at a great disadvantage as it renders him more and more a consumer of high-priced manufactured articles. The planter is in effect a colonial at the mercy of an imperialist. It is the imperializing industrialist who is ultimately to blame for the lowering of the tenant's status which Mr. Raper calls exploitation. The planter has been forced to adopt a cash relationship toward his tenants, and it is really not altogether his fault, or the fault of his system, that the cash relationship has not for a long time been bounteous.

Mr. Raper has nothing to say about such matters. He does not discourse upon the economic dependency of the South, although his contemporaries, Mr. Vance and Mr. Odum, have made much of it. In *Southern Regions* we may find that the Southeast, with about twenty-one per cent of the nation's population, has only nine per cent of the nation's income. Mr. Raper does not consider the role of the tariff, of foreign markets, of world prices vs. domestic prices in the cotton economy. He does not instruct us in the matter of how recent increases in taxation have helped to drive Southern agriculture down hill, although Mr. Odum has collected figures to show that the largest percentages of tax increase in the nation have occurred in the Southeast.[20] And there is also the new "High standard of living," which is to be figured in the same decline.

It is true that in his chapter, "The Exodus," Mr. Raper tells of enormous

---

19. Vance, *Human Factors in Cotton Culture: A Study in the Social Geography of the American South* (Chapel Hill, 1929).

20. Odum, *Southern Regions*, 125–27.

areas that have been sold for taxes or have fallen into the hands of loan companies. By 1934 or thereabouts, 17,000 acres in Greene County and about 20,000 in Macon County had been taken over by loan companies. In Green County the John Hancock Life Insurance Company had become the largest single landowner. But Mr. Raper considers these figures only in relation to Negro migration and the operation of the New Deal. In general his economic facts fail to get a broad and realistic interpretation. He cannot relate the shabbiness of tenant houses to the glorious upsurge of the Empire State Building or realize that the thirty or forty cents a day paid to the Negro wage hand may, in a sense, represent what is left when tribute has been paid to Detroit, Wall Street, and the American Federation of Labor.

These failures of interpretation grow out of Mr. Raper's predilections and his specialized sense of injustice. I should never want to fall into his error and say that such failures are inherent in sociology as a system. But sociologists, absorbed in their abstractions, sometimes do not realize how their great structures of fact may be invalidated by wrong assumptions. And that is the moment when sociology becomes dangerous. We must respect the sociologist when he is giving us real facts upon good assumptions, or perhaps upon no assumptions. For then, if his facts should prove to be in error, they can be corrected. But when his factual presentation is linked with false assumptions, he is not presenting facts at all; he is mythologizing. And it is extremely difficult to correct myths, all the more when they come to us in the disguise and with the great prestige of science. The whole thing is summed up in Blake's aphorism: "A truth that's told with bad intent / Beats all the Lies you can invent."[21]

Out of the same cause as the failure of interpretation arises also a failure of vision. Mr. Raper does not see, or certainly he leaves out, some of the pertinent facts. He has no urge to go a-socializing among the planters themselves. He is credulous toward the Negro point of view, and lets it alone. That is probably one reason why he fails to tell us that there is a marked difference between plantations, some being, let us say, good agrarian plantations, others being speculative, commercial, almost industrial. And there are many other little items about the housing, clothing, feeding, fueling, and doctoring of Negro tenants that he passes over lightly or simply omits.

What did Mr. Raper intend *Preface to Peasantry* to be: a sociological study, upon which, after mature verification, social changes might be based; or the

---

21. William Blake, "Auguries of Innocence" (1803), lines 53–54. See David V. Erdman, ed., *The Complete Poetry and Prose of William Blake,* rev. ed. (Berkley, 1982), 491.

program itself of social change, with supporting argument and evidence? If he intended the former, he has injured a valuable and ambitious study by being doctrinaire and emotional. This is a pity, for Mr. Raper is a good writer, and there are few books of sociology in this special field, that are as lucid and systematic as his book is. But invariably, somewhere in the course of his smooth and matter-of-fact exposition, the cold pointing finger of the expositor suddenly becomes the clenched fist of the propagandist. Thus, at the end of an admirable discussion of the status of churches, white and Negro, one is told that

> the churches of both races are doubtless no more materially handicapped by economic conditions than they are paralyzed by race dogmas which rest upon the premise that Negroes are something less than normal human beings. Though they have adjusted their theology and philosophy to include their racial dogmas, the rural whites dislike to be faced with the Negro question, and but few of them can discuss local race conditions without some show of excitement, or resentment, or even rage. [372]

And neither can Mr. Raper forget his own dogma, blended as it is with his militant humanitarianism, nor can he quite stifle his own rage.

Is the book then a program? It is. Or rather it is two programs. One, the program of small ownership implied in the title of the book, though its practicality is doubtful in Macon County, is a program openly offered, and in line with the new tendency to apply such a remedy to regions weakened by a high percentage of tenancy. The second program, nowhere openly avowed, but continually hinted in scattered outbursts and frequent innuendoes, can hardly look toward anything else than a radical change in the Negro's social status and a resounding attack upon the South's bi-racial system, with its firmly established discriminations and segregations. What else can be implied in Mr. Raper's indignation at Negro disfranchisement, at the separateness of white and Negro in public institutions, at the workings of "white supremacy" and Negro "obsequiousness"? Mr. Raper would remedy discrimination against Negro relief projects by seeing that the Negro is represented on county boards and school boards. He regards the spread of automobile ownership with satisfaction, for the following reasons: the Negro tenant who owns an automobile, no matter how ramshackle, learns about machinery; the car entitles him to half the road, no matter who is coming on the other half; it sets him free to roam incognito and uncommanded; it affords him an escape from "the irritations of the unequal transportational facilities provided by train and bus and plane" [175]. Such references, with the never-ending emphasis upon the inequality of Negro circumstances as compared with white, the ironical reiteration of such phrases as "the poorest folk work the richest land," [22] and the large display of photographs carefully selected to contrast plantation house with meanest cabin and splendid white school with most wretched Negro school—all this leaves little doubt that Mr. Raper's hopes, prayers, and designs look beyond a simple advocacy of an ownership program to lift the Negro out of mere economic debasement.

The "peasantry" to which Mr. Raper thinks the decay of the plantation system is a preface is the base for a general maneuver, the object of which is apparently to set the Negro up as an equal, or at least more than a subordinate member of Southern society. The second, or unavowed, program is the new form of abolitionism, again proposing to emancipate the Negro from the handicaps of race, color, and previous condition of servitude. It seizes upon small ownership for purposes of rationalization and, neglecting all else, offers it as a panacea. Once the panacea was simply the abolition of slavery. But when the pure principle of emancipation failed to solve the problem, the right of suffrage was added. When suffrage also failed, education became the universal panacea, and after that, interracial committees. The new fashion calls for small ownership.

Let us grant that Mr. Raper's sympathy with the lot of the Negro is admirable. But an entirely admirable interest in Negro welfare, which many Southerners would share with him, leads him to extremes. If small ownership by Negroes means what Mr. Raper apparently wants it to mean, it is unattainable as long as the South remains the South, or is to be attained only at such a cost as would make Mr. Raper out to be not a sympathetic but a ruthless person.

But is small ownership for Negroes practicable, in a more modest sense, as a program aimed simply at improving the economic position of the Negro tenant? In some parts of the South, yes. But, even if we grant the competence of the Negro as owner and the willingness of the Federal government to provide long-time loans for such a purpose, there is still reasonable doubt that the scheme could be worked out on a considerable scale in a typical plantation region of the Deep South. Aside from other obstacles, the great and insuperable obstacle is the large excess of Negro population. To establish large numbers of Negro owners on good land would result in the ultimate eviction of white owners. These would be evicted either directly, by a process of purchase and government subsidy, or indirectly, through a process of competition, like that by which the Japanese peasant infiltrated into California. The bad race relations brought about by the coming of the Japanese peasant, who had a low standard of living, into a region of white farmers who had a high standard of living, indicate what would happen if such a competitive element ever became a part of the plantation scene. Race relations would be worse, not better. Nor would such irritating competition be eliminated by the conversion of Negro tenants into Negro owners to a degree moderate enough to establish a relative scarcity of tenant labor and so, as Mr. Raper hints, to raise the wage scale. What would then happen is shown by what happened in the South under the NRA: white owners, obliged to pay more wages, would turn to white labor. Thus another serious cause of friction would be created. It is indeed already a potential cause of friction in Macon County, where distant loan companies have imported white Alabamians from the uplands to farm lands they have taken over.[22]

Yet Negro ownership is practicable and, in fact, already exists in regions of the South where the Negro population is a minority. Or, as Mr. Raper notes, it may well occur even in Greene and Macon counties where circumstances may be specially favorable to it, and may have good effects. But it has good effects and may occur only where Negro ownership does not imply disturbance of the time-honored economic arrangements and social conventions which have resulted from the gradual adjustment of both races to the artificial, difficult, post–Civil War situation.

What the solution of the race problem may be, who knows? Maybe there is no possibility of a solution unless the American people can some day bring themselves to define a place for the American Negro as special as that which they have defined for the American Indian. Certainly the Negro derives no benefit from being a bone of contention, flung passively hither and thither. The Negro's acceptance (which so piques Mr. Raper) of the role the South has given him would seem to indicate that he prefers an inferior status, if it be real, to being a bone.

The general Southern view would be, I imagine, that any program of agrarian reform which really helps the farmer will also help the Negro tenant. Everybody knows that the tenant needs help. And everybody with sense knows that programs of agrarian reform must proceed with due regard for the special conditions of regions and localities.

Such measures cannot begin on the assumption that the plantation is a useless anachronism in Macon County, about to collapse of its own inherent rottenness. Elsewhere that assumption might apply. Even before the 1860s there were regions of the South where the plantation, especially the large plantation, represented a temporary agricultural phase and often was, indeed, an economic monstrosity. From such regions the plantation has long since vanished. But in Macon County, as in regions of the same general character, the plantation has shown singular vitality. The very fact that it has survived, even through periods of terrible agricultural disability, should lead the social scientist to ask whether it may not be specially adapted to its local situation and should not, therefore, constitute a notable exception to the general and widespread necessity of remedying agricultural disability by checking tenancy and distributing ownership more widely.

In so far as Mr. Raper's book may direct attention to the need of agrarian reform and so, by that means, may improve the Negro's lot, it will accomplish good and will, as I said at the beginning, get results. But in Macon County Mr. Raper has obtusely chosen the worst possible example to sustain his own argument. The more I think of the months that I spent in the land of Eden, the more incredible it seems that Mr. Raper ever came there to illustrate his thesis, or, having been there, could continue to argue it. In the part of Macon County around Marshallville, to which Mr. Raper devotes no special attention, are some of the best farmers in America, and certainly some of the best plantations in Georgia. By contrast certain other parts of Georgia seem a waste land of ruined fields and human unhappiness. I should not have been surprised to find the Marshallville region cited as an object lesson for those who might be interested in knowing whether a plantation system could justify itself. The planters of that region, despite the old dominance of cotton and a none too happy excursion into peach-growing, have practiced for years all the farming methods now so much talked about: diversification, contour-plowing, terracing, soil-building, crop rotation. They have even tried cooperative marketing and small industry. They have a good deal of the old, self-sufficient, agrarian tradition. Such methods, administered by a kindly and generous people, have made that little area, relatively speaking, an Eden. If a sociologist makes it out to be a Hell, then that sociologist had better begin to sociologize himself, for there is something wrong with him.

---

22. Whether they owned their farms or were tenants or sharecroppers, black Southerners suffered disproportionately during the New Deal era. The racial tensions Davidson referred to were often exploited by landowners to disrupt protests like that of the Southern Tenant Farmers' Union. See Harvard Sitkoff, "The Impact of the New Deal on Black Southerners," in James Cobb and Michael Namorato, eds., *The New Deal and the South* (Jackson, Miss., 1984), 117–34, and Donald H. Grubbs, *Cry from the Cotton: The Southern Tenant Farmers' Union and the New Deal* (Chapel Hill, 1971).

Donald Davidson

An Agrarian Looks at the New Deal

Donald Davidson performed his examination of the New Deal just as Franklin D. Roosevelt's popularity struck its lowest ebb. By late 1937, hopeful economic signs had vanished, the country was back in the throes of severe recession, and many Americans were aghast at the president's attempt to "pack" the United States Supreme Court with justices sympathetic to the programs the standing Court had struck down as unconstitutional. Amid the apparent failure and confusion, Davidson called for an explanation of the "working gospel," the "political philosophy . . . upon which the New Deal is supposed to be acting."

Using historian Charles A. Beard's isolationist call to action, The Open Door at Home *(1934), as a loose structural guide, Davidson commended the efforts of Roosevelt and his planners to restore morality to American life, to act for the "national good." The Agrarians—along with Beard and the president himself—viewed the calamity of the Great Depression as a "crisis in thought," and the United States' future depended on how that crisis was resolved. That much agreed, the New Deal and Agrarianism parted company. Davidson, who viewed the federal apparatus as a leviathan unable to discriminate between good and evil, repudiated liberal welfare state ideology. A good society could not, he explained, be "superimposed by an act of will," nor, certainly, by an act of Congress. For national salvation, Americans must look not toward the government, but to their souls, to their traditional communities, and to the land.*

Reprinted from *Free America* 2 (1938): 3–5, 17.

In the history of the New Deal nothing has been more remarkable than the ineptitude and shallowness of the public discussion that it has provoked. Both the critics of the administration and its friends have displayed a talent for confused discussion that is unparalleled even in a country like ours, where for a very long time the rule of public discussion has been: the more confused, the better. The climax of disorder and befuddlement, surely, was reached during the fight over the reorganization bill[1] when on the one hand we might hearken to Dorothy Thompson, Frank Kent, and Walter Lippmann shrieking in high-C against an imminent *coup-d'état,* and on the other hand witness Messrs. Barkley and Rayburn[2] patrolling the aisles of Congress and urging the radio-deafened, telegram-bombarded guardians of democracy not to repudiate the personal leadership of the President.

The Lord of Misrule himself could not have devised a more cacophonous exhibition of democracy at its worst. Yet as we look back we must confess that we have been moving deeper and deeper into confusion as the New Deal became less and less new. We have not had a discussion of the New Deal upon a basis of principle—not, at least, from the politicians or from the great national newspapers and periodicals, the very agents who are supposed to define and clarify the real issues. We do not even know, with certainty, what the political philosophy is upon which the New Deal is supposed to be acting, but all, or nearly all, is rumor, wild opinion, prejudice, conjecture, or simply froth.

There are many reasons for this awkward and discouraging situation, but I shall suggest only two, as of some considerable importance. First, the Roosevelt administration has had to buy itself with expedients before it could systematically define its working principles; and it was the worse off because

---

1. The 1938 Reorganization Bill proposed a reconfiguration of federal agencies to improve governmental efficiency. Following on the heels of Roosevelt's court-packing fiasco, the bill reawakened fears of dictatorship and failed to pass. A stripped-down version won congressional approval in 1939.

2. Dorothy Thompson (1893–1961) in 1938 wrote "On the Record," a column on national and international politics for the *New York Herald Tribune.* A moderate conservative, she was married to novelist Sinclair Lewis. Frank Kent (1887–1958) of the *Baltimore Sun* wrote the conservative syndicated column "The Great Game of Politics." Kent criticized the New Deal's augmentation of federal and presidential powers. After 1935, Walter Lippmann (perhaps the era's best-known political journalist) was frequently antagonistic to New Deal policies. He endorsed Roosevelt's challenger, Alf Landon, in the 1936 election. In his 1937 book, *The Good Society,* Lippmann accused the New Deal of listing toward the kind of collectivist, totalitarian political structure he saw devouring European democracy (Ronald Steel, *Walter Lippmann and the American Century* [Boston, 1980], 315–17, 321–26). Alben G. Barkley (1877–1956), a Democratic senator from Kentucky and a New Deal supporter, was the Senate majority leader in 1937. The Democrat Samuel Taliaferro Rayburn (1882–1961) represented Texas in the House of Representatives and had served as speaker 1931–33. He remained loyal to Roosevelt even during the fight over the unpopular Reorganization Bill.

it came into office sponsored by a party that had let its old principles fall into desuetude and had no sharply defined new ones. But, second, the principles were not there anyhow, in the shape of ideas and issues clearly formulated and familiar to the public. We are now paying the penalty for having long been unself-conscious, innocent-minded, heedless of fundamentals even in the highest quarters.

Where, then, shall we turn for a discussion of principles? Where can we find a statement of principles? I believe we must fall back on the students of history and political science, for they were concerned with the situation, or saw its coming shadow, before the politicians or the press waked up. Even so, they have been a little tardy in formulating their ideas. We should be better off if we could have had access, say, during the Wilson administration, to conceptions now clearly outlined. But there is no use regretting that defect. It is still not too late to ask what the principles are and where they are best stated.

Passing by many possible candidates, I incline to choose the works of Charles A. Beard as a likely *fons et origo* [source and origin] of the principles upon which a New Deal government, such as we now have, might be conceived as operating. I claim no direct connection. I do not nominate Mr. Beard as the Colonel House of the Roosevelt administration. But certainly such a book as Mr. Beard's "The Open Door at Home" (1934)[3] represents a school of political-economic thought so closely resembling the New Deal pattern as to invite serious study. At any rate, to examine the Roosevelt administration in the light of Mr. Beard's conceptions is a useful approach, which may have the value of disinterestedness and perspective.

The Beard of this book is a political philosopher who has apparently repudiated, or at least to some extent set aside, Beard the historian. In 1927, when he published his great popular work, *The Rise of American Civilization,* Mr. Beard seemed to incline strongly toward economic determinism— though of course he guarded his interpretations with many a discreet or sardonic *if.* Certainly his work at that time gave most comfort to those who believed in a continuous flow of industrial production as the mark of national health and progress, and least comfort, surely, to fantastic persons who might doubt that very process because it damaged the national life in such

---

3. The Texas-born Edward Mandell House (1858–1938) was Woodrow Wilson's trusted political adviser. In *The Open Door at Home: A Trial Philosophy of National Interest* (New York, 1934), Beard argued for isolation and national economic independence as a way to avoid the kind of debt and market entanglements that had precipitated the international Depression. In the early 1930s, Beard began spending part of each year in Washington, D.C., advising politicians and the Roosevelt administration (Ellen Nore, *Charles A. Beard: An Intellectual Biography* [Carbondale, Ill., 1983], 144–46).

intangible departments as ethics and aesthetics. Yet Beard the political philosopher now seems ready to take his seat with those very fantastic persons.
He will now subordinate economics—and with it other determinants once
thought to be fixed—and make room at the very top of national policy for
the ethics and aesthetics long exiled from political thinking.[4] The former
economic determinist not only sets up "values" but establishes a hierarchy of
values.

Politely concealing our surprise, let us ask how and where, in a process already described to us as mechanistic, do ethics and aesthetics enter the scene
as salutary intervening forces. Mr. Beard's answer to this crucial question
comes at the end of a brilliant negative analysis, in which he demonstrates
how lame has been our dependency upon certain assurances derived from
the nineteenth century.

Science in general has failed, he says, and the social sciences in particular
have failed in their series of attempts to establish laws, equivalent to the laws
of physical science, for the prediction of human conduct and the control of
human affairs. The sciences remain useful instrumentally, but have none
of the authoritative merit that the nineteenth century ascribed to them.
They are not leaders or guides, but tools. They must now join the old ruling "elites"—monarchies, aristocracies, clergies—which they once hurled
from the seats of power. We have reached a "crisis in thought." We are back
at first principles again.

> Deprived of the certainty which it was once believed science would ulti-
> mately deliver, and of the very hope that it can in the nature of things disclose
> certainty, human beings must now concede their own fallibility and accept
> the world as a place of trial and error, where only those who dare to assume
> ethical and aesthetic responsibility, and to exercise intuitive judgment, while
> seeking the widest possible command of realistic knowledge, can hope to di-
> vine the future and mold in some measure the shape of things to come. [20]

And so ethics and aesthetics appear as categorical imperatives in the new
statecraft. They enter into the formation of national policy when it becomes

---

4. Charles A. and Mary Beard, *The Rise of American Civilization*, 2 vols. (New York,
1927). Indeed, Charles A. Beard underwent an evolution in his thinking about history
and politics during the Great Depression. *The Rise of American Civilization* stressed the
importance of economic interest to human action (and thus history) and approached the
past as a knowable realm subject to discoverable laws. By the 1930s, Beard was questioning positivism, and he cautioned that science and reason could not always supply
solutions to political and economic problems. For more on this intellectual shift, see
Nore, *Charles A. Beard,* chap. 12.

clear that the old imperatives of theology and science have failed, carrying with them into ruin industrialist statecraft and something that Mr. Beard calls "agrarian" statecraft.[5] Neither a high tariff, laissez-faire, industrial imperialism of the old order, nor the low tariff, "free trade" type of agrarianism that has been its foe can any longer avail us. Laissez-faire, imperialism, and communism all fail in their attempt to set up premises and deductions comparable to those of science. They fail in grounding policy upon material interests and in rejecting ethical and aesthetic interests. It must be the task of the statesman to restore the neglected elements to their place in national policy. But, since there is no absolute ethics—and, I suppose, no absolute aesthetics—the statesmen can reintroduce them only by forming his vision of what the good life ought to be in America. He must mount above the special interests represented in industry, labor, and agriculture, or even the dangerously vague general interest represented in the current forms of internationalism, and outline his concept of the ideal nation, recognizing on the one hand the affiliation of the special interests with the quest for security and stability, and yet not neglecting "the body of professed values" in the cultural heritage of the United States [152]. He may use science as the instrument of his purpose, but he must realize that "our duty, our form of action . . . is written in no known iron law of destiny, in no statistical curves showing past performances" [135]. He must seek in short what ought to be, form his plan, and then, working in the spirit of 1783–1787, submit it to the people.

The relation of this bold conception to what we know of the working gospel of the New Deal at its best is clear enough without going into Mr. Beard's more specific statements about the line of national policy. Mr. Roosevelt has indeed attempted, as Mr. Beard would say, "to cut the knot" [135]. Despite the enormous pressure of specific economic tasks and matters of sheer political expediency, his is the only administration since the early days of the republic which has worked steadily at a *general* program, quite evidently planned to touch eventually all the great cruxes of our national problems. Behind the numerous legislative acts of the New Deal even the harshest critic cannot fail to discern a real endeavor to formulate some conception of the national good, seen in terms of a "good life" rather than of merely material benefit. Mr. Roosevelt has shown, too, a readiness to use science instrumentally—hence his "brain trusters" and experts; but it is equally evident that he has proceeded intuitively and experimentally, not scientifically, not with any affectionate regard for a special brand of economics or limited party

---

5. Beard, *Open Door at Home,* chap. 4.

creed. The "ethical" aspects of his program may be found in such phrases as "fair practices," "the good neighbor," and so on. But even more significant is the fact that in his speeches and papers he has emphasized—though not always with the gift of eloquence that belonged to such presidents as Lincoln and Wilson—the ethical aspects of his program. His "must" legislation derives from a genuine ethical *ought*. And doubtless much of his impatience, when checked by courts or critics of the new-born opposition, derives from his annoyance that obstructionists fail to recognize the categorical imperative of a human *ought* behind the political devices got up to instrument it. He has assumed that his program would work ethically because he has conceived it as founded on ethical principles. When the contrary has happened, he has been astonished and angry, and then, resorting to expedients to save the program, has been forced to make a fight for expedients rather than principles, at great cost to the effectiveness of his program and to the prestige of his administration.

The trouble evidently lies deep. Mr. Roosevelt seems to assume, with Mr. Beard, that ethical qualifications may be superimposed by an act of the will, without changing the conditioning elements that have already destroyed the human impulse to do right and impaired the American tradition of fair play. The New Deal would alter the *ends* for which the machinery of industrial civilization has been operating, substituting love of the general interest for love of the special interest and putting the ideal of the good life, conceived in national terms, above the baser motives of mere luxury, profit, power. Can this be done by the identical means long used for other ends?

Mr. Beard talks approvingly about medieval attitudes toward work, profits, usury. He even applauds Ruskin's criticism of nineteenth-century industrialism [148]. But he does not mention Ruskin's doctrine that ethics and aesthetics must be inherent in the task, the tool, the organization, the society, and cannot be superimposed except, at great hazard, by the use of a force strong enough to reduce human society to servility.[6] Both Mr. Beard and the New Dealers seem to occupy a position comparable to that of the humanists of several years ago, who sought to impose ethical restraint upon modern art without consideration of the culture that produced it. But ethics fuses with action and makes a social harmony only when it is already present at the base

---

6. John Ruskin (1819–1900), the English critic of art and architecture and an Agrarian favorite, was known for his opposition to that watchword of the nineteenth century, "progress." For Ruskin's comments on industrial depravity and the way to true art, see "The Nature of Gothic," in *The Stones of Venice* (1851–53), vol. 2; *Unto This Last* (1862); and *The Two Paths* (1859).

of society. As was said in *I'll Take My Stand,* it cannot be "poured in from the top."[7]

If this view of ethics (which is an agrarian-distributist view) is adopted, the nature of Mr. Roosevelt's difficulties becomes plain. For example, despite some scattering talk against monopoly, the New Deal, with Mr. Beard, seems to accept "bigness," on the assumption that, by changes of mechanism or of regulation, large industrial operations can be made to deliver technological benefits and at the same time behave ethically. But big business, a little mended, a little regulated, and heavily supported, has merely taken advantage of its spell of security to line its pockets in the old manner. The consumer has his gadgets (and is in debt as before), business has its profits, and the ethical principle is right where it was. Now that a recession has occurred, Mr. Roosevelt finds his administration attacked by the very persons to whom he supplied the opportunity, as it is being said, "for taking the cream off the business revival." Under the Triple-A [Agricultural Adjustment Act], the big planters and corporate farms enjoyed their allotments and insured prices without marked ethical regard for the little people or the national interest. Organized labor, finding its special interest also guaranteed, seized its chance to enlarge its power without caring how its operations affected either the labor movement or the national interest. And so on down the line. We do not seem to have advanced, morally speaking. Right now, we seem to be occupied mainly in arguing about what practical means may be used to save the economy once more from the unedifying debauch in which we indulged in 1936–37.[8] If the issues continue to have this coloring, Mr. Roosevelt will be driven more and more toward a policy of force, in one form or another. That is, his administration will have to continue to seek means of making the economy behave ethically despite its obvious predisposition to do otherwise. The means now in use is the government's money power—a form of force. The next might become more drastic kind of regulation than has yet been tried.

Agrarian statecraft is not what Mr. Beard has represented it to be— another form of business, less rapacious than industrialism only because its special interest is more domestic, less imperialistic. A true agrarian—or agrarian-distributist—statecraft holds that high-minded statesmanship is all but impossible where the people are corrupted or cast into abstraction and

---

7. *ITMS,* xliii–xliv.

8. Davidson probably referred to the contraction of government social spending in 1937, a contraction the economy was too fragile to withstand and that sent the country back into recession.

dissociation, by the very character of their occupations. Agrarian statecraft would seek to make its expedients conform to this principle: that the inculcation of ethics begins in the daily task of the worker, the farmer, the business man. It would use the power of the government to restore gradually to American life a system of tasks and functions which within themselves beget ethical ends. The point cannot be expanded here, but it need not be, for it has been made before. This statecraft is in contrast with Mr. Beard's statecraft, wherein ethics is a synthetic substitute for economic determinism, an *eidolon* which people are bribed into worshipping, by an uninterrupted flow of goods and services. But I cannot close without observing that, though Mr. Roosevelt's administration has been in trouble through accepting Mr. Beard's *eidolon,* there has always seemed to be more room for the agrarian-distributist conception in the spirit and practice of the Roosevelt administration than in Mr. Beard's too rigidly hopeful theory; and that in Walter Lippmann liberalism, or Marxianism, or common Toryism, there is certainly no room at all.

Donald Davidson

The Class Approach to Southern Problems

"The Class Approach to Southern Problems" rests at a complex intersection in South-
ern intellectual history. In the essay, Donald Davidson pitted his views and those of
his conservative peer, Frank Owsley, against work by two more progressive Southern-
ers: historian C. Vann Woodward and Jonathan Daniels, the influential editor of the
Raleigh News and Observer. *Situated somewhere between these traditionalist and*
progressive versions of Southern thought — and being pulled toward each — was Her-
man Clarence Nixon, whom Sarah Shouse has rightly called "both a conservative and
a liberal." Davidson's essay shows how the Agrarians struggled to keep Nixon in the
fold without embracing his collectivist proposals for agrarian reform. As early as
1935, Allen Tate explained why the editors of the sequel to I'll Take My Stand *hes-*
itated to solicit Nixon for an essay: "We had the impression that he had gone some-
what cooperative, if not pink, in the last few years, and we were afraid of him." But
the Agrarians were also acutely conscious of Nixon's clout with the architects of the
New Deal. "I am glad we have him on our side," Owsley confessed to Tate, "for he has
developed into a power and has the keenness and wit to do us damage. . . . I let him
know pretty frankly that we would get his scalp if he went communist or socialist and
began to talk about 'the class struggle' and 'the dictatorship of the proletariat.'" Yet
even after the publication of Nixon's Forty Acres and Steel Mules *(1938), when it*
was no longer possible to deny that he had become a full-fledged liberal distressed by
the economic oppression of poor Southerners of both races, Davidson — as the follow-
ing essay confirms — was loath to excommunicate Nixon, whom he had brought to the
movement ten years earlier.[1]

Reprinted from *Southern Review* 5 (1939): 261–72.

---

1. Sarah Newman Shouse, *Hillbilly Realist: Herman Clarence Nixon of Possum Trot* (University, Ala., 1986), 13; Tate to Owsley, 26 Sept. 1935, Owsley Papers, Vanderbilt

By the law of averages the book called *I'll Take My Stand* ought long since to have been entombed under the debris of changing events and tumbling systems. It was planned ten years ago and published nine years ago. By the measures now common it is a veritable antique—pre-Depression, pre-Hitler, pre-Roosevelt, pre-New Deal, pre-Popular Front.[2] Yet still it seems to be a very present factor in the minds of Southerners who write about the South. Still it is being refuted, as of old, by people who have not read it. And still new voices keep crying out that it must not shake its gory locks at them. Among these new voices are, for example, Mr. Jonathan Daniels and Mr. C. Vann Woodward.[3]

In the Spring issue of *The Southern Review*[4] Mr. Frank Owsley reviews *A Southerner Discovers the South* and in doing so notes that Mr. Daniels is

---

University Library; Owsley to Tate, 12 Nov. 1935, quoted in *Hillbilly Realist*, 70. Shouse, to whom we are especially indebted for an illuminating chapter on Nixon's relationship with the Agrarians and the Chapel Hill liberals, argued that "[a]mong the twelve Agrarians, a group of strong individuals who displayed a variety of sociopolitical views, Nixon would acquire the most liberal outlook and Davidson the most conservative. . . . Nixon was a good barometer of the tensions inherent in the Agrarian critique of modern society." In 1933, added Shouse, "Owsley and Davidson were predicting a sectional revolt of South and West against East. Nixon disagreed and warned that dangers existed of a class revolt of peasants and workers against the 'industrial owning-and-dominating class with the initiative possibly being taken by the urban proletarian leaders'" (*Hillbilly Realist*, 66, 68).

2. The "Popular Front" was a coalition government elected in Spain shortly before the Spanish Civil War (1936–39) broke out.

3. Like his father, Josephus Daniels, Jonathan Daniels (1902–81) was a progressive journalist. A New Deal Democrat, he assumed editorial control of the *News and Observer* of Raleigh, North Carolina, in 1933. See Charles W. Eagles, *Jonathan Daniels and Race Relations: The Evolution of a Southern Liberal* (Knoxville, 1982). The preeminent historian of the New South, Comer Vann Woodward (1908–99) was born in Vanndale, Arkansas. After earning degrees at Emory and Columbia, he received a doctorate from the University of North Carolina, Chapel Hill, in 1937. From Johns Hopkins, he moved to Yale University, where he taught 1961–77 and then became Sterling Professor of History Emeritus. His many works include his paradigm-creating work of historical revisionism, *Origins of the New South, 1877–1913* (1951), and a Pulitzer Prize–winning edition of Mary Chesnut's diaries, *Mary Chesnut's Civil War* (1981). In spite of his ideological affinity with the progressive sociologists at Chapel Hill, Woodward maintained cordial personal relations with the Vanderbilt Agrarians (Woodward, *Thinking Back: The Perils of Writing History* [Baton Rouge, 1986], 18–19) and told Davidson he was "not a Marxian" but "an agrarian sympathizer" (Davidson quoted in O'Brien, *IAS*, 200).

4. Founded in 1935 at Louisiana State University by Robert Penn Warren and Cleanth Brooks (the Vanderbilt-trained literary critic who would contribute to the sequel to *ITMS*), the *Southern Review* became one of the most important Agrarian organs. See Thomas Cutrer, *Parnassus on the Mississippi: The Southern Review and the Baton Rouge Literary Community, 1935–1942* (Baton Rouge, 1984).

"perturbed over agrarianism."[5] Although out of a certain cordial impulse of reciprocity I have not yet read Mr. Daniels' book, I can bear witness to his perturbation. Mr. Daniels called me out one evening from a none too inspiring Ph.D. oral examination, and we sat down to discuss agrarianism. It was not long before I discovered that, to Mr. Daniels' mind, I was virtually entombed, either among nostalgias or actually dead things. He was gentle with me, and sympathetically inquiring, but it was evident that he was a little uneasy. He would be happiest if he could go on thinking of agrarians as *only* ghosts; but it would be a bother to be haunted by ideas in the flesh.

There must be a fearful pleasure in visiting a ghost—in studying it, watching it shake its gory locks, hearing it talk history and economics; in being a little frightened yet not really hurt. Mr. Daniels, opening his mind to full capacity, was obviously having such a pleasure, and it would have been a shame to deny him. But there is also a pleasure, known to romantic poets as the "pleasures of melancholy." That pleasure was mine. We played ghost; and I was the ghost. It was a pensive evening. We mourned a good deal and were properly nostalgic. Then Mr. Daniels went to his hotel and shortly thereafter wrote a book. I bit my tongue and crawled between the sheets without waiting for cockcrow. Somehow I feel under no compulsion to add anything more to the record—unless it might be to issue an invitation to Mr. Daniels to repeat his visit. I get few opportunities to be nostalgic.[6]

To pass from the sphere of the marvelous to the sphere of the merely abstruse, here is Mr. Vann Woodward's provocative discussion (also in the Spring issue of *The Southern Review*) of H. C. Nixon's *Forty Acres and Steel Mules*.[7] There is a good smack of wire grass and wool hat about Mr. Woodward. One would hardly expect the author of that sound and sturdy book, *Tom Watson: Agrarian Rebel*,[8] to be worried by anything so insubstantial as the spooks that ride with the speed-artist, Jonathan Daniels. But Mr. Woodward is ha'nted too. He is uneasily conscious that Mr. Nixon, whom he praises for his realism, once consorted with the agrarians in their spookish and nostalgic rites. Since this is not a respectable activity for a plainspeaking

5. Jonathan Daniels, *A Southerner Discovers the South* (New York, 1938); Frank L. Owsley, "Mr. Daniels Discovers the South," *SR* 4 (1939): 665–75 (670).

6. Daniels's less than flattering account of his interview with Davidson appears in *Southerner Discovers the South*, 111–19. To make matters worse, Daniels's book "overshadowed" Davidson's *Attack on Leviathan* (1938), which appeared at the same time (O'Brien, *IAS*, 195).

7. Woodward, "Hillbilly Realism," *SR* 4 (1939): 676–81. Herman Clarence Nixon, *Forty Acres and Steel Mules* (Chapel Hill, 1938).

8. See Woodward's "Preface to the 1973 Reissue" of *Tom Watson: Agrarian Rebel* (New York, 1938), vii–viii.

realist—especially one who is assisted by photographic documentation—Mr. Woodward sets out, by selective quotation and studied emphasis, to dissociate Mr. Nixon from his former participation in the symposium, *I'll Take My Stand.* Yet the spooks are all over the place, anyhow. The South of the 1930s is having a new fit of sectionalism, and Mr. Woodward (if I interpret him correctly) is inclined to think that agrarians may have supplied some of the animus behind the new outbreak. He therefore emphasizes the "class approach" as opposed to the sectional approach. He likes Mr. Nixon's book because it holds that the exploitation of the South as a colonial dependency of the North is now less important than the exploitation of three overlapping classes: farmers, laborers, Negroes.

Though the implications of such views are perhaps startling enough to raise the dead, I would never attempt to play ghost with Mr. Woodward. I will therefore discontinue the exercise in fantasy and try my hand at realism.

First, Mr. Woodward seems to dissociate Mr. Nixon from his old companions, the agrarians of *I'll Take My Stand,* and he does so with the implication that while Mr. Nixon has changed his former (maybe partly nostalgic?) views, the old, die-hard agrarians have not. This distinction is conveyed mainly in the following passages from Mr. Woodward's review:

(1) "Mr. Nixon is quite prepared to admit that ten years *do* make a difference, and that there is a 'discrepancy' as well as 'kinship' between his present views and his views of the 'agrarian' twenties. To those who lift an eyebrow at discrepancy, he is disposed to quote a country woman's dictum, 'What I am, I am, and nobody can't make me no ammer.'"[9]

(2) "If Mr. Nixon rejects the heady romanticism of the Southern promoters, expanders, and industrialists, with their rosy visions of the future, he is equally as wary of the romanticism of the type that envisions a charming agrarian past of a golden age. Such a view, he cautions, 'overlooks the fact that the charming life was at no time the privilege of more than a few thousand families, while slaves, "poor whites," yeomen farmers and small slaveowners constituted the millions of the population and furnished the concealed reality of Southern economy.'"[10]

(3) "Mr. Nixon would not give assent to the view expressed in a work to which he was a contributor—the view that 'The inferior, whether in life or in education, should exist only for the sake of the superior.'"[11]

---

9. Woodward, "Hillbilly Realism," 677–78.

10. Woodward, "Hillbilly Realism," 680.

11. Woodward, "Hillbilly Realism," 681; John Gould Fletcher, "Education, Past and Present," *ITMS,* 119.

These passages reveal a great deal of confusion in Mr. Woodward's mind and perhaps some in Mr. Nixon's, too. Agrarianism, so called, has never been a dogma requiring of its adherents the rigid "orthodoxy" insisted upon by Marxians and their fascist opponents. Mr. Nixon was never asked to swear an oath affirming that he would be forever true. The agrarians do not believe in purges, and have never asked Mr. Nixon or anybody else to stay in or stay out of their extremely informal association. The impression of real solidarity that they have nevertheless given arises, first, from their spontaneous refusal, in 1930, to accept the superficial diagnoses of the Southern situation which were then current; and second, from the "Statement of Principles" with which they prefaced their symposium and which individuals have since elaborated in various ways. Though those participating in the book agreed in a general way on these principles (which I think do not need restatement here), no attempt was made to secure uniformity in the articles from various contributors. They did not, and still do not, agree closely on the methods or "program" which would best realize the principles. Their great hope was and still is to give a definite statement of fundamental questions and to stimulate really serious debate. But meanwhile they have always hoped (as I note Mr. Nixon still hopes) that the South will not unthinkingly take over the large-scale industrialism which was and is being used as the sole means of salvation.

For these reasons, there was "discrepancy" among the various articles contributed to *I'll Take My Stand*—as later in *Who Owns America?* Discrepancy as great, say, as will be found in Andrew Lytle's "The Hind Tit" and Stark Young's "Not In Memoriam But In Defense"; or between the relatively enthusiastic interest of some, later on, in cooperatives, and the relative skepticism of others. If Mr. Ransom or Mr. Tate or any of those who spoke out in 1930 were now to write about the South, their present views would inevitably show some discrepancy with former views. And all could cheerfully say, with Mr. Nixon, "What I am, I am, and nobody can't make me no ammer."[12] It is only giant industrialism and its related isms which compel people by bayonet, bomb, strike, boycott, or plan to be "ammer" than they want to be.

This much for one of Mr. Woodward's intimations. Other differences to which he refers seem to be errors of interpretation and have no basis in fact. Nowhere in *I'll Take My Stand* or in later discussions have any of the "agrarians" envisioned "a charming agrarian past of the golden age."[13] That great

---

12. Nixon, *Forty Acres and Steel Mules*, v.

13. Woodward, "Hillbilly Realism," 680; Woodward paraphrased Nixon's sentence, "When the South looks at its past it looks at a charming 'agrarian way of life,' which was

magnolia stink is of hoary antiquity. Its sentimental history runs at least as far back as *Uncle Tom's Cabin*. It is the perennial taunt flung against the Southerner who happens honestly to doubt New England transcendentalism, or the behaviorist psychology, or the piety of Wall Street, or the reality of progress, or the divine inspiration of Karl Marx. It has been diligently pinned upon the agrarians by Northern (and often Marxian) critics, and by Southern journalists like Gerald Johnson and George Fort Milton and Jonathan Daniels who do not or can not understand what the agrarians are talking about. It always implies, of course, that the upholders of the "charming agrarian past" are trying to conceal horrible facts, like tobacco worms, outdoor privies, and illiteracy, or are suppressing sinister bits of Southern history. I challenge Mr. Woodward to produce a significant item of Southern or American history which the "agrarian" writers have intentionally or ignorantly glossed over, obscured, or distorted in order to make the picture of an agrarian South seem fairer than it ought in fact to seem.[14] Or perhaps I ought to chide Mr. Nixon for embodying this wicked little phrase in his book—as if his old friends did not know as well as he does how truly the South of past and present is a mingling of plantation, farm, and frontier, with both the imperfections and bounties that such a mixture implies. The truth is that the agrarians of 1930 put the emphasis exactly where Mr. Nixon now puts it: on the farm rather than the plantation; on the real plantation rather than its fictional image; on democracy rather than aristocracy; on the little fellow rather than the big fellow (and without shirking that hardest of problems, the Negro).

The third passage noted above contains an error of false generalization. The "Statement of Principles" in *I'll Take My Stand* does not say anywhere that "the inferior . . . should exist only for the sake of the superior." The quotation has been taken (isolated from its context) from an article by one of the individual contributors.[15] Mr. Woodward, in using this quotation, rather leaves the implication that Mr. Nixon himself disagrees ("would not give

---

made possible by rivers and river bottoms, a commercial agriculture, and the labor of human slaves" (*Forty Acres and Steel Mules,* 9).

14. This comment is ironic in light of the major role Woodward's subsequent works played in helping overturn the racist school of history that the Agrarians borrowed from prominent historians of the early twentieth century. In *Thinking Back,* Woodward warned white Southerners against relying "for regional identity on the old 'Central Theme' of white supremacy—'the cardinal test of a Southerner,' Ulrich B. Phillips called it. . . . That is what the antebellum South did with slavery in the first Lost Cause, the Agrarians on an intellectual level in a second, and the racists on the popular level in a third" (142).

15. Fletcher, "Education, Past and Present," 119.

assent") with the "view" of *I'll Take My Stand* ("a work to which he was a contributor") on an apparently cardinal point of agrarian doctrine. But I cannot find any place in *Forty Acres and Steel Mules* where Mr. Nixon quotes the sentence cited or says anything to justify Mr. Woodward's specific attribution of nonassent to him.[16] Mr. Woodward is talking here, not Mr. Nixon. But if Mr. Woodward were going to use the passage, he ought to have had the goodness to say which individual contributor said this, and in what context. The truth is, again, quite different. The agrarians hold no such view as Mr. Woodward suggests, and never have done so. Almost without exception they have followed Jefferson in politics, economics, and social interpretation. If *one* agrarian, in passing, has used the saying of a Chinese sage or some rationalization of Harper and Dew,[17] that is no reason for attributing the sentiment to all, and thus subtly smearing them with the charge of snobbery— or does Mr. Woodward imply something even more sinister than snobbery? I would like to know what he does mean.

I begin to hope that I do not know what he means when I turn to his major distinction between Mr. Nixon and the agrarians. The sectional approach, Mr. Woodward seems to think, has been important in the past but is not now adequate. Mr. Nixon's special virtue lies in his realism, and his realism had to do with his willingness to use the "class approach" (Mr. Woodward's phrase). Mr. Woodward quotes and emphasizes the following passages from *Forty Acres and Steel Mules*:

[T]he ills of the South are the ills of class more than of region or section. . . . It is too easy and too simple to charge the ills of the South up to extra-regional control. It is more to the point to say that the South has disproportionately large numbers of the three overlapping groups of Americans who have been most consistently exploited by the "American system." These three overlapping groups are farmers, including tenant farmers; laborers,

---

16. Nixon did say, "There is not only kinship but discrepancy between the present study and my chapter in *I'll Take My Stand,* and I wish to anticipate any possible critic in making this point. I participated in the 'agrarian' indictment of the American industrial system of the nineteen-twenties, but I seek a broader program of agricultural reconstruction than I read into the writings which have come from most members of that group since 1930. It should be said that what I have here written is by way neither of conformity nor of dissent. My ideas or observations must speak for themselves" (*Forty Acres and Steel Mules,* v).

17. The University of South Carolina chancellor William Harper (1790–1847) and the College of William and Mary professor Thomas R. Dew (1802–46) were pro-slavery essayists whose writings appeared in *The Pro-Slavery Argument* (Charleston, 1852).

including unorganized laborers; and Negroes, including many farmers, especially tenant farmers, and laborers.[18]

One way of discussing Mr. Woodward's contention would be to summarize (as he has not done) the contents of *Forty Acres and Steel Mules*. I invite the reader to compare Mr. Woodward's review with Mr. Nixon's book, page by page, chapter by chapter, as I have done, and endeavor to find just where the author has emphasized the "class approach" and, still more important, where he has demonstrated its efficacy. Hardly more than a half-dozen pages out of a hundred contain any reference to the "class approach." It assumes a slight prominence only in the last two or three pages of the book (from which most of Mr. Woodward's striking quotations, including the passage above, are taken).

In general the book does not diverge greatly from the established pattern of books about Southern problems. It is hardly revolutionary. Rather, to a very large extent, it is a synthesis of studies made by various individuals and agencies and of views drawn from various sources including the agrarian. It is a compact introduction to social problems rather than a special plea. And it carries weight because it is made by one of the ablest of contemporary Southerners, who can draw on his own personal experience, add his own salty aphorisms and anecdotes, and make his own untroubled assessments. The leaning, throughout, is toward the New Deal economics of planning and centralized control, but at many points Mr. Nixon writes far more realistically than most of the official New Dealers that I have seen in action. The originality of the book ought to have been in its presumptive theme, implied by the title. Mr. Nixon knows more than most people about the effects of machines upon agriculture, both from within and from without the farm. I should have liked to hear him on that point, but unfortunately he does not follow the theme very far. He turns to other topics, among them the relation of towns, villages, and small cities to an agricultural economy. This seems to me the most valuable part of the book. But Mr. Woodward makes no comment on it, or on the "steel mules."

It would have helped matters if Mr. Woodward had at least indicated that the "class approach" is by no means the only element in Mr. Nixon's book. Possibly his interest in Populism has led him too enthusiastically toward this one approach, just as the same interest, perhaps, has occasionally led Mr. Nixon into inept historical pronouncements, as when he says that the

---

18. Nixon, *Forty Acres and Steel Mules,* 95, quoted by Woodward in "Hillbilly Realism," 678–79.

civilization of the antebellum South was "socially too much like that of Russia before the World War and sure to fall sooner or later"[19]—a statement which certainly ignores the findings of recent historians and the analyses of such men as Rupert Vance,[20] who insists upon a multiplicity of "Souths." And the assertions about "class ills," like the historical judgments, are not supported by demonstrations. They are merely assertions. Mr. Nixon does not say just how class ills are to be remedied by dropping the sectional fight and "seeking a national policy for the good of all sections and all classes."[21] Neither does the approving reviewer, Mr. Woodward, although he goes to the trouble, in three introductory paragraphs, of advancing a theory that Southern history has been an alternation "from an emphasis on section-consciousness to an emphasis on class-consciousness, or, if one will, from sectionalism to nationalism."[22]

The flavor of such interpretation seems to me almost inevitably Marxian, if it will tend to be taken as such, things being what they are nowadays. It is a surprise to find the author of *Tom Watson, Agrarian Rebel,* in this role. If he really means it, and is not just playing with words, then he ought to go back and revise the earlier chapters of the Watson biography. There Mr. Woodward clearly—and I think properly—indicates that the temper and structure of Southern society have been rather Jeffersonian. Distinctions in Tom Watson's day were not very sharp, and were not based on economics. Family, or perhaps clan, mattered; not "class." It was not a very class-conscious Georgia which followed, in the rapid shifts of those days, Alexander Stephens, Bob Toombs, Ben Hill,[23] Henry Grady, and so on. The relatively quick failure of Populism and the easy triumph of the New South Bourbons might have been due to a Populist tendency to begin to make a "class approach." More specifically, the Populists ran into trouble when they crossed the color line, solicited Negro support, and permitted the slogan of white supremacy

---

19. Nixon, *Forty Acres and Steel Mules,* 10.

20. Rupert Bayless Vance (1899–1975) was a progressive sociologist at the University of North Carolina, Chapel Hill. Vance's significant books include *Human Geography of the South* (1932).

21. Nixon, *Forty Acres and Steel Mules,* 92.

22. Woodward, "Hillbilly Realism," 676.

23. Alexander Hamilton Stephens (1812–83) was a Georgia legislator who became vice president of the Confederacy in 1861. Robert Augustus Toombs (1810–85) was a Georgia legislator who in 1861 served briefly as secretary of state of the Confederacy. Benjamin Harvey Hill (1823–82) was a Georgia legislator elected to the senate of the Confederate states in 1861; he later served as a U.S. senator 1877–82. All three men became active critics of Republican rule during Reconstruction.

to be used against them.[24] In his review, Mr. Woodward recognizes the continuing possibility of such reactions, but he omits reference to the dangers inherent in the race question.

I may be reading too much into Mr. Woodward's review. I should be glad to have it proved that I am doing so. Nevertheless, it does seem that considerations not apparent either in his own biography of Watson or in Mr. Nixon's present book have made him somehow hospitable to the "class approach." And so he has reviewed the book with that emphasis, and has been willing to renew the old game of tossing labels and epithets at the agrarians rather than to get down to the business of meeting their contentions with solid arguments.

In all friendliness, and only for the sake of clarity, I will offer another view of the "class approach." I feel, with Mr. Herbert Agar, that critics would do the agrarians a service if they would only attack a real position instead of some "queer warped notions of their own."[25]

The Marxian notion of "class" and "class struggle" arises out of the growth and decline of industrial capitalism in Europe. It is an arguable question

---

24. Davidson seemed to ignore Woodward's praise of the young Watson for attempting to integrate the Populist movement. Of his exploration of Watson's early race attitudes, Woodward has written, "On this I went so far as to say that 'Tom Watson was perhaps the first native white Southern leader of importance to treat the Negro's aspirations with the seriousness that human strivings deserve' and that 'never before or since have the two races in the South come so close together' as under his leadership of the Populists. Even further, I said that in years when racial violence was at its peak, and Georgia led the country in lynchings, Watson 'faced his problem courageously, honestly, and intelligently,' and 'met each issue squarely.' He vowed to 'make lynch law odious to the people,' to prove that 'the accident of color can make no difference in the interests of farmers, croppers, and laborers,' and to assure black people their full political and legal rights and participation in his party" (*Thinking Back,* 36).

25. Herbert Agar (1897–1980) was a Princeton-trained author and columnist who became allied with the Agrarians in the mid-1930s. After Seward Collins invited Tate to review Agar's Pulitzer Prize–winning *The People's Choice* (1933), a conservative reading of American history, Tate was so impressed by the book that he invited Agar to contribute to the sequel to *ITMS,* the anthology Tate and Agar wound up coediting as *Who Owns America? A New Declaration of Independence* (1936). Agar, who would be appointed editor of the *Louisville Courier-Journal* in 1940, was a close associate of Judge Robert Worth Bingham, publisher of the *Courier-Journal* and ambassador to England 1933–37. The Agrarians were ecstatic when Agar promised to help them publish a weekly newspaper and to gain the president's ear via Ambassador Bingham. Davidson here misquoted Agar, who wrote, "[O]ur critics can then attack our actual program (which might be valuable to us), instead of merely attacking some queer misshapen notions of their own" ("But Can It Be Done?," *WOA,* 103).

whether the Marxian terms are perfectly applicable even in Europe, especially in light of recent developments. But let us grant that they are. Although European Marxians have been a little inclined to admit that America is an "exception," American Marxians have disliked "exceptionalism." But they apply the terms "class" and "class struggle" by analogy, without much consideration of whether the analogy fits. The weakness of trade unionism, the fluidity of our social structure, the prevalent sense of social equality even in the face of economic inequality, and the prevalent tradition of individual independence—all these obvious facts suggest that the analogy may not apply. There is reason to think that terms like *bourgeois* and *proletarian* tend to be, among us, just figures of speech, catchwords, war cries, rather than exact designations.

But even if we grant a tendency toward "class struggle" in the highly industrialized North, it seems out of order to look for "classes," in the Marxian sense, in the less industrialized, more agrarian areas: the South and the West. The Marxians seem to be arguing that since industrial capitalism must run its fatal course anyhow, we had just as well anticipate the process and hurry up to generate some class consciousness whether we have it or not. This is about the position at which Mr. Woodward would have Mr. Nixon to be arriving.

The agrarians go at the argument from the other side. They say that the Marxian analogy will not hold, is indeed ridiculous, especially in the South, with its heavily agrarian population. For Jeffersonian politics and economics planted deeply in America, almost from the beginning, a conception of what the Marxians claim to be striving for—the so-called "classless society." Under industrial capitalism that conception has been terribly abused and even endangered, but it is still virile. The advance of giant industrialism may produce conditions that invite the Marxian description. But in that case it seems more rational and practical to attack the disruptive industrial regime than to endanger the American experiment and throw away all our advantages, as we do if we imagine ourselves bound by European imperatives. The industrial regime can be limited and curtailed and finally transformed; negatively, by withdrawing the subsidies and protections legally extended to monopolistic industry and continued even under the New Deal; affirmatively, by fostering farm ownership, "production for use" at home, and like measures that diminish the hold of the money economy. Such processes will change *industrialism,* or gradually destroy it; they will not destroy *industry,* or machinery, or bathtubs! (Mr. Nixon himself makes almost this distinction.)

The sectional (or regional) issue comes into the argument naturally. The South and the West, as "agrarian" areas, are already strategic centers of resistance to industrialism and strong adherents to the Jeffersonian conception, but their very adherence makes them victims of "colonial" exploitation as long as a pseudo-national policy supports the centralized industrial regime. As long as such a policy continues, the sectional fight is forced upon such areas. It would be better to have a true national policy—that is, one not exclusively pro-industrial—but, failing to get that, a section must fight either for reciprocity or protection. Those who take the other view ("cooperation," so called) are in fact assuming the position of the industrial capitalists, for they apparently think that the benefits of a restored industrialism will "trickle down" to the exploited sections very much as Hoover prosperity was supposed to "trickle down" to the masses. In effect they are saying that the debtor can catch up with his debts if the creditor is saved from bankruptcy and given a new subsidy. This looks entirely too much like the post-Versailles hocus-pocus of German reparations.

This is the outline, and only the outline, of an agrarian argument—if I understand agrarianism. The agrarians want to cut the economic system to fit the society rather than the society to fit the economic system. Their immediate "program" grows out of such a fundamental conception. For the South it is basically land reform, as Mr. Frank L. Owsley has set forth, in brief summary, on page 671 of the Spring issue of *The Southern Review*.[26] Or in more extensive form it will be found in *Who Owns America?* and in sundry articles, some of which Mr. Nixon lists in his "Selected Bibliography."

Agrarianism rejects the "class approach" on principle. On the evidence of past and present, it would seem wise also to reject the "class approach" on

---

26. Owsley wrote, "The basic agrarian economic doctrine, as the name implies, is land reform: it is strongly advocated that tenant farmers and share croppers be homesteaded at government expense—though not at an expense that would entail the building of a four thousand dollar dwelling house and expensive outbuildings. Next in importance is an advocacy of the decentralization, wherever feasible, of industry both as to ownership and physical structure—always, however, making use of the best technical equipment. Wherever national defense or physical necessity makes decentralization questionable, some of the agrarians advocate government ownership or government control; others are opposed to either. The original agrarians—with the exception of one who is reported to be a fellow traveler with the communists at the present [Owsley apparently referred to H. C. Nixon]—have always advocated a balanced economy for the South, where agriculture would be the leading occupation, but where there would be industry enough for regional self-sufficiency wherever such self-sufficiency would be economical. They object to a high tariff, freight rate discrimination, and most passionately to absentee ownership of Southern industry and resources. Politically, they still believe that the doctrines of Thomas Jefferson and the Declaration of Independence are valid in most instances. In all matters they are regionalists and are opposed to the exploitation of one section by any other" ("Mr. Daniels Discovers the South," 671).

sheer practical grounds. The class approach failed to make the Populist uprising into a farm-labor party; instead it put Cleveland, the Gold Democrat,[27] into the White House, and then came McKinley, Mark Hanna's boy.[28]
It threw the South back into the hands of the industrial Bourbons. More
recently, the "class approach" of Mr. Roosevelt, in the "purge" fiasco, sent
Cotton-Ed Smith and Walter George back to their seats in the Senate, and
prepared the way for the worst congressional defeat that the New Deal has
experienced.[29] The hue and cry which followed the meeting of the Southern
Conference on Human Welfare in Birmingham, in 1938,[30] illustrates the
kind of weapons which the "class approach" puts into the hands of "reactionary elements."

---

27. As opposed to the Populists, who in 1892 pressed for the inflationary, credit-
easing coining of "free silver," Democratic Grover Cleveland (1837–1908), who served
as president of the United States 1885–89, won reelection in 1893 by embracing the
gold standard and pleasing Republican financial interests in the East.

28. Marcus Alonzo Hanna (1837–1904), an Ohio-born U.S. senator 1897–1904,
was best known as a wealthy, pro-business, Republican power broker; Hanna twice
helped to nominate and elect William McKinley (1843–1901) to the presidency over
William Jennings Bryan.

29. Ellison DuRant ("Cotton Ed") Smith (1864–1944), a conservative Democratic
senator from South Carolina, helped found the Southern Cotton Association and fought
Roosevelt's Fair Labor Standards Act in 1938. Walter Franklin George (1898–1957), a
long-term U.S. senator who represented Georgia, was another major critic of the president. In the summer of 1938, Roosevelt, who was frustrated by the efforts of Smith,
George, and other Southern conservatives to block legislation, launched a personal
campaign to prevent their reelection; the "purge" failed, however, when the two legislators and other conservatives won their races. William E. Leuchtenburg reported that
"[t]he Roosevelt coalition received another heavy blow in the November 1938 elections.
Republicans picked up eighty-one seats in the House, won eight in the Senate, and captured a net of thirteen governorships. Although the G.O.P. polled only 47 per cent of
the House vote compared to 48.6 for the Democrats, it made a decided gain over its
39.6 per cent showing in 1936." Nevertheless, added Leuchtenburg, "[i]t is by no means
clear that the 1938 elections marked a rejection of the New Deal" (*Franklin D. Roosevelt
and the New Deal, 1932–1940* [New York, 1963], 271).

30. Nixon played a major role in organizing the racially integrated Southern Conference for Human Welfare (SCHW), which brought Eleanor Roosevelt and Southern
progressives together in Birmingham, Alabama, 20–23 Nov. 1938 to discuss poverty,
civil rights, and labor issues. "The most persistent problem the SCHW faced," Shouse
judged, "was countering charges that it was a communist front. No one had denied that
a few communists were present at the Birmingham meeting and perhaps a score of communist sympathizers. Reactionaries seized this fact, coupled it to the integration issue, and branded the organization as communist" (*Hillbilly Realist*, 111–12). See also
Thomas A. Krueger, *And Promises To Keep: The Southern Conference for Human Welfare,
1938–1948* (Nashville, 1967), and Linda Reed, *Simple Decency and Common Sense: The
Southern Conference Movement, 1938–1963* (Bloomington, 1991).

One practical weakness in the "class approach" to Southern problems is that it assumes (as Mr. Nixon in his closing pages seems to assume) that the interests of Southern labor and Northern labor, or of Southern farmers and Northern labor, are identical: that their cause is the same cause. It assumes the Southern farmers, including tenant farmers, white and colored, and Southern labor, white and colored, are to make one party with similar elements in other sections and thus are to determine "national" policy. I do not believe such assumptions will hold good, or have ever held good since the time when industrialism concentrated power in the North. Southern farmers and laborers cannot make common cause with Northern farmers and laborers on Southern terms, or even on some middle ground; they must accept Northern terms, in the social and economic sense. Over against Mr. Nixon's wise statement that "today an employer of Atlanta may have more in common with an employer of Boston than with an employee of Atlanta"[31] one can set the equally correct statement: a Northern employee has more in common with a Northern employer than with either a Southern employee or a Southern farmer. The high wage scale of the Northern laborer, no less than the dividends of the industrialist, works to the disadvantage of the Southern farmer and laborer. The Detroit factory worker who gets five dollars a day and up is no less than Henry Ford an exploiter of the South. The clash of interests cuts across "class" lines. Nor has any permanent method as yet been found, in industrial terms, even under the friendly Roosevelt administration, of avoiding this clash of interests. But any emphasis on "class lines" only too quickly arouses antagonisms and divisions of which the solid forces of reaction can, as of old, readily take advantage.

The difficulty is enormously increased if the "class approach" means, as it generally seems to mean nowadays, the obliteration of the color line in the South. Southern experience shows that the introduction of the race issue into general problems inevitably confuses all issues, postpones the solution of general problems, and renders any solution of the Negro problem more difficult than ever. This alone is a solid and sufficient reason for the traditional Southern insistence that the Negro be put in a separate category and that his problems be treated separately. Such a policy should not mean injustice to the Negro; it does not mean, as Mr. Woodward, interpreting Mr. Nixon, seems to suggest, any denial of the Negro's "humanity." In retrospect, it seems that it would have been a wise course, at the time of Negro emancipation, to remove the race question from politics by giving the Negro a status at least as special as that of the American Indian. At any rate, there is no reason to think that needed benefits can be secured for the Negro

---

31. Nixon, *Forty Acres and Steel Mules,* 93.

by mixing up the race issue with the class issue. To argue that in this important matter the South must discard "sectionalism" for the supposedly broader "class approach" is simply to meet serious and indeed tragic facts with rhetoric. Once more it is time to say that the South, like Mr. Nixon's country sibyl, "can't be no ammer."

Andrew Nelson Lytle

The Small Farm Secures the State

This lyrical portrait of the "livelihood farm"—Andrew Nelson Lytle's own term for subsistence farming, which he thought had the "bad odor" of hardscrabble—illustrates more clearly than many other Agrarian essays the movement's overwhelmingly masculine point of view. Indeed, in letters, the Agrarians often saluted one another as "Brother" or "Bre'r" and referred to the group as the "brethren." To later critics, the invisibility and near irrelevance of women to their vision of agrarianism is arresting.[1] Lytle believed life on a small farm offered the best shot at personal contentment and strong social morality, and by way of argument packed his essay with details—the sounds, smells, and labors of agricultural routine. Lytle spoke at least in part from experience. Cornsilk, his father's farm in Guntersville, Alabama, was his haven in the 1930s. There he wrote, tended strawberries, and hosted fellow Agrarians. "No place have I loved so much," Lytle declared in his family memoir. "During the Depression the T.V.A. drowned the place under waters. Since that time I have felt in exile."[2]

Reprinted from Who Owns America?, 237–50, by permission of the author.

For the first time since the great war of the 1860s there is official political recognition that agriculture must have equal consideration with the other

---

1. See, for example, Lytle to Tate, 19 May 1931, *The Lytle-Tate Letters,* ed. Thomas Daniel Young and Elizabeth Sarcone (Jackson, Miss., 1987), 43. Carol S. Manning, "Agrarianism, Female-Style," *Southern Quarterly* 30 (1992), 69. For more on gender and the Agrarians, see note 46 to the introduction, above.

2. Lytle, *A Wake for the Living* (New York, 1975), 259.

powerful interests. This is a step toward a sensible political economy. It is a return to older policies and natural alliances. Mr. Roosevelt, better than all those in authority now, unless it is Senator Bankhead or Secretary Wallace, recognizes this.[3] In his Chicago speech before the American Farm Bureau Federation (December 9, 1935) he says that it is "necessary to bring agriculture into a fair degree of equality with other parts of our economic life. For so long as agriculture remained a dead weight on economic life, sooner or later the entire structure would crash."[4]

This is true; it has always been true; and, as long as man may hunger, it will remain true. For agriculture, to paraphrase another great ruler, Napoleon, is the life of the people, industry is its comfort, and commerce its luxury. When this relationship is upset, we must expect the mechanics of civilization to come to a dead stop, as they did on March 3, 1933.[5]

To recognize agriculture as a great business interest, trading its commodities for the goods and services of other interests, is a policy the soundness of which cannot be questioned by rulers who have the common well-being at heart. But this policy does not go far enough. *Agriculture* is a limited term. A better one is *farming.* It is inclusive. Unlike any other occupation, farming is, or should be, a way of life. Its business side is important surely, and in the modern world it has reached a degree of consideration never before seen in Christendom. Perhaps this is inevitable. But it is also inevitable that the State, to endure, must have internal security; and this security is best maintained when its citizens have a stake in the commonwealth; and the lasting kind of stake is property, and the most durable kind of property is a small farm.

There are many reasons why, from the point of view of a stable society, the small farm is necessary. It is the norm by which all real property may be best defined. The basis of liberty is economic independence. And in what

---

3. Henry Wallace (1888–1965) was born in Iowa and served as secretary of agriculture under Franklin Roosevelt. He implemented the Agricultural Adjustment Act and urged the opening of foreign markets to American farm products. The Alabama senator John Bankhead (1872–1946) specialized in rural and agricultural legislation. He helped formulate the Cotton Control Act, and defended aid to farmers via the Commodity Credit Corporation and the 1937 Bankhead-Jones Farm Tenancy Act, which enabled some farmers to purchase land with low-interest loans. Lytle may also have been referring to the Agrarians' hope that the TVA would assume some responsibility for supporting small farms, an ideal Owsley articulated in "The Pillars of Agrarianism." See Walter Creese's discussion of this proposal in *The TVA's Public Planning: The Vision, the Reality* (Knoxville, 1990), 87–90.

4. For a text of Roosevelt's speech, see the *New York Times,* 10 Dec. 1935, 12.

5. On 3 March 1933, Roosevelt declared a national bank holiday.

other occupation is there so much independence? The man who owns a small farm has direct control over the life-giving source, land. The three prime necessities, food, shelter, and clothing, he may command because he has a small inexhaustible capital. The fact of possession gratifies his sensible demands, and because of the nature of his occupation his home and his living are combined in the same physical surroundings. Since the family's living is made by the family for itself, the small-farm economy, unlike the larger commercial farm, has less to do with the forces of trade. And yet it shares in the general practices of the trading world.

It is a form of property, therefore, that the average man can understand, can enjoy, and *will defend*. Patriotism to such a man has a concrete basis. He will fight for his farm in the face of foreign or domestic peril. And if a man has nothing to fight for, he has little to live for.

The kind of farm which must be kept in mind is not the amphibian of Mr. Henry Ford, where the family works part of the time in the factory and part of the time on the land. Such an arrangement is industrial. It is an attempt to better factory labor's condition, and as such there is much to be said for it. But it is not farming. Nor can the subsistence farms being established by government agencies, such as the T.V.A., be rightly called farming. A bad odor attaches itself to the word *subsistence*. It implies a lower standard of living in relation to what an American might be expected to demand. It has many of the marks of a desperate and temporary expedient to be indulged until the industrial mechanism of the country becomes readjusted to the "highest standard of living the world has ever seen" of the 1920s. Indeed, it is a form of dole. This is said in all due respect to those experiments which are proving themselves in many ways successful. They are a move in the right direction, but how timid and coy are their steps! And this is because the people responsible for the experiments have chiefly the commercial aspect of farming in mind: the swapping of the goods of the great industries for their mutual benefit. As has already been said, this parity between agriculture and industry is fairer and better than the old relationship when the earth and its cultivators were the contemptible but useful sources of a legal peonage. But it fails to recognize that too much commercialism has bankrupted agriculture and deprived farming of its freedom.

Our hope for the betterment of country life demands that these casual experiments be turned into a real offensive. And the offensive must be carried on primarily by those of us who live upon the land, well supported by our Government. Any life which has the vitality to endure must move from the *inside out* and not from the *outside in*. The moral and spiritual centers of a way of life will decide what kind of house, for example, a man will build for himself, how he will conduct himself in all his relationships: they will, in short, determine the cultural values of the community. These cannot be brought in as "uplift."

Let us look at the proper sort of small farm, a plain man's home and the good citizen's seat. A type will be aimed at, but with the understanding that where farming is concerned, there is no type. Just as liberty presupposes equality of opportunity and inequality of function, so does farm life expose wide differences. This is its chief virtue; and this makes for its stubborn resistance to regimentation. It is the agricultural corporation that sacrifices the security and the benefits of country living for the factory method, the money crop, the bank lien, and, inevitably, the sheriff's sale.

Let the real farm be called, for the want of a more descriptive name, the livelihood farm. The word is old and in good standing. It goes far back in the history of our common culture. Livelihood: to give the means of living. But what is it to live? It is to eat surely, but is that all? The economy of modern times—and how short and modern they are when we relate them to the centuries which enclose Western culture—has assumed that the greatest good lies in the alternate stuffing and purging of a man's belly. Well may a hearty meal seem to the hungry the whole purpose of living. But famine and want, except as occasional features, do not appear in a healthy society. And surely it is the healthy society that the great body of Americans would like to see again. For what is health? When we are sick, we know what it is. When a man is abed, all his natural action is stopped. He cannot eat well; he cannot work. His senses live on a fever. He cannot move about as he is accustomed. And when society is sick, all things are out of joint.

And when we are sick, what do we do? We look for somebody or something to make us well again. Sometimes we are desperate and we listen to quacks, especially if we are impatient to get up. And like men, society may listen to quackery. But a better way is to follow the course of nature and assist it with a few long-tried and simple remedies. And is there a better remedy than setting up conditions where life will be free? I do not think so. Nor does the history of human conduct show any other way.

The livelihood farm has those simple features which will secure to the simple man as good a living as he is able and willing to stand. First of all, it allows him to make his bread by the grip of his hands, the bent of his will, and the sweat of his brow. These are no new-fangled principles. They are habits that experience has proved good. And they find their surest expression in working the land with the knowledge that the harvest will be gathered and stored away in cribs and barns against the barren winter. Such a farmer should have as many acres as will keep him in comfortable circumstances. This will vary according to the location, the richness of the soil, and the size of his family. He must have fields for cultivation, land for woodlots, and for pasturage. The farm should not be so large that he cannot know the fields intimately, nor so small that he will fear want. He must work hard without becoming a slave to the earth.

Removed from the public thoroughfare, upon a good situation, in a grove of trees if they are available, his house will stand. If it is a new one, it should not bear the stamp of a typical architecture. It should fit the local traditions or be adapted to them. The early American builder considered the demands of climate, taste, and needs, using the materials to be found easiest to hand. The dwelling should not be built hastily but to last. This is one of the surest signs of a conservative people. Thus will the physical and spiritual demands of a home be gratified. The farmer has no rent to pay and no fear of having his family thrown out on the big road because some new machine has taken his job away. Only death can do that; even then the man is removed, and the job remains for the son and heir. This is the security of shelter.

Then there is the security, already spoken of, against hunger. Near the kitchen the garden will lie. In the spring, summer, and fall it fills the pots and supplies the table always with fresh, crisp vegetables. The surplus, and there is always a bountiful surplus in a well-tended garden, may be put away in cans and jars. But even after the frosts fall, the farmer's wife may follow the path toward the richest spot of ground on the place and pick collards and greens. High mounds of potatoes, both kinds, will rise under dirt and leaves to fall gradually before the coming of spring; and turnips, if there is a taste for them. The canning is no easy job, coming as it does in the hottest weather. It might be simpler to buy the cans from the nearby town, except that this will involve the budget and endanger the family's security. It will also force upon the family a lower standard of living, for goods put up for the general public cannot consider special tastes. And it is this very matter of seasoning and taste which defines, in cookery, the special quality which makes for high living. Food must not only be nourishing; it must also be palatable.

Back of the house the farm orchard will spread its branches, shake out the first blooming of spring, slowly bud; and, as the season turns, hang red with cherries, the furry peach, the heavy apples and the russet pears. The vineyard may cover the walk to the well, or it may line the garden fence. But, wherever set, the fresh fruits will fill out the plainer diet of the garden and the surplus go into jellies, preserves, cider, vinegar, and the heady wines. In the fence corners, harboring birds, the wise farmer will let the native fruits grow wild, or he may cultivate the blackberry, the strawberry, the cantaloupe, the melon, the quince, and somewhere the classic fig.

There can be meats according to the family's likes and dislikes: chickens, broilers and frying size; fattened hens who are outlayed by the pullets; and all the year their fruit to make bread and cakes and desserts, or come to the table scrambled, fried, or in omelet. For the three summer months, if the neighborhood is established in its practices, twelve farmers may form a beef club (there is one in Middle Tennessee a hundred years old, whose membership has jealously descended from father to son). Once a week a fat beef is killed and divided into twelve parts. The parts go to the members by progression so that, beginning with the head, the family by the time summer is ended, has eaten a whole cow. Then, if this is not enough meat, the farmer may raise in the proper season sheep for lamb and mutton, guineas, turkeys, ducks, and geese to vary the diet. And with the cold weather comes hog-killing time, the rich surfeit of the greasy meat for a short spell, the salting down, the hanging in the smokehouse, and the long curing. As a by-product the stands of lard will take their places in the pantry; and if there is more than can be used, it may be turned into cash.

But we must not forget the spring house and the dairy nearby, for the choicest possession of the livelihood farm will be its milk cow or cows. They must be bred with care, so that always the milk will flow from bountiful udders and, sweet and sour, stand in the high pitchers with rich yellow pats of butter lying between. This will take good management, to have a fresh cow coming in as the old one goes dry. The young bull calves can be fattened and turned into beef; and if the heifers are promising, they can be kept for milkers. Thus the physical necessities of the farm family are supplied in the most direct way. It is well housed and well fed. For the cover of clothing the small money crops may be sold and exchanged with the output of the factory.

But it must be understood that the supply of physical needs is no easy matter, nor can it always be of the same degree of excellence. There are two things which qualify the degree of plenty: the imagination and will-to-work of the farmer and the exigencies of nature. It seems almost a waste of type to reaffirm such old and stubborn truths, but the fact is that we are like drunkards who must reassure themselves that the sidewalks really lie solid underfoot, that in the morning the lamppost that is swaying like an elephant's snout will be found upright and immovable. These truths give the assurance, when a farmer fails, that his failure is his own, that in the conflict with natural forces either his manhood has been found wanting, or in the inscrutable ways of Providence he has been marked for special disaster. In either case he has no complaint to make of society. But under present conditions great injustice is done the competent, those who hunger after living, for it is impossible to separate these men from the dullards and the shirkers. Those who have been deprived of their birthrights and those who never had any are lumped together through the necessities and fears of an artificial deprivation of occupations.

This loss of occupation among the many is the most damning betrayal of all. To take away bread and meat is to deny life, but to take away a man's occupation is to deny the desire and joy of living. And in the consideration of a remedy for this condition of affairs the small livelihood farm offers the easiest and the surest way out, at least for a large fraction of the population. The act of providing the security of shelter and the security against hunger passes beyond the care for material needs. In the back of the farmer's mind is the knowledge that he must furnish the physical necessities; but unconsciously, for he is not a man of many words, he gets great joy in the doing of it.

He does not suffer the spiritual sterilization, and often the physical, which comes from the modern technique of factory and city labor: the dissociation between work and the life of the sense, where work is a necessary evil, and pleasure is to be bought with a part of its wages. What does the farmer feel when he begins the day's work? He is not rudely startled from sleep by the strident factory whistle or the metal whang of the alarm clock. At break of day he is found sleeping beside his wife in that deep and resting sleep which only the combined fatigue of the body, the mind, and the senses can induce. At first, the night turns blacker and the air grows chill with such a chill as settles the last of the frosts deep upon the low grounds, thinly skimming the high places, softening the earth for the spring's breaking. This holds for a short spell; then gradually the darkness thins, pales, and slowly sifts in through the windows to settle on the goodman's eyes. By degrees the darkness lifts from the closed lids; light sinks through to the pupil; gently, with never a jarring, it stirs the blood, warns the senses that rest must end. As yet the mind still sleeps. Nature is like a passionate but no[t] rude lover. It spent nine months to prepare this man for his first light and now it moves in its complex way to rescue him from the shorter night. In the distance a rooster crows, a dog barks. There is an answer from the nearby barn. The turkeys lift their heads, stretch, and fly down from the tall pine. The chickens, the good layers, for the fat lazy hens are the last to leave the roosts, are down and scratching for the worm or corn that was missed the night before. The cows move about. The work stock shake themselves in their stalls. The hogs grunt, or the sows fall before the squealing pigs. The song birds chirp. The sky grows brighter, and the world is full of familiar noises. And these sounds, like the unfolding of a drama, penetrate the house and the ears of the sleepers. Suddenly like a gay fan snapping open, the heavens run with color to announce that the high lord of day approaches. The goodman, the master of a few acres, suddenly finds that his eyes are open. He yawns, and the saliva flows to tell him he may taste. He stretches, and his fingers tell him he may feel. He breathes deeply, and the fresh morning air, sweeping before the sun, shows how good it is to smell. His wife stirs beside him; gets up and dresses; calls the girls. Soon blue smoke from the kitchen stove rises over the house like a Byzantine column. The man is still in bed, enjoying the luxury of keen senses come alive and with no thought as to whether he may spend another five minutes without missing the car, being late for work, and possibly losing his job. He lies there, giving no thought to the tremendous ceremony that has gone into his morning levee. He is thinking of the day's work, for soon he must be up and with the boys feeding the stock, drawing water, and milking. Then he will have no time for planning. Like a good general, once he is dressed, his thoughts are of tactics not strategy.

As complicated as the beginning of the day is, it is only one day in a lifetime of years. There is continual variety. There are the seasonal changes, the time changes, the imperceptible lengthening and shortening of light hours, the variable weather. The richness of these phenomena defies the hardening of a rigid routine. It is a scene in nature's drama, a complete pattern in itself and a part of the larger pattern, the constant performance of death and renewal. Each morning the farmer wakes to some new action. There is the time for breaking the ground, the time for planting, the exciting moment when the crops begin to show themselves, palely green, upon the surface of the earth, the steady progress toward the ripe harvest, or it may be a barren harvest. He may wake, day after day, in a drought, when the sun is hateful. The terrific suspense, the sullen face of the world in a dry time when even the cattle in the fields catch the common fear, he must withstand. How often do the eyes seek the north, the flash of lightning, for the sign of rain. And the thanksgiving when in the sultry night a wind blows and the gentle rain falls on the hot shingles and down the crevices of the hard-cracked earth. The farmer, the farmer's wife, the children listen to know whether it will be a delusive shower or a real season. Then, when the patter becomes steady, restful sleep falls upon the house. Next morning with what joy does the farmer breathe in the crisp damp air. No perfume would possibly so exalt this one sense of smell. And his eyes look upon the world and see it come to life; see the brown ruin leave.

Or it may be there is too much rain, and the overhanging clouds encompass a rotting world. Then what a sight it is when the sun drives down the morning mist and sucks the fields dry. How busy is everybody killing the grass and saving the moisture. But this work must be done at the right time, for if the cultivator is hasty, is illy disciplined, he may plow the ground too heavy and not only injure the crops but do such damage to the soil as many seasons may fail to heal. Without conscious knowledge of the part he is playing, the farmer is dignified by this continual struggle with nature, with the seed time, the growing season, the gathering time, the storing away, and at the end the great dénouement with its relieving catharsis, for if there is death, he has learned that always it makes for new life. It is not possible to distinguish the needs of the flesh, the senses, and the spirit, for when the farmer thinks of making a good living for his family, this good living means physical, sensory, and spiritual welfare.

This is why the genuine farmer (and it takes a proper society to make a genuine farmer) never loses his belief in God. And the greatest flowering of formal religion will be found when society has the right understanding of this natural drama. When religion grows formless and weak, it is because man in his right role as the protagonist in the great conflict is forgotten or disbelieved. He becomes vainglorious and thinks he may conquer nature. This the good farmer knows to be nonsense. He is faced constantly and immediately with a mysterious and powerful presence, which he may use but which he may never reduce entirely to his will and desires. He knows of minor successes; he remembers defeats; but he is so involved in the tremendously complex ritual of the seasonal drama that he never thinks about idle or dangerous speculations.

In isolation such farming would be of no force in the common life. There must be enough of such livelihood farms to restore a conservative balance to the country community. Like the individual, no farm can stand alone; but— and this is the important issue—it must stand as a part of a healthy country life, not as a division of an internal colonial province to be exploited according to the irresponsible desires of commerce which, like a barn fire, increase the more they are fed. The livelihood farm is proof against exploitation. By giving security, it makes a self-respecting and stable citizen. It will have its influence, also, on the larger farms, of necessity having to do more with money crops. Seeing these semi-independent farm units about them, the large farmers will have a constant warning against the ruinous influence they have followed for over three quarters of a century, the ruthless and speculative demands of foreign trade, the sole interest in the money crop, and a bad system of tenantry—bad for the proprietor as well as for the worker, since he is the tenant to the credit system as the cropper is the casual worker of the land.

But even under a bad system, the livelihood farm will show virtues and make for stability. In hard times unrest and suffering will be reduced to the minimum, since these freeholds will always secure first the necessities of life. Depressions and public peril can only deprive them of comforts and some few luxuries. Good times can add only material comforts, vanities, and bought luxuries. And if the State is overturned in revolution, the freeholders are the last to be swept into chaos. Having something very definite to risk by change, such men will be slow to follow the demagogue, whereas, the tenant will be quick to follow him, since the tenant has been reduced to squeezing all he can from a system that gives him at best enough to eat and wear. In the seasonal drama which gives purpose and dignity to the small proprietor the tenant plays the part either of a churl or buffoon.

There are other negative virtues to a program of encouraging the livelihood farm. By taking much land out of the money crops and repopulating it with people instead of with wheat, cotton, and tobacco, with people who will consume most of its produce, the overproduction in the major crops will be naturally reduced, not artificially as the AAA orders.[6] At the same time the problem of distribution will be simplified. Food, housing, and to an extent clothing will not have to follow the wasteful process of being gathered into large centers and wastefully redistributed, for every hand that passes goods about must take its share. *Such commodities will be produced and consumed at the same place.* And without too great a disruption of the present trading set-up, for although the measure of each farm unit's produce for the general trade will be small, over and above its living consumption, its multiple will be large enough to maintain a healthy traffic between industry and agriculture, supporting the trade of the larger commercial farms, small merchants, the local professions, and the community of artisans.

It must be understood that everybody is not fit to follow the life of the livelihood farm. There will always be men incapable of responsibility and ownership of property, even on so small a scale, just as there will be other men whose wits and wills and imaginations demand larger possessions and the honor of command. Regional, climatic, or cultural differences would forbid that so large a territory as the United States should all be divided into yeoman farms. But if our country might boast even one fourth or one third of the population so situated, rural life and therefore the life of the nation would by present comparison become wonderfully stable. And the commercial farms, instead of a machine tenantry, held steady by such a leaven, could be served by that large body of people who are unfit for responsible ownership or who by ill-luck are reduced to the state of temporary dependence. On such a basis foreign and internal trade would find itself confined to a more constant and less variable rise and fall in prices. But the greatest good to result from such an economy will be its more natural living conditions. This should be the important end of polity, for only when families are fixed in their habits, sure of their property, hopeful for the security of their children, jealous of liberties which they cherish, can the State keep the middle course between impotence and tyranny.

------

6. The 1933 Agricultural Adjustment Act was designed to control production and maintain the prices of agricultural products, chiefly by decreasing the number of acres planted. In exchange for not planting, or in some cases plowing under and slaughtering livestock, farmers received government payments.

Herman Clarence Nixon

The South in Our Times

In 1934, Herman Clarence Nixon found himself in an ideological straddle. "The South in Our Times"* applied aspects of Agrarianism, Southern liberalism—even radicalism—toward the sticky issues of race and class that would ultimately draw him into what his biographer called the "radical fringe" of Southern thought. He had assumed an advisory role in New Deal agricultural policy and had joined the Southern Regional Committee, which funded scholars studying Southern problems and arranged conferences geared to regional reform. In part because of these experiences, Nixon demonstrated a command of the South's agricultural and economic predicaments the other Agrarians never matched. Nixon's more liberal social views, along with his quantitative methods, likely gave him greater political credibility. The essay's remarks on the plight of African-American farmers may appear perfunctory to readers today, but in 1934 few white Southerners defended black citizens' right to a fair portion of the New Deal.[1] Even more significant, in view of the direction Nixon's career would

---

*H.C.N. note originally appended to the title: An address presented at the luncheon conference of the Agricultural History Society on the occasion of the concurrent meeting of the various historical societies at Urbana, Illinois, on December 28, 1933. [Owsley also attended the conference, where he presented "Scottsboro, The Third Crusade," reprinted here.]

1. Several months after the appearance of this article, Nixon wrote W. T. Couch, editor of the University of North Carolina Press, and distinguished his views on the race issue from those of other Agrarians: "I can not go with them in their unwillingness, as I understand them, to give the Negro a square deal; that's carrying damn-yankee-ism too

take in the later 1930s, are the essay's astute observations about Southern textile mill workers and the labor movement.[2]

Reprinted from *Agricultural History* 8 (1934): 45–50, with the permission of Mrs. H. Clarence Nixon.

The "New South" has passed from quotation marks into eclipse with a tentative admission of the paradoxical advantage of backwardness. It has moved out of the mud into the red and is willing to exchange the shibboleth of States' rights for any three letters of the endowed alphabet.

In spite of the boasting about industrialism and in spite of the increasing role of industrialists in the public affairs of the South from 1875 to 1929, this section remained essentially agrarian in population, occupation, outlook, and consciousness. But by 1928 it was rather rapidly picking up an industrial spirit and viewpoint, yielding to an industrial invasion and an industrial revolution. In other papers,* I have pointed out that Herbert Hoover, the industrialist, carried the new centers such as Houston, Dallas, Birmingham, Atlanta, and Chattanooga in 1928, while [Democratic presidential candidate] Alfred E. Smith carried such old centers as Galveston, San Antonio, New Orleans, Mobile, Montgomery, Savannah, and Charleston, though one might say that the per capita consumption of liquor and religion was about the same in the old and in the new centers. Industrial-mindedness was the differentiating factor. But since there was no industrial Santa Claus, the whole South slid back into an agrarian consciousness by 1932 and voted solidly for the Georgia farmer-New York governor, who also knew how to harvest votes in the West.[3] It did not have far to slide and did not have to

---

far for me" (quoted in Sarah Newman Shouse, *Hillbilly Realist: Herman Clarence Nixon of Possum Trot* [University, Ala., 1986], 74).

2. In the late 1930s, Nixon devoted much of his time to investigations of labor violence in the South, and in 1938 he resigned from his teaching post at Tulane, where his activities had been frowned upon (Shouse, *Hillbilly Realist,* 95–119).

*H.C.N. note: "The Changing Political Philosophy of the South," *Annals of the American Academy of Political and Social Science* 153 (January 1931): 246–50; "The Changing Background of Southern Politics," in *Social Forces* 11 (October 1932): 14–18.

3. Roosevelt's Georgia "farm" consisted of some twelve hundred hilly acres surrounding Warm Springs, the resort he purchased in 1926 and continued to visit throughout his political career. Tenants raised livestock and grew crops. See Otis Graham Jr. and Meyhar Robinson Warden, eds., *Franklin D. Roosevelt: His Life and Times: An Encyclopedic View* (Boston, 1985), 450–52. Pete Daniel described the impact of the AAA in Meriwether County (where Warm Springs was located) in "The New Deal, Southern Agriculture, and Economic Change," in James Cobb and Michael Namorato, eds., *The New Deal and the South* (Jackson, Miss., 1984), 47–48.

meet such serious jolts to the ways of life as did the regions of the Middle West. Its backwardness had kept down farm mortgages, and it is estimated today that two-thirds of Southern farm lands by area or three-fourths by value are free from mortgage.* There were wonderful shock absorbers for the depression in the share-cropper tenant farmers, who lost several years of their slow advance in their low standard of living without making themselves heard.

The South, in prosperity or depression, has a combination of regional problems which have been developing over recent years and which deserve urgent attention. In the transformation and partial industrialization of agri-culture, the Southeast has not kept pace with the Southwest. Cotton acreage and production expanded extensively in the Southwest at the expense of the Southeast in the 1920s, with Arkansas coming closer to Texas in the rank-ing and Georgia leading the Southland in the reduction of acreage and the abandonment of farm lands, showing an estimated abandonment of more than three million acres. During this decade people were tending to leave hilly lands, while on the other hand there was rapid spread of mechanized farming on the Western Plains where agriculture was somewhat a matter of long furrows and a sedentary occupation. The hills cannot compete with the plains in the large-scale use of expensive farm machinery. Texas increased cotton acreage in the 1920s about twice as fast as Georgia decreased it, and some of the red old hills of Georgia became inadequate to support crops ei-ther of cotton or county politicians, with consequent demands for the reor-ganization of agriculture and local government.[4] Incidentally, the migration from the rural regions of Georgia to Florida and other States was sufficient to hold the Georgia population practically at a standstill between 1920 and 1930, in spite of heavy natural increase.

While the Southwest was gaining on the Southeast in the cotton economy, the white population was gaining on the Negro population in the general agricultural role. The increases in farm populations were often predomi-nantly white, while many communities with declining farm population re-flected a large decrease in Negro population. At the same time there were distinctly white communities among the rural hills reflecting net losses

---

*H.C.N. note: Gus W. Dyer, "Dangers of Radical Inflation," *Southern Agriculturist* 63 (November 1933): 4.

4. Nixon probably referred to the Georgia governor Richard Russell's (1897–1971) reform efforts, particularly the 1931 Reorganization Act consolidating state agencies. Meanwhile, the ravages of the boll weevil were leading Georgia farmers to shift slowly from cotton to other crops such as tobacco and peanuts (Kenneth Coleman et al., eds., *A History of Georgia* [Athens, Ga., 1977], 310, 267).

through migration to level fields from which Negroes were moving to urban centers, near or distant. A Georgia experiment station study shows that between 1910 and 1925 certain counties in that State lost from sixty to seventy-five percent of their Negro farmers.* Between 1920 and 1930, Georgia and South Carolina lost one-third of the farms operated by Negroes, reversing the tendency prior to the World War, while Negro farm owners in general have had less success than white owners in the struggle to prevent forced sales for debts or taxes in the period of depression.

The rural State of Mississippi lost in Negro population between 1910 and 1920, while between 1920 and 1930 the number of whites caught up with the number of Negroes. Many highland whites came down to the Delta region of that state to locate on more productive soil, adopt newfangled machinery, and supplant the Negro farm population. Bolivar County, in the Delta, increased its number of white farmers nearly threefold between 1920 and 1930. These shifts do not mean a decrease in farm tenantry in the South, but an increase particularly in the proportion of white tenants. The proportion of tenant farmers ranges above sixty percent in a few Southern States, including Georgia, South Carolina, and Mississippi. It is also true of this section that share croppers "formed more than four tenths of all tenant farmers in 1930—about one third of the white tenants and considerably more than one half of the colored tenants."†

The Southern hills, with low incomes and high birth rates, have also been an important source of labor for the textile mills which have been coming South to find individualistic "Anglo-Saxon" workers. From independent mountain farms, it seems, not a few laborers of stamina have come, and it is significant but natural that the labor elements from this source have been the most active in staging textile strikes in the last few years, though working in districts where wages were relatively high for the South. In the mill villages of the lower South, however, where wages have often been lower than in the uplands of Virginia and North Carolina, a larger proportion of the white labor has been drawn from tenant farm families and has tended to be more docile.[5] During the depression much of this textile and other industrial labor

---

*H.C.N. note: Conference on Unemployment, Washington, D.C., 1921, Committee on Recent Economic Changes, *Recent Economic Changes in the United States; Report of the Committee on Recent Economic Changes, of the President's Conference on Unemployment* . . . (New York, 1929), 2:573.

†H.C.N. note: Leon E. Truesdell, "Farm Tenancy; United States," in the *Encyclopedia of the Social Sciences* (New York, 1931), 6:123.

5. Farm ownership could affect textile workers' labor militancy. Although workers did not triumph in their 1929 strike against the Bemberg and Glanzstoff rayon companies,

has been thrown back into the rural hills to increase the ranks both of the tenant and marginal independent farmers, with a resulting importation of Western mules and the tilling of lands only recently abandoned. The families of such migratory farmers at times live in barren shanties, from which one might study astronomy through the roof and geology through cracks in the floor.

The depression conditions which have brought about this back-to-the-farm movement have tended to disturb the general labor relations between the races in the South. The Negroes have fared rather worse than the whites in local relief and in the distribution of jobs under the National Recovery Administration, though fortunately, they are getting a square deal in the dispensing of Federal relief, both through the Emergency Relief Administration and the Civil Works Administration.[6] Federal relief may tend to check the recent increase of pellagra and illegitimacy among Southern Negroes.[7]

Southern agriculture is directly or indirectly the basis, in the supply of raw material or in the role of consumption, of most of the manufacturing which has developed in the South, such as cotton textiles, cottonseed-oil milling, tobacco manufacturing, sugar refining, the mixing of commercial fertilizers, and, in part, the manufacture of lumber, especially by many small migratory sawmills. Nearly all of this manufacturing is low-stage or coarse-stage processing, with relatively low value added to the product by manufacturing.

---

they were emboldened and supported by the fact that "many . . . commuted to the mills from their hillside farms, and they could count on help not only from their families but from the small country merchants who relied on those families for their trade" (Jacquelyn Dowd Hall et al., *Like a Family: The Making of a Southern Cotton Mill World* [New York, 1987], 213–14).

6. A more recent study challenges Nixon's assessment of these New Deal programs' records on race: both the Works Progress Administration and the Federal Emergency Relief Administration had policies against discrimination. In practice, however, relief work wages were racially determined and "[t]hroughout the South officials registered blacks only when all white applicants had been provided for." One Mississippi county's Civil Works Administration official "imported white workers . . . even though eight hundred local blacks clamored for employment" (Roger Biles, *The South and the New Deal* (Lexington, Ky., 1994), 115–16.

7. Nixon probably overestimated the New Deal's leeway to assist black Southerners—much less address "pellagra and illegitimacy." According to Biles, "The federal government supplied a modicum of relief, but always under the watchful eye of local authorities." Relief programs helped Southern black citizens get by, but hardly produced a ripple in the prevailing racial order (*South and the New Deal*, 103, 113–24). See also Harvard Sitkoff, "The Impact of the New Deal on Black Southerners," in Cobb and Namorato, *New Deal and the South*, 117–34, and Sitkoff, *A New Deal for Blacks: The Emergence of Civil Rights as a National Issue* (New York, 1978).

Much of the cotton-yarn milling, for instance, is a comparatively low addition to an agricultural value for shipment to New England, where the final processing takes place. The South performs a relatively large part of that kind of manufacturing which is mainly dependent on cheap labor.* There may be other reasons for cheap labor, as in the recent lumber code for the South.[8] This code allows a minimum wage of twenty-four cents an hour, in comparison with forty-two cents for the Pacific Northwest, the grounds for the differential being the limited use of machinery in Southern logging and sawmilling because of small mills, small trees, and small patches of timber. Another reason not emphasized by the Southern Pine Association may be the weakness or lack of labor organization in this industry.[9]

Southern industry can hardly begin to absorb the released man-power, if a restrictive policy of agriculture is to be definitely adopted, unless a drastic reorganization of the whole economy is effected. Texas, more than the Southeast cotton section, seems to have been turning eyes toward foreign markets and noting the serious decline in exports, especially cotton, in the last four years. The Houston Cotton Exchange has issued a resolution favoring the termination of the intergovernmental debts as a method of stimulating foreign consumption of cotton. The *Texas Weekly,* edited by Peter Molyneaux of Dallas, has been preaching vigorously and constantly for months and years for a disposition of the debt question and all other problems which seem to stand in the way of foreign trade.[10] Molyneaux, who uses comparative statistics so eloquently that he has been called "Per Capita Pete," points out that Texas exports in former days of prosperity ran far ahead of those of New York on a per capita basis, and furthermore, that Texas cannot raise or maintain a standard of living in the face of excessive declines in farm exports. Increase in consumption, not decrease in production, is his gospel, and he branded the original proposal to take about one-fourth of the cotton land out of cotton production as a landlord's code, destined to displace two hundred thousand tenant families, embracing a total population of approximately one

---

*H.C.N. note: Clarence Heer, *Income and Wages in the South* (Chapel Hill, 1930).

8. In the summer of 1933, the lumber industry conceded to regulation under the National Recovery Administration. See William E. Leuchtenburg, *Franklin D. Roosevelt and the New Deal, 1932–1940* (New York, 1963), 66.

9. For a fuller description of the lumber industry's relationship to labor, see James E. Fickle, *The New South and the "New Competition": A Case Study of Trade Association Developments in the Southern Pine Industry* (Urbana, Ill., 1980), chap. 9.

10. Born in New Orleans, the *Texas Monthly* editor Peter Molyneaux settled in Texas and became vocal in agricultural planning issues, especially surrounding cotton. See his *The Cotton South and American Trade Policy* (New York, 1936).

million.[11] He has support from observers who fear that a restrictive policy will only result in an increase in the production of non-American cotton, as during the Civil War when the world's supply of American cotton was limited, though experts note that it may take more than two years for the world, particularly Brazil, to offset any American restriction.

However, the hilly cotton region east of the Mississippi must take restriction more seriously, for if not government restriction, there is the Texas competition, with a production per man (regardless of the production per acre) far above that of the Southeast. The Tennessee Valley venture is an experiment in planning and balancing a regional economy in a section where farmers cannot generally hold their own with the West and where there have not been adequate non-agricultural pursuits for the released farm population, even in prosperous times. A general agricultural reform is also under way in the Eastern Cotton Belt, not only as to scientific farming, but in rural economy and politics in the broad sense. Recognizing that economic laws or trends are at work on Southern farms, subscribers have rallied to the support of an agricultural press with a boost rather than a decline during the depression. This interest suggests the agricultural reform in Virginia led by Edmund Ruffin before the Civil War under the stimulus of the keen competition from the newer South of his day.[12] One Southern agricultural paper, with subregional editions, has something like a million readers, while another has about three-quarters of a million, with a twenty-five thousand increase in the past year. Half a dozen boast a circulation of one hundred thousand or more.[13] These journals would have remained in economic clover if the "Damn Yankees" had not cut down the advertising. They are an index of

---

11. In a drastic attempt to shore up cotton prices, the AAA had mandated crop destruction, for which farmers would be compensated by the government. Despite AAA regulations prohibiting it, landowners often took advantage of croppers and tenants. Cheated of their share of federal subsidies—or simply evicted—they were often forced into wage work. See Daniel, "The New Deal," 50; Donald H. Grubbs, *Cry from the Cotton: The Southern Tenant Farmers' Union and the New Deal* (Chapel Hill, 1971), 17–24; Sitkoff, "Impact of the New Deal," 121–22.

12. The Virginia planter and pioneer agricultural reformer Edmund Ruffin (1794–1865) published the *Farmer's Register* and demonstrated how, using fertilizer and other techniques, depleted land could be revitalized. Avery O. Craven described Ruffin's agricultural successes sympathetically in *Edmund Ruffin, Southerner: A Study in Secession* (1932), 49–72.

13. *Progressive Farmer* (founded 1886), which published regionally targeted editions, was the largest of the agricultural papers. Two older Southern agricultural journals, *Southern Planter* (founded 1841) and *Southern Cultivator and Farming* (founded 1843), also boasted subscriptions in the hundreds of thousands.

improved livestock, tick eradication, land and timber conservation, and currents of change now taking place in farm methods; they are spreading the teachings from Washington, D.C., and from the agricultural colleges and experiment stations; and they are lining up with some success for better organization and government administration in the South. They are vehicles of encouragement in the direction of social progress, and they clearly indicate that Southern agricultural reform, though it has a long road to travel, is at least on the way.

Herman Clarence Nixon

Farm Tenancy to the Forefront

Herman Clarence Nixon rejected the Vanderbilt Agrarians' anti-collectivist stance in order to embrace, if somewhat critically, the economic policies of the New Deal. Indeed, by 1936, he was playing an important role in shaping federal agricultural policies affecting the South. Nixon's biographer noted that in addition to his teaching and administrative duties at Tulane, where he was chairman of the Department of History and Political Science, "he was leading the Southern Policy Committee's lobby for the Bankhead-Jones Farm Tenancy Bill and conducting hearings on the Agricultural Adjustment Administration (AAA) cotton tenancy program."[1] In the crop-curtailment program cited by Nixon below, cotton planters were paid by the government either to plow under their crops or to leave their fields fallow. The policy was widely held to have benefited landowners and to have aggravated the economic plight of tenant farmers.[2]

Reprinted from *Southwest Review* 22 (1936): 11–15, with the permission of Mrs. H. Clarence Nixon.

---

1. Sarah Newman Shouse, *Hillbilly Realist: Herman Clarence Nixon of Possum Trot* (University, Ala., 1986), 69.

2. See David Eugene Conrad, *The Forgotten Farmers: The Story of Sharecroppers in the New Deal* (Urbana, 1965); Donald H. Grubbs, *Cry from the Cotton: The Southern Tenant Farmers' Union and the New Deal* (Chapel Hill, 1971); H. L. Mitchell, *Mean Things Happening in This Land: The Life and Times of H. L. Mitchell of the Southern Tenant Farmers' Union* (Montclair, N.J., 1979); Frank Freidel, *F.D.R. and the South* (Baton Rouge, 1965); James Cobb and Michael Namorato, eds., *The New Deal and the South* (Jackson, Miss., 1984); and Paul K. Conkin, *Tomorrow a New Deal: The New Deal Community Program* (Ithaca, 1959).

The depression and the crop-curtailment program of the Government have combined to center national attention on the farm-tenant problem, which is most acute in the cotton country but nevertheless prevalent in other sections, especially in the Middle West. Yet the census figures have been telling the tale of increasing tenancy for decades; the trend has persisted through good times and bad. In the South alone the number of white tenants increased 200,000 between 1920 and 1930, although Negro tenants showed a decrease of two thousand during the decade.[3] In 1930, sixty percent or more of the farmers of eight Southern states were tenant farmers.[4] No net decrease of tenancy occurred in the first half of the nineteen-thirties. Though slight decreases were registered during the depression in certain areas devoted to basic crops, there often were increases in areas of marginal and inaccessible lands, where squatters might be least disturbed in an unhealthy back-to-the-land movement.

The South has more farm tenants than any other part of the country, just as it has more farmers. It has poorer tenants, just as it has poorer farmers. It is the land of share tenants and of share croppers who in reality are risk-taking laborers working for a share of the crop. The share-cropper plantation has many characteristics in common with the Southern slave plantation of former days, including the exploitation of land and labor and the serious risks for the planter; the landlord's automatic crop lien takes the place of the older title to human chattels.

It has proved almost impossible to devise a governmental crop program which is ethical and workable within the landlord-tenant relationship prevailing in the South. Rupert B. Vance and Charles S. Johnson have made this difficulty strikingly clear in their factual field studies, while Henry I. Richards, in his Brookings Institution study *Cotton and the AAA,*[5] makes the pertinent observation that the initial governmental cotton program had to favor the landlords, for otherwise it could not have been adopted and put into operation. No amount of planter rationalization can explain away these criticisms, although the planters themselves must be included in the picture of disparity in recent years between agriculture and industry.

Agriculturists, students of rural life, and practical observers have long

---

3. These figures appeared in Charles S. Johnson, Edwin R. Embree, and W. W. Alexander, *The Collapse of Cotton Tenancy: Summary of Field Studies and Statistical Surveys, 1933–1935* (Chapel Hill, 1935), 5.

4. A table compiled by Rupert Vance showed these states to be Alabama (64.7 percent), Arkansas (63.0 percent), Georgia (68.2 percent), Louisiana (66.6 percent), Mississippi (72.2 percent), Oklahoma (61.5 percent), South Carolina (65.1 percent), and Texas (60.9 percent) (*Human Geography of the South* [Chapel Hill, 1932], 191).

5. Henry I. Richards, *Cotton and the AAA* (Washington, D.C., 1936).

known that the Southern type of short-term tenure leads to unbalanced farming, low productivity, soil-robbery, decline of community life, and extreme backwardness in the important sphere of cooperative enterprise. Reformers have been exposing the ills of farm tenancy and absentee landlordism in the South ever since the days of Henry Grady's trenchant journalism. But new angles of the problem have recently come into view. One is that farm tenancy in the South is becoming increasingly a white man's problem, with Negro tenants dwindling into a minority of about forty percent of the total. Another is that the "agricultural ladder," by which a farm laborer might progressively become a cropper, a tenant, and a landowner, almost disappeared in the nineteen-twenties and has not been restored in the days of depression. "Once a share cropper, always a share cropper" became too uniformly the rule, whether for social or for economic reasons. Southern farm tenancy is fostered by a high birth rate and an inadequate outlet for an increasing labor supply. The whole problem is complicated by comparatively great poverty and illiteracy, particularly in the Southeast, which encourage the mouthings of rural demagogues. The twin evils of poverty and illiteracy are not entirely foreign to the western end of the cotton country, but the farm tenants of that section have been more articulate and have attained a slightly higher economic level than those of the Southeast.

The Southern tenant problem has faced the New Deal since the first plow-up campaign in 1933.[6] The AAA, the Federal Emergency Relief Administration, the Resettlement Administration, and other Federal agencies have had to reckon with it. Rural unions have sprung up to demand a square deal for tenants and share croppers. Muckraking journalists have pointed out the sore spots of the cotton belt. Research studies have been made, conferences have been held, and committees have been appointed to study the subject. The Southern Policy Committee[7] and its conferences have insisted that land

6. Conrad explained the New Dealers' reasoning: "The plan was simple. The AAA would pay farmers to plow under 10 million acres of cotton, a fourth of the crop, so that the market would be less glutted at the end of 1933." The AAA advocated the policy despite "the obvious fact that if a fourth of the crop were destroyed, approximately one-fourth less labor would be needed to cultivate and harvest what was left" (*Forgotten Farmers,* 43).

7. Originated in 1935 by the liberal Virginian Francis Pickens Miller, the Southern policy committees were served by progressive academics and journalists interested in improving relations between the races and conditions for tenant farmers. When Nixon was named chair of the Southern Policy Committee's umbrella organization, his relationship with the Nashville Agrarians grew even more strained. When the committee met at Lookout Mountain, Tennessee, in 1936, Tate and the conservative Agrarians became embroiled in a disagreement with William Amberson, a socialist associated with the Southern Tenant Farmers' Union. See Shouse, *Hillbilly Realist,* 78ff.; Francis Pickens

tenure and land policy constitute the greatest set of issues confronting the South today.

The first major step toward doing something with the problem was taken by Relief Administrator Harry Hopkins in a program of "rural rehabilitation." This program was first announced at a regional conference in Atlanta in March of 1934.[8] It was an inspiration to attend this conference, which was blessed by Mr. Hopkins's official pledge of millions, scores of millions, to bring about a new day for distressed rural families. The group of families to be aided would be drawn largely, though not entirely, from farm tenants and farm laborers. Another assault on tenancy was made at the same time through a number of village homestead projects of the Relief Administration and of a division of the Department of the Interior, while the TVA[9] was also experimenting with rural planning and reconstruction. But of course only a few hundred rural families could be established in planned village-colonies, although other hundreds were moved from sub marginal lands to better individual locations.

The most extensive work connected with this program was the supplanting of pure relief, or the dole, with rural rehabilitation on a basis of tenancy rather than ownership. It was made possible for thousands upon thousands of families to rehabilitate themselves as farm tenants and get off or stay off the regular relief rolls. This program had several shortcomings. The funds

---

Miller, *Man from the Valley: Memoirs of a 20th-Century Virginian* (Chapel Hill, 1971), 79–84; Wilma Dykeman and James Stokely, *Seeds of Southern Change: The Life of Will Alexander* (Chicago, 1962), 281; Mitchell, *Mean Things Happening,* 127; and Jonathan Daniels, *A Southerner Discovers the South* (New York, 1938), 81–88.

8. Harry L. Hopkins (1890–1946) headed the Federal Emergency Relief Administration, established by Roosevelt in 1933 to channel federal funds to individual states for distribution to the unemployed. See Henry H. Adams, *Harry Hopkins* (New York, 1977), and George McJimsey, *Harry Hopkins: Ally of the Poor and Defender of Democracy* (Cambridge, Mass., 1987). Nixon was elected "a member of the Rural Rehabilitation Committee, an ERA subcommittee charged with lending to rural families and providing livestock, feed, and other basic supplies to the most destitute" (Shouse, *Hillbilly Realist,* 77). See Conkin, *Tomorrow a New World,* 133ff., and Lawrence Westbrook, "The Progress of Rural Rehabilitation of the F.E.R.A.," *Journal of Farm Economics* 17 (1935): 89–100.

9. The Department of the Interior added the Division of Subsistence Homesteads in August 1933 (Conkin, *Tomorrow a New World,* 98). Nixon's research for *Forty Acres and Steel Mules* entailed trips to inspect these planned village communities for farmers; according to Shouse, seeing the villages "made Nixon a cooperative Agrarian" (*Hillbilly Realist,* 77–78; also see *Forty Acres and Steel Mules* [Chapel Hill, 1938], 65–70). Funded by Congress in 1933, the Tennessee Valley Authority was a massive federal project to generate energy, conserve soil, and control flooding in the Southern states adjacent to Tennessee.

were too limited for actual reconstruction in view of the excessive number of rural families needing aid. So much attention had to be given to so many families at the bottom, or below the bottom, of the agricultural ladder that little could be done toward elevating families who might be holding positions a rung or two higher. There were also many difficulties in making arrangements for leasing suitable lands which had AAA quotas for basic cash crops. But the program justified its existence, under the circumstances, and was taken over by the new Resettlement Administration,[10] which also inherited various village and community projects. It is of some importance to the South that the successor to Dr. Rex Tugwell as head of the Resettlement Administration is Dr. Will W. Alexander, a practical-minded Southerner who understands the problem of tenancy.

Appreciation of the magnitude and national importance of the problem, and realization of the inadequacy of the existing agencies and funds, led to the formulation of the Bankhead-Jones farm tenant bill in 1935. This proposal was designed to transform worthy tenants, croppers, and farm laborers into land-owning farmers under government financial sponsorship with low rates of interest and long terms for payment. The bill passed the Senate, but a legislative jam prevented its coming to a vote in the House. Nevertheless, the proposal served to focus the attention of the press and of political leaders, including President Roosevelt and Secretary [of Agriculture Henry] Wallace, on the problem of tenancy. Correction of the ills of farm tenancy became one of the trump cards of the New Deal. After the last campaign and election, the President appointed a commission on farm tenancy, embracing both experts and publicists. This commission has conducted five regional hearings, including one at Dallas and one at Montgomery, Alabama. The Bankhead-Jones bill in modified form has been reintroduced, and definite legislation in behalf of farm tenants is expected from the present Congress.

It should be noted that the correction of ills of farm tenancy does not mean immediate and complete abolition of tenancy and setting up every farmer with forty acres and a mule.[11] For one thing, it would take too many billions of dollars and too much bureaucracy to carry out such a gigantic program. Forty acres and a mule will work in many cases, and will undoubtedly be applied on a gradual but progressive scale. But all farming can no longer

---

10. Founded in 1935, the Resettlement Administration made loans to farmers and relocated rural Americans living in abject poverty.

11. Eric Foner has speculated that the phrase "forty acres and a mule" dates to an 1865 military edict of General William T. Sherman's in which he ordered that each freed slave receive mules and forty acres of South Carolina land (*Reconstruction: America's Unfinished Revolution, 1863–1877* [New York, 1988], 70–71).

be done by individualists with only this equipment, and our farm tenancy should yield to a flexible system of improvement. It has taken the South and the nation more than a generation to get into the present land-tenure mess, and it may take a decade or two to get out of it. Denmark and Ireland got rid of the ills of farm tenancy through governmental action. But they did it in a generation, not in a day. Farm tenure can be shifted from the share-tenant-cropper system to a definite lease system in such a way as to secure many of the advantages of ownership, including the opportunity for cooperative activities and for production credit at low cost. It should be possible to abolish or reduce the share-cropper evil without making every farmer immediately a landowner.

The South needs both more land-owning farmers and more farm tenants with a definite tenure or status. These two changes should make possible more effective soil conservation, larger production, and a higher rural standard of living. It must be borne in mind that the correction of the ills of Southern farm tenancy can be achieved only as one phase of a general improvement in Southern farming. If Southern farmers are permanently to improve their lot as farmers, they must produce more beef or other meat and eat it, more milk and drink it, more feed and feed it, more cotton or other money crop and sell it. Southern farmers must go in for more subsistence farming and more cash farming. They must correct the disparity between agriculture and industry on a basis of plenty, not on a basis of administered scarcity. And before such a correction can be brought about, there must be a diffusion of ideas as well as of land ownership. The problem is one of education as well as of economics.

Herman Clarence Nixon

Southerntown

In contrast to Donald Davidson's vituperative response to John Dollard's Caste and Class in a Southern Town, *Herman Clarence Nixon's style in this brief review of the same book seems sober and detached.*[1] *Though Nixon had by 1938 shed many of the racist attitudes he once shared with the Agrarians, he still bristled at Northern criticism of life in the South. Nixon, like Davidson, questioned the methodology applied by Dollard, whom he chastised for being "ever conscious of being a Northerner, a sociologist, and a disciple of Freud." Nixon had gained sufficient objectivity about the South to see the value of Dollard's book, but he could not resist making a parting jibe at social scientists—and giving a backhanded compliment to Dollard. "Perhaps this is a book which sociologists prefer," he concluded, "but one might wish that such an important study could be given a more direct lay appeal."*

Reprinted from *Virginia Quarterly Review* 14 (1938): 154–56, with the permission of Mrs. H. Clarence Nixon.

Southern race relations furnish a subject of enduring inquiry to many social scientists, especially sociologists. Southern towns likewise are topics

---

1. See Davidson, "Gulliver with Hay Fever," as well as the review of Dollard's book by fellow *ITMS* contributor Lyle H. Lanier, "Mr. Dollard and the Scientific Method," *SR* 3 (1938): 657–72. Like Nixon, Lanier adopted a cool, academic tone in his review, although his conclusion—which put forward as a goal not better race relations but individuals' progress within the "biracial cultural pattern" (672) of Jim Crow segregation—was far less liberal than Nixon's.

172 / Herman Clarence Nixon

of interest to students of human relations. In *Caste and Class in a Southern Town,*
Dr. John Dollard, a sociologist, has undertaken to make a combined study
of race and of town life in the South. He spent five months in the town he
writes about and had numerous interviews with men and women of both
races. He acknowledges a "debt of analogy" to Robert S. and Helen M. Lynd,
whose *Middletown* had grown in importance since its appearance in 1929.[2]
"Southerntown," like "Middletown," is a fictitious name for a real center.[3]
The location, according to all the internal evidence of the volume, is in a
Delta county of Mississippi, a county in which Negroes constitute seventy
percent of the population. This race ratio makes the town typical of only
a part, though an important part, of the South, and, consequently, the interpretation must not be accepted as applicable to the whole Southern or
Southeastern region. The author dispenses certain bits of information which
seem rather strange to the reviewer, who was born and reared in a Southern
county in which the whites, not the Negroes, constituted a substantial majority.[4] Dr. Dollard gives emphasis, for instance, to a rigid taboo against
whites' shaking hands with Negroes and tells of his embarrassment on that
account in meeting Negro informants [7]. I have never felt the effects of such
a taboo, though I shake hands with Negroes, even on a town square or in
other public places. A taboo in Mr. Dollard's Southerntown is merely a restricted practice in my town.

The Dollard study is both more and less than the Lynd study. We get a less
intimate and less thorough report of the total goings-on in the town than the
Lynds have given for their town. But we get incident on top of incident and
analysis on top of analysis in the sphere of inter-racial and intra-racial attitudes, feelings, and activities. Much of the information collected in the town
on the subject of race concerns other towns and other sections; this somewhat minimizes the importance of the work as a town study and increases its
value as a racial study. It seems fair to say that the book is pointed toward
an understanding and explanation of the thinking, culture, and status of the
Negro, but that it gives attention to the other race because of the author's
realization "that whites and whiteness form an inseparable part of the mental life of the Negro" [1]. Each race is approached under a three-fold division

---

2. *Middletown: A Study of American Culture* (New York, 1929) by Robert and Helen
Lynd was the path-breaking comprehensive sociological study of community life in
Muncie, Indiana.

3. Indianola, Mississippi.

4. Nixon spent his early life in the hill country of Merrellton, Alabama (Sarah Newman Shouse, *Hillbilly Realist: Herman Clarence Nixon of Possum Trot* [University, Ala.,
1986], chap. 1).

of classes: upper, middle, and lower. But Dr. Dollard gives chief attention to middle-class and lower-class Negroes and to middle-class whites. In a forty-page appendix, Leonard W. Doob,[5] who also visited Southerntown, presents a scholarly but somewhat tentative discussion of "Poor Whites: A Frustrated Class" [445–84]. This essay reveals more directness of statement and more clearness of perspective than does the main study.

Mr. Dollard writes of his Southern investigation with a considerable degree of self-consciousness. He seems ever conscious of being a Northerner, a sociologist, and a disciple of Freud. He makes rather frequent comment on his own reactions to this and that experience, and he takes many pages for an introductory treatment of research site, methodology, bias, historical attitudes, and the like, getting around to the discussion of caste and class in Southerntown at the beginning of Chapter Five. He makes at least seven references to Freud without working in Adler or inferiority and superiority complexes, which his title might suggest.[6] He gives no little emphasis to the incidents and the incidence of sex in race relations, presenting facts, supported conclusions, and guesses. He shows how inter-racial sex violence by white men tends to bring about insecurity to Negroes of both sexes. He piles up cases and case histories, on which a sensitive Mississippian might call for a statistical check. He discusses the economic gains and losses of the caste system, touching upon the plight of the Negro in this respect. He works in extensive footnote dissertations, with quotations "by permission" from the writings of Donald Young, Charles S. Johnson, Arthur Raper, Howard W. Odum, E. B. Reuter, A. H. Stone, Paul Lewinson, R. R. Moton,[7] and others. These learned observations add their own quality to the study but seem

---

5. Leonard William Doob (1909–) was a professor of psychology, sociology, and African studies at Yale University.

6. Alfred Adler (1870–1937) was an Austrian psychiatrist who helped found modern psychotherapy, but whose work challenged several central Freudian principles.

7. The sociologist Donald R. Young (1899–1977) directed the Social Science Research Council 1932–45. Dollard frequently referred to Young's 1932 book, *American Minority Peoples*. Edward Byron Reuter (1880–1946), a native of Missouri, received his Ph.D. in sociology from the University of Chicago and spent much of his career debunking the widely held assumption that interracialism would cause a decline in civilization. See his *The American Race Problem: A Study of the Negro* (New York, 1927) and *Race Mixture: Studies in Intermarriage and Miscegenation* (New York, 1931). Born in New Orleans, Alfred Holt Stone (1870–1955) lived in Mississippi as a planter between 1893 and 1931, when he became involved in cooperative agricultural organizations and, later, New Deal farm policy. He also wrote regularly from the 1890s onward about racial issues. See his *Studies in the American Race Problem* (New York, 1908). Paul Lewinson (1900–) had published *Race, Class and Party: A History of Negro Suffrage and White Politics*

to limit it as a succinct report on Southerntown. Perhaps this is a book which sociologists prefer, but one might wish that such an important study could be given a more direct lay appeal.

---

in the South (New York, 1932). The educator Robert Russa Moton (1867–1940) was born in Virginia and graduated from Hampton Institute. In 1915, he succeeded Booker T. Washington as principal of the Tuskegee Institute. A founding member of the Commission for Interracial Cooperation, Moton published *Finding a Way Out: An Autobiography* (New York, 1920) and *What the Negro Thinks* (New York, 1929).

Frank Lawrence Owsley

Scottsboro, the Third Crusade:
The Sequel to Abolition and Reconstruction

While Southern history was a touchstone for all Agrarians, Frank Lawrence Owsley, more than any other number of the movement, framed the economic, political, and racial dilemmas of the contemporary South within a historical narrative—and with a positivist's belief in his own accuracy.[1] But, as Owsley later confessed to Robert Penn Warren, his judgments sometimes owed more to emotion—and less to scholarship—than he liked to admit, and might propel his reasoning "outside the limits of history."[2] But in 1933 he had no such qualms, and, not content to let this essay languish in a little read, non-academic journal (the American Review*) he carried it to Urbana, Illinois, where the American Historical Association held its 1933 meeting, and delivered it as a conference paper—a decision that continues to mar his academic reputation.[3]*

---

1. Introduced by the French philosopher and sociologist Auguste Comte (1798–1857), positivism dominated late-nineteenth-century philosophy. Comte proposed that human thought passed through ascending stages (from religion through metaphysics and culminating in science). This scheme coincided with widespread Western confidence that scientific and technological progress would in time overcome human failures. Agrarians, among other conservatives, tended to reject positivism's reliance on the idea of progress as well as its enthronement of science as the greatest means of discovering truth in the natural and social orders.

2. Owsley to Warren, 24 Feb. 1938, quoted in O'Brien, *IAS,* 173.

3. On Owsley's reputation, see O'Brien, *IAS,* 172. Owsley himself recognized the risk he took by writing "Scottsboro." In 1935, Owsley explained to Herbert Agar his mission "personally and through my students" of "digging at the abolition roots of American history and its writing. Until recently, I have got mighty far under some of these

Conceived in fear, punctuated with sarcasm and bitterness, the essay is a direct response to the racial crucible of the Scottsboro case.[4] Owsley advanced his theory that a train of Northern "crusades" (abolition, Reconstruction, and now communist agitation) had been launched to destroy the South, and had come perilously close to success.[5] With each Northern attempt, he argued, violence and disorder had resulted; such explosions could be avoided in the future only if the nation granted recognition to a white-ruled South with full local control. Long sections of the article detail what he considered the egregious assaults of abolition and, especially, Reconstruction. Owsley could rely for his conclusions on the work of then respected historians (in particular those associated with the pro-Southern revisionism of Columbia University's William Archibald Dunning); other sources were just becoming available from scholars beginning to rewrite the Dunning version of Reconstruction.[6] In the third, contemporary

---

roots without being distrusted or accused of bias or motive—other than desire to set forth the truth—, but I detect a certain suspicion." In writings such as "Scottsboro," Owsley felt he had "told the unvarnished truth in unvarnished language," which "may serve immediate ends and afford a great deal of personal satisfaction; but it undermines one's authority as a historian" (Owsley to Agar, 1 Oct. 1835 [carbon], Tate Papers, AM 19629, 9:20, Princeton University).

4. The Scottsboro case involved nine African-American youths arrested 25 March 1931 in Paint Rock, Alabama, following a fracas on a passing train. Two white women accused the blacks of rape, and only weeks later eight were sentenced to death. The case went through appeals and was retried in 1933 while Owsley wrote his Scottsboro article. The International Labor Defense, a group associated with the Communist Party, handled the appeals, which heightened publicity for a case that had already sparked nationwide debate. Evidence weakening the state's case soon emerged: the two women were found to be prostitutes—a circumstance that in 1933 immediately placed their testimony in doubt. More important, one of the alleged victims, Ruby Bates, confessed to perjury in 1932, and in March 1933, she testified in court that the rapes had never occurred. See Dan T. Carter, *Scottsboro: A Tragedy of the American South* (Baton Rouge, 1979), 186–87, 232. James Goodman's *Stories of Scottsboro: The Rape Case That Shocked 1930's America and Revived the Struggle for Equality* (New York, 1994) threads together the experience and meaning of Scottsboro from multiple perspectives, including those of the defendants, their lawyers, the accusers, the activists, the white liberals, the local authorities, and the commentators who recorded their views of the case. Among these was Frank Owsley (113–15, 170).

5. Owsley was not the only Agrarian to speak out about Scottsboro. In a letter to the editors of the *Nation,* John Gould Fletcher denounced the negative coverage the case had received (particularly in the Northern press) and threatened a second secession. Before the South allowed outsiders to alter its racial system, he thundered, Southerners "will again take up arms in our cause" (letter from Fletcher and editorial reply, "Is This the Voice of the South?," *Nation* 137 [1933]: 734–36).

6. Kenneth M. Stampp's "The Tragic Legend of Reconstruction" supplies an admirably succinct review of the Dunning school historiography in *Reconstruction: An Anthology of Revisionist Writings,* ed. Kenneth Stampp and Leon Litwack (Baton Rouge, 1969), 3–21. (The volume also contains helpful corrective essays by Lawanda and

crusade, Owsley identified whites again as the victims, with black Southerners as the pawns, in an anti-Agrarian campaign waged by a daunting phalanx of communists and industrialists determined to reduce the section to one great factory.[7]

Reprinted from *American Review* I (1933): 257–85, with the permission of Mrs. Harriet C. Owsley.[8]

History is the collective experience of a people. Wisdom counsels man to focus this experience upon the present so that he may escape the mistakes of the past and be able to gauge somewhat the future. To ignore the past, or to be too contemptuous to master it, is to choose folly as a guide.

America makes less use of the past than any civilized country in the world. It might almost be said to be an American cult, this contempt and ignorance of the past. Ceaseless shifting of individuals, the rapid growth of populations, the coming of hordes of aliens, the idea of "progress" which scorns things of yesterday, have tended to destroy community life and with it a sense of historical continuity. Without this sense of continuity between past and present, history becomes to a people the advice of a wise father to a wayward and inexperienced youth—the words of a dotard. In America the same mistakes

---

John H. Cox, Vernon Lane Wharton, and W. E. B. DuBois.) Owsley relied heavily on Walter Fleming, *The Sequel of Appomattox* (1919), and Claude Bowers, *The Tragic Era: The Revolution after Lincoln* (1929), for his version of Reconstruction. The most recent exhaustive study of the Reconstruction era is Eric Foner, *Reconstruction: America's Unfinished Revolution, 1863–1877* (New York, 1988); see also Leon F. Litwack, *Been in the Storm So Long: The Aftermath of Slavery* (New York, 1979). The *Journal of Negro History* was founded in 1915, providing a forum for historical dissent from the Dunning school. W. E. B. Du Bois's revisionist *Black Reconstruction in America* (New York, 1935), with its path-breaking exposé of racist historical distortions, remains a crucial source but was not yet available to Owsley. See particularly its final chapter, "The Propaganda of History," 711–29.

7. Many white Southerners were susceptible to this argument, especially when it was placed on a continuum with whites' highly charged mythology of Reconstruction. Faced with Scottsboro, Southern liberals worked behind the scenes but with little success, since almost any critic of the Scottsboro case was vulnerable to accusations of being in league with the defense, which meant with the Communist Party. For a fine assessment of the awkward reaction of the Commission on Interracial Cooperation, and subsequent liberal responses, see Goodman, *Stories of Scottsboro,* 53–59, 163–72.

8. At the request of the late Mrs. Harriet C. Owsley, Frank Owsley's widow, the editors add this note from her book, *Frank Lawrence Owsley, Historian of the Old South: A Memoir* (Nashville, 1990), 84: "Frank thought as did many other Southerners that the Scottsboro trial that charged the blacks with raping the two white women was another unfair attack on the South. He responded with the article that condemned the attack as part of a spiritual crusade against the South. Frank died before it was discovered that some of the evidence had been withheld and medical records showed that the two women had not been raped. Frank always tried to be fair; had he known of the suppression of evidence, he would have supported the defendants in the case."

are committed frequently and at close intervals, with no apparent knowledge of former mistakes; and the intelligentsia has led the field, ignorantly plunging over the same precipices where its fathers and grandfathers plunged.

If I may suggest that an act is a mistake when it is followed by results either opposite to what was intended or bad as judged by the accepted rules of ethics, I shall be so bold as to assert that the mistake most often repeated has been the interference of the North—usually the Northeast—with the relationship between the whites and blacks of the South. This interference has continued since 1819, when the Missouri Compromise debate began, until the present day, with periods of respite. Twice, indeed, it has developed into war upon the South: the abolition crusade of 1819–1865 (including the Civil War); and the period of reconstruction. In the present epoch the interference is again rapidly assuming the proportions of a war upon the South. The Scottsboro and Dadeville cases,[9] Judge James Lowell's action in the case of the Negro refugee murderer from Virginia,[10] and the widespread agitation involved, are some manifestations of the third crusade.

I feel fairly certain that most of the intellectuals of the East who are leading the third major crusade against the South, and the public whose opinion is being formed by these intellectuals, are quite unaware of the relation between the abolition crusade, reconstruction, and the Scottsboro case. The ignorance and indifference to experience and to human nature which the intellectuals have shown in these crusades in incredible; yet grievous errors committed in sincere pursuit even of ideas of abstract justice might be condoned. But the sincerity of the crusaders is under suspicion; in fact, they

---

9. Owsley may have been referring to either of two incidents involving shoot-outs between sharecroppers and law enforcement authorities in Alabama. In July 1931, Ralph Gray, a black farmer who had helped organize agricultural workers in the Croppers' and Farm Workers' Union, died of gunshot wounds. The International Labor Defense, which also defended the Scottsboro Boys, assumed the defense of the sharecroppers, who had been rounded up and accused of conspiracy following the gun battle. In the other case, which also took place in Tallapoosa County, Alabama, three black members of the Sharecroppers' Union died in December 1932 after they tried to prevent a landowner from seizing the property of an indebted cropper. Both cases were tried in the county seat of Dadeville (Robin D. G. Kelley, *Hammer and Hoe: Alabama Communists during the Great Depression* [Chapel Hill, 1990], 40–43, 49–52).

10. In 1933, Judge James A. Lowell (1869–1933), a U.S. district judge in Massachusetts, provoked Southern white resentment when he refused to extradite George Crawford, a black man accused of a double murder in Virginia. The NAACP based its argument on Crawford's behalf on the impossibility of his receiving a fair trial from an all-white Virginia jury—the same strategy lawyers eventually used to defend the Scottsboro Boys. See Richard Kluger, *Simple Justice: The History of Brown v. Board of Education and Black America's Struggle for Equality* (New York, 1976), 147–48.

leave little doubt that when they have not been sentimental or fanatical dupes, they have been hired tools cloaking motives of material gain in robes of morality. It is ignorance and guile parading as God.

The precise way in which those who are attacking the South today, at Scottsboro, at Dadeville, in Judge Lowell's court at Boston, and in the Northern press generally, are intellectual children and grandchildren of the abolitionists and reconstructionists may not be obvious. Indeed, if I can demonstrate the analogy both of technique and motive between the present agitation for "justice to the Negro" as exemplified in the Scottsboro affair, I shall consider that I have performed a patriotic duty. For I am exceedingly anxious and seriously alarmed over the present agitation. I am aware that a poisoned apple is being thrown, once again, for the two races to fight over; that direr consequences than those of the abolition crusade or reconstruction may be in store for the South and for the nation; and that the relationship between the two races will be more greatly strained than ever by the conflict that is being prepared by outsiders for them.

The American Federal Union was established in the full knowledge that two distinct social, economic, and political systems were being brought together under one government. The founders of the Union were deeply conscious of the dangers of housing the capitalistic commercial East under the same roof-tree with the agrarian South. But compromises and mutual concessions satisfied both sections that the peculiar interests of each were properly safeguarded. The capitalistic East, however, soon found the compromises and limitations of the Constitution irksome and unprofitable, and it very properly considered the benefits of peaceful withdrawal.[11] Before a withdrawal could be effected the industrialization of the East changed the attitude of that section. New men, raw, uncultured, hard and aggressive, lacking, as the bourgeois class everywhere lacked, any sense of social responsibility, ushered in the Era of Machinery.

These men were ignorant and unashamed, contemptuous of human experience. There was no yesterday for them nor was there any tomorrow in its ultimate sense, only an extended present. Their scale of values was the dollar. Ruthless and pushing, they did not propose to withdraw the industrialized East from the too narrow confines of the Union, but, seeing wide-flung lands paying them tribute as the ruling power in government, they girded themselves and their section to do battle for the control of that Union. They would wipe out the sectional compromises and guarantees, stretch the

11. The secession or "peaceful withdrawal" Owsley referred to was contemplated by some New England states at the Hartford Convention, December 1814.

narrow bounds of the Constitution, and remake the Federal Government. In the accomplishment of this objective it would be necessary either to subordinate or to destroy the agrarian South—the decision was to be left to chance. The New Order had sucked in the politicians and intellectuals of the Old Order in the East—poets, preachers, teachers, novelists, and statesmen. These fashioned for the industrialist East a philosophy of society and government in keeping with its larger ambitions. Webster called the new philosophy nationalism and thereby clothed it with sanctity; in reality, it was a greater sectionalism of exploitation.[12]

The two sections had preserved a careful balance of power during the Old Era. In order to subordinate the South it would be necessary to destroy that balance. But the industrialists, carefully coached by their lawyers and statesmen and "intellectual" aides, realized the bad strategy of waging a frank struggle for sectional power; they must pitch the struggle upon a moral plane, else many of the intelligentsia and the good people generally might become squeamish and refuse to fight. Shibboleths and moral catchwords must be furnished. It was therefore found convenient to attack slavery as an evil and the slave holder as a criminal, in fact to impugn the morality of the South, in order to create opinion in the East and North in favor of the industrialists' plans of Southern restriction. The practical program of the industrialists was to prevent further creation of slave States from the vast territories which had been acquired by the United States from France, Spain, and Mexico. The political history of the period from 1819 to 1860 is largely the story of the exclusion of the South from the Territories. To hold public opinion to the support of this program the abolition crusade against the South was waged for over forty years. The Garrisons, Emersons, Sumners, and Phillipses—moralists and intellectual leaders—ignorant of the South and of much of human nature, were the spokesmen of the New Order.[13]

---

12. The celebrated New England statesman and lawyer Daniel Webster (1782–1852) consistently opposed Southern ambitions aimed at tariff reduction and sectional autonomy. Conservative, pro-union, and pro-industry, Webster helped pass the Compromise of 1850. In defending the Compromise, he claimed to speak "not as a Massachusetts man, nor as a Northern man, but as an American."

13. Owsley supplied a roll call of abolitionists and legislative reformers who had helped end slavery and establish rights for former slaves. William Lloyd Garrison (1805–79) was among the most radical abolitionists. He enraged Southerners by calling in his newspaper, the *Liberator,* for immediate emancipation and denouncing not only slavery but the Constitution and all it touched. The transcendentalist poet, essayist, and lecturer Ralph Waldo Emerson (1803–82) spoke against slavery and helped finance John Brown's 1859 raid at Harper's Ferry, Virginia. The Massachusetts senator Charles Sumner (1811–74) vigorously opposed the Fugitive Slave Law and the extension of slavery

They were the uncritical propagandists of a system of society as vulnerable, more vulnerable when tested by humane standards, than the society whose overthrow they were preaching.

At the time when Wendell Phillips proclaimed to the world that the South was "a great brothel where half a million women are flogged to prostitution," when Stephen S. Foster denounced the Southern Methodist Church as "more corrupt than any house of ill-fame in the city of New York," and when the Reverend George Bourne insisted that it would be better "to transfer the in-mates from the state prison and the pander from the brothel to the pulpit" rather than permit a Southern minister to preach in a Northern church [14]—when, in other words, the moralist crusaders of the Northeast were painting a picture of universal prostitution and miscegenation in the South, informa-tion was available to these same moralists which showed sexual degradation in the factories of the East to have reached depths hitherto unknown in the experience of a modern civilized nation.

Illegitimacy was more common in the industrialized East than in any other country in the world. Yet these crusaders offered little criticism of a society which forced young girls into semi-prostitution. The professional abolition-ists and their transcendentalist brethren of literature and religion glibly pictured the Southern masters as brutes; they drove their slaves to heart-breaking and unrequited toil, beat them like wild beasts, fed them poor and insufficient food, clothed them in filthy rags, housed them in hovels unfit for stabling horses. At the time when these men who had no knowledge of the South, but who spoke with omniscience of that country, were drawing such an indictment, the most appalling conditions of labor and wages existed in the industrial belts of the East. Children began work in the factories at age six and toiled fourteen hours or more under the lash. Women worked even

---

into new territories and states in the decades before the Civil War. He later spearheaded Congress's Reconstruction-era efforts to secure civil and political equality for African Americans. Wendell Phillips (1811–84), the Boston reformer, orator, and abolitionist, denounced the U.S. government and its Constitution for being tainted by its compro-mise with slavery.

14. Phillips, "The Philosophy of the Abolition Movement," in *Speeches, Lectures, and Letters* (Boston, 1884), 108. An abolitionist activist and lecturer, Foster (1809–81) grew up in New Hampshire. Owsley quoted from Foster's *Brotherhood of Thieves, or A True Picture of the American Church and Clergy* (New London, Conn., 1843), 7. George Bourne, *Slavery Illustrated in Its Effects upon Women and Society* (Boston, 1837), 116–17. An English-born Presbyterian minister, Bourne (1780–1845) became an early advocate of immediate emancipation and lost his Virginia ministry because of his opposition to slavery. Both Bourne and Foster received extensive attention in Arthur Young Lloyd, *The Slavery Controversy 1831–1860* (Chapel Hill, 1939).

longer hours under the most degrading and unhealthful conditions. Wages afforded the barest existence; there was no chance to accumulate funds for sickness, old age, and times of unemployment. Able-bodied foreign girls were brought in ships which rivaled the slave-ship of the "middle passage" to take the place of native-born girls who might show less tractability or demand better wages. Unemployment, sickness, old age, had no avenues of escape save prostitution, thievery, and the poorhouse. No sense of security existed among these four million working people (four million in 1860). Yet in the South, which the moralists were attacking, Negro children did not work in the fields before they were ten or twelve years of age; old Negroes were retired from active labor when they began to show signs of feebleness; and both old and young were secured against want and illness. But the crusaders offered little objection to the conditions of labor in their own social system. They and their followers, waging war against a section and a society about which they knew nothing, were immensely satisfied with their own system of society about which they knew much. Their reforming zeal—as that of many in the present day—lay outside the bounds of this society.[15]

The effects of this first crusade against the South were the curtailment of the expansion of that section; the overthrow of the balance of power and the secession of the South in an effort to escape its doom; and finally the Civil War itself. The relationship between the blacks and whites had suffered greatly by 1860 as a result of this outside attack. The incendiary language of the abolitionists was generally believed to be directed toward bringing about a slave uprising and massacre of the whites such as Nat Turner's revolt and John Brown's raid.[16] Their attack resulted in restrictive regulations and closer surveillance of the Negro. He could no longer be freed without the consent of the Legislature; teaching him to read was made a serious offense—lest he read abolition literature and massacre his master; he could not travel without a pass; his religious activities were curtailed lest abolition

---

15. In the foregoing passage, Owsley repeated many of the ideas developed by George Fitzhugh (1808–81) in *Sociology for the South* (1854) and *Cannibals All!* (1857), which presented Southern slavery as a humane alternative to Northern industrialism. Fitzhugh and other Southern white intellectuals struggled to formulate a morally based reply to anti-slavery forces. For analysis of the pro-slavery movement, see Larry Tise and Paul Finkelman, eds., *Proslavery Thought, Ideology, and Politics* (New York, 1989), and Larry Tise, *Proslavery: A History of the Defense of Slavery in America, 1701–1840* (Athens, Ga., 1987).

16. Fifty-five whites were killed by slaves during Nat Turner's 1831 rebellion in Virginia's Southampton County. This uprising, along with the establishment of Garrison's *Liberator*, greatly alarmed white Southerners, and many states passed stricter rules for the treatment and movement of slaves. John Brown was supported in his raid on the federal arsenal at Harper's Ferry by well-to-do Northerners.

propaganda be spread; in short all the liberties and privileges which he had gained through the years of civilizing influences were greatly lessened— though his master continued to treat him kindly as an individual. Finally, the South was forced to spend its energies defending an institution which, before the crusade began, it had thought to abolish; gradual emancipation of the Negro with its period of adjustment for both master and slave—a thing which probably would have taken place in the South long before the close of the nineteenth century—was frustrated, and the Negro was finally thrown unprepared as a child upon the world by his sudden emancipation, an act which had the effect of bringing about the ruin, for many years, of both himself and his former master.[17]

Neither the destruction of the balance of power nor the defeat of the South in the Civil War assured industrialism of its permanent control of the Federal Government. The agrarian West, though non-slave-holding, had usually allied itself with the agrarian South in the days before the war, and the alliance of these two sections after the war would have turned all the victories of industrialism into ashes. That alliance must be prevented. As long as it threatened, the triumph of industrialism—"the fruits of victory," as Sumner and Stevens were wont to say—was exceedingly doubtful.[18] Once more the blending of moral force and political expediency was resorted to. The enfranchisement and civil and social equality of the Negro were the ostensible aim of this second crusade. The real aim, of course, was to gain political control of the South by the exploitation of the Negro: the Negro was to be alienated from the Southern whites and taught to regard them as his oppressors—a thing which the abolitionists had not succeeded in doing. When

---

17. Historical studies have not supported Owsley's argument that slavery would have died a natural death. Most have concluded that despite considerable anti-slavery feeling in the South, slave-holding was too profitable and/or adaptable to perish without intervention. For the economic viability of the institution, see Drew Gilpin Faust, "The Peculiar South Revisited," in *Interpreting Southern History,* ed. John B. Boles and Evelyn Thomas Nolen (Baton Rouge, 1987), 81–86; Alfred H. Conrad and John R. Meyer, "The Economics of Slavery in the Ante Bellum South," *Journal of Political Economy* 66 (1958): 95–130; Robert Fogel and Stanley Engerman, *Time on the Cross: The Economics of American Negro Slavery* (Boston, 1974); and Keith C. Barton, "'Good Cooks and Washers': Slave Hiring, Domestic Labor, and the Market in Bourbon County, Kentucky," *JAH* 84 (1997): 436–60.

18. The Pennsylvania congressman Thaddeus Stevens (1792–1868) cast one of only two votes against the 1861 Crittenden Resolution, which stipulated that the Civil War was not intended to destroy the South or slavery but to preserve the Union. After the war, he enthusiastically pursued land confiscation and advocated military rule in the South in order to establish full political and civil rights for blacks.

this was accomplished the Negro was to be enfranchised and the Southern whites disfranchised to give the Negro a safe majority at the polls. The Negro would be taught—in fact coerced if need be—to vote for the industrial party, now the Republican Party. This would create an alliance of agrarian South and industrialist East.

Such daring plans could not be carried until the public was won to their support—and the Northern public in 1865 would have risen and thrown out the radical leaders had such plans been baldly disclosed at the time.[19] Just as in the abolition crusade, moral aims were now pushed into the foreground. The white man was re-enslaving the Negro, cruelly using him, committing even greater wrongs against him than in the days of slavery. Soon every Northern newspaper was dripping with sorrow for the poor Negro. The intelligentsia was again leading in the pack of propagandists. It did not take long to educate Northern opinion by such strategy. By the fall of 1866 the public was in full support of the Sumner-Stevens program of Negro rule in the South.[20] As for the Negro, he was made to feel that his former master was his deadly enemy. Freedman's Bureau clerks,[21] missionary schoolteachers, carpetbag politicians, all emissaries of the Radical Republican Party—radical only in the South—gathered the Negroes together, as armed for battle, in secret societies known as Union Leagues, where in the dead of night, protected by heavily armed guards who were ordered to shoot any Southern white attempting to approach, they preached to the naive and childish blacks incendiary doctrines calculated to rouse the wildest passions against their former masters.[22] They urged the Negroes "to use the torch because the blacks were at war with the white race," says W. L. Fleming. They incited them, says the same author, "to kill some of the leading whites in each

---

19. Indeed, a Republican would not have captured the presidency in 1860 if voters had believed that he or his party supported abolition. For a discussion of Republican Party ideology on race and slavery, see Eric Foner, *Free Soil, Free Labor, Free Men: The Ideology of the Republican Party before the Civil War* (New York, 1970), chap. 8, 9.

20. On the contrary, the proposals by Sumner and Stevens "went far beyond what the average white man, North or South, was ready to support" (Kenneth Stampp, *The Era of Reconstruction* [New York, 1965], 90, 29–97).

21. From 1865 to 1869 the Freedmen's Bureau provided relief and protection for Southern blacks during the transition from slavery to freedom. A thorn in the side of many whites, it distributed food and supplied medical assistance and mediated freedmen's work contracts. The bureau also established schools for black children and special courts to resolve disputes between whites and blacks. For an assessment of the Freedmen's Bureau, see Stampp, *Era of Reconstruction*, 131–35.

22. The Union League, which began as a patriotic organization during the Civil War, provided an umbrella for anti-establishment political activity in the postwar South. Owsley's portrait of the Union League derives largely from the work of historian

community as a warning to others"; the white carpetbaggers, who had heard Thaddeus Stevens urge the same thing, promised that the property of the whites would all be confiscated and given to the Negro. The government, they said, would give the black man "forty acres and a mule" if he deported himself as the radical instructed him. In short, they encouraged the Negro to commit universal pillage, murder, and rape.[23]

Aroused by his white leaders, the Negro marched forth from his league meeting in military formation to commit many acts of violence—though never as many as were urged upon him, for the average Negro was more kindly than his Northern preceptor. The missionary preacher, aside from his work in the Union League, set out to make use of his religious office to rouse the Negro against the Southern white and "to teach the Negroes that every man that was born or raised in the Southern country was their enemy," that "Christ died for Negroes and Yankees, not for rebels."[24] The Freedman's Bureau encouraged the Negro in a similar fashion; so did the schoolteacher. The industrialist political leaders, of course, set the pattern for the moralists and intellectuals. Thad Stevens, who characterized the Constitution as "a bit of worthless parchment," urged that the South be treated "as conquered provinces." Let us, he declared, "strip a proud nobility of their bloated estates; reduce them to a level with plain men," or better still "exterminate or drive out the present rebels as exiled" and turn their land over to the blacks.[25] His advice was typical of the doctrines which Congressmen and intellectuals of the East proclaimed. They promised to give the Negro social and political justice—at the cost of Southern white extermination, if need be.

Promised the lands of his white neighbors, promised political control

---

Walter Lynwood Fleming (1874–1932), his fellow Alabamian and Vanderbilt colleague, who viewed the League as the epitome of Republican diabolism. Michael W. Fitzgerald rejects such hysterical accounts as Owsley's in *The Union League Movement in the Deep South* (Baton Rouge, 1989).

23. Fleming, *Sequel of Appomattox*, 185–86. Although Owsley drew most directly from Fleming, the extensive work of the Dunning school historians supported this view of Reconstruction. As a graduate student at the University of Chicago, Owsley had nearly gone to study under the renowned William Archibald Dunning (1857–1922), whose long career at Columbia secured the school's reputation in the field of history (O'Brien, *IAS*, 164). For more on the Dunning school, see note 72 to the introduction, above.

24. Fleming, *Sequel of Appomattox*, 205.

25. Stevens quoted in Fleming, *Sequel of Appomattox*, 59. In the original speech, Stevens called for bringing former slave owners "to level with plain republicans." The speech was published in the *Congressional Globe*, 10 March 1866, and reprinted in Fleming's *Documentary History of Reconstruction: Political, Military, Social, Religious, Educational and Industrial, 1865 to the Present Time*, 2 vols. (Cleveland, 1906–7), 1:151.

of the South, promised equality and in some instances promised white skins, the Negro was fully ready within two years to vote for any program his "benefactors" presented. With the North thoroughly committed to the radical plans of reconstructing the South, and the Negro ready to vote as he was told, the objective of the second "crusade" was easy to accomplish. The enfranchisement of the blacks and disfranchisement of the whites on a large scale resulted quickly in bringing the South under Negro rule which was supported by Federal troops.

The South thus reconstructed probably had no counterpart in the history of the world. The *New York Herald* pictured the situation graphically: the South was forced "by a secret and overwhelming revolutionary force to a common and inevitable fate. They are all . . . to be governed by blacks spurred on by worse than blacks. . . . This is the most abominable phase barbarism has assumed since the dawn of civilization. . . . It is not right to make slaves of white men even though they have been former masters of blacks. This is but a change in a system of bondage that is rendered the more odious and intolerable because it has been inaugurated in an enlightened instead of a dark and uncivilized age."[26] James S. Pike, a Republican journalist, gave a vivid description of a State Legislature during reconstruction: "In the place of this old aristocratic society stands the rude form of the most ignorant democracy that mankind ever saw, invested with the functions of government. It is the dregs of the population habilitated in the robes of their intelligent predecessors, and asserting over them the rule of ignorance and corruption. . . . It is barbarism overwhelming civilization by physical force. It is the slave rioting in the halls of his master and putting that master under his feet. . . . The Speaker is black, the Clerk is black, the door-keepers are black, the little pages are black, the chairman of the Ways and Means Committee is black, and the chaplain is coal black. At some of the desks sit colored men whose types would be hard to find outside the Congo; whose costumes, visages, attitudes, and expressions, only befit the forecastle of a buccaneer."[27]

---

26. Owsley quoted from Fleming, *Sequel of Appomattox,* 148. Fleming did not cite his source in the *New York Herald.*

27. The Maine-born journalist James S. Pike (1811–82) was the *New York Tribune's* Washington correspondent 1850–60. He opposed slavery and after the war traveled southward, publishing in *The Prostrate State: South Carolina Under Negro Government* (New York, 1874). Pike's report on the South Carolina legislature is from *Prostrate State,* 12, reprinted in Fleming, *Documentary History of Reconstruction,* 2 : 53–54, and *Sequel of Appomattox,* 227–28. In its full context, Pike's portrait of the South Carolina Reconstruction-era legislature was far less damning than it appears here. Pike continued, "It is not all sham, nor all burlesque. They have a genuine interest and a genuine earnestness in

The South was now a rotten borough controlled by the East. Thus reconstructed the agrarian South and industrial East became allies. This, said Stevens, "would insure the ascendancy of the union party" (the Republican Party).[28]

Even with Negro governments—controlled by carpetbaggers—installed in the South and the way apparently made easy, the industrialists did not confiscate the lands of the Southern whites, divide them among the Negroes, and thereby fulfill their major promise. Nor did the Federal Government buy any of the millions of acres which were sold for taxes or mortgages (in Mississippi alone an area as large as Massachusetts and Rhode Island was sold for taxes) and give the Negro his forty acres. The land in the South which was sold for taxes would have been sufficient, without violating any property rights, to give every Negro family at least forty acres and thereby a real economic freedom and independence. The failure to fulfill this promise was due to the discovery that the alienation of the Negro from the Southern whites insured the Negro's vote for the Republicans without further expenditure of money.

Yet this was the only promise held out to the Negro that carried any substantial benefits; social equality and political enfranchisement, for the black man so recently emerging from savagery, were delusions. No one knew this better than the "crusaders." Their failure to carry out their only worthwhile pledge to the Negro convicts them of the insincerity of the abolitionist crusaders: they had no real interest in the welfare of the Negro; he was no more than a pawn.

The results of the "reconstruction crusade" upon the relations of the Southern blacks and whites, as has already been partly anticipated, were bad indeed. The hatred against the Southern white engendered in the hearts of the guileless black by the radical agitators in order to get the Negro vote resulted, as I have already noted, in many violent deeds. The black

---

the business of the assembly which we are bound to recognize and respect. . . . They have an earnest purpose, born of conviction that their conditions are not fully assured, which lends a sort of dignity to their proceedings" (quoted in DuBois, *Black Reconstruction,* 419). For other responses to the slanders hurled at black politicians during Reconstruction, see DuBois, *Black Reconstruction,* 417–19, 469–70, 490–91, 498–99, 515–17, 528–29; and August Meier, "Afterword: New Perspectives on the Nature of Black Political Leadership during Reconstruction," in Howard Rabinowitz, ed., *Southern Black Leaders of the Reconstruction Era* (Urbana, 1982), 393–409.

28. Fleming, *Sequel of Appomattox,* 138. Stevens's speech in support of the 1866 bill for military reconstruction (*Congressional Globe,* 3 Jan. 1867) is reprinted in Fleming, *Documentary History of Reconstruction,* 1 : 150.

governments—in one State there were two hundred Negro trial judges who could not read their names[29]—gave legal sanction to such violence. The white man, especially the small farmer and the poorer classes, returned the hatred of the Negro with interest. The slave-holder of former days was more tolerant of the Negro's irresponsible acts, for he regarded the Negro as a juvenile race badly advised; but being human, he came to distrust and in many cases to hate the Negro. Despite the military support given the Negro governments, retaliation was frequent and violent.

When the Federal troops were withdrawn, when Northern opinion no longer supported the industrial program in the South, and Negro and carpet-bag rule collapsed, the unfortunate Negro who had been taught by outsiders to hate the whites now found himself alone to face those who had come to hate and distrust him.

The Negro should have learned then that in the end the relationship good or bad between himself and the white race of the South must be settled between them and that no outside power could dictate permanently the terms of this relationship. He was quickly disfranchised by direction—and constitutionally, for the Supreme Court has not been able to void the legislation by which it was done—driven from politics, brought under rigid social discipline, in short, completely subordinated socially, economically, and politically.[30] The white race disciplined him severely for his conduct during reconstruction. At length, however, with outside interference largely removed, old friendships were renewed between the races; new ones were formed until something of the old affection which had existed between the black man and white man returned. His condition gradually improved; though he has never yet been given back the ballot nor allowed to sit on juries. The experience of reconstruction was too bitter to be soon forgotten. It has formed and will continue for many years to form the background of Southern social and political attitudes. In considering any political action either state or national, the Southern white first considers how that action will ultimately affect the relationship between the races. It has crippled and at times destroyed the political value of the South in the national councils; it has created and will indefinitely perpetuate the solid South, solid against the Republican Party.

The third crusade against the South is now under way. Not that industrialism has not found it necessary since the days of reconstruction to keep alive that

---

29. Fleming, *Sequel of Appomattox*, 225.

30. In the case of *Williams v. Mississippi* (1898), the Supreme Court condoned that state's plan to minimize black voting. For a thorough examination of the rise of segregation and disfranchisement, see Woodward, *The Strange Career of Jim Crow* (New York, 1974).

dislike of the South which had been cultivated in the former attacks, in order to keep the agrarian West under control. The method is familiar: holding the South up to ridicule as backward, ignorant, unprogressive; waving the bloody shirt during political campaigns; instructing recalcitrant Westerners to "vote as your fathers shot," and giving wide currency to race conflicts and lynchings in the South, while ignoring such difficulties in the North as the Chicago (1919) and St. Louis (1917) race riots.[31] But until the last few years there has been no serious interference from the outside with race relations and adjustments. Industrial control seemed so well assured that such interference was probably considered unnecessary.

Within the last two years, however, a disturbing attack has commenced in the East. Great publicity is given to alleged injustices committed against the Negro. This new attack does not place so much emphasis upon lynchings as upon unfair trials. That is to say, the administration of justice by the courts of the South is being challenged wherever Negroes are concerned. The common factor in the attacks upon Southern courts is the charge that the Fourteenth Amendment is being nullified in the Southern States by the exclusion of Negroes from juries. The three outstanding examples at the present moment which involve this common factor are the Dadeville (Alabama) case; the case of the Negro murderer from Virginia in Judge Lowell's court in Boston; and, most prominently advertised, the Scottsboro case. As a matter of fact, there are numerous others, such as the murder-rape case in Birmingham, in which the Fourteenth Amendment is probably being used as a basis of interference in the administration of justice.[32] I am not here concerned with the guilt or innocence of the Negroes—though I wish justice done; I

---

31. Owsley here belittled a problem of tragic consequence. In 1933, twenty-four black Southerners were lynched. Between 1880 and 1930, according to Fitzhugh Brundage, 732 whites and 3,220 blacks were lynched in the South (*Lynching in the New South: Georgia and Virginia, 1880–1930* [Urbana, Ill., 1993], 8, 292). See also Michael Newton and Judy Ann Newton, *Racial and Religious Violence in America: A Chronology* (New York, 1991), 404–7. More than 80 percent of the victims were African Americans. Owsley had available a body of documentation on lynching that included Arthur Raper's *The Tragedy of Lynching* (Chapel Hill, 1933) and the work of an early anti-lynching activist, black journalist Ida B. Wells Barnett (see her *On Lynchings* [New York, 1969]). The NAACP leader Walter White also described the ongoing, brutal practice in *Rope and Faggot: A Biography of Judge Lynch* (1929). Racial violence in the North is examined in William M. Tuttle Jr., *Race Riot: Chicago in the Red Summer of 1919* (New York, 1970), and Elliott Rudwick, *Race Riot at East St. Louis, July 2, 1917* (New York, 1972).

32. See Kelley, *Hammer and Hoe*, 82–84, 89–90. In this case, in the Scottsboro appeals, and in the Dadeville cases, the International Labor Defense employed a legal argument based on the Fourteenth Amendment that no trial was valid in which blacks were excluded from potential juries.

am interested in pointing out the meaning of these cases and of the general emotional disturbance in the East over the "injustices" committed in the South against the Negro. I wish to examine the relationship between this new attack upon the South and the former attacks, and by doing so gauge the probable motives and the final results.

One sees the familiar spectacle of the intelligentsia taking the lead in this new thrust between the white and black man of the South. One reads emotional columns in reviews and newspapers. Such diatribes as that of Mrs. Mary Heaton Vorse in the *New Republic* on the Scottsboro case [33] sound alarmingly like the pages out of a Northern journal during the days of reconstruction; and one might well suspect, in the light of history, that the public mind in the North is being prepared for the identical program. The robes of morality are having the dust and wrinkles shaken off for the intelligentsia and good people to march forth in. One feels assured that industrialism has found the agrarian South once again an obstacle in the way of its control of the Federal Government. But today there are two sets of industrialists: the capitalist-industrialists on the one hand and the proletarian-industrialists or Communists on the other.

The capitalist-industrialists control the Republican Party, which has for the time, at least, fallen into desperate straits. They have within the last few years seen the South and West gradually coalesce until in the autumn of 1932 this alliance overthrew their industrialists' party. [34] The South with its Western allies offers a serious menace to industrialism's control of the Federal Government just as it did before the abolition crusade or reconstruction. That the industrialists have within their inmost secret councils decided for the third time within a century that "Carthage must be destroyed" seems entirely reasonable. [35] Partly ignorant of what their fathers and grandfathers have attempted and completely indifferent as to the consequences—because

---

33. Mary Heaton Vorse, "The Scottsboro Trial," *NR* 74 (1933): 276–78. For more on Vorse (1874–1966), who grew up in Massachusetts and became known for her coverage of the labor movement in the U.S., see the introduction to a collection of her journalistic writings, *Rebel Press: The Writings of Mary Heaton Vorse,* ed. Dee Garrison (New York, 1985), 7–27.

34. The Democratic Party coalition forged by Roosevelt in 1932 included states in the South and West, as well as strong support from urban areas and immigrant groups.

35. After the defeat and death of the Roman general Hannibal, Cato the Elder dramatized the danger posed by the economic revival of Carthage in a speech to the Roman senate by flourishing a fresh bunch of figs picked in Carthage only three days earlier and insisting, "Ceterum censeo Carthaginam delandam esse" (I consider that Carthage must be destroyed). Thereafter, he ended all his speeches with this phrase, until the Third Punic War accomplished his ambition.

they feel certain that the consequences will affect only the South—they commence their third "Carthaginian War." It must be pointed out, however, that the complete overthrow of the South by abolitionism, war, and reconstruction has been a major disaster to the North itself. The elimination of the South and the political subjugation of the agrarian West by sectional propaganda has had the same effect upon the North as the loss of the "governors" on a steam engine. The North has spent the greater part of seventy years in running wild.

While the ostensible object of the new attack upon the South is the betterment of the status of the Negro, the real object is, as before, to gain power at the expense of both the whites and blacks. The Fourteenth and Fifteenth Amendments, which were used to secure Negro government and Republican control of the South, but which, as we know, failed in the end, are now to be resuscitated. Under the Fourteenth Amendment Congressional representation and the electoral vote of the South can be cut by one-third; under the Fifteenth Amendment, should the Supreme Court do its part, the Negro could be re-enfranchised. In the first case the importance of the South would be greatly reduced in national politics; with the "enforcement" of the Fifteenth Amendment, the industrialists might hope again to control the South by means of the Negro, who is once more being estranged from the white man.

That the industrialists have declared war upon the South is a conclusion based partly upon circumstantial evidence and analogy. But the Communists who represent the base of industrialism leave us no doubt of their intention. I have their program before me in printed form as I write. They are furnishing the greater part of the energy in this new crusade against the South, at Scottsboro, at Dadeville, and in other places, while their enemies, the capitalists, ignorant of the fact, are acting as allies in spreading damaging reports concerning the Southern white man's treatment of the Negro. This alliance, let me pause to say, presents one of the most amazing situations in history. It is filled with the irony of divine comedy. The cause of our economic collapse is easy to understand when our captains of industry thus prepare their own funeral pyre; for the South is probably the greatest obstacle to Communism. Certainly the Communists—the few who have a sense of humor—must derive enjoyment from the discovery that these capitalists supposed to be fierce and cunning wolves appear to be only dumb sheep in wolves' clothing.

The technique of both Communists and industrialists is the same as that of the former crusaders. It is to discredit the South in the eyes of the North so as to gain support for their Southern programs; while at the same time they are creating as much friction between the races in the South as possible, so as to furnish further outrage-propaganda which the moralists, poets, novelists, journalists—the intelligentsia—may pass on to an increasingly indignant public.

Those engaged in this new crusade of "justice for the Negro" in Southern courts may be divided into the four classes so characteristic of abolitionism and reconstruction: first, the industrialists themselves, either capitalists or Communists, with their smart lawyers and publicity advisers, retained on salary, who work out the program; second, the journalists, publicists, novelists, poets, preachers, professors, who work as paid propagandists (the recent power-lobby investigation indicated that an alarming number of such intellectuals were for sale as propagandists in any cause); third, those who, being victimized by stories of Southern outrages, take up their pens to write in anger against the South, against which they already harbor an animosity inherent from former attacks; finally, the public at large, uncritical, lacking in either historical information or historical sense, ready because of its inherited dislike of the South to believe the worst of that section.

The Communist and industrial leaders, using the same propaganda, the same dupes, are working the uncritical public into a froth about unfair administration of justice in the South. This they do while their own Rome is burning; while the third degree—medieval torture—is used in Northern courts to extort confessions; while counsel is frequently denied the accused until the police and detectives have beaten him into "confession"; while witnesses are "taken for a ride" so frequently that the conviction of a gangster is an exceptional thing; while business daily pays tribute to racketeers as the price of immunity from bombing and machine-gun squads; while kidnapping of children and their frequent murder is a common occurrence; while, in short, the underworld, aided by unscrupulous lawyers, renders the administration of justice in the North a cruel farce.

Once again, from a social system open to every form of criticism—which in fact Europe looks upon as incredible in the twentieth century—comes the attack upon the social system of the South, which is bad indeed as judged by European standards, but which knows little of kidnapping; makes little use of the third degree or torture to extort confessions; does not take witnesses for "rides"; and is not acquainted with the gangster or racketeer except when Capone and such underworld kings of the North pass through.[36]

This propaganda in the North is calculated, as I have said, to prepare pub-

---

36. The Brooklyn-born Chicago outlaw Alphonse Capone (1899–1947) used his violent organized crime syndicate to keep a hold on the city's liquor business during Prohibition.

lic opinion for a program. I have already suggested the possible program of the industrialist leaders. The Communists (proletarian-industrialists) have for their larger objective the conversion of the United States into a Bolshevik State. This is well known. But this program is dependent upon the attainment of many lesser objectives. Should they be able to carry the population of the industrial centers of the North with them, they would still not be able to control the greater part of the United States. The agrarian West and South would still hold, perhaps, thirty-nine States composing the greater part of the territory of the present Union. But Communism, as any other form of industrialism, must have large rural populations to exploit. The industries must have raw material—cotton, iron, copper, coal, petroleum, et cetera; must have food—grain, hogs, cattle, sheep, vegetables, et cetera. In short, Communism, like capitalist industrialism, is dependent upon agriculture, cannot, in fact, exist without it. Though changing names, industrialism under the title of Communism would face the same irrepressible conflict with agrarianism as existed under the old capitalistic industrialism.[37] What is good for the one is harmful to the other. As the industrialist East in 1819 set out [via the Missouri Compromise] to subordinate the South—and West, so the Communistic East now sets out upon a similar course. That is, it must either weaken and eventually gain control of the South as the abolitionists and reconstructionists did or its program will largely fail.

But the Communists are quite conscious that agriculturalists as a class, and Southerners in particular, have a very strong sense of property. For property in an agricultural society is more tangible than in an industrial society; it is made up of definite pieces of land, with old family graveyards where relatives lie; of trees and creeks and landmarks which for generations have been the daily companion in nature of those who quietly wait in the cemeteries for the Last Day. This sense of property which identifies man and nature so strongly in the South, even yet, cannot be broken down by the philosophy of Communism. When it is realized that this feeling is strong and not only among the owners of land, but among the landless tenants, black and white, as well, Bolshevism finds it necessary to weaken and gain control of the South otherwise than by converting its people to Communist doctrines. It has a weapon already at hand, fashioned for it by the capitalist industrialists—the race question. A land of thirty million whites and nearly ten million blacks can be rendered helpless, can be thrown into chaos, so they reason, if the black and white races are set against one another in deadly conflict; they might even

---

37. See "The Irrepressible Conflict," Owsley's contribution to *ITMS*.

destroy one another, and thus leave the South, as Thad Stevens had advocated during reconstruction, to be peopled with new men.

When one examines their Southern Program, published at Headquarters in New York City (under the title *The Communist Position on the Negro Question*), it becomes evident that inflammatory literature is being circulated among the Southern blacks. This literature does not advocate any form of socialism; the Communist leaders admit that they have sounded out the Southern Negro on that question and found him strongly attached to property. He is land-hungry. So the literature promises him land. It urges the Negro to rise and seize the lands of his oppressors and divide them out. It promises to confiscate and give him these lands should the Communist Party succeed in gaining control of the Federal Government. It even promises to create a Negro State out of the Southern black belt and grant the Negro autonomy to allow him to secede from the Union. That is, it offers to help the Negro set up a black peasant state formed out of the confiscated or expropriated lands of the white man who is to be either exterminated or completely subordinated to the black race. The Communist Party instructs its agents in the South as follows:

> The white revolutionary workers, who understand the powerful revolutionary potentialities inherent in the struggles of the Negro masses, would answer in the following manner: "This land on which you and your ancestors have slaved for centuries rightfully belongs to you. The bosses' government in this territory is a government of foreign slave drivers; it is our enemy as well as yours. We recognize and support your right to organize your own government, to elect your own officials, to organize your own militia, and your unqualified right to separate from the United States. Moreover, we, the white revolutionary workers, will prove our sincerity right now, at the present time, by helping to organize a struggle to bring about those conditions in which you will be able to exercise your right to self-determination."[38]

---

38. Harry Haywood, "The Theoretical Defenders of White Chauvinism in the Labor Movement," in *The Communist Position on the Negro Question: Equal Rights for Negroes: Self Determination for the Black Belt* (n.p.: n.d. [probably 1932]), 39–40. This pamphlet, a collection of speeches and articles, was designed to demonstrate the Communist Party's commitment to and its plan for black liberation. The highest phase of class consciousness, members were warned, could not be reached until (white) workers banished racism from their hearts. Scottsboro had supplied a perfect opportunity to spread the party's message: "Today . . . we are rallying the workers, Negro and white, in a fight for nine black boys—a fight which attacks the system of lynch law and national slavery at its very roots; we are penetrating the South; we are drawing hundreds of thousands

Or again:

> In the South, the fight must be fearlessly developed against the thievery and robbery of the Southern Capitalists and landlords; against their whole system of enslaving the Negroes based on Jim Crowism and lynch terror. . . .
>
> In the first place, our demand is that the land of the Southern white landlords, for years tilled by the Negro tenant farmers, be confiscated and turned over to the Negroes. This is the only way to insure economic and social equality. . . .
>
> Secondly, we propose to break up the present artificial state boundaries . . . and to establish the state unity of the territory known as the "Black Belt." . . .
>
> Thirdly, in this territory, we demand that the Negroes be given the complete right of self-determination; the *right to set up their own government* in this territory and the right to separate, if they wish, from the United States.[39]

In order that the Negro may be properly aroused to undertake such a task, no chance of stirring his passions against the Southern white is to be overlooked. The Communists in this handbook on their Southern Program admit their authorship of the trouble leading to the Dadeville trial. These Negroes were tenants who had, like all other tenants in the South, mortgaged their crop in advance for supplies for themselves and stock. When time came to pay up, they barricaded themselves in a house and without warning shot down four deputy sheriffs who had come to serve writs of attachment. Incendiary literature issued from Communist headquarters was found in the house, thus identifying—if identification were necessary—this race conflict with the Communist program. At present the trial has been appealed so that it is on the way to the United States Supreme Court. Irving Schwab,[40] the lawyer for the defense, employed admittedly by the Communist Party, is appealing the case on the basis that the Negro is not represented on the jury as he has a right to be under the Fourteenth Amendment. In the Birmingham

---

of white workers into the struggle for Negro rights; we are ferreting out and driving from our ranks those who are hopelessly imbued with the poison of white superiority" (Elizabeth Lawson, introduction to *Communist Position on the Negro Question*, 2).

39. C. A. Hathaway, "Who Are the Friends of the Negro People?," speech delivered at the nomination of Communist James W. Ford to vice president of the United States, 1932, in *Communist Position on the Negro Question*, 28.

40. Irving Schwab (1904–43), the New York attorney for the International Labor Defense, established the group's branch office in Atlanta. In the decade before his death, he concentrated on helping "anti-Fascist refugees" (by which he meant European Jews) obtain asylum in the U.S. (*New York Times*, 18 April 1943, 48).

case, the Negro who killed two white girls and shot a third first made his victims a speech which was identified as coming from incendiary literature of the Communist Party.[41]

As for the Scottsboro case, it bears the earmarks of the Communist Party from the beginning to the present. These young Negroes, while it is said they are not Communists themselves, had been embittered and inflamed against the Southern whites before the alleged attack upon the two white women. Certainly since the beginning of the case the Communists have made every possible use of it to incite these and other Negroes to do violence against the whites. They say in their Southern Program that the Scottsboro case is their most strategic point in the world at the present time. They call attention to the wide-spread support given them in the North by people who are not Communists—in fact, who are thoroughly unaware that they are helping a Communist program. At the present time the "Scottsboro boys," as the Communists love to call them, are holding levee in the Birmingham jail. Hundreds of Negroes, not Communists, of course, but Negroes who have been aroused by the incendiary literature meant to set the blacks to fighting the whites, visit the jail. The "Scottsboro boys" riot at will: refuse to go to their cells, arm themselves with pieces of plumbing and window fixtures, while the jailer and sheriff, lest they be accused in the Northern press of cruelty and mistreatment, stand impotent.[42]

The Negro is incited to attack the white man, is promised his property, is promised an independent state where he will either rule or destroy the white man—is promised in effect the same things which the industrialists offered him as the price of his support during reconstruction.

Once again, the unfortunate black is being used as a pawn. If he were able to destroy or subordinate the white man with outside aid, as during reconstruction, he would not be given the white man's land; or if he expropriated it during the contemplated race struggle, he would not be permitted to keep it. One only has to remember the strategy of the Communist Revolution in Russia with reference to the landless peasantry to predict the fate of the proposed Negro peasant and his newly acquired lands. It will be recalled that the

---

41. The case against Willie Peterson was appealed by lawyers backed by the NAACP. The court refused to hear the appeal, the prosecution's concocted evidence notwithstanding (Kelley, *Hammer and Hoe,* 83–84, 89–90).

42. In April 1933, following defendant Haywood Patterson's second trial (which again ended in a death sentence), the staff at the Jefferson County Prison in Birmingham tightened restrictions. In protest, the prisoners did as Owsley described, and successfully won back basic privileges. The Scottsboro defendants were nevertheless subject to frequent brutality (Goodman, *Stories of Scottsboro,* 155–56).

Russian peasant was promised in 1916 the lands of the nobility if he would quit the battle front. He did so, made his way back to his village armed with his rifle, helped mob the landlords, seized their property, and when the smoke had cleared up lo! the land was not his, but belonged to the State. He found himself no longer a free peasant, for the State took his wheat, barley, wool, flax, nearly everything he made, and left him hardly enough, and frequently not enough, to live on. He had become a State slave and has so remained in Russia until this day. This, of course, must necessarily be the fate of any agrarian population, black or white, which comes under the control of a Communist State; that is to say, it will be even worse than the fate of the agricultural populations under the capitalistic industrialist regime, where the farmers are slaves to insurance companies, banks, and merchants.

No, it is impossible to believe in the sincerity of the promised of "justice," land, and self-determination which the Communist Party holds out to the black man of the South. Nor can one believe that the Communists want "justice" for the "Scottsboro boys" or the Negro men on trial at Dadeville or the Negro murderer in Judge Lowell's court. They would prefer that the "Scottsboro boys" be executed by the State of Alabama and that all the other cases be decided against the Negroes in the end. What they want is a lengthy period of violent agitation against the South, a chance for such speeches as those which Lawyer Leibowitz delivered at the trial in Decatur or in New York, in which he characterized the people of Alabama as "lantern jawed morons and lynchers," swayed by bigotry and race hatred, "creatures" with "sordidness and venom in their hideous countenances,"[43] or for articles by such facile pens as that of Mrs. Mary Heaton Vorse in the *New Republic*. After they have rung the changes on the trials, it then would be a fitting end to have the Negroes executed. This would create another group of martyrs, another period of violent propaganda, in which the Southern people, their courts, their governments, would be held up to ridicule and Northern opinion further prepared for a Southern program; while more fuel would be added to the race antagonisms in the South.

---

43. Samuel Simon Leibowitz (1893–1978) was a Romanian-born New York criminal defense lawyer whose pro bono work for the Scottsboro case ultimately led to the Supreme Court ruling that the exclusion of blacks from juries was unconstitutional. Upon his return to New York after a second all-white jury had convicted Haywood Patterson of rape and sentenced him to die in the electric chair—despite the recantation of charges by one of the alleged victims—Leibowitz was asked by a reporter how a jury could have found Patterson guilty. Of the jurors, he replied, "If you ever saw those creatures, those bigots, whose mouths are slits in their faces, whose eyes pop out at you like a frog's, whose chins drip tobacco juice, bewhiskered and filthy, you would not ask how they could" (*New York Herald Tribune*, 11 April 1933).

I believe that Communism will fail in its ultimate goal of converting America into a Bolshevik state. Modified and practical State Socialism will be experimented with during the near future and it will probably meet the emergency. If Bolshevism should be successful in winning the Negro in the South to its Southern Program, and then fail to gain control of the Federal Government, it would leave the Negro in a worse plight than he was after reconstruction. He would find himself face to face with an embittered white race, outnumbering his race three to one, with whom he would have to make his peace; and the terms would probably be more severe than before.

But in the meanwhile, before the issue is settled, Communist agitation— and such conduct as Judge Lowell's—is creating a dangerous situation in the South. The criminal Negro, seeing those who have been accused of murder or rape such as the "Scottsboro boys" or the defendants on trial at Dadeville assiduously championed by an outside group, seeing them granted immunity in Judge Lowell's court or, perhaps, even in the Supreme Court, is bound to feel that he himself is above the reach of the law in a Southern State. It is hardly to be supposed that the Southern whites will tolerate such a situation. One has only to read the history of the abolition crusade or more particularly the history of reconstruction to be able to predict what will follow such flagrant interference either by the capitalist industrialists or by Communists. An extra-legal government would quickly spring into existence and such cases as that of the "Scottsboro boys" would be tried in courts whose decrees could not be appealed to a Federal tribunal. In other words, the outside interference with the relationship of the whites and blacks in the South can result in nothing but organizations like the Ku Klux Klan and in violent retaliation against the Negroes—themselves often innocent. Such interference makes justice difficult, not only by creating friction between the races, but by arousing anger against those who interfere: Lawyer Leibowitz and those who sent him were more on trial at Decatur than the Negro boys. The boys might have been cleared by a native lawyer on the second trial.[44]

---

44. In a letter to the editor, Leibowitz rebutted this allegation, pointing out that in fact the defense team included a "native lawyer," the Chattanoogan George W. Chamlee (1872–1958), previously the attorney general of Hamilton County, Tennessee, whose father was a celebrated Confederate soldier and who was himself a member of the Sons of Confederate Veterans. These qualifications did little to protect Chamlee, Leibowitz said, for he was subjected to taunts and humiliation by fellow Southerners during the trial. See Leibowitz, "Scottsboro Case Defense," *New York Herald Tribune,* 30 April 1933, 8.

Frank Lawrence Owsley

The Pillars of Agrarianism

Although Frank Lawrence Owsley preferred interpreting the Old South, in "The Pillars of Agrarianism" he proposed a concrete land reform policy for the South of the 1930s. Owsley's article is akin to those of Donald Davidson in its defensive desire to set critics — especially H. L. Mencken — straight about the Agrarian principles in I'll Take My Stand. *In the specificity of its economic proposals, however, the article is more suggestive of the work of the liberal sociologists at the University of North Carolina.[1] Owsley was undoubtedly ecstatic when the Southern Policy Committee reprinted the essay and had it disseminated to New Dealers as powerful as Alabama's Senator John Bankhead, architect of the Bankhead-Jones Farm Tenancy Act. The article thus achieved a duality of purpose: a fellow Agrarian such as Allen Tate could tout it as one of the most accurate summaries of Agrarianism,[2] while advocates of land redistribution in the South could cite it as evidence that even conservative Southerners were calling for intervention by the federal government. Paul Conkin has called Owsley's article "the closest the [Agrarian] group ever came to endorsing specific remedies for agricultural distress in the South."[3]*

Reprinted from *American Review* 4 (1935): 529–47, with the permission of Mrs. Harriet C. Owsley.

1. O'Brien, *IAS,* 162–84, 174–78.

2. Tate identified three papers as containing the most genuine Agrarian doctrine: Owsley's "The Pillars of Agrarianism," Ransom's "Happy Farmers" (*AR* 1 [1933]: 513–35), and Agar's "The Task for Conservatism" (*AR* 3 [1934]: 1–22). Tate to Gilbert Seldes, 29 April 1935, Allen Tate Papers, 39:8, Princeton University Library.

3. The essay "was truly agrarian in the sense of proposed limitations on acreage and new means of opening access to land. The proposals, close to ideas that Nixon and Owsley had frequently discussed, reflected their mutual concern over the evils of sharecropping and tenancy" (Conkin, *SA,* 113).

Since the appearance of *I'll Take My Stand* in 1930, the Agrarians have been subjected to a fusillade of criticism. I suspect that our philosophy as set forth in that book and in later essays, published in certain periodicals, especially in the Distributist-Agrarian[4] *American Review,* has irked the devotees of our technological civilization. Venturing an even stronger word, it begins to appear that the doctrines announced in *I'll Take My Stand* have actually *infuriated* these people. Just recently, on an important examination for a certain scholarship, it seems that the Committee inquired of each candidate what he thought of agrarianism. It was noteworthy that the successful candidate summed up his opinion by saying that the advocates of such a system were "cockeyed." One of the candidates who was not only rejected, but was urged not to apply again on the grounds of age (he has just celebrated his twenty-second birthday, and the age limit of the scholarship is several years above this age) answered that as far as he understood it he heartily approved of agrarianism. The most recent and, perhaps, the most violent attack upon the advocates of an agrarian state is that of H. L. Mencken.[5] While Mencken's attack is so violent and lacking in restraint that it does not fall far short of libel, I have no desire to single him out as a critic worthy of an answer. However, I must confess that Mencken's attack, because it is typical — outside of the billingsgate — of those coming from the pillars of Industrialism, has prompted, to a certain extent, this essay.[6] Such essays as his, appearing with amazing regularity, have without doubt troubled the mind of the neophyte, and, in many cases, have utterly confused him and made him lose sight of the principles and specific objectives of agrarianism.

---

4. Conkin explained that Seward Collins "cemented a working alliance between the Southern Agrarians and the English distributists. Soon they shared the same general platform, with the Agrarians applying it to the specific problems of the south. The small distributist movement originated in the work of Hilaire Belloc, who published his opening manifesto, *The Servile State,* in 1911. By the 1930s he had gained a considerable following in England, with an organized movement and a small journal. Collins recruited an aging Belloc for the first numbers of the *American Review,* publishing in six installments what amounted to a book, 'The Restoration of Property.' In England, Belloc had long advocated the restoration of a rooted and stable English peasantry as an antidote to an otherwise inevitable socialist or fascist form of totalitarianism" (*SA,* 111–12).

5. In "The South Astir," *VQR* 11 (1935): 53, Mencken called the twelve Southerners "Agrarian Habakkuks."

6. According to Shapiro, "The original draft of this [Owsley's] essay contained an extensive attack on Mencken, but Davidson and Ransom convinced Owsley to remove much of this criticism because they feared Mencken would reply in kind" ("The Southern Agrarians, H. L. Mencken, and the Quest for Southern Identity," *American Studies* 13 [1972]: 87).

Few, if any of the Agrarians have expended any effort in answering the criticism of those who attack our principles. From the beginning we have pursued the attack rather than the defense; nor have we—if I may continue the military figure of speech—seen fit to consolidate our positions. However, it seems to me very proper, at the present time, for the sake of those who have been confused, or those whom we hope to draw into our way of thinking, to restate and elaborate the fundamental economic and political principles on which an agrarian society will probably have to rest in the United States, and most particularly in the South.

I shall not attempt to restate and discuss all the principles and programs of our hoped-for agrarian society, for this, as John Crowe Ransom has said in another connection, would indeed institute an infinite series. My purpose is to confine my discussion to the five great pillars upon which this society will have to rest. Before going into an exposition of the foundation of a restored agrarianism in the South (or other regions), it will be well to restate our definition of an agrarian state as set forth in the introduction of *I'll Take My Stand:*

> Opposed to the industrial society is the agrarian, which does not stand in particular need of definition. An agrarian society is hardly one that has no use at all for industries, for professional vocations, for scholars and artists, and for the life of cities. Technically, perhaps, an agrarian society is one in which agriculture is the leading vocation, whether for wealth, for pleasure, or prestige—a form of labor that is pursued with intelligence and leisure, and that becomes the model to which the other forms approach as well as they may.[7]

I shall edit this definition. We had in mind a society in which, indeed, agriculture was the leading vocation; but the implication was more than this. We meant that the agrarian population and the people of the agricultural market towns must dominate the social, cultural, economic, and political life of the state and give tone to it. Today, the Scandinavian countries are fair examples of such a state. France before the World War was a most beautiful example, where 30,000,000 people lived on the land and 10,000,000 lived in the towns and cities engaging in commerce and industry. Even today, after the disastrous War and its effects upon mechanization of industry, France presents the best balanced economic system of any first-class nation in the world. The ownership of property is more widely distributed there than in any nation comparable in wealth and population. Governments may rise and fall, but the French peasant and farmer seems eternal when compared to

---

7. *ITMS,* xlvi–xlvii.

those of the United States. Today there are about 350,000 persons unemployed in France as against hardly less than 12,000,000 in the United States. Yet the United States has less than three times as large a population as France.

Before entering into the details of our fundamental program, let me say that we are not exotics, nor a peculiar sect living in a vacuum, untouched by public affairs, merely irked by the noise of factory wheels and machinery. We fully realize that our program cannot be put into operation until matters affecting the nation as a whole are set aright. Everything which affects the agrarian interests also touches industry, finance, and commerce. Our program, therefore, intimately involves national problems. We are on the side of those who know that the common enemy of the people, of their government, their liberty, and their property, must be abated. This enemy is a system which allows a relatively few men to control most of the nation's wealth and to regiment virtually the whole population under their anonymous holding companies and corporations, and to control government by bribery or intimidation. Just how these giant organizations should be brought under the control of law and ethics we are not agreed. We are, however, agreed with the English Distributists that the most desirable objective is to break them down into small units owned and controlled by real people. We want to see property restored and the proletariat thus abolished and communism made impossible. The more widespread is the ownership of property, the more happy and secure will be the people and the nation. But is such a decentralization in physical property as well as in ownership possible? We are confident that it is, however much we may differ among ourselves as to the degree of decentralization that will prove desirable in any given industry. We are all convinced, though we hold no doctrinaire principles as to method, that these robber barons of the twentieth century will have to be reduced and civilized in some form or other before any program can be realized by our state and Federal governments.

While we are deeply interested in the whole nation, yet, as Agrarians and Southerners, we are not desirous of launching a crusade to convert or coerce the other sections of the country into our way of thinking. We, therefore, while inviting all who wish, to go with us, have a fundamental program for the South to which I have referred as the five pillars of agrarianism.

The first item in our agrarian program is to rehabilitate the population actually living on the soil. This farming population falls into several categories: large and small planters; large and small farmers, both black and white; black and white tenants who own their stock and tools, and rent land; black and white tenants who own no stock or tools, but are furnished everything and get a share of the crop for their labor. Finally, there is the wage-hand either colored or white who is furnished a house, and perhaps food and a certain cash wage.

Today the farm population in the South whether wage-hand or large planter is in a precarious and often miserable state. The exploitations by the industrial interests through high tariffs and other special favors from the Federal government, which force the farmer to buy in a protected market and sell in a world market, and the periodic industrial depressions following in close order since the Civil War, have greatly oppressed the Southern agricultural population. The majority of the planters do not really own their lands; the real owners are the life insurance companies or the banks. The payment of interest on his mortgage leaves the almost mythical landowner little on which to subsist. Repayment of the principal is out of the question. Actually, most of the planters are without credit, and are no better off than the tenant or share-cropper. In fact, the renter and share-cropper frequently come out of debt with some cash, their corn, sorghum, potatoes, pigs, cows, and other live stock above the board. The fate of the small or large farmer is much better. As a rule he is thrifty, owes less than the other classes, and lives to a great extent off his farm. Sometimes he sends his children to college, especially the agricultural college. His house is usually comfortable and sometimes painted. For the farmer as a class, there is less need of state intervention in his affairs than in the affairs of the tenant and planter classes. Yet a new political economy is necessary for him as well as the planters and tenants, or he will eventually lose his land and status. This new political economy will be discussed later. As for the planter class, there are many whom even the new political economy cannot save. Their equity in the once broad acres which they held in fee simple is too small. It will be best for them to liquidate and begin over as small farmers under the plan which I shall presently offer in connection with the tenant farmers.

The most serious problem, however, is not the bankrupt planters but the tenant-farmers, black or white, because of their great number. I do not know the exact ratio between the tenant-farmer class and the landholding class; but I have heard it said that 75% of the population living on the land in the South are tenants. If this estimate is too high, it will not long remain so unless strong measures are taken, for the tenant class has been increasing so rapidly in recent years that it threatens to engulf the entire agricultural population of the South. Most of the white tenants were once landowners, but have been thrust near to the bottom of the economic and social order by the loss of their lands through industrial exploitation, depression, and, frequently, through high pressure salesmanship of radio, automobile, and farm machinery agents. Industrialism has persuaded, or created a public opinion which has virtually driven, the farmer to accept industrial tastes and standards of living and forced him to mortgage and then to lose his farm. Battered old cars, dangling radio aerials, rust-eaten tractors, and abandoned threshing machines and hay balers scattered forlornly about are mute witnesses to the tragedy of Industrialism's attempt to industrialize the farmer and planter.

A portion of the lower class of white tenants, especially the adults, are beyond redemption. Through diseased tonsils, adenoids, unbalanced rations, tuberculosis, hook worm, malaria, and the social diseases, many have been made into irresponsible, sometimes—but not often—vicious people who are lacking in mental alertness and the constancy of will to enable them to till the soil without close supervision. Such people would not be able to make a living on land which might be granted or sold to them on easy terms by the government. However, the county and state public health departments should be enabled to take steps necessary to salvage the children of such families in order that they may be owners of small farms and good citizens when of proper age. It is this class of whites in particular, who own no stock, plant no gardens, raise no chickens, who are frequently and perhaps accurately described as the "po' white trash."

The higher class white tenants, those who own their stock and cattle and have their gardens and truck patches, are ready to become the proprietors of farms. Frequently they are good farmers and send their children through the high schools. They are probably in the majority in most of the Southern states and, as I have suggested, their families have been landowners: they were, in short, once a part of the Southern yeomanry; and for a nation or section to allow these people to sink lower and lower in the social and economic scale is to destroy itself.

As for the Negro tenant class, the majority of the Agrarians agree that the really responsible farmers among them who know how to take care of the soil and who own their own stock and cattle, should be made proprietors of small farms.

The planters and large farmers who are left after liquidating their debts will still have an abundance of tenants who work well under supervision. In the South, the wage-hand is usually the son of a tenant. He is frequently young and more intelligent than the lower tenant class. He should, where his intelligence and sense of responsibility permit, be homesteaded like the better-class tenant. Otherwise, he should be kept where he is, under the supervision of one who has good judgment and a sense of responsibility.

Now, instead of the Federal or state government spending $2500 in building a house for the homesteaders, with whom they are very gingerly experimenting, and several hundred dollars on small tracts of land, let the national and state governments buy up all the lands owned by the insurance companies and absentee landlords—which are being destroyed rapidly by erosion—and part of the land owned by the huge planters who are struggling to save a portion of their lands, and give every landless tenant who can qualify, 80 acres of land, build him a substantial hewn log house and barn, fence him off twenty acres for a pasture, give him two mules and two milk cows and advance him $300 for his living expenses for one year. By this means 500,000 persons can be rehabilitated in one year at $1,500 a family or $300 per person. An outright gift of the land is advocated to the homesteader with one condition attached: the land must never be sold or mortgaged, and when abandoned it should automatically escheat to the state which should be under immediate obligation to rehabilitate another worthy family.

The next step would be to bring the technologically unemployed, intelligent city people back to the country. First, those who have had experience as farmers should be rehabilitated; next, but relatively few at a time, those without experience should be permitted to become tenants on plantations, whereupon, if such tenants and their families should feel that they would like to go on, the government should grant them a homestead with sufficient stock and cattle and enough cash to subsist them one year. It seems quite clear to the Agrarians that technological unemployment is destined to increase with rapid acceleration until the majority of the population once employed in industry will be thrown out of the system. The government will be faced with perhaps three alternatives: it could put these permanently unemployed on a dole—until the government becomes bankrupt or an orderly slave state is established; it could refuse the dole and have a revolution; or it could rehabilitate the unemployed by giving them small farms. We, as interested citizens of the United States, urge this last policy upon the government as the only permanent relief from permanent technological unemployment. As Agrarians we urge it as an opportunity to restore the healthy balance of population between city and country which will aid in the restoration of agrarianism and in the restoration and preservation of civilization.

Next in order of importance but simultaneous with the first step should be the rehabilitation of the soil. We, in common with the agricultural colleges of the country, urge that small and large farmer, small and large planter, regard the enrichment and preservation of the soil as a first duty. Those who own the soil must be held accountable in some way for their stewardship. Undrained, unterraced, single-cropped land, and lack of reforestation, should be *prima facie* evidence that the homesteader is not a responsible person and his land should, after fair warning and action in Chancery Court, escheat to the state. As for those farmers and planters who acquire their land by purchase or inheritance, a heavy suspended fine should be imposed upon them; and unless the planter or farmer remedies the abuses within a reasonable time or gives good reason why he has not been able to do so, the fine should be collected. The county agent and three men appointed by the state department of agriculture, should serve in each county as a kind of court to pass on such matters, and appeal from their decision should be allowed to go to Chancery Court. In short, land must be conserved for future generations and not exploited, as has too often been the practice, by the present owners. Another drastic proposal which would aid in conserving the land as well as preventing its being alienated or becoming encumbered with debt, is that by state constitutional amendment, no land could be mortgaged, except by consent of a court or equity; nor should any kind of speculative sale be permitted. It must become impossible for land to be sold to real estate and insurance companies or banks. In thus making alienation of the soil difficult and its proper management necessary, I am suggesting a modified form of feudal tenure where, in theory, the King or state has a paramount interest in the land.

When the rehabilitation and conservation of the soil and stability of tenure have been provided for, the next consideration must be the products of the soil.

Subsistence farming must be the first objective of every man who controls a farm or plantation. The land must first support the people who till it; then it must support their stock. In the olden days when there were no money taxes or mortgages to meet, nor automobiles and fine carriages to buy, nor life and fire insurance to keep up, and when the priest and the teacher were paid in kind, this type of farming, if carried on with the scientific knowledge available today, would have supported the grandest of establishments. But today, a minimum outlay of cash is necessary even for those fortunate souls who are without debts: taxes, insurance, clothing, certain articles of luxury, and medical attention require cash.

After subsistence come the money crops. In the South these crops, too often planted at the expense of the subsistence crops, are peanuts, rice, sugar cane, tobacco, and cotton. Cotton and tobacco, the two leading staples, can be raised in the South in almost limitless quantities and must always depend, to a large extent, upon the foreign or world market. Considerable talk has been going its rounds concerning the danger of losing the foreign market because of crop limitation. Crop limitation, however, has no bearing at the present time, at least, upon the problem of cotton and tobacco. There are between nine and twelve million surplus bales of cotton and large quantities of tobacco above current crops, stored in the United States; and there can hardly be any question about loss of world markets because of crop limitation when we are unable to dispose of this terrific surplus. Further, considerable alarm has been expressed concerning the inability of American cotton growers to compete with Russia, Egypt, Brazil, Turkey, China, and India. This is a groundless fear, for even in the days when the South produced the scrub variety of cotton, the world depended largely upon American cotton, because, with the exception of limited areas in Egypt, the Sudan, and South Africa, no part of the world could raise as much cotton per acre or as good a fiber as the American South. Now that Coker of South Carolina and other planter breeders have produced an upland staple with a fiber about two inches in length, which will grow on any soil in the South, and which is being rapidly introduced everywhere, there can hardly be any serious competition with the South, as far as cheapness of production, quality, and quantity are concerned.

Everything being equal in the world markets, the South could soon drive its competitors out, as it did until past the turn of the century when other factors entered. These factors will have to be dealt with intelligently by the government of the United States or by the regional governments to be discussed later, else the South will be wiped out economically. One factor is that within the last twenty years America has ceased to be a debtor nation and has become a creditor. As a debtor we shipped cotton to England, France, or Germany which created foreign exchange with which to pay the principal and interest on our debts and purchase foreign goods. The South could raise large cotton and tobacco crops and be sure that the world markets would take all. As soon as we became a creditor we could no longer ship our cotton and tobacco crops with assurances of a sale. England and Germany and France and even Japan, wherever possible, have bought cotton from those countries which owed them money. This loss of a foreign market was seemingly made permanent by the rising tariff scale in America, which effectually cut off foreign goods from our markets, and thereby destroyed the chief sources of foreign exchange in this country with which Southern staples could be bought. The tariff, which was a guarantee of the home markets for the industrial interests of the country, principally located in the East and a belt following the Great Lakes, has been the greatest permanent factor in destroying the foreign market on which the South chiefly depended.

It must be said, at this point, that such a situation was envisaged in 1833 when South Carolina nullified the tariff law of 1832, and again when the Southern states seceded from the Union in 1861. The belief that industrialism, as soon as it got control of the Federal government, would not only exploit agriculture but would destroy the South was behind the whole secession movement. Today, we Agrarians witness the fulfillment of the jeremiads of Robert Barnwell Rhett[8] and John C. Calhoun. We, however, are not hoping for or advocating another break-up of the Union; but we are demanding a fair hearing for the fundamental cause of the South—now that slavery can no longer befog the real issue. If the industrial interests continue the monopoly of the home market and thereby cause the agricultural South (and West) to pay a much higher price for goods than the world price level, we must have a *quid pro quo:* a subsidy on every bale of cotton and pound of tobacco or other important agricultural products shipped abroad, based on the difference between world and domestic prices. In order that foreign countries shall have sufficient American exchange with which to purchase our staple farm exports we further insist that all farm products and raw material shipped into the United States be used in creating foreign exchange with which cotton and tobacco may be purchased and exported. (James Waller in *A New Deal for the South* suggests this technique of establishing parity between agriculture and industry.)[9] In short, the South—and, if I may be so bold as to speak for the agrarian interests of another section, the West—must have agriculture put upon the same basis as industry.

With such political economy the South would soon become one of the most important parts of the world, and it would add much to the prosperity of the other sections of the country. It is doubtful, however, whether such intelligent legislation is possible under a government so dominated by particular sectional interests.

---

8. The fire-eating South Carolina congressman and senator Robert Barnwell Rhett (1800–1876) actively promoted secession.

9. The Nashville-born attorney, businessman, and economist James Muir Waller (1900–1971) trained at Vanderbilt (1922), Yale, and the University of North Carolina, Chapel Hill (Ph.D. 1957). In 1935, Waller resigned from Nixon's Southern Policy Committee when African-American sociologist Charles S. Johnson was elected a member. "I do not feel," Waller wrote, "that cooperation with educated members of the race would be prevented or even hampered by their not having official representation on the Committee. Furthermore, I believe the inclusion of negro members would automatically and immediately destroy a large part of the possible effectiveness of the Committee in attempting to mold and reflect Southern opinion. It would, I feel, make the Committee be regarded by a tremendous percentage of people in the South as a semi-communistic and racial equality group somewhat akin to the American Civil Liberties Union. While such a judgment might be totally unjustified, it would, nevertheless, in my opinion, be practically impossible to overcome" (quoted in Sarah Newman Shouse, *Hillbilly Realist: Herman Clarence Nixon of Possum Trot* [University, Ala., 1986], 81). Waller contributed "America and Foreign Trade" to *WOA*.

For that reason—which is founded upon the history of the last one hundred and forty-six years—we are striving for a new constitutional deal which will help put the several sections on equal footing and prevent the exploitation of one by the other. We are in the front ranks of those who insist that the United States is less a nation than an Empire made up of a congeries of regions marked off by geographic, climatic, and racial characteristics. It has been suggested that New England would form a distinct region, the Middle Atlantic another, the Middle West another, the Rocky Mountain and Pacific States another, perhaps, and the South another. Of course the region to which a state wished to affiliate would be determined by a plebiscite. W. Y. Elliott of Harvard [10] suggests that the regional governments be granted the present powers of states, and that the states themselves be deprived of anything save administrative functions. He further suggests that one set of courts should serve both as Federal and state courts, thus eliminating the maze of courts by which justice is delayed and defeated and encouragement thereby given to lynch law.

Mr. Elliott suggests that in the new set-up the Federal government retain its present powers much more clearly defined. He further urges that all concurrent powers be eliminated. As far as I know, Mr. Elliott is not an agrarian; but his plan is essentially what the Agrarians have urged constantly, except in the matter of division of power between the Federal and regional governments. His plan seems very reasonable and conservative. Something like it will have to be adopted if the United States is to endure. The Agrarians, I believe, advocate that, in the redivision of powers in a new constitutional convention, the regional governments should have much more autonomy than the states have ever had. The Federal government should have supreme control over war and peace, the army and navy, interregional or even interstate commerce, banking, currency, and foreign affairs. On the other hand, the sections should have equal representation in the Federal legislative body and in the election of the president and in the cabinet. The legislative body should be composed of a senate only and should be elected by the regional congresses. Finally, the regions should have control of the tariff: that is, the several regions should have an equal share in making the tariff,

---

10. The Tennessee-born author William Yandell Elliott (1896–1979) graduated from Vanderbilt in 1917, contributed to the *Fugitive,* studied at Oxford as a Rhodes scholar, and spent almost his entire career as a professor of government at Harvard. Owsley alluded to Elliott's *The Need for Constitutional Reform: A Program for National Security* (New York, 1935); Davidson discussed Elliott's book in *The Attack on Leviathan: Regionalism and Nationalism in the United States* (Chapel Hill, 1938), 121 ff.

which would be in the form of a treaty or agreement between all the sections, somewhat in the fashion of the late Austro-Hungarian tariff treaties. In case one region, say the South, failed to agree to the tariff treaty, then the South should be exempted from the operation of the law until an agreement could be reached. Such an arrangement does not mean there would be interregional tariffs; it does mean that, if the South should have a lower tariff than the other regions, goods imported through the South from abroad would have to pay an extra duty on entering the other regions operating under the treaty. There would be some smuggling across the Potomac and Ohio, but not any more than through Mexico and Canada.

The Supreme Court, like the proposed Senate, should have equal representation from all the sections, regardless of political parties, and the members of the Supreme Court should not be the creatures of the Senate or the President, but, like the Senate, should be appointed by the regional governors subject to the ratification of the regional legislature, which also should be only a senate. The courts—that is, the courts of appeal and circuit courts—should be constituted regionally, but should be considered both Federal and regional, sitting one time as Federal and one time as regional.

In our Agrarian program, not only does it seem necessary to grant more local autonomy because of differences of economic interest, but because of differences of social and racial interests as well. Under such a government, the Civil War would not have been possible, nor would Reconstruction and the ensuing difficulties and hatreds have arisen. And what is more to the point at the present time, Communist interference in the Southern courts, and even conservative interference from other sections, would hardly take place. In other words, the Agrarians—who come nearer representing the opinion of Southern people than do newspapers largely subsidized by Northern-owned power companies and Wall-Street-owned banks, or the Southern liberals fawning for the favor of these corporations or of other powerful Northern groups—believe that under regional government each section will find it less difficult to attend to its own social and economic problems, and thereby will be encouraged to restore the old friendships which were crippled or destroyed under our present system.

Let me sum up. The five pillars on which it would appear that an agrarian society must rest are: (1) The restoration of the people to the land and the land to the people by the government purchasing lands held by loan companies, insurance companies, banks, absentee landlords, and planters whose estates are hopelessly encumbered with debt, and granting to the landless tenants, who are sufficiently able and responsible to own and conserve the land, a homestead of 80 acres with sufficient stock to cultivate the farm, and cash enough to feed and clothe the family one year; (2) The preservation and restoration of the soil by the use of fines and escheat, and by making land practically inalienable and non-mortgageable—that is by restoring a modified feudal tenure where the state had a paramount interest in the land and could exact certain services and duties from those who possessed the land; (3) The establishment of a balanced agriculture where subsistence crops are the first consideration and the money crops are of secondary importance; (4) The establishment of a just political economy, where agriculture is placed upon an equal basis with industry, finance, and commerce; (5) The creation of regional governments possessed of more autonomy than the states, which will sustain the political economy fitted for each region, and which will prevent much sectional friction and sectional exploitation.

Once this foundation is securely built, the agrarian society will grow upon it spontaneously and with no further state intervention beyond that to which an agricultural population is accustomed. The old communities, the old churches, the old songs would arise from their moribund slumbers. Art, music, and literature could emerge into the sunlight from the dark cramped holes where industrial insecurity and industrial insensitiveness have often driven them. There would be a sound basis for statesmanship to take the place of demagoguery and corrupt politics. Leisure, good manners, and the good way of life might again become ours.

Frank Lawrence Owsley

The Foundations of Democracy

In his essay for Who Owns America?, *the 1936 sequel to* I'll Take My Stand, *Frank Lawrence Owsley directed his Agrarian critique at the fundamentals of the nation's political economy—as it once was and as it had become. The topic lay near to his heart, for the focus on the South's "plain folk," and his faith in a Jeffersonian yeoman state—both amply expressed here—culminated in his final work of major historical scholarship.*[1] *Relying in part on Charles A. Beard's reading of the Constitution and its flaws, Owsley advanced the radical recommendation that the entire document be scrapped. A falsely conceived instrument (beginning with its secret convention), the Constitution as Owsley saw it was so perverted by the forces of wealth and an over-active judiciary as to have lost all validity. According to his thesis, the trouble began early, with Alexander Hamilton's economic plan to encourage manufacturing; the Constitution's ill fate was sealed in 1886 when Hamilton's intellectual descendants on the Supreme Court granted the "corporation the status of a person." This perfidious sleight of hand, Owsley contended, had ever since weakened the very "keystone" of the Jeffersonian state, which was "private property, widely distributed." A new constitution would be friendly both to states' rights and to the property-owning interests of the small farmer. The ongoing crisis of the Depression amplified Owsley's natural pessimism, leading him to predict that without reform the United States would devolve into a "fascist or communist totalitarian state, which guarantees security and denies freedom."*[2]

Reprinted from *Southern Review* 1 (1936): 708–20, and *Who Owns America?* (1936), with the permission of Mrs. Harriet C. Owsley.

---

1. Owsley, *Plain Folk of the Old South* (Baton Rouge, 1949).
2. The Agrarians, along with journalist Walter Lippmann, were some of the first American intellectuals to seize upon the danger of totalitarianism, a little-used term in the 1930s. On Lippmann and other intellectuals' views of totalitarianism, see

Neither Congress, President, nor Supreme Court knows at this moment what is the Constitution of the United States; and it can hardly be proved that the remaining 130,000,000 inhabitants of the United States possess any greater certainty about their Constitution than the three departments of the Federal government which are sworn to uphold, maintain, and defend it. We are indeed in a constitutional fog which has constantly grown thicker since the original document was presented to the country for ratification in 1787.

Let me point out a few of the leading factors which have caused the people and their organs of government to become thus enveloped. It will be recalled that the convention which drew up the Federal Constitution in 1787 was in essence a revolutionary, secessionist body. Its actions were in violation of state instructions and of the Articles of Confederation, which at the time, were the Constitution of the United States. It performed its work in secret, and the document which it presented to the country in 1787, while it contained many fine principles of government, was essentially reactionary and undemocratic. The president was to be chosen by uninstructed electors, who in turn were to be chosen either by a suffrage based upon property qualifications or by state legislatures based upon a similar suffrage. The Federal senate was to be elected by these same legislatures, which usually held office—as today in many states—by the approbation of the county court or some other local political hierarchy which was in practice self-perpetuating. The Federal judiciary was to be chosen by the president with the consent of the senate. The social philosophy of the Constitution was in keeping with its undemocratic mechanism. In short, the original Constitution was so contrived as to remove the Federal government as far as possible from the sound of *vox populi* and to place it in the hands of the few men of wealth.

The vote upon this document could scarcely be called a plebiscite: out of a population of four million or more, only about 165,000 voted. Cajolery, trickery, and bribery were used to obtain ratification, and even so, the margin in favor of ratification was only a few thousand.[3] A constitution obtained by such methods and one which repudiated many of the fundamental principles for which the American Revolution had been fought only a few years before could not be regarded by its contemporaries, or by a well-informed, intelligent person today, as *sacrosanct* or as falling within the same category as the Ten Commandments.

Stephen J. Whitfield, *Into the Dark: Hannah Arendt and Totalitarianism* (Philadelphia, 1980), esp. 9–14.

3. Although Owsley drew his own, more radical conclusions, his complaints against the Constitution derive from Beard, *An Economic Interpretation of the Constitution of the United States* (New York, 1913), 324–25.

214 / *Frank Lawrence Owsley*

The impending dissolution of the American State and reconquest by England brought many liberal leaders like James Madison to support such a constitution. But even so—and despite the doubtful methods used to obtain ratification—the friends of the Constitution would have failed had they not pledged the immediate incorporation into the Constitution of the first ten amendments, which contain, to a great extent, the Bill of Rights, or the rights of man, for which the intellectual leaders of the American Revolution had contended, and for which the common man had thought the War was fought. But the incorporation of the rights of man within a document reactionary in its philosophy of human society as well as in its mechanism could only thicken the fog which had already been raised. On the face of it, it appears to have been an attempt to fuse in one short charter the philosophy of plutocracy and that of democracy, a fusion which was the impossible proverbial mixture of oil and water. In reality, as I have suggested, it was the hope of the old revolutionary leaders, soon to be called Jeffersonians, that the Bill of Rights would, by mere force of principle, correct the undemocratic features of the main body of the Constitution. Tacked on at the end and forming no organic part of the whole, the Bill of Rights was a liberal postscript added to an illiberal document.

Fortunately for the plutocratic philosophy that government is in essence the executive committee of great wealth, the Federalists, under the leadership of Alexander Hamilton, secured control of the executive branch of the government for twelve years and the legislative during most of this time. But most fortunately of all, the Federalists for forty years held possession of the judiciary, which arrogated to itself the power to declare laws of Congress unconstitutional and in general to declare the law and the Constitution. For a brief period, under Chief Justice Taney, the Jeffersonians gained control of the Court. With the Civil War the Court came again under the control of jurists who professed the Hamiltonian philosophy.[4]

After the Civil War, during so-called Reconstruction, the Federalists, now bearing the Jeffersonian name "Republican," obtained two amendments, the Fourteenth and the Fifteenth, which were intended to change, and did change to a certain extent, the fundamental nature of the original Constitution. Now, all the historians of Reconstruction except three Negro writers and one carpetbag ex-governor agree that these two amendments were incorporated into the Federal Constitution by open fraud and violence

---

4. In 1835, President Andrew Jackson appointed Marylander Roger Brooke Taney (1777–1864) to the Supreme Court to replace John Marshall. Taney's "Jeffersonianism" consisted of a higher regard for states' authority, as in the Charles River Bridge case (1837) and the Dred Scott case (1857).

supported by Federal troops in the South, and congressional legislation which even the Federalist Supreme Court would have thrown out had it not been intimidated by the Radical leaders.[5] Regardless of what may be thought of the desirability of such amendments—and that irrelevant question is not to be raised here—no self-respecting, well-informed American can look with reverence upon this portion of the Federal document. But I wish to call attention, in passing, to the fact that it is the Fourteenth Amendment which corporate wealth holds next to the Jeffersonian Fifth Amendment, most sacred and most dear. Among other things, the Fourteenth Amendment guarantees that the state can deprive no person of life, liberty, and property without due process of law. By giving a corporation the status of a person, the Federalist judiciary has caused these colossal bodies of organized wealth to become the undefeated champions of personal liberty! The irony of these two amendments is withering. One was honorably secured by the Jeffersonians as a safeguard for the liberty of the white man; the other, violently and corruptly secured by the Republicans, ostensibly in behalf of the liberty of the black man: both—like other Jeffersonian amendments in behalf of human liberty—have been erected by the Supreme Court, not into bulwarks of human freedom, but into impregnable fortresses of corporate wealth.[6]

I have pointed out, thus far, various factors which have obscured the meaning of the original Federal Constitution and the Jeffersonian amendments, and which deprive that document of any claim to sacredness: the

---

5. The consensus described by Owsley has since eroded (see Eric Foner, *Reconstruction: America's Unfinished Revolution, 1863–1877* [New York, 1988]). By "three Negro writers and one carpetbag ex-governor," Owsley likely meant W. E. B. Du Bois (*Black Reconstruction in America* [New York, 1935]), John Roy Lynch (*Facts of Reconstruction* [New York, 1913]), Carter G. Woodson (*The Negro in Our History* [Washington, D.C., 1922]), and Albion W. Tourgée, not an ex-governor but a superior court judge in North Carolina and author of *A Fool's Errand* (1879), an account of Reconstruction's racial politics.

6. In 1885, Roscoe Conkling, the former New York congressman and senator who served on the committee that drafted the Fourteenth Amendment, was arguing a railroad case before the Supreme Court. He alleged that the amendment—ostensibly written to guarantee due process and equal protection to freedmen—was in fact also designed to extend such safeguards to corporations. As "persons," corporations would thus be shielded from state and local regulatory incursions. Conkling's claim was picked up by Charles A. Beard in *The Rise of American Civilization*, 2 vols. (New York, 1927), a text Owsley knew well. The argument was reviewed and rejected in Howard Jay Graham's "The 'Conspiracy Theory' of the Fourteenth Amendment," in *Reconstruction: An Anthology of Revisionist Writings*, ed. Kenneth Stampp and Leon Litwack (Baton Rouge, 1969), 107–31. Bernard Schwarz has further contended that "corporate personality antedated the Fourteenth Amendment. . . . When the ultimate protection of person and property was transferred by the Fourteenth Amendment from the states to the nation, the

unconstitutional procedure of the Convention of 1787; the secrecy of its operations; the trickery and fraud used in the adoption of the Constitution (1787–9) and in the adoption of the Reconstruction amendments; the packing of the judiciary with Federalists when Jefferson was elected; the doubtful assumption of power by the Supreme Court to declare a Federal law unconstitutional; and above all, the interpretation placed upon the Fifth and Fourteenth Amendments. Another factor of paramount importance in darkening the glass through which we view the Constitution is, or was, the sectional interpretation of the original document. One has only to remember New England's threats of secession during the Jeffersonian Embargo, or the War of 1812, or even at the annexation of Texas; or the Southern threat of secession in the Virginia and Kentucky Resolutions, the Nullification movement, and the final secession in 1860 — all centering around the meaning of the Constitution — in order to see that sectional interpretation was a major factor up until 1865, in creating doubt as to the meaning of the Constitution.

I wish to comment further upon the role of the Supreme Court in befogging the meaning of the original Constitution and the amendments. Under the Hamiltonian philosophy that government is run for and by the rich, the supreme judiciary has stretched the Constitution of 1787 and the amendments in many different directions; meanings have been read between the lines, into the lines, and beyond the lines; lines have been added, subtracted, divided, and multiplied to fit the exigencies of the occasion and to benefit great wealth (and destroy small wealth). One reads many of these decisions and looks about himself in vain for a familiar constitutional landmark. The Constitution, he feels, has been made to serve God and Mammon, human liberty and human bondage. The Supreme Court has rendered hundreds of decisions which have defined the Constitution in all its aspects; yet, despite the fact that this high court has usually been in the hands of jurists who are disciples of Hamilton, the hundreds of decisions which it has rendered are consistent chiefly in this one principle: excessive amiability toward those who possess great wealth and great indifference toward those who own nothing or small private properties. Outside of this excessive amiability to great wealth, the decisions of the Supreme Court, which cover about twenty thousand pages and over 290 volumes, are confusion and contradiction piled upon confusion and contradiction: here we behold a constitutional tower of

---

judicial trend in favor of the corporation also became a national one." In a separate case (*Santa Clara County v. Southern Pacific Railroad Co.* [1886]) the Supreme Court relied on the amendment when it ruled in favor of the railroad (Schwarz, *A History of the Supreme Court* [New York, 1993], 169, 169n).

Babel. Yet it is these twenty thousand pages of decisions, rather than the document printed in the backs of our textbooks, which are the working constitution of the United States. It is out of this welter of decisions that the executive, legislative, and judicial branches of the Federal government select the precedents on which they estimate the constitutionality of a bill or law. It is possible, of course, to go back to the original Constitution itself and ignore the principle of *stare decisis;* but it is too much to expect of our jurists.[7] The Supreme Court has determined and will determine the constitutionality of a measure in accordance with its social and political philosophy, for the justices will have little difficulty in finding precedents to support their positions. The personnel of the great judiciary determines everything. In view of this I am strongly tempted to assert that the Constitution of the United States is not the original document adopted in 1789 or the twenty thousand pages of decisions, but the Supreme Court itself. Such an assertion would be equivalent to saying that we are living under a judicial despotism.

This perennial uncertainty as to what is our constitution has been one of the most dangerous and disruptive forces in our history; and now that the economic, social, and political systems of the world are in chaos, such uncertainty adds to the uneasiness among all classes. While the Hamiltonians have the Court today and are rejoicing that the Constitution has been saved, people are asking, "What constitution?" Tomorrow, the Jeffersonians may control the Court and save still another constitution. But eventually the fascists or communists may gain control of the Court, and what constitution will they save?

It seems impossible to escape the conclusion that we need a new constitution which will reconstruct the Federal government from center to circumference. Such a reconstruction must take into consideration the realities of American life, past and present; and one of the greatest realities is sectionalism or regionalism; and above all, it must be based upon the eternal verity that while man must eat, he does not live by bread alone.

While I wish to put myself on record here as being an advocate of the reconstruction of the American State, and most particularly the Federal judiciary

---

7. *Stare decisis* (Latin for "to abide by, or adhere to, decided cases") is the legal tradition by which courts are bound by judicial precedent (*Black's Law Dictionary,* 6th ed. [St. Paul, 1990], 1406). A strict constructionist, Owsley complained that a court invoking the principle of *stare decisis* was effectively unrestrained because the variety within existing precedent gave it an unlimited and even contradictory selection of earlier decisions by which it could be "bound."

in all its branches, it is not my purpose in this essay to propose a plan of re-construction. Rather do I wish to urge this: it is high time that we—and this applies most pertinently to our judiciary—re-examine the principles upon which the American State was founded in 1776. Lincoln and Seward,[8] as spokesmen for those interests which found the Constitution as interpreted under the Jeffersonian Chief Justice Taney too narrow for their full expansion, called upon a "higher law," and it was upon this "higher law"[9] that the Republican Party came into power. The interests which Seward consciously and Lincoln, perhaps innocently, represented were industrial and corporate wealth, located chiefly in the East. These great industrial and financial groups had set good, but ill-informed, men upon a crusade against slavery in the South, where it was already destined through economic causes to disappear rapidly.[10] The ends of abolition could not be obtained within the Constitution; so the "higher law" was invoked. It was only after Lincoln's death that it became apparent that the "higher law" had been invoked to bring freedom and happiness, not to the slave, but rather to the great bankers, railroad magnates, and industrialists—freedom to gambol between the great walls of the Fourteenth and Fifth Amendments! In short, it was in reality the industrialists and corporations who invoked the "higher law" to gain control of the national government and make it over according to their desire. The abolitionists were futile, ill-informed idealists who were ruthlessly brushed aside when their services were no longer useful.[11] Today, because we do not know what is the Constitution—unless it be the Supreme Court—and because if it were the simple document of 1787 it would be absolutely inadequate and would always have been so even during the horse-and-buggy stage, we

---

8. William H. Seward (1801–72) was a New York senator, active abolitionist, and Abraham Lincoln's secretary of state.

9. Seward coined this phrase in a speech to the Senate on 11 March 1850 on the admission of California to the Union ("Freedom in the New Territories," in *Works of William H. Seward,* 7 vols., ed. George E. Baker [New York, 1853–84], 1:74).

10. See note 17 to Owsley, "Scottsboro, The Third Crusade," reprinted here.

11. The abolitionists' historical reputation has fluctuated widely. From the turn of the century until the 1960s, historians anxious to mend the wounds of the Civil War found more in the movement to criticize than to praise. From the early 1960s until the mid-1970s, abolitionists were given a more positive reading. A later group of historians criticized them not, as Owsley did, for their radical actions, but rather for the movement's overall timidity, paternalism, and, in some cases, racism. See the introduction to Lewis Perry and Michael Feldman, eds., *Antislavery Reconsidered: New Perspectives on the Abolitionists* (Baton Rouge, 1979), vii–xvi. For a discussion of how some abolitionists made the transition from agitation to freedmen's aid, see Willie Lee Rose, "Iconoclasm Has Had Its Day: Abolitionists and Freedmen in South Carolina," in Martin Duberman,

invoke the "higher law" against those same interests who falsely invoked it to destroy the South and reduce both South and West to the status of proconsular provinces of the old Roman Empire. The "higher law" is inherent in the fundamental principles upon which the American State was founded, the early American principles which became known, as I have said, as Jeffersonian principles. It is time that we re-examine and reassess these principles. Such principles, thus disinterred, should control the constitutional reconstruction of the United States, which must ultimately come; and in the meanwhile they must be made to guide our political action and our conduct of government. Otherwise we cannot escape the communist or fascist totalitarian state.

The whole body of founding fathers subscribed to these principles, to this "higher law," some with mental reservations, others with deathless devotion. Among the greatest of these were: James Otis and Samuel Adams of Massachusetts; George Mason, Patrick Henry, James Madison, and Thomas Jefferson of Virginia; John Dickinson of Pennsylvania; and Christopher Gadsden [12] of South Carolina. The leadership of Thomas Jefferson, which lasted over half a century, attached his name to these principles. He embodies and symbolizes them. These principles upon which the American State was founded fall into one great category which in turn contains at least five cardinal principles; from these five cardinal principles numerous other principles stem like the branches of a tree. This great category was and is the absolute denial of the totalitarian state: neither kings nor parliaments, foreign or domestic, had complete sovereignty over the individual. "Thus far shalt thou go and no further" was said to government. The founding fathers drew their principles from the experience of the English race; from the Anglo-Saxon days when God was supposed to have made the laws and the king and his council only declared what they were; from the charter of Henry I, who acknowledged

---

ed., *The Antislavery Vanguard: New Essays on the Abolitionists* (Princeton, 1965), 178–205. For an overview of the movement during the war, see James B. Stewart, *Holy Warriors: The Abolitionists and American Slavery* (New York, 1976), 178–79, 192–203.

12. James Otis (1725–83) was an early spokesman for independence and a Revolutionary leader. Samuel Adams (1722–1813), a proponent of colonial independence and Revolutionary politician, later opposed the Constitution of 1787. George Mason (1725–92) wrote Virginia's Bill of Rights and advocated the addition of such a bill to the Constitution. The Revolutionary leader and orator Patrick Henry (1736–99) vehemently opposed the 1787 Constitution. The politician and Revolutionary leader John Dickinson (1732–1808) served as a delegate to the Constitutional Convention of 1787. The politician Christopher Gadsden (1724–1805) helped frame South Carolina's state constitution.

the supremacy of immemorial customs and laws; from King John, who signed the Magna Carta; and from all the kings who came after him who, in a similar fashion, admitted that their sovereignty over their subjects was limited. The jurists Coke, Littleton, and Blackstone[13] confirmed the limitation of sovereignty and Browne, Hobbes, Milton, and Locke, the philosophers, stated in broad abstract terms the theories of limited sovereignty.[14] The philosophers of the American Revolution stated these principles more clearly, and as I have said, they made these principles the foundation of the American State. They were called "natural rights." There were five great rights which no government could legitimately destroy: the right to life; the right to liberty; the right to property; the right to pursuits of happiness (so long as the exercise of this right did not encroach upon the rights of others); and the right to self-government—that is, government was made to serve man, man was not made to serve government, and when government failed to serve man it should be changed, peaceably if possible, forcibly if need be.

These principles, as I have said, were partly repudiated by Alexander Hamilton and many of his followers; but on the other hand, Jefferson and many of his colleagues clung to the original American doctrines and founded a party upon them. There can be no doubt that liberty in all its magnificent meaning was to Jefferson the greatest of the five principles; liberty was indeed the flowering, and end of being, of the other cardinal principles; freedom of thought, freedom of conscience, freedom of speech, all the things, indeed, which we call personal liberty, were parts of that freedom which Jefferson and his colleagues visualized. The other four principles were both ends in themselves and instruments by which *liberty* could be secured. What

---

13. Sir Edward Coke (1552–1634) was an English judge known for his rulings against royal prerogative and his strict devotion to common law. The jurist Sir Thomas De Littleton (1407–81) produced the earliest work on English land law, *Treatise on Land Tenure* (n.d.). The *Commentaries on the Laws of England* (4 vols., 1765–69) by the legal scholar and judge Sir William Blackstone (1723–80) propounded the legal and historical foundations of English institutions. Blackstone's work was used by generations of law students in Great Britain and the United States.

14. It is unclear whom Owsley had in mind when he listed "Browne." The Scottish philosopher Thomas Brown (1778–1820) was admired by John Stuart Mill. William Browne (?1590–1645) was a poet, not a philosopher, but Milton praised his work. Thomas Hobbes (1588–1679) outlined his political philosophy in *Leviathan, or the Matter, Form, and Power of a Commonwealth, Ecclesiastical and Civil* (1659). The poet and intellectual John Milton (1608–74) produced numerous works defending republicanism, civil liberties, and religious freedom. In his *Treatises of Government* (1690), John Locke (1632–1704) helped disseminate the idea of government for the people as opposed to the divine right of kings.

seem to be three additional principles which have been attached to Jeffersonianism almost to the exclusion of the others are state rights, strict construction, and laissez faire. Any student of Jefferson and his like-minded colleagues is aware that the doctrine of state rights was only another form for the cardinal principle of self-government. The knowledge gained from experience as English colonists demonstrated irrefutably to these men that government from a great distance, by legislators not equally affected by their laws with the people for whom they were legislating, was ignorant government because it had no understanding of the local situation; and it was despotic government because the opinion and wishes of the people for whom the laws were passed were not considered or even known. Any believer, then, in the right of a people to govern themselves would naturally adhere in the early days of our history to the doctrine of state rights. This doctrine was also an instrument by which the other Jeffersonian principles could be obtained or protected; particularly so when the Hamiltonian philosophy dominated the government. The Virginia and Kentucky Resolutions and the Nullification movement are good illustrations of the use of state rights and state sovereignty as defense weapons, for sectional protection as well as for the protection of the five cardinal principles already enumerated as the basic Jeffersonian principles.

The strict construction doctrine was primarily an instrument of defense against the Hamiltonian philosophy. Like state rights it was meant to preserve local and, therefore, self-government; and uphold the other great principles of human rights. It was not an end or a virtue in itself, for when Jefferson and his successors were in power they violated the doctrine of strict construction and added to the territory of the United States until it reached the Pacific,[15] and they undertook many other measures which only a loose construction of the Constitution could justify. What I wish to make clear is that state rights and strict construction either were aspects of the great principles of the right of self-government or were defense weapons against what the Jeffersonians believed to be inimical to the basic principles of the American State. If Jefferson and Samuel Adams were here today they would hardly be state rights advocates. They would, probably, according to their own logic, advocate *regional governments;* and realists as they were, they would hardly be able to look at the 290-odd volumes of Supreme Court decisions and remain strict constructionists. Without doubt they would de-

---

15. The Louisiana Purchase did not stretch to the Pacific Ocean, although Lewis and Clark soon reached the ocean on their expedition into Oregon Country.

mand a new constitution which guaranteed unequivocally the basic principles of democracy.[16]

Jefferson's doctrine of laissez faire, that the best government was the one which governed least, has been most ironically appropriated by the Hamiltonians, just as have been the Fifth Amendment and the Fourteenth as another sanctuary for great wealth. To hear the United States Chamber of Commerce or the House of Morgan or the Liberty League[17] quote Jefferson, whom they hate, to prove that government should not interfere with business, is the perfect example of the Devil's well-known facility in quoting Scripture. There is one part of Jefferson's statement concerning the so-called laissez faire doctrine which the corporations and their political representatives fail to quote: he specified that there should be enough government to prevent men from injuring one another. It may be supposed that in a simple agricultural society where land and natural resources were plentiful and every factory hand could quit his job and move West, little national or state government would be necessary. Such has often been the assumption of historians who have not studied closely the career of Jefferson and that of his aides. It is thus that Jefferson's so-called laissez faire doctrine has so often been explained. But a careful study of Jefferson will disclose that he found a tremendous amount of government intervention necessary, even in an agricultural society, to prevent men from injuring one another. Jefferson's career as a legislator in Virginia during the American Revolution and as President of the United States should be contemplated by those who quote the great democrat in support of the nonintervention of government. Jefferson, Pendleton, and Wythe[18] drew up a new code which was calculated eventually under the leadership of Jefferson, Mason, and Madison to revolutionize the social and economic fabric of Virginia. The laws of primogeniture and entail were abolished, with the result that a redistribution of landed property took

---

16. According to O'Brien, another call for reform that may have influenced Owsley came from political scientist William Yandell Elliott, who had taught at Vanderbilt in the 1920s and whose *The Need for Constitutional Reform: A Program for National Security* was published in 1935 (*IAS, 175*).

17. J. P. Morgan and Co., the New York banking giant, saw its power greatly diminished as a result of New Deal reforms stipulating the separation of investment and commercial banking. See Ron Chernow, *The House of Morgan: An American Banking Dynasty and the Rise of Modern Finance* (New York, 1990), xii and chap. 18. The American Liberty League was founded in 1934 by conservatives anxious to counter New Deal policies and promote free enterprise.

18. Edmund Pendleton (1721–1803), a Virginia Supreme Court judge, presided over the 1776 Virginia Convention. George Wythe (1726–1806), a signer of the Declaration of Independence and a law professor at the College of William and Mary, was previously the chancellor of Virginia.

place not unlike that which resulted from the French Revolution.[19] Jefferson was thoroughly familiar with the destruction of the yeomanry in England by entail, primogeniture, and the enclosure acts. Tidewater Virginia was in his day rapidly developing into a country not unlike England, which Goldsmith was describing as a land "where wealth accumulates and men decay."[20] Under the influence of Jefferson the Episcopalian Church was disestablished, its property appropriated; he introduced bills to establish a system of public schools the like of which had not been dreamed of since the days of Plato. He lived to see the University [of Virginia] and part of the lower system established. The embargo of 1808–1809 upon all commerce, laid down at the behest of Jefferson as president, was the strongest intervention of government in business known in American till 1917. These are fundamental illustrations of the Jeffersonian conception of the role of government in the affairs of man. He was unafraid of government except when it was in the hands of the enemies of free government.

I have said that the cardinal principles of the Jeffersonian or early American doctrines of government, were the rights to life, liberty, pursuits of happiness, self-government, and property, and that these rights were great ends in themselves, and that in turn each was an instrument to secure the others. The greatest of these instruments, indeed, the *sine qua non,* for making possible the other rights, was the right to own property. If they had thought of the great political principles enumerated as stones in the arch which upholds the state, then the Jeffersonians would have considered private property as the keystone of the arch, without which the whole thing must fall. But what was the Jeffersonian conception of private property: not great corporations, trusts, monopolies, banks, or princely estates—in brief, not great wealth concentrated in the hands of the few, but land and other property held or obtainable by all self-respecting men. Such property thus widely held must, of course, in the very nature of things be *personally controlled,* or it would cease to have much value as the basic instrumentation of the right to life, liberty, the pursuits of happiness, and self-government. The *ownership* and *control* of

---

19. Jefferson hoped that by overturning these feudal customs, America would foster a natural aristocracy based on talent, not wealth (A. Whitney Griswold, *Farming and Democracy* [New York, 1948], 42–43). Primogeniture, which required that estates be handed down intact and undivided to the eldest (male) heir, was common in the Southern colonies. Virginia, following Jefferson's urgings, outlawed the custom in 1785, and by the end of the century the rest of the states did the same. Entail limited the willing of property to any but a property-holder's blood heirs. In 1776, Virginia abolished entail and thus helped discourage the establishment of a landed aristocracy.

20. Oliver Goldsmith, *The Deserted Village* (1770), line 52. In fact, Goldsmith described an Irish, not English, village.

productive property sufficient for a livelihood gave a man and his family a sense of economic security; it made him independent; he was a real citizen, for he could cast his franchise without fear and could protect the basic principles of his government. Jefferson regarded stocks and bonds as an insecure economic basis for a free state, for even in the eighteenth century directors and presidents of corporations understood, perfectly, the art of avoiding the payment of dividends to small stockholders who had no voice in directing the management of the business. The insecurity of citizens who depended upon such property over which they no longer had control was doubtless a strong factor in the Jeffersonian advocacy of the agrarian state. Perhaps the Jeffersonians believed that city life was not a good life, but the loss of economic independence and security which accompanied this life was what made the great Virginian and his colleagues fear urbanization and look upon land as the best form of private property and the only safe basis of a free state.

The Hamiltonian conception of property was great wealth concentrated in a few hands, and he and his disciple Marshall[21] and their disciples proposed, and propose, that government and society be run in the interest of the rich and well-born.[22] Under the Hamiltonian philosophy, Dives may throw crumbs to Lazarus and permit his dogs to lick the sores of Lazarus; but that is the end of his obligation.[23]

If one combines the economic and social unbalance created by technological development with the friendliness of government to great wealth, which I have just sketched, he has in his hands the principal factors which have produced conditions from the worst consequences of which we may not be able to escape. Primarily as a result of government by and for great wealth, private property has almost been destroyed. Forty or fifty million American citizens are living on an economic level hardly more comfortable and less secure than that of the caveman of twenty thousand years ago. Another fifty million are desperately, and with a constant sense of insecurity, struggling to

---

21. The Federalist John Marshall (1755–1835) exercised his nationalist views for more than three decades as an associate and chief justice of the U.S. Supreme Court. His opinion in *Marbury v. Madison* (1801) established the principle of judicial review, thus greatly expanding the court's authority. He championed Hamilton's national economic program and struck down attempts to strengthen states' rights.

22. This depiction suggests the extent to which Owsley relied on Claude Bowers for his dichotomous (and virulently anti-Hamiltonian) view of American economic traditions. Bowers cited Hamilton's "contempt for democracy" and his "ideal of government" as "the rule of 'gentlemen'—the domination of aristocrats" (*Jefferson and Hamilton* [Boston, 1925], 29).

23. Dives is the rich man to whom the beggar Lazarus came for relief in the parable in Luke 16:19–31.

meet the daily needs of existence. Perhaps the other twenty or thirty million are living well, but I challenge that. As for the two hundred corporations and the few thousand men who own the bulk of the resources of the United States, at least it can be said that they are able to meet their desires; but they are living in great insecurity because they fear that they will be heavily taxed, and that there may be danger of communism. From top to bottom, from rich to poor, there is a feeling of insecurity. No one but a fool feels safe.

In simple words let me repeat that private property, widely distributed, which formed the basis of the early American State has all but disappeared. The keystone of the arch which supported the free state, the property state, which was able to challenge the theory of the totalitarian state, whether the absolutism of a monarch by divine rights, an absolutist British Parliament, or a modern fascist or communist state, is crumbling. With the disappearance of private property has disappeared much of the popular reverence for property. The average man does not truly know what property is. To him—in a vague way—it is something he can touch or see or comprehend with his sense; but he is dispossessed of such. Stocks and bonds and banks and securities are meaningless. He owns none and his friends own none. In any case, he has no control over his property.

The propertyless folk of Italy, Russia, Germany, and even Japan have given up claims to freedom, or any of the human rights, which the Jeffersonians thought of as the natural rights of man, in exchange for economic and social security or promise of such security. In America, where the tradition of freedom still persists, such an exchange would not be made so readily and openly; yet millions—I dare not contemplate how many millions—of Americans are this day ready to trade in (as they would trade in the battered remains of an old car which will not run and which they doubt can be made to run) the residue of abstract liberty which they still may lay claim to, in exchange for bread and circuses; and millions more are half decided, while the great mass of American people must, within no distant time, come to the conclusion that it is better to be well-fed slaves with their families secure than to cling to a freedom which leaves them upon the streets and their children to die of exposure or grow up as beggars and their franchise to be bought for a cup of coffee.

The right to life, the right to liberty, the right to the pursuit of happiness, the right to govern oneself, the right to own property—all natural rights according to the founders of America, beyond which the state cannot go, which deny the complete sovereignty of the state, must give way to the fascist or communist totalitarian state, which guarantees security and denies freedom, unless private property is put back into the hands of the disinherited American people.

John Crowe Ransom

Land! An Answer to
the Unemployment Problem

*In the early 1930s, John Crowe Ransom, who had become increasingly interested in
the study of economic theory, began work on a book titled* Land! *He completed part
of the manuscript in Great Britain while he was spending a year as a Guggenheim Fellow and delivering a series of highly successful public lectures on economics. The popularity of Ransom's economic theories did not, however, extend to the American publishers to whom he submitted his new work. At least three firms—Harcourt, Harper's,
and Scribners—rejected* Land! *Reluctantly, Ransom was forced to admit that he
did not have "the economist's air, flair, style, method, or whatnot." Forecasting his
growing disillusionment with agrarianism, he mused, "I'd better stick to poetry and
aesthetics."*[1]

Before abandoning Land! *in late 1932, Ransom published excerpts from the manuscript in periodicals. In the following essay, he lamented the conversion of America's
agricultural lands into large, profit-oriented businesses run by capitalistic farmers
forced to take on debilitating debt. Ransom blamed unemployment—a related problem in his view—on industrialists such as Henry Ford, whom he believed had lured
independent, "homemaking" farmers into overproductive factories only to lay them off.
(In another article adapted from his proposed book, Ransom outlined tax incentives*

---

1. Ransom to Tate, 19 May [1932], in *Selected Letters of John Crowe Ransom*, ed.
Thomas Daniel Young and George Core (Baton Rouge, 1985), 208; we have also drawn
from Thomas Daniel Young, *Gentleman in a Dustcoat: A Biography of John Crowe Ransom*
(Baton Rouge, 1976), 228–69, and O'Brien, *IAS*, 127–28.

for non-commercial agrarianism in order to preserve soil, curb production, and keep prices high without the direct government interference that became central to the New Deal. Farmers could then be "happy.")[2] *However prescient Ransom's indictment of industrial America and its impact on agriculture, his assessment of farm life during the Great Depression is more wishful than factual. The farmers he idealizes magically acquire fertile lands immune not only to the unpredictability of nature, but to economic reality.*

Reprinted from Harper's Magazine 165 (1932): 216–24.

Humanitarians are much concerned with relieving the unemployed, in the sense of finding money and handing it to them to live on. That is the least we can do for them at the moment. But economists are concerned with restoring them to livelihood and making it unnecessary to resort to philanthropic drives for their relief. More employment for the unemployed, less employment for the humanitarians.

Let us conceive the economic problem of our society in its simplest sense as an occupational problem: how to find occupation for those who have none and how to find remunerative occupation for those whose occupation has become only a formal or waiting one. The chief desideratum of any political economy at this moment is to assign a really economic function to every member of the economic society.

We are an overproductive society. Our productive plant on its capital side is overbuilt and has too many owners to support, and on the side of working personnel it is overmanned and has too many employees to support. I do not mean necessarily that our overproduction is an absolute one, a production of more goods than people need or more goods than people will some day, under happier conditions, be able to buy. But it is an effective one, since we evidently produce more goods than we can make the money to buy! How this paradoxical situation can be is a puzzle, and I shall not waste a moment in offering my analysis when the best economists are not agreed in theirs. I shall only suggest that one occupation is quite available for those of us who need it, and that, in fact, it is where we are least likely to look for it, or right under our noses.

Before naming it precisely, I should like to ask the question, From where did all these superfluous men, now squeezed out of their nominal occupations, originally come? The number of them is large, but they are the excess of workers in a plant that is huge. This plant produced in 1928, the last full year of our prosperity, something like five times as much as its nearest com-

---

2. Ransom, "Happy Farmers," *AR* 1 (1933): 513–35.

petitor. It had expanded to these proportions rather rapidly, making tremendous drafts as it did so upon a manpower somewhere that it needed for operation. It recruited from several different sources. There was first of all the "natural increase" in the given industrial population. But this was far behind the rate of increase which the expanding plant demanded. There was immigration, which recruited from European populations on a very large scale. Even so, the immigrants who entered the American labor market were not, after a certain point, the chief source of supply and as a matter of fact, they finally ceased to be needed at all. After the World War we legislated immigration nearly out of existence. Already we were feeling crowded, and the problem of occupation was presenting itself. Another accession of personnel was that made by the negro. In increasing numbers the negroes left the South and entered the industrial occupations of the East and Middle West. They made a considerable item.

But the chief source of manpower for our scheme of production was unquestionably the native American population that had been living quietly and a little bit primitively on the farms. The accession made by the negroes belongs really under this head, for they came out of country life. It was because the old-fashioned farmers of America went industrial, and migrated in a steady stream to the towns, that the capitalistic community was finally swamped beneath a personnel greater than it could assimilate to its economy. That, I think, is a fact worth pondering when we study the grievous failure of occupation today.

In theory the farmers were well within logic in making the move. It promised to increase their own personal fortunes and, incidentally, the wealth of the nation at large. Industry is more productive than old-fashioned farming. But unfortunately it sometimes proves too productive; it steps up production faster than it can develop its market. Capitalistic society has not learned how to operate its productive plant smoothly, but is subject to dislocations and stoppages that cost the economic lives of many of its members. The old-fashioned farmers in joining this society were gambling a secure if modest living against a precarious prospect of wealth, and for some of them it now definitely turns out to have been a poor gamble. There was room in the productive plant for some of them, but not for all who crowded into it. They taxed its accommodations, and presently it broke down under the strain.

But let bygones be bygones. The question is, What will these unwanted industrialists do next?

It is only on its present scale, of course, that the occupational problem is a new one. It used to be easy for the man whose occupation failed him to fall back upon another one which made all comers welcome and which he could reasonably count upon to support him. What was the admirable occupation which was always ready in this manner to save the economic society from its own mistakes? Nothing more or less than agriculture—the common occupation, or the staple one, even in a society which had developed many; and by long odds the most reliable one, or the stable one.

Let us imagine the old-fashioned country community of size enough to make a fairly self-contained economic unit. The bulk of its population consisted of farmers, who took their necessities from the land for immediate use. They found it too laborious, however, to practice a perfect self-sufficiency, and so they developed a capital city, or a country town, to which they sold some of their produce, and from which in turn they bought the services necessary to complement their own labors. We speak of self-sufficient farmers, but we must understand that never in American history, at least since the earliest pioneer days, have the farmers been entirely self-sufficient. Nobody wanted them to be. In addition to feeding themselves, they had to feed the business and professional populations of the towns. They made the staples of their own living, but they made some money crops besides and sold them. They took their stuff to town, and with the proceeds of sale they secured their law and government, their professional needs, their tools and machine-made articles, the sugar and coffee and spices or other primary products which they could not take from their own soil; and they even made transactions with one another in the native products of the region. Some of these services had to come, of course, from larger towns elsewhere and from remote countries, and implied the national and international economic order, which was a money order. But the national and international order was fairly subordinate to the agrarian or community order in that the main reliance of the citizens was upon their own home-made products; and in a pinch they could manage with these alone.

Suppose now that a bright farmer felt it to his taste to stop farming and set up as a merchant in the town. He would be abandoning his self-sufficiency in favor of an economy in which he must live by trade and patronage rather than by the direct fruit of his labors; he would become a social creature rather than an independent. But the town with its friendly human relations was not foreign to him altogether. He was throwing himself upon the mercy of a small homely society, not a great impersonal one. Nevertheless, the town might not really need another merchant; in which case he would struggle for a time, doing damage meanwhile to other merchants, but eventually might have to admit failure and give up his business. Where would he go? There is no doubt that the community would expect him, and if necessary assist him, to go back to farming; and the land, when the prodigal returned to it, would be as kind as if he had never left it. So far as America is concerned, there always was land enough for him to till; there was no such problem as overpopulation. The sons of the landed aristocrats, who were sometimes numerous, might not inherit as much land as they wanted, and some of them were rather expected to go into business and the professions. But when they failed they could always return to the land in some sort of capacity. They could go to the frontier and take up large areas of free or cheap land if they felt so ambitious, but it was not necessary to feel too sorry for them if they went home into a humbler status. Many professional men played both ends of the economic game, and did not know whether they were professional men and, therefore, retainers of society, or independent planters. The commonest kind of intuition, reinforced by the voice of tradition, told them they had better not get too far from the land. It was a landed community.

The country towns of an older generation—the English used to refer to them very accurately as "market" towns—have changed beyond knowing, which is to say that they have about vanished from the American scene, the casualty of a great economic "advance." The farmer who now goes to town to start in business does not set up his own store so often as he accepts employment with a national chain or a big concern whose business is national though its plant may be situated in the town. Big business has succeeded little business, and the town is caught up into the cycle of the national economy, prospering as it prospers and going down when it has a depression. It has scarcely any control over its own economic life. It is only an outpost of empire. And no farmer moving to town today will be making himself a member of a kindly, independent, and shock-proof society. He will fail in business when everybody is failing, and the day when the failures came one at a time and could be absorbed by the community has gone perhaps forever. Let us not take the time to mourn for the lost town.

But the land is with us still, as patient and nearly as capable as ever. This brings us to the query: Why is not the land perfectly available today for its ancient use as a refuge individually for those who have failed in the business economy, when such a refuge is needed as never before?

It is still available. That is the answer, though nobody is prepared to believe it. We no longer think kindly of the land when we think as economists, and we would look almost anywhere else first for our economic salvation. That is because we have seen the landed life in our time degraded and its incomparable economic advantage disused and nearly forgotten. There is just one thing that town men know for certain about the contemporary farmer: that he has the most underpaid occupation in our whole society. The farm owners stagger under mortgages and produce crops often in spite of the fact that the prices they receive will not pay the cost of production. Their employees are lower than the robots of the cheapest factories in the wage scale, lower than the women in the sweatshops. But behind this condition is a price of ruinous economic folly.

The American farmers in "going productive" did a thorough job of it; they went in more senses than one. Some of them, as we have seen, made a clean break with the land and went into the factories and offices of the towns. But even those who stayed at home ceased to farm in the old self-subsistent way, by which they had made a living first and a money crop second; now they began to devote themselves exclusively to their money crops, expecting to take the money and buy themselves a better living out of the stores than they could have made with their own hands. Think of farmers buying hams and bacon, garden stuff, eggs and butter, jams and pickles and preserves, and labor to whitewash their fences, prop up their porches, and prettify their lawns! Townspeople have always bought such things, but it is a novelty for farmers. Nothing less than an economic revolution swept over the American farms. It consisted in the substitution of the capitalistic or money economy for the self-subsistent or agrarian economy. The change, like the migration to a town, required a period rather than a single date; it was under way when the War began and it was virtually complete when the world settled down to peace.

The capitalistic, or money economy, is "efficient" on the farm as it is in the factory. It implies specialization of function rather than the completeness and independence of the individual, each function contributing to the whole and taking its remuneration in money. When applied to farming, it assigns to each piece of land its special use, equips its farmer with the best tools to work it regardless of expense, and expects him to devote himself with perfect concentration to obtaining maximum output in the specified product. If a nation is rather short of a supply of land, capitalistic farming will make the most of what there is, and old-fashioned agrarian farming cannot be tolerated because it is wasteful. The old farmer, whose object was first of all to supply himself, and only then to cater to a market, was a sort of Jack-of-all-trades, like some strange producer who had elected to run a one-man factory, and consumed his own production. That is not the scientific or modern theory of business, which means essentially big business, and is based on the willingness of everybody to forego producing his own independent living and to produce something strictly to sell to others, even at the risk of disaster when his particular product cannot be sold. The difference in efficiency between the two economies on the land is such that the following is scarcely an exaggeration of facts already exhibited: the same land might support a million self-subsistent farmers, or it might support a society of twice the number if farmed properly for money, and yet require only five hundred thousand of them to live and work on the land, leaving the other million and a half to perform the more industrial functions in the towns; and the latter society would be not only richer in the aggregate, but richer in per capita wealth. That is a familiar type of argument and lies either as an intuition or as an open theory behind our whole capitalistic development.

But it would be miraculous if every new member of the capitalistic society should fly unerringly to his proper economic station and live there and prosper forever. There are a great many mistakes made in assigning the occupations in so intricate a society, and a great many persons get hurt. The ex-farmers who went to town know all about that. But what happens now to the farm population that is left, reduced though it may be, when it repudiates the old way of farming for independence and security and applies the money economy finally, and rigorously, to the land itself?

Farming exhibits now a greater percentage of failures, or a greater excess of personnel, than any other large American occupation. Farmers are not able to go to the stores with money jingling in their pockets to buy freely of the comforts and decencies of life. Their houses are tumbling down in a manner which would have mortified their grandfathers, because with all their money-cropping they have not made the money to hire the carpenter and the painter. They furnish their tables in a style quite unworthy of the tradition of farmers' plenty. They worry themselves to death over their unhappy relations with the bank or the loan company that holds the mortgage, and the hardware firm that equipped the farm with modern machinery. And all this was true in 1928 as well as in 1931. Ever since the farmers became money-makers they have had nothing but unsuccess. We were reading about the farmers' sufferings long before the papers began to fill up with news of a depression for everybody. The farmers have complained of their situation, naturally, and loudly, and there is plenty of sympathy for them, or was at least before everybody had troubles of his own. But every reform movement which they advocate, or which their economist patrons advocate for them, is only another artificial and privileged way to make more money than they can possibly make under the natural operation of economic laws.

There is a simple reason why farming as money-making, or as an industry conceived in terms of capital and income, cannot flourish in America. This industry is overcapitalized and overproductive from the beginning; all the tillable land is in capital, and its productive capacity is two or three times greater than its market. Under these circumstances an excess of farm products, and therefore an excess of farmers, is not the exception but the rule.

The capitalistic doctrine, nevertheless, swept all before it in America, including at last the farmers. It was perhaps not so strange if farmers grew envious of the quick wealth it created, tired of their home-made security, and trekked in ever larger numbers to the city; or even if, where they stayed on the land, they applied to it at last the capitalistic technique and farmed it exclusively for money. But it was also not strange if, when they had made a capital instrument out of their land, they found it so unprofitable that their migration cityward was accelerated; economic compulsion was behind that. Almost any other occupation looked better than farming to the amateur capitalistic economist.

At this moment, however, an alteration has come over the economic landscape. The money-making farmers, who are making no money, are looking as usual at the other occupations to see if there is no room for them somewhere else, while the other occupations are looking back at the farmer and wondering if there is really no chance on the farm, with neither party finding the slightest ground for encouragement. There is no migration from the farm to the city because the city has no more occupation to spare. And there is little enough migration in the opposite sense; yet there is a little. Some eccentric persons move to the country to escape from an overproductive society and make a primitive living in comparative peace. More important than that, proposals are heard now and again in America for the relief of some local unemployment by colonizing the unemployed on the nearest unoccupied land; precisely the thing which the Austrian government is said to be doing, and some of the unemployment committees of the German municipalities, though land is rather scarce in Germany.

In just such a movement as this lies, I think, our readiest and surest economic deliverance provided we will conceive it on a large scale and work it hard. We shall not be making much use of it so long as we think of it as a makeshift measure which for the time being will furnish the needy with some wretched and uncomfortable sort of subsistence that is better than starvation. I am afraid that it is felt that a man reduced to raising his own potatoes and chickens has about the rating of the cow turned out to pasture; which is rather ridiculous considering the generations of men who, till quite recently in the world's history, lived in what they often regarded as comfort and dignity on the soil without the use of a great deal of money for purchasing goods upon the market.

We have unsuccessful men of business today, but we have more of them, for reasons not subject to their determination; but that does not matter. Such men used to go back and be reabsorbed in the landed occupation they had come from. It is precisely what they should do today. It is hard to say why they do not, in numbers sufficient to make a movement, except that they, and we who might be helping them, now understand the landed occupation in an improper sense. But that misunderstanding, though it is general, can be remedied.

I venture to suggest to the patriots and economists that they try to re-establish self-sufficiency as the proper economy for the American farm, and thus save the present farmers; and at the same time try to get back into this economy as many as possible of the derelicts of the capitalistic economy who are now stranded in the city. I suggest an agrarian agitation, sponsored by people who may speak with authority, and leading to action on the part of people who are already on the land or who may return there.

I have defined a general proposition briefly, and I shall add only a few remarks in detail. But I mean economic remarks strictly. It is tempting to write like a poet, philosopher, or humanist about the aesthetic and spiritual deliverance that will come when the industrial laborers with their specialized and routine jobs and the business men with their offices and abstract preoccupations become translated into people handling the soil with their fingers and coming into direct contact with nature. There are virtues special to the landed life that will always appeal powerfully to certain temperaments. But there is enough merit in an agrarian movement if it will perform the pure economic service of restoring the superfluous men to livelihood.

I remark first that the new agrarian farmers will be the most innocent and esteemed members of the economic society because they alone will not injure one another through crowding and competition. If there is land for all, they cut nobody's throat by farming it in this way; and in America there is land for all. Any man who temperamentally cannot bear to hurt his needy neighbor by holding on to his economic function had better take to the agrarian way of living, and any political economist who deplores the inevitable inhumanity of the competitive scramble at such times as these might well approve a movement which is capable of enlisting productive personnel and planting it in an economy which is not essentially competitive.

We shall always have a capitalistic, or money-making, community, herding for the most part in cities, even though this fraction of the population may be due for a permanent reduction. The members of this community will attend to their respective specialties, and they will have to buy food and farm stuffs, which means that in the future, as in the past, the farmers will sell their country wares in the city and buy capitalistic products with the money. In other words, whether farmers are on the capitalistic or the agrarian basis, they will sell produce and make money. But probably they will be able to sell about the same amount of stuff one way as the other. Though they turn and spend all their time on their money crops, they do not as a class sell any more, as the event has abundantly proved. This is a fact for farmers to ponder both individually and collectively.

Nearly every economist in prescribing for the present distress of farmers feels obligated to advise that they reduce their acreage and cut down a production which is always an overproduction. Both experience and logic would suggest that this advice is thrown away; it cannot be taken so long as farming is conducted for money alone. You cannot ask some of them to go out of business and commit economic suicide in order that the others may prosper. The only way to reduce production is to get them to do something else instead which it would pay them to do. This something else, according to an agrarian theory, is the business of supplying just as much of their own living as they reasonably can. It is an undertaking that would be progressive as they learned to secure new articles of food and new conveniences of living of the homemade kind. Having this sort of occupation in the first place, the individual farmer would reduce the volume of his market production with advantage to himself; and in the degree that the agrarian doctrine spread there would be just that cut in national farm production which the economists covet.

A better job of agrarianism ought to be done today than formerly, because the technique both of farming and of living has advanced. I am not content to use the "argument from our grandfathers" which is to the effect that if our grandfathers could wrest their living from the soil, so can we. We should improve on them. To go agrarian may yet become for many people the regular alternative to starvation, but it will scarcely arouse enthusiasm if it means that they must live like primitives, or frontiersmen, or even grandfathers.

The difference lies in the advance of the industrial revolution, and the almost universal distribution of its benefits. Most occupations are less laborious because of new machines and processes, and domestic life is furnished with new conveniences. There is no reason why the farmer should not take some advantage of the improvement. It is true that modern equipment for his farm and his house will hardly consist in articles which can be homemade; they are the products strictly of capitalistic industry, and cost money; and the agrarian farmer will always have less money at his disposal than a man of equal intelligence and zeal in some capitalistic occupation. The commodities that the farmer will want to purchase are such as electricity and water supply, truck and pleasure car, radio, modern farm machinery. It would be arbitrary to say in advance that all of these commodities are out of his reach. It is only necessary to say that he must go slowly, not expect to get everything at once, do without any item that he cannot afford, and *try to keep out of debt*. Indebtedness for indiscreet purchases of modern products has doubtless been the ruination of as many farmers as the deliberate adoption of revolutionary farming theory. When a farmer is deeply in debt he is obliged, no matter what his theory of farming may be, to think about increasing his money crops in order to pay out and keep the title to his land; though the likelihood is that he will thereby lose it.

Mr. Ford[3] is an indefatigable amateur economist as well as a master professional capitalist. He has expressed himself about the farm problem, as all economists do sooner or later, and his proposition is that the farmers may expect to prosper when they not only raise their crops in the growing seasons, but work in factories in the winter. It is a good proposition to lay down as a basis of discussion, and I shall compare it briefly with the agrarian proposal.

It implies in the first place that a farmer's crops do not give him a year-round occupation, and do not afford him a sufficient income. Mr. Ford is thinking of money farmers, and for that kind of farmers the point must be granted. He would supplement their farming with industrial occupation in the hope that by having two alternating occupations they could be as fully occupied and in receipt of an appropriate income.

The proposal that farmers go agrarian contains a similar implication. They do their money crops very well indeed, and it is hard work while it lasts, but it leaves them with insufficient income to go through the winter on. But if the farmer does not stop with his money crop, or does not even start there, but produces whatever he can for his own consumption, winter consumption included—if he is his own carpenter, painter, roadmaker, forester, meat packer, woodcutter, gardener, landscape gardener, nurseryman, dairyman, poulterer, and handy man—then he has a fair-sized man's job on his hands which will occupy him sufficiently at all seasons. His hard work will come in the spring and summer, but if his work slackens after that, no confirmed lover of nature will begrudge him a little leisure time for hunting, fishing, and plain country meditation. Though his factory occupation might bring in a little revenue equal or even superior to buying those services which he would otherwise supply with his hands directly, it would present the objection that it would be altogether different from his normal occupation and possibly distasteful. He would be partly a farmer and partly an industrialist, which would seem to be tending to an unnatural disintegration of his personality.

---

3. Henry Ford (1863–1947) was a Michigan-born automaker, philanthropist, and Ford Motor Company president. With the assistance of Samuel Crowther, Ford wrote a series of self-aggrandizing books in which he celebrated industrial mechanization and pontificated on the American economy. The Agrarians would have found distressing any number of passages in these books.

But the conclusive argument against the Ford farm plan is that it does not relieve but aggravates the present economic situation, of which the distressing feature is unemployment due to overproduction. In what factories would the farmers elect to labor? Hardly in the Ford factories, for Mr. Ford is periodically obliged, like other owners, to lay off a great many of his own men. An agrarian movement would aim not only at providing for the farmers without increasing their production or decreasing their number, but even at taking superfluous or unemployed men out of the industrial community and off the consciences of their former employers. Mr. Ford would save the farmers only at the expense of his own or somebody's factory employees, but an agrarian plan would expect to save the farmers and the Ford employees too.

A last remark—about America and her future. Is there no relation between the economic destiny of these States and their peculiar natural resources? We have a large population, but an area more than large enough for it, and well blessed in soil and climate. The acreage in fact is excessive if we intend to put it to work producing foodstuffs and raw materials scientifically and capitalistically like a factory; on that basis the country population which tends it is overproductive and the victim of insufficient occupation in the strictest economic sense. But nothing could be more absurd to the bird's-eye view of some old-fashioned economic realist than the phenomenon of men actually sitting down to unemployment in the country; though he might expect some unemployment in the cities, which have grown like mushrooms. What then, is our land good for? Is it for picnics and camping parties, is it for scenery? Is it for Boy Scouts to play on? It used to be thought good for homes. Unfit for intensive money-making, because of its very excellence and abundance, it is ideal for homemaking. That happens to be the very thought which inspired the fathers to found the colonies, then the Union, then one by one the successive new States. It is remarkable that an admirable and obvious thought like that should ever have slipped out of our notice, but it will be as good as ever if we will entertain it again. There is nothing the matter with it. Perhaps we shall like it better when we set it beside the thought that not all the nations have such a brilliant opportunity as we do. In Britain, for example, they cannot afford agrarianism; they have not the land to provide homes for all that need them; and I, and most people, are sorry. In America we may realize an economic destiny more secure than has generally been allotted to the people of this earth.

John Crowe Ransom

Sociology and the Black Belt

*A number of essays in this collection display the Agrarians' suspicion of sociology —
both as a method for understanding cultures generally, and specifically as a tool
for highlighting Southern "problems." John Crowe Ransom's review of* Shadow of the
Plantation—Charles S. *Johnson's study of black citizens of Macon County, Alabama—stands in marked contrast to Donald Davidson's reviews of other sociological
forays into Dixie.*[1] *Johnson tabulated statistics describing family, economic, educational, and health characteristics of the black population, but he interspersed such
facts with the words of individual residents. Their voices were, and remain, potent.
Caught off guard, Ransom was swept into the poetry and excruciating sorrow expressed
in one mother's narrative of her child's death, probably of syphilis. While he did not
take up the crux of Johnson's argument—that the county's contemporary economic life
and race relations "were set in the economy of slavery,"*[2] *having come down through
the generations, almost unaltered, from antebellum times—Ransom confessed that
"the reader, perhaps unexpectedly, finds in himself a complete sympathy with these
black folk, and a respect for their dignity." The "sympathy" did not, however, trans-
late into agreement for Ransom. Whereas Johnson looked toward national social reform and economic relief as the most promising way to improve his subjects' lives, Ransom offered Agrarianism, for, he contended, "it is the intrusion of industrial action . . .
that has produced the present situation."*

Reprinted from *American Review* 4 (1934): 147–54.

---

1. See the preface and note 3 to Davidson, "Sociologist in Eden," and Nixon,
"Southerntown," reprinted here.

2. Johnson, *Shadow of the Plantation* (Chicago, 1934), 16.

Even the general reader would accord several stars of merit to Professor Johnson's *Shadow of the Plantation;* all the more gladly considering its classification. It is a sociological survey, but not an ordinary performance in that character.

A survey of what? Of precisely 612 Negro families and quasi-families, mostly cotton workers, in a section of Macon County, Alabama, with respect to such broad features as domestic relations, economic life, schooling, religion, play, and health.

Professor Johnson has accomplished a masterpiece of fact-finding. He concludes his chapters of fact, where it is possible, with tabulations. But the evidence and the tabulations are about all; he offers few comments, and may be said to be extremely chary of generalizations. He brings in Doctor Robert E. Park, a veteran sociologist, to undertake the Introduction, which presents the general concepts. Doctor Park is eligible for this task for two good reasons: he is one of those who think out the philosophy of sociology, having both inspired and indoctrinated many of our younger social workers in his former classes at the University of Chicago; and he knows Macon County, having once been at Tuskegee in that county, and served as Booker Washington's right hand.[3]

To confess here to a misgiving. Perhaps the present reviewer is not the right man for this book, being habitually a little irritated with sociologists. But it may be that this irritation is not entirely without objective foundation. Sociology is at the same time a struggling infant science and, by strong preference, a self-contained one. Its devotees do not always bother much about a background. It possesses for their discipline no dialectical tradition like that which keeps in the straight path a philosopher, or a philologist, or a natural scientist, or even a literary critic.

The apprehensions which another sociological treatise arouses in the critical reader are at least partly realized in this Introduction. Doctor Park is a good writer, if it is possible to say so with the reservation that he is still a sociological one; that is, one who uses a highly technical jargon and yet manages to write loosely.

For instance, he makes a wise and admirable observation when he writes: "It is evident, in spite of all that has been written of human nature and of human behavior, that the sources of joy and sorrow are still obscure. It is

---

3. Park (1864–1944) was not only the leading sociologist at the University of Chicago, which dominated the field until after World War II, but was also Johnson's former professor. Johnson received his Ph.D. from Chicago in 1922. For more on Park, see Fred H. Matthews, *Quest for an American Sociology* (Montreal, 1977).

evident also that, as Stevenson says . . . 'to miss the joy is to miss all.'"[4] One would not think it necessary to improve on [Robert Louis] Stevenson's saying. But the godless Stevenson has to be translated into sociology, with the following effect: "That is to say, if you miss the joy you miss the one aspect of a people's life which more than anything else gives vitality to cultural forms and ensures their persistence, possibly in some new and modified form, under changed conditions" [xvi]. The elaboration here is by way of pure invention; it is such writing that makes hard reading, and an esoteric "literature," out of sociology even when it is substantively thin. Does sociology exist by virtue of the multiplication of entities beyond necessity? It is too easy to catch it in the act of watering its stock.

But this passage is connected with the development of an important topic: the meaning of caste. Whether it is due to the excellence of his own intuitions, or to his professional ideology, Doctor Park makes what in substance is a fine statement, and says what looks like the ultimate truth:

> It has been observed that as long as their social institutions are functioning normally, primitive peoples ordinarily exhibit an extraordinary zest in the life they lead, even when that life, like that of the Eskimo in the frozen North or the pigmies in the steaming forest of Central Africa, seems to be one of constant privation and hardship.
>
> On the other hand, when some catastrophe occurs which undermines the traditional structure of their society, they sometimes lose their natural lust for life, and that euphoria which enabled them to support the hardships of their primitive existence frequently deserts them. That catastrophe may be, and frequently is, the sudden advent of a more highly civilized people intent upon their improvement and uplift by incorporating them in a more highly organized industrial society.
>
> Under such circumstances, a people may be so completely obsessed by a sense of their own inferiority that they no longer desire to live as a people; and if they live as individuals, they will prefer to identify themselves, as far as they are permitted to do so, with the invading or dominant people.
>
> It is in some such way as this, i.e., by the incorporation of defeated or merely disheartened people into some larger and more complex social unit, that castes are formed. [xv–xvi]

---

4. Robert Louis Stevenson (1850–94), the Scottish novelist and poet, was most famous for his masterful storytelling in *The Strange Case of Dr. Jekyll and Mr. Hyde* (1886) and *Kidnapped* (1886). The Stevenson phrase quoted by Johnson and, in turn, by Ransom is from "The Lantern Bearers," reprinted in *Robert Louis Stevenson, 1850–1894, Works*, 24 vols. (1909), 15:247.

Here we have the essential inner tragedy of the Negro's present condition, and it may be of his permanent destiny, in our America.

Professor Johnson's exhibit, which is the body of the book, is a distinguished one. The distinction does not lie exactly in the thoroughness and orderliness of his facts, nor in the sociological presuppositions, though these seem perfectly competent. It lies in the peculiar quality of document used to attest his facts; Doctor Park defines and commends it as a "human" document. Professor Johnson gives the direct testimony of the Negroes whom he has questioned. He is obviously a man of rare tact to have elicited it, and he has the good taste to give it in the vernacular, not censored, and not whittled down to fit the topic under discussion. The effect is more like that of an art than of a science: sociological interest gives way and aesthetic understanding is born; and the reader, perhaps unexpectedly, finds in himself a complete sympathy with these black folk, and a respect for their dignity. If this is sociology, then sociology is something less than a science, but at the same time it is something a good deal more. For it is a technique of impression and feeling rather than moralization and will, and its project is wide and difficult at the cost of being not entirely practical. A pure science cannot afford to objectify its material as faithfully as this.

Sometimes a single piece of testimony illuminates a whole group of abstract topics—"mortality, morbidity, illegitimacy, illiteracy, poverty, insufficiency of food and clothing" [204]. I quote a part of one statement:

> When my third baby was coming, his father jumped up and married another girl. She was in a family way and I wondered why he married her 'cause she was in a family way and he didn't marry me when I was in a family way too. This girl was a school teacher and he married her one month before she got down. Then when he started coming back round, I told him, "I ain't going to fool with you no more; you done fooled me enough." I got real mad. I got mad about him, so I told him to stay away 'cause I felt bad about it . . . and I was 'specting to marry him.
>
> He left here and went to Montgomery. Then he sent me money to come to him but I was so hungry that I took the money and bought us something t'eat. I guess I'd a went if we hadn't been so hungry. After he married, he would give me rice and things for the chillen every time he saw me in town. He just seemed to be in love with the chillen. They say now that he is living with another woman. His wife died when she was getting down the second time. He had left and went to Montgomery to work but they wasn't separated. It was after she died that he sent for me to come to him. . . .
>
> Just when I thought I got my chillen well, my oldest boy died. He just rotted to death. This is how he got sick. He started with a headache. He said

his head nearly bust open and Br'er got some salts and give him and he didn't complain no more for about two weeks; then he went to school one morning and the next morning they didn't have no school and he got up and it started with a hurting right here (just inside the elbow bend). He said it was itching first, then hurting, and he just starting running 'round having fits. He just went crazy. We rubbed and greased his arms and we rubbed him good, but he just went crazy and tore up the things in the house. The doctor give him some medicine when we took him to him and he said it was pellagacy but I ain't seed where it done him a bit of good. He told one man down here that it was the curriest pellagacy he ever seed in his life, and he told somebody up there that he didn't know what it was; but he told me it was pellagacy.[5] Well, that boy would run away and I'd hear him calling way up on the hill. He just come unjointed. It all just rotted off—all his hands and arms. He bit one of his fingers off and he never was in his right mind after he first went crazy. He would take the bed down and when you ask him what he was doing it for, he'd say he wanted to put it up on a hill. He swold up and just come in two. He died in two weeks.

When I got sick I went to Dr. —— and he told me I needed shots but that he couldn't give them to me 'cause I wasn't able to pay. He asked me if I had any property and I told him no. He said he just couldn't give 'em to me then. He said, "If you just had a cow to put up against it!" [205–6]

To have presented this material would seem to be, primarily, a literary achievement. But sociology intends to be, one supposes, for the most part, a science; it has practical aims. So here is a wretched population inviting improvement; where shall we begin? Most of us would proceed at once to the character of the economic determination behind this sort of exhibit.

Professor Johnson devotes much attention to presenting fairly the facts of the economic status of the black cotton worker. He is usually a tenant farmer, still entangled in the plantation system—a system which flourished, if it ever flourished, a hundred years ago and now is in complete decay. The condition of Southern tenant farmers, both white and black for that matter, is economically the lowest to be found in America, and constitutes the most urgent of all our permanent economic problems.

Analysis has not generally proved so easy as to render Professor Johnson's admirable account commonplace. The Negro tenant is sometimes simply exploited by his unscrupulous landlord; but perhaps not generally;

---

5. The sharecroppers Johnson studied were plagued by pellagra, a potentially fatal vitamin B deficiency generally brought on by a corn diet. In fact, as Johnson suggested, the child probably suffered from congenital syphilis.

the author thinks that this is not quite the account of the matter, as a whole. The Negro tenant is the victim of the plantation system, and it is symbolized for him in his landlord. But the landlord in his turn is the victim of the same system, and it is symbolized for him in his banker. And it might be too naive to stop there, and to identify the system at last with the banker's evil machinations; for the banker may be himself a helpless victim of the system, with a bogey of his own to fear. What then is the plantation system? A casualty of our money economy; that is, of our modern industrial system; that is, of that blind economic organization which governs almost the whole of our business life, and has the following characteristics: defining narrowly the income-producing functions, and turning all the members of society into functionaries dependent on money-income; then tending increasingly to make one big business world out of all the little business communities until it is impossible for the functionaries to figure their markets, or even to find the responsible parties with whom they might hold discussion, make agreements, and lodge complaints. Here I suppose I go beyond Professor Johnson's analysis, but I do not in any sense controvert him.

What is to be done about it? Sociologists rarely speak as economists; but here is a case where sociology must wait on economics; probably going on making other surveys in the meantime, for I have heard it observed that of the making of surveys there is in sociology no end. The practical conclusions which Doctor Park reaches upon reading this book are as follows:

> What the findings of this survey suggest, then, is: (1) the necessity of a wider—in fact, a world-wide—and comparative study of the cotton plantation not merely as an economic and industrial but as a cultural unit; and (2) a comparative study of the actual conditions of the world in which people on the plantation live. [xxii]

That seems rather pusillanimous. A non-sociologist is in a position to pay a higher compliment to Professor Johnson's book, by saying that it carries conviction and suggests the need, not necessarily of further books, but of a little action. Of political-economic-social action, comprehensive, "totalitarian"; the hardest kind of action to which in our modern enfeeblement we could turn. If the section is still capable of action, then it will never find a better occasion for it than here in the plight of the tenant farmers, black and white. But it is clear that effective action will have to be of that tenor known as "agrarian." For it is the intrusion of industrial action into a field unfit for it that has produced the present situation.

John Crowe Ransom

What Does the South Want?

With the publication of Who Owns America?, *the Agrarians attempted to broaden their appeal by incorporating ideas from congenial intellectual movements overseas and by reaching out to other groups and regions in the United States. In "What Does the South Want?," Ransom's essay for the new symposium, he argued that independent businessmen, workers, Midwesterners, and Westerners would all benefit if subsistence farmers were granted enhanced property rights and tax relief. With his indictments of "modern mechanized labor" and thoughtless "forces of progress," Ransom reaffirmed the underlying principles of Agrarianism. Yet scholars have correctly interpreted this essay as evidence of a growing disenchantment with Agrarianism that would ultimately impel Ransom to renounce the movement.[1] In the following essay, one finds an Agrarian who embraced the federal union, who praised massive New Deal programs—Social Security, unemployment insurance, rural electrification—and who advocated modern plumbing and paved roads for farmers. When Ransom did resort to the more traditional Agrarian credo—as in his concluding claim that the South's "prejudices" would ensure its salvation (and thereby the nation's)—he seems*

---

1. The half-hearted tone of "What Does the South Want?" is discussed in O'Brien, *IAS*, 133–34, and Conkin, *SA*, 124. Ransom waited until 1945 to publicly disassociate himself from Agrarianism, by which time he had been for some years professor of English at Kenyon College and editor of the highly regarded *Kenyon Review*. He had made peace with the structure, if not all the effects of the modern (industrial) economy, and looked upon his former enthrallment with Agrarianism as a "fantasy" (Ransom, "Art and the Human Economy," *Kenyon Review* 7 [1945]: 686).

not only blind to the harmful manifestations of such traditions in Southern culture, but unable to disguise his own ambivalence.

Reprinted from *Virginia Quarterly Review* 12 (1936): 180–94, and *Who Owns America?*

It is my impression that Southerners do not have inhibitions against speaking up, and that what they like to speak about is the South. They now seem to concede that the South is a member part of an organic Union, and that in this relation will come what future happiness may be in store for the section. They begin to speak more importantly, or so it sounds, more prophetically, about what the South proposes to be and to do. But they speak with many voices, so that a listener is bewildered, and asks, What constitutes a proper spokesman, and, Which is the real South?

I cannot answer these questions; or rather, I cannot demonstrate that the answers I should like to offer are the correct ones. So various are the attitudes taken by Southerners toward Southern history, so various the views held about Southern policy, and so uncertain the future. The unitary South has passed; not even in a bare electoral sense is the South solid any more. The unitary South has been gradually disintegrating, ever since Reconstruction days. In war, the South lost her army by attrition. In peace, when the political defenses were down, there has been another process at work: the gradual, uneven, insistent penetration of the region by foreign ideas.

Consider the contiguous States of Virginia, Tennessee, and North Carolina. They were, respectively, the last, the penultimate, and the antepenultimate States to join the Confederacy. The first two had considerable Unionist populations. All three were mindful that, in the event of war, the position of a border State would be uncomfortable. (North Carolina would be a border State if Virginia did not come in.) But all joined. The war was fought principally in Virginia and Tennessee, as was bound to be, and North Carolina was spared the presence of armies on her soil, but contributed as if for compensation more soldiers to the Confederacy than any other State. And today? No State is quite identifiable with a doctrine, or policy, since each State contains within itself all the doctrines. But a little may be said towards a distinction. Virginia, of all States in the Union probably the most conscious of her history, has a highly ambiguous present position. Virginia's policy, so far as one may be predicted, is unrelated to Virginia's history. The history, aggressively, self-consciously Southern; and the policy? I only know that important Virginians say, "Virginia really has more Eastern affiliations than Southern ones; we are not exactly one of your regular Southern States." Which means to me, to the extent that this is official Virginian talk and feeling, that Virginia is bidding for a place in the imperial Eastern big-business economy. And as for North Carolina, there is the fact that the Piedmont region is visibly industrialized far beyond other Southern regions, and is less distinctly Southern. In North Carolina they have had their Walter Hines Page, a John the Baptist preaching in the wilderness to prepare the way for the new ideas; and in the excellent University of the State [Chapel Hill] they have a group of able modernists expounding the real thing.[2]

In Tennessee there are certainly many persons who agree with the Virginia and Carolina modernists. In 1929 the biggest and most high-powered promoters in the whole South—or at least the ones that made the biggest crash—had their headquarters in Nashville.[3] But in Nashville also was the nucleus of the so-called Agrarian group. The movement which these last initiated was not measurably a very big one, yet surprisingly it seemed to engage the public imagination as the counter-attack, or the belated offensive, of the old or traditional South. But for the possibility that it would be reading too fateful a history into the event, I should say that it was as if the State had essayed to assume a leadership that was not coveted by her elders. Not by Virginia, who is oldest, nor by North Carolina, who is the mother of Tennessee. The assumption would miss being a presumption because the leadership was going by default.

Hitherto the Agrarians have addressed themselves principally to their fellow Southerners, with the result that they have sometimes been fairly unintelligible to readers from other sections. But it must be supposed that they would welcome all reasonable affiliations, and indeed seek them if they knew how. (After all, the Agrarians are mostly harried college professors, with neither time nor gift of public relations; brain trusters.)[4] They have nevertheless been pleased to find some friends; as, among New Englanders who have seen land and power pass from the original possession into strange

---

2. Chapel Hill figures such as President Frank Porter Graham, the university press editor William Couch, and the sociologist Howard Odum gave the university a reputation for liberalism and reform (Daniel Singal, *The War Within: From Victorian to Modernist Thought in the South, 1919–1945* [Chapel Hill, 1982], 115–52, 265–301).

3. Nashville in the 1920s was known as the "Wall Street of the South" for its high concentration of banks, insurance companies, and securities firms. See Don H. Doyle's *Nashville in the New South, 1880–1930* (Knoxville, 1985). Chapters 9 and 10 and the epilogue help reconstruct the economic and business context against which both the Fugitive poets and the Nashville Agrarians rebelled.

4. A group of New York college professors had been recruited by Roosevelt as advisers to his campaign, earning the nickname "brain trusters." After the election, Barnard political scientist Raymond Moley, with Rexford Tugwell and Adolf Berle Jr. of Columbia, were given prominent roles in the administration, thereby establishing a model of academic-government collaboration Agrarians aspired to imitate.

hands and strange uses; and among Westerners and Middle Westerners who have never known their real interests to be pursued by their nominal patrons who controlled things in New York and Washington. The Southern Agrarians would like to see all these sympathetic elements combine, for the sake of power; that is, for the sake of common protection, and the preservation of American institutions. America has been dominated, financially, industrially, politically, from the East. Behind this dominion there was no idyllic purpose ever pretended, but there was the promise that it would make all Americans rich, and "civilize" them in the hard materialistic modern style. It made many Americans richer, indeed, and then its magical power suddenly failed, and even the favored Americans became very much poorer. The Eastern idea is not exactly working. There must be as many persons begrudged against by this imposed economy as there are persons who still feel easy and hopeful under its grandiose ministrations.

The South has a body of prejudices—I think that is the precise name for them—which are yet far from dead.[5] They have to do with the way to live, and the way to conduct business. These prejudices do not consist with the recent economic doctrines but they do consist with the new skepticism and discontent. In other words, the South, by virtue of being moved by a tradition, is capable of bringing passion to the support of a policy which other regions begin to come to by rational and very diffident processes. That is why, as I hope, the South may be a valuable accession to the scattering and unorganized party of all those who think it is time to turn away from the frenzy of big business towards something older, more American, and more profitable.

I shall try to calculate what sort of economic establishment the South would approve most naturally, in the light of these prejudices. If the Agrarians have in the past had most to say about an economy for farmers, there are also just as instant prepossessions in the South in the matter of the right economy for other estates. There are businessmen and laborers, as well as farmers, equally to be defended. I shall refer to each class in turn.

An orthodox capitalism for the South would be an economy with a wide distribution of the tangible capital properties. That is the thing with which the South is still best acquainted. The business transacted under it is business on the small scale—many owners, little businesses. The philosophy behind

---

5. Contrary to the common definition of "prejudice" as a negative, ill-considered, or irrational viewpoint, Ransom—perhaps ironically influenced by H. L. Mencken, who called his collections of essays *Prejudices*—used the word to indicate a neutral predisposition or characteristic.

it I will argue briefly as a philosophy which most plain Southerners would understand.

Ownership of property is one of the best privileges and one of the most sobering responsibilities that citizens can have under a free state. It is all but an indispensable qualification for the complete exercise of citizenship. But I refer to that kind of property which the owner administers, not to a paper ownership which does not entail any part in the management. The fathers of the nation were at pains to write into the constitution the inviolability of the person, and then at pains to write into it the inviolability of property; of property in the sense I have said, which was nearly the only sense of it they had. These are the principles of original Americanism, North and South. Because of them the constitution may still be regarded as an instrument worth fighting for, provided it can be held to its intention. The Southern heresy, as many "advanced" or "liberal" thinkers regard it, lies in the constitutionalistic bias of the region.

With the advent of the modern economy, however, the little businesses merge into the big business, and the fact of property takes on a new meaning; a meaning very much poorer in content, and encouraging some vicious propensities. For, what becomes of the original small owners, those responsible and therefore ideal citizens, in the age of big business?

They may become employees in the big business. But in that event they lose their economic freedom, for they become hired men, though they wear white collars, taking orders. The bigger and more efficient the business, the more meticulous the orders. Under big business the real economic initiative rests upon a few choice heads, which may be very strong heads indeed; it is these who lay out the program, for the others. The owners of all the other heads cannot find a first-rate occupation for them, and do not become the better men for it, though they may enjoy an increased productivity.

Or, as an alternative, they may become paper owners in the big business; but if this is their only function in the public economy it is a strange one. It involves no responsibility, or one so slight and indirect that it does not seem worth trying to exercise. Among the incidents in the growth of the scale of business organization—which defines somewhat the development of the modern economy—is the increase in the fluidity of capital, which means that there is more and more of free capital to hire out at interest for purposes with which the owner has no concern, and possibly very little acquaintance.

Is it necessary to persuade Americans to guard the right to administer their own property? We are singularly enfeebled if we now resent the thought of such a bother. Yet our economic "progress" brings the steady increase of a class of persons who might be defined as economic geldings; they are the *rentiers*, or the investors. The bad repute which once attached to the usurers when usury was nothing but interest was born of the plain man's notion that the lender of money, dissociating himself from the pains and pleasures of capital production, was dodging his responsibilities, and really was too deficient to relish the taste of them.

Many of the ablest men of this country, however, as judged either by heredity or by education, have been gelded. In the South also they are to be found, often the handsome and charming members of the old families. They would define their economic occupation as "watching the market"; meaning the fluctuations of security prices on Wall Street. Their technical ownership in a company does not imply an interest in its actual business problems. If it gets into trouble, they are far from feeling any proprietary concern. They telephone their brokers to sell.

Who, then, runs the big businesses? The executives, the officers, the directors, a small company of men, all in the position of trustees for the invisible and putatively brainless owners. Assume that they are honest trustees, as they probably are. What is honesty in a trustee? The virtue of a business executive is like that of a statesman, it consists in getting all he can for his wards. The standard of international morality is lower than the standard of personal morality, and the code of big business is lower than that of little business. The most charming statesmen are prepared to tell lies and break treaties and wage unjust wars in the name of their country, and amiable gentlemen on becoming business executives proceed to cut the throats of their small competitors and hire labor for the company on terms that sacrifice the dignity and elemental needs of the laborers. We have been informed that the "economic man," who used to be cited by economic theorists as the man who acts strictly in the pursuit of gain and is immune to moral and personal considerations, was an abstraction that never existed. He does not exist in small business, or at least he is hard to find there, but he is the regular thing in big business. The true economic man is the corporation, whose multitude of owners enjoy limited liability and leave the business to agents to run with maximum efficiency. Under big business and limited liability the spirit of *noblesse oblige* has disappeared from the working habits of the rulers of society. If it remains somewhere within consciousness, it ceases to apply at the place where it would do the most good, for in the economic world a technique has been devised which will prevent it from having any effect.

These are human and moralistic scruples, it must be conceded. But by a coincidence the associated doctrines of big business, mass production, and maximum efficiency begin to encounter suspicion from the pure economists. I shall not attempt to reproduce their arguments. They observe:

1. That the superior productivity claimed for big business seems to have been overestimated, and to be by no means the invariable rule. At the least,

a very expert analysis is demanded. And it is certain that the destruction of little business by big business does not always prove the latter's superior economy, for often it means that the superior capital of the big business has been used to advantage in unfair trade practices.

2. The superior efficiency of big business may be clearly demonstrable, by beautiful statistical exhibits, and by theory of perfect cogency, and still it seems to be a question whether big business does not head inevitably for the graveyard. There is the strange phenomenon of 1929–32 to its credit. There is the contemporary phenomenon of "rapid recovery" without serious diminution of unemployment.[6] Of what use is a brilliant system that cannot keep on its feet?

Now there is practically nobody, even in the economically backward South, who proposes to destroy corporate business. Least of all, it may be, in the South, which wants to see its industries developed, so that it may be permitted to attain to regional autonomy. Corporate business is essential to the production of many things that we demand, it is institutionalized in our economy. But every day or so it seems to Southerners, when they reflect upon it, to have exceeded its limits and become predatory. It preys on all little independents. But it is peculiarly vulnerable to attack because it is primarily, and will very largely remain, an Eastern instrument, preying on the West and South. Here is the modern sectionalism that makes inflammable tempers take fire. The South is perhaps more sensitive to that kind of piracy than the West, but perhaps the West will be glad to have a Southern alliance as soon as it sees how opposed to its own interests are the Eastern business interests, and how impossible it is to bring the Eastern interests to terms by the exercise of nominal functions in a ruthlessly Eastern political party. It seems to me certain that coming economic issues will array section against section very openly.

Specifically, I should think that the South, when it has a definite program which is consistent with its customary attitudes, will make at least two major requirements towards the recovery of responsible business direction: a review of the easy bargain which the charter-granting power now makes with the absentee owners of capital properties; and every possible legal assurance to the small independents of their right to compete against the corporations without being exposed to conspiracies.

---

6. Ransom referred to the ups and downs of the Great Depression. Following Roosevelt's election in 1932 and the swift passage of his programs for economic relief and stimulus, the economy did improve. But, as Ransom noted, even the much heralded "rapid recovery" failed to restore jobs, and by 1937 the economy took another dive from which it did not recover until World War II.

And now the farmers. Farming has remained a private business; the joint stock companies engaged in agriculture in this country are as exceptional as their economy is doubtful. Farmers are far ahead of the so-called business men in the unanimity of their independence. Even the tenant farmer takes his contract on broad terms which leave him free to plant, tend, gather, and sometimes even sell, at his own discretion; and even the day laborer does not submit to anything like the bossing of a factory foreman; that is not at present his peculiar grievance. Farmers are much the most important bloc of free spirits who have survived the modern economy. They should be regarded as the staple of our citizenship.

Yet with respect to pecuniary reward farming is a miserable business, in the South as elsewhere. The conclusion is forced upon the realistic observer that agriculture in this country is not an ordinary business, but one that suffers from an immense and peculiar disability. "Agrarians" take the realistic view, and propose the following theory.

In the modern "efficient" society business is highly specialized, and both owners and laborers live by the money income which they net from the sale of their special goods and services. But agriculture, pursued on strictly business principles, will always be insolvent, and the class dependent on it will always have an insufficient income.

The reason for this is that agriculture is an overcapitalized business, therefore an overproductive business, and therefore an unprofitable one. Its capital is the land, which is fixed by nature, and which is greatly in excess of our needs. How much in excess, it is impossible to say. The land is several times too abundant at least; under the circumstances it will never attain anything like its maximum productivity, so that we shall never know how great that is. Yet practically all of this land is in business; that is, in the hands of private owners waiting to produce. These owners will raise crops for the market as fast as they see any chance to dispose of them at cost, and as a matter of fact always a little faster. In the same way the railroads, or the cotton textile mills, must cease to prosper if there is a marked excess of fixed capital engaged in the competition. But the doom of agriculture is really worse, for it is perpetual. The supernumerary railroad or mills might be abandoned, or scrapped. The land cannot be destroyed, and it cannot even come out of the hands of private owners until the present constitution ceases to govern the American society.

But light is shed upon the special position of agriculture as soon as we ask the question, How, then, do farmers remain upon the land when they are by definition bankrupt and destitute? They do it by virtue of the fact that they practice not one but two economies. The one to which I have been referring is the money economy, in which farmers as a class would certainly fail if they had no other recourse; but the other is the individual economy of self-subsistence, upon which farmers can always fall back and by virtue of which farmers are invincible. The mistake which farmers in America have made is in having been taken in by the brilliant (if wayward) spectacle of the money economy, so that they concluded to rely on money-farming alone; they were betrayed into this decision by unrealistic advisers, including for the most part their instructors in the agricultural schools and experiment stations. It is not by money-farming that farmers can hold their property and live in decent comfort; it is by the combination of subsistence farming and money-farming. This was the burden of what the Agrarians had to say to farmers.

The special position of agriculture in America presents these features therefore: Liability, a natural and perpetual capitalization which is grievously excessive, and which makes it impossible for it to survive as a money-making business; and assets, first the rare privacy and independence which attaches to its pursuit, and second the unique advantage of subsistence without regard to money income.

But something must be said as to income, and the things that income and nothing but income will secure to farmers. (They will not live by bread alone, nor even by bacon, dairy products, and garden truck.) At this writing, the Agricultural Adjustment Act for enhancing farmers' income by arbitrary government subsidy has been ruled out by the Supreme Court.[7] That is well. Much as the farmers need money, it is too precarious to depend on receiving it in the form of a bounty, and it does not help their morale. Still worse, they cannot submit to government control as the condition of receiving it; farming ceases to be farming when its direction becomes external and involuntary; and farmers would have eventually rebelled against AAA in the name of their constitutional rights if the processors had not anticipated them.

It seems idle also to expect much of foreign trade as a means of disposing of surplus farm products. The world does not need additional exports of American farm products, and economic nationalism is certainly the only logical status which a country may look forward to when it does not need imports. Even the Southern cotton farmers, who look to the foreign markets as no other farmers do, begin to be pessimistic about relief from this source, and to consider other uses for their cotton acreage.

---

7. In *United States v. Butler* (1936), the Supreme Court struck down the Agricultural Adjustment Act of 1933, which gave federal subsidies to farmers who curtailed crop production.

But in view of the special liability of agriculture in this country, and the fact that farmers are a class whom the nation should delight to honor, there should be a special treatment for them. It should take the form of basic yet indirect bounties, which would give them the advantages needed for the exercise of good citizenship: government services. The farmer should receive greater and not lesser services than he now receives, and yet he should be relieved entirely or nearly of his present land taxes; for these are not paid with produce but with income from the land, and the income from the land does not justify them.

Among these services must be listed good roads. Another will be a free domestic market on which he can buy with his limited income at competitive prices, and not, as at present, at prices fixed by business combinations. Another will be first-class educational advantages for his children; it is the lack of these which has driven many of the best farmers from the land. They should not have to leave the land for that reason; the farmers of the poor Scandinavian countries have not had to do it.

A not unimportant service would consist in electricity delivered cheap at his door. It is just possible that the name of the thirty-second President will go down in history chiefly as associated with this philanthropy. It is electricity which makes most of the difference between the comforts of the city and the comforts of the country, and yet no commodity is more negotiable. The Agrarians have been rather belabored, both in the South and out of it, by persons who have understood them as denying bathtubs to the Southern population.[8] But I believe they are fully prepared to concede the bathtubs.

The South cannot view human labor in the classical economic sense, as a commodity, or a cost. Labor is men laboring. The men who labor are, on the

---

8. Ransom referred here to Grace Lumpkin's notorious 1936 interview with *American Review* editor and Agrarian supporter Seward Collins, which included the following passage:

Q. You wish to live as people did [in medieval times]?
Mr. Collins: Yes, do away with the automobile and go back to the horse.
Q. You wish to do without conveniences?
Mr. Collins: Yes.
Q. Without bathtubs?
Mr. Collins: I never use a bathtub.
Q. You don't bathe?
Mr. Collins: (dignified) I use a shower.
("I Want a King," in *FIGHT against War and Fascism* 3 [1936]: 3, 14, quoted in Albert E. Stone Jr., "Seward Collins and the *American Review:* Experiment in Pro-Facism, 1933–37," *American Quarterly* 12 [1960]: 16)

whole, those who are backward in economic initiative and intelligence; more rarely, those who have an apprenticeship to serve, who lack nothing but economic opportunity and experience. But they are men, and if they are too helpless or too docile to defend their human dignity they must be assisted.

The indignities of modern mechanized labor are marks of slavishness, not freedom; they affect principally the spirit, then incidentally the body, and the purse. But the cure which the passionate partisans of labor generally propose is an odd one. They would destroy the freedom of the owners in order to bring about the propertyless state in which nobody is to be free. Before that stage is reached they suppose that bigger wages, or a larger share in the spoils of production, is all the compensation for servility that can be thought of; or that it does not really matter how the laborer has to labor if it enables him to ride in a car after working hours.

In the South I believe it is generally assumed that there will always be the men whose courage and intelligence entitles them to own, and also the men whose natural quality fits them to work for hire. Otherwise the ordinary pattern of economic society is not possible, or at least it is criminally wrong, and we must find a new one; though it is very likely that the present large scale of wage-slavery misrepresents the actual proportion of this latter class in our society. In opposition to this assumption, the writers of recent proletarian literature have become irrational and a little maudlin in their glorification of the workingman.[9] They have gone mystical. They have broken bread with laborers, and communed with them over their beers. They have liked the thrilling odors from the armpits of men who work with their hands, and they have admired the ox-like strength of laborers, and still more the ox-like herding together in comradeship, and in the gregariousness of simple creatures they have seen the sublime consummation of human society. But by an oversight they have forgotten to make room for the most distinguishing of the human qualities, which is—intelligence.

Such realistic expressions as these may not seem to promise much for labor; they hardly compare with those of the left-wing authors for quixotism. On the other side I shall try to imagine some of the advantages which the South may want to realize for its labor population as its new industrial establishment rears itself. But there is first one more reservation to make, for the sake of honesty. The income receivable by wage-earners is like that

---

9. Among the most enduring examples of this Marxist-oriented 1930s literary and critical movement are John Steinbeck's *The Grapes of Wrath* (1939), John Dos Passos's *U.S.A. Trilogy* (collected 1938), and the journals *The Masses* and *The New Masses*.

receivable by farmers. It must depend more on economic forces than on leg-islation. Nevertheless there are minimum advantages which laborers as citi-zens should enjoy. It should be possible, by a combination of law, public opin-ion, and labor union policy, to improve the conditions of labor almost beyond recognition.

The tenure of the job should be secure; that is, if the job fails, there should be a fresh source of income, a fund in reserve, to fall back upon.[10] In other words, the South is entirely sympathetic with our incipient national and State program in this direction.

The houses and premises, so far as they are provided by the company, and perhaps with the assistance of the State and the community, should be brought up to a standard of decent habitableness. The houses should have plumbing; and what is even more important, a minimum of room, both indoors and out, which means privacy, which means personal dignity to the inhabitants. The section should be paved, planted in trees and flowers, pro-vided with playgrounds and parks, and such other advantages as are urged nowadays by welfare workers. But I should be a little wary of the professional welfare workers, and not let them drill the population too hard in play-habits and social functions. I should give the labor community its rights and let it make the most of them. There must be adequate medical and hospital ser-vices, and provision for good education.

Finally, the labor machine itself should not be more monstrous than the nature of the machine positively requires it to be. The principal relief from the absurd monotony of some forms of machine-tending must consist in stopping frequently; and the labor should not be performed at the fastest possible pace in the first instance. Here the Southern temperament discloses a peculiarity which sets the region quite apart from others as a field for indus-try. Southern labor will not work as fast as other labor. It is even a matter of pride to the laborers, and I have heard manufacturers discuss it. But it is not the orthodox and approved direction for laborers' pride to take. Generally it is the "efficiency" of American labor companies, who are naturally well dis-posed to it, until it is taken up by the laborers, and eventually becomes the official boast of the American Federation of Labor. American labor works faster than British labor; but I believe it is exceeded now in this respect by Japanese labor; and the Japanese in turn are excelled by the red ants, who probably are proud of knowing how to run without ever having learned how to walk.

---

10. The Social Security Act was passed in August 1935, creating a fund for retire-ment pensions and unemployment compensation.

Is the tempo of Southern labor to adapt itself to that of Eastern labor, or is it to become the new standard of American labor generally? I hope the latter. Otherwise the term "labor-saving" refers to labor in its old invidious sense, as meaning nothing more than one of the costs in production.

Private property versus corporate property; the excellence of homely country life; the rights and natural limitations of hired labor; here are issues upon which Southern prejudices seem to have something to say. How strong are the prejudices? Evidently they are disappearing, they are being mined away. But that may mean one of two things.

It may mean that times have changed, and the conditions do not now permit the Southern attitudes and policies. Evidently the enemies are strong, and evidently sometimes they go by pretty names: Business as It Is Today, Maximum Efficiency, and Habit of the Modern Mind. Perhaps the enemies are too strong. But let us not be too sure; let us wait and see.

For it may mean, principally, that prejudices are simply out of date, no matter how good are their prescriptions. Prejudices are traditions, and traditions work in pious ages when we act upon doctrines without having to argue them out; but this is the age of reason when everything has to be argued out. In that event the economists and statesmen must do as the moralists and the parents—they must argue patiently upon the merits of all proposals. I venture to hope that the policies I have defined are not without rational supports; and that their opponents, if they have the honor of attracting any, will not dispose of them by saying, "These are only prejudices, and we have expunged that term from the bright lexicon of the forces of progress."

John Crowe Ransom

The South Is a Bulwark

Throughout the 1930s, the conservative wing of the Agrarian group battled not only liberal social scientists, but leftist literary critics. Disagreements with the literary left usually centered on the function of art in modern society. While the leftists called for a new American literature that would celebrate the proletariat, those Agrarians who were poets were promoting the art-for-art's-sake theories that prefigured the New Criticism.

When Scribner's Magazine *invited John Crowe Ransom to debate V. F. Calverton,[1] the Marxist critic, author, and editor, the result was a heated exchange on the state of the South. Opening the debate, Calverton lambasted the region for its religious fundamentalism, anti-intellectualism, and overall provincialism. The majority of Southern writers, he argued, take on the "petty-bourgeois outlook" and "either retreat to imaginary towers of their own construction or to a romantic past." He noted that the Agrarians had "declaimed against the petty-bourgeois South," but their essays in the* American Review *were to him the writings of fascists who wanted "to return to a form of pre-capitalist economy, in which horse and buggy transportation will supplant that of the automobile and the steam locomotive, and handicraft production will replace that of machine production, all of which is not only most reprehensibly naive and fantastic but most dangerously reactionary."[2]*

---

1. Victor Francis Calverton (1900–1940) edited the *Modern Monthly,* which he founded as the *Modern Quarterly* in 1923.

2. Calverton, "The Bankruptcy of Southern Culture," *Scribner's* 99 (1936): 294–98 (297, 298).

Ransom responded to these charges by laying out an agronomic plan for the United States. He was now willing to admit that the Southern farmer should no longer "be expected to live as a self-subsistent primitive." Yet he still believed that the state and federal governments had a duty to help individual farmers resist the big-business agriculture he considered tantamount to Soviet collectivism. Charging the Marxists with an idealized notion of economic progress, he defended the agrarian South as "a real bulwark against those revolutions under which men surrender their general integrity and become pure functions, or abstractions, or soldiers in an army."

Reprinted from *Scribner's Magazine* 99 (1936): 299–303.

Herodotus, the father of history, told wonderful stories about such things as the search of the one-eyed Arimaspians for gold, and the manners of the rude Scythians.[3] He had a good chance to spread himself because in those days the Greek cities had no sort of contact with the remote barbarian nations. Mr. Calverton, though a modern historian, is ingenious too. His imagination is all the more remarkable since he lives in the age of communication, and at the trade center of the world's largest free trade area, and writes what is technically domestic history, and still is not inhibited.

It would be an error of literary judgment to argue with Mr. Calverton's pretty fancies. He is a serious and sincere thinker, but not I believe with respect to Southern culture in the ordinary sense of the word.

I must construe Mr. Calverton from a distance, for my acquaintance with him is as documentary or theoretical as is his acquaintance with the South; so I may be wrong. His real cultural interest, I gather, is precisely what Karl Marx's was: limited to a very special interest in the political economy of the region. The South is too "petty bourgeois" for him; that emerges as his real concern; which means that the South has not yet gone in wholeheartedly for giant business organizations in the place of small ones, and therefore is not yet ready to be propositioned by the Marxians. The thesis of the Marxians is that the rich must become richer and the poor poorer before the class struggle can attain violence enough to accomplish anything. For that reason they approve of plutocracy if it is nicely "bloated," of high finance, mass production, and technology if they produce depression and unemployment, and of bankers, landlords, and employers if they are so strong and greedy as to arouse the hatred of a multitude of victims. These ifs they think will be sufficiently realized under any high-powered version of the modern industrial society. Big business is the stage precedent to revolution. The South's backwardness slows up the program and postpones the millennium.

Mr. Calverton's enthusiasm for the old plantation aristocracy is rather

---

3. Herodotus (ca. 484–ca. 430B.C.), *Histories*, 3.116; 4.13, 27, 59ff.

more uncritical than my own, and also, I believe, than that of Mr. Donald Davidson. It is charming, almost disarming. But I reflect that Mr. Calverton is deep, and I remember that any great gulf between the classes is good from a Marxian view because it sets the stage of the revolution, and that a privileged aristocracy, if fat and "gay" enough, would serve the purpose as well as a plutocracy.[4] Unfortunately the gay planters did not wait until the Marxians could appear upon the scene, they went down with the rest of the economic establishment of the region and were superseded by a society of small owners; a nut that Marxianism cannot crack. So was the French Revolution of 1789 premature too, in that there was no Marxian leadership to direct its outcome. The French aristocracy gave way to a petty bourgeoisie, and there it is today.

So there is an issue between Mr. Calverton and the South, and it is worth discussing. But many other Americans besides Southerners are on one side of it, just as many others besides Mr. Calverton are on the other side of it, and the future of the country depends on which side is going to have its way. Mr. Calverton is the spokesman for certain "forces of progress," the nature of which we can read between the lines. He senses the Southern opposition infallibly. There is plenty of it elsewhere, but it is peculiarly stubborn and substantial in the South. I believe it may be said that if the Union has to be defended against the sort of program which Mr. Calverton would put forward, this section is a very bulwark.

The merest tourist, at 300 miles per day, can tell you ways in which the South differs from other sections. Perhaps he notices the unusual degree of warmth, or he may call it curiosity and garrulousness, on the part of the leisurely natives with whom he trades for a sandwich, or a fill of gasoline, or a lodging. They seem determined to import personal relations into business transactions, a habit which is clearly the enemy of maximum efficiency.

Another observation, more to the point, may not be unrelated to this one: the smallness of scale in the objectified economy of the region. The cities are not imposing, the skyscrapers are not high. The biggest residences are not so big, indicating that the richest Southerners are not so rich. The railroads are slow and the automobiles are cheap. The country clubs do not glitter.

Statisticians will confirm his findings, and contribute others which are not so visible. The public schools run on lower per-child expenditures than elsewhere, the public libraries are classified as inadequate, the colleges are below standard in enrollments, libraries, endowments, and other measurable

---

4. Ransom alluded to Calverton's assertion that the plantation era "represented the gayest life in America" (Calverton, "Bankruptcy of Southern Culture," 296).

properties. There are no great publishing houses, and no great weekly or monthly journals to act as distinguished organs of public opinion; not money enough for such things.

There may be exceptions to the rule of small effects—a big factory here, a big country estate there. The chances are that the capital or the income which floats the thing is imported Northern money. The South has been discovered in recent years by enterprising capitalists as a good place to plant capital in, and by retired capitalists as a good place to live in. In Virginia, for example, many of these latter have restored the architecture and the superficial form of the old plantations, and are playing at country squire; but the gesture is not significant, since there is no economic reality behind it.[5]

The South simply has less income at its disposal than other regions have, and it is correspondingly backward in the statistical evidences of "culture." But there should never be an extended discussion of this point without some remark about its historical background. Seventy years ago the South, seeking not aggression but peaceful separation, was defeated by force of arms, and then by the same force "reconstructed." The two operations were continuous and lasted from ten to twenty years. The economic result of this disruption was that the South became a sort of colonial dependency of the East at the time when the latter entered upon its industrial expansion. The South was fixed in the role of a primary producer. It took its punishment, precisely as a vegetable economy always does when trading with a mineral economy; I am borrowing Professor Beard's recent terms.[6]

But a principle of compensation works, though it may be slowly and darkly, in the interest of the vegetable economy. The profits of the mineral economy must have somewhere to go and earn, and they are bound to go eventually back into the vegetable economy, to take the form of naturalized capital plant, and to initiate industrial processes there too. So far as the South is concerned, political and sectional attitudes at first stood in the way of this development; but, after all, the South has more than its share of mineral resources and, a great thing now, water power. If capitalists are so enterprising and capital is so mobile as the classical economists have supposed, then the industrial development of the South is assured; and in fact it is well started. The financial and industrial domination of the East has seen its last days, and I suppose even now the financiers and captains of industry in New York

5. Ransom may have had in mind the multimillion dollar restoration of Colonial Williamsburg funded in the 1920s and 1930s by John D. Rockefeller Jr.

6. Beard borrowed the terms from Erich W. Zimmermann; see Charles A. Beard, *The Open Door at Home: A Trial Philosophy of National Interest* (New York, 1934), 122–23. Agar reviewed the book in "A Plea to Mr. Charles A. Beard," *AR* 4 (1935): 297–309.

begin to be acquainted in a faint premonitory manner with the feeling of holding a bag.

I do not know anybody in the South who thinks that industrialization can be stopped where it is, or wants it stopped there. The Southerners with whom I am acquainted want economic independence for their region, and the wish seems modest enough not to rate as treasonable. To its attainment the planetary influences are now entirely favorable, if I am an astrologer. Nevertheless, I think that industrialization will be a little different in the South. The South, as Mr. Calverton says, is rather a petty-bourgeois community.

In the Carolina Piedmont region, and at other places in the South, industrialization has been taking place very fast and the forces of progress have been jubilant. The North Carolina patriots used to welcome this development without any qualms. They seemed to go on the theory which I believe is Mr. Calverton's own, that culture is a function of income, or of the material advantages which money will buy. The Carolina thinkers wanted a big income for the South, and could name very noble reasons: the increase of libraries, publications, schools and colleges, government services; the breeding of big philanthropists. Some liberal-minded Carolinians wanted to see the income widely distributed, too; they were aware as soon as anybody else of the now well-published necessity of distributing the purchasing fund. But they did not want to see it come to the workingman in the form of richer crumbs from the employer's table, but in the form of obligations acknowledged and written into the contracts. To that end they were ready even to stand for militant unionism, and their courage and realism must be honored.

But income is not enough, and the distribution of income is not enough. If these blessings sufficed, we might as well come to collectivism at once; for that is probably the quickest way to get them. In Russia they are building up almost overnight a productive plant like that which it took America many years to secure, and they are distributing its benefits more widely than has ever been known in an industrial society. Mr. Calverton, the realist, might not at all object to our taking the Russians for our guides. I think the liberal Carolinians would come to it eventually too; some of them have been coming very rapidly to it. The subtle Marxians see exactly what can happen very easily to a big business economy, even to our own. Thus: the system collapses in labor violence, or perhaps it collapses in depression; yet the productive plant is there still, and the population is there still, already trained and drilled in obedience to orders, already regimented. So the state takes over the plant and assigns the personnel to its posts; the revolution has been accomplished. In the degree that the business organization has done a good job already in enforcing the habit of subordination, the revolution may even be a tolerably bloodless affair.

Another group of Southern minds, if Mr. Calverton will allow the term, has for its locus Tennessee rather than Carolina. They believe that freedom and human rights are as important for happiness as money and goods, and that the advocates of "progress," who applaud the virtues of income and of standards of living as measured statistically, are not the natural interpreters of the section. Considering the genuine public zeal manifested by the Carolinians, they would observe further that big libraries, big educational plants, and unlimited public services all put together do not make a fair price for the loss of private freedom.

There may be an opposition between maximum productivity and private freedom. But there is no fixed opposition between private freedom and a great deal of material welfare, a considerable productivity; these do not exclude one another. The per capita natural wealth of this country is all but beyond comparison greater than that of other nations, and it is astonishing to find economists concluding that its development can proceed only by tactics which are harsh and sacrificial of human rights. I mean this: by the police tactics of the Soviet republics, or even by the impersonal and "strictly business" tactics of our own big corporate businesses.

Nowhere on earth is there a society so well able as ours to afford the luxury of freedom. We are not as Italy, to whom Il Duce, in the name of what we would call the planned society, addressed his famous remark, "Italy cannot afford freedom."[7]

The Nashville Agrarians have been most concerned with the farm economy. They pitched on that as a central problem for the South, which is a rural section, and in which the occupational status is something like sixty percent agricultural; perhaps also because of their own personal background and taste. But at this moment most of the original writers are making a fresh appearance in a second symposium, *Who Owns America?* With them are presented a still larger number of other writers, who are not so interested in the agricultural as in the business economy, and correspond to those British economists who call themselves Distributists; they propose "the restoration of private property" in America. Each group, the Agrarian and the Distributist, thinks that it requires the complementary assistance of the other, and that no change in its own principles is involved; for neither the farmers nor the business men can flourish in a society in which both these estates are not at once comfortable and secure.

The new book is not written with peculiar reference to the South. If its authors are not mistaken, it advances doctrines 100 percent pure American;

---

7. Il Duce was Benito Mussolini (1883–1945), fascist dictator of Italy 1922–43.

though not exactly the kind of doctrines which seemed to be orthodox in 1929.[8] I shall tell in my own terms the position taken by most of the writers upon the problem of the land, and also upon the problem of industry and business. This position looks almost congenial to Southern habits of mind. But I should describe it also as "early American," and again "constitutional."

As for the land, the Agrarian theory has a fresh statement. It is my impression that it is the only theory that has ever made a realistic approach to the very peculiar problem of American agriculture.

The most obvious thing to say about agriculture in America is that, as a business in the ordinary sense, it can never prosper. Speaking of bankruptcy, there is no bankruptcy like that of Southern cotton planters trying to earn money which is not there to earn; unless it is that of some other group of farmers raising an American staple. Here is a field in which common business principles cannot apply. The common business principles are based on the understanding that each business is a special function in a society of delegated functions, and that those engaged in it make a money income by selling their goods or services to society and then live on the income. Each business tries for maximum efficiency; that is maximum productivity at minimum cost of labor, material, and capital equipment. But agriculture cannot successfully play this part among the other businesses. It has a unique disability.

The disability is this. The volume of productive land is out of proportion to the wants—whether this means the wishes or needs—of the American community. The land is the fixed capital of agriculture, but it is fixed by nature and not by man, therefore fixed indeed. No European nation in modern times has had to worry with this peculiar condition, and therefore no pattern for handling it is discoverable in European economic, or in any other economic derived from European writings. Technically, the excess of American land is overcapitalization, and an overcapitalized business is always an overproductive one.

The extent of an overcapitalization is not determined by the size of the marketable surplus of goods produced. In an old business subject to calculation, production will probably not greatly exceed the demand for any given year, since many producers will gauge the prospect accurately and stay out

---

8. Ransom apparently used the term "100 percent pure American" not as it was used by nativists after World War I (see John Higham, *Strangers in the Land: Patterns of American Nativism, 1860–1925* [1963], 204 ff.); his use of the phrase more likely reflects the Agrarians' desire in the mid-1930s to gain an audience beyond the South.

of production. But until these producers abandon their capital plant, they are waiting their first chance to produce, they are a menace, and they see to it that the ordinary condition of the market shall be one of glut, and the ordinary condition of the business one of insolvency. Most farm economists, however, prefer to measure the overproductiveness of American farmers by the actual surplus, and so they deceive the statesmen legislating for the farmers, and the farmers too, as to the dimensions of the problem. For example, it is suggested that the eating of two extra loaves of bread a year by each American person will cure the plight of the wheat farmers. It is the overcapitalization and not the visible overproduction that counts. The precise excess of American land will never be known; so long as the population stays under a hundred and sixty millions, as it is calculated to do, we can only say of it that it is indefinitely great. The land might easily support several times that population, but naturally it will never set in to prove this for the benefit of doubting economists. It is perfectly natural that American land should be farmed extensively and inefficiently, rather than intensively and according to the principles of agronomy; that is the easiest way to farm it, and it is more than efficient enough. There is always a great deal of marginal land waiting to come in as soon as the good land is earning, and by all means there is a higher productive capacity which the good land is waiting to realize as soon as profits begin to show.

The Agrarians have reluctantly come to the conclusion that the foreign markets offer no prospect of employing that unused capacity of American land. They do not endorse the somewhat vindictive program of Mr. Peter Molyneaux, of Texas, who seems desirous of breaking down the American tariff walls no matter what it means to American industry, on the ground that it was American industry which ruined the Southern farmers, and that the ruin of industry must now save them. The South once had a strong case in making this argument, but that was definitely yesterday. It was mostly nature which ruined the farmer in the South, and it is certainly nature which keeps him ruined now.[9] Europe is finding elsewhere cheaper farm stuff than we can supply, and that is about all there is to the argument. The time may come when all American farmers, even the cotton ones, will be thankful for a tariff which protects not only the industrialists but themselves. In any case, it is inevitable that a country which does not require imports will finally have to abandon exports, and work out its economy on a domestic basis, farming included.

---

9. This essay, published in the twilight of his Agrarian phase, demonstrates Ransom's more realistic understanding of the environmental problems faced by farmers during the 1920s and 1930s.

The late lamented AAA was an ignoble though humanly natural experiment. Southern farmers accepted its benefits as cheerfully as others, and doubtless with fully as much secret consciousness that the arrangement was slightly disreputable. If the Constitution had not intervened, I imagine that one of two things would have happened before long. It would have been established that it was profoundly uneconomic, and too expensive for the government of the United States, to guarantee income on a fixed capital whose excess had never been computed but was close to the fabulous. Or, if the government continued to deal only, and arbitrarily, with that group of farmers who happened to be caught producing in the year that Triple A took effect, the reasonable and constitutional desire of others to enter this privileged business, working fresh land or working the given land much more efficiently, would have raised clamor enough to wreck the scheme.

There is no hope for American agriculture as a business, with its fatal incubus of too much land; governmental action foreign or domestic cannot save it. But observe a paradox. In spite of this fact farming is a fine and tolerably secure occupation for the right sort of farmers. And here is the secret. To compensate for its peculiar disability, farming has the peculiar advantage that it lends itself not to one economy, as other businesses do, but to two economies. The farmer does not have to live entirely in either one. So the farmer is, now, a money-maker, requiring an income, exposed to the hazards of cost and competition like all the others; very much underprivileged in this economy, as we have seen. But, again, he is in a private economy of his own, producing his own subsistence without money transactions. He is an amphibian and cannot be destroyed.

I have given the order wrong, so far as the American farmer is concerned. He should produce his own necessities first, and then consider his money crops. His present misery is mostly due to the fact that he has learned to put his money crops first, and then more often than not forgotten to produce for himself; he has never had pointed instruction to the effect that agriculture in America is not one of the ordinary businesses, and does not permit this. Naturally he is in a desperate situation. This is what the Agrarians recently have been saying with probably wearisome iteration. In their own section the oral tradition which handed down the detail of the dualistic farm economy is not yet quite dead.

Yet the state should delight to honor the farmer, and to assist him so far as it does not involve direct bounties, or privileged treatment, or a burden of expense which the state cannot bear. The farmers are the freest citizens in this country; the most whole, therefore the most wholesome. Nobody bosses their jobs meticulously, even if they are hired men. If they are owners, they are the perfect examples of the propertied man; the man who actually administers as he pleases a property he owns; whose business relations are personal, moral, and neighborly, not impersonal, legalistic, and corporate. They should be regarded as the staple of our citizenship; and if the South has a large proportion of them in its population then the South is a real bulwark against those revolutions under which men surrender their general integrity and become pure functions, or abstractions, or soldiers in an army. The socialists and communists are quite aware they can do little with the farmers, who like too well their status.

But the farmer needs income; he should not be expected to live as a self-subsistent primitive. The state—I do not mean to specify which of the hierarchy of his governments—can do several things. First, it can nearly or wholly cease to tax his land. The tax is payable in money, not in kind, but the land is not productive of much money. Then it might assure him of his right to buy in a really competitive domestic market, so that his limited funds will go as far as possible; now he has to spend them in a market largely determined by monopolies and combinations. Southern farmers applaud Senator Borah's stand on this matter fully as much as Western farmers do; incidentally, they also share his regard for the Constitution.[10]

The farmer cannot expect to have his income enhanced by government dole. But there is good reason for asking the state to provide him with certain services which are practicable, and also essential to his good citizenship. I am thinking of such services as good roads; provision for first-class general education, as good let us say as Denmark gives its rural population; provision for agricultural or technical education under instructors who know more about farming than how to make money crops; and possibly electricity delivered cheap at the front gate. This last may not have to be strictly a governmental service, but the corporate utilities will have to be hustled if they are

---

10. A six-term Republican senator who represented Idaho, William Edgar Borah (1865–1940) battled monopolies, condemned the Agricultural Adjustment Administration's crop curtailment program, and supported a protective tariff for farmers. "Give the farmer a fair market," he wrote, "—a market in which he can realize the cost of production with reasonable profits—and he will return the check, take back the idle acres, fight for the life of his pigs, and chase away the first representative of bureaucracy appearing at his barn gate, with a pitchfork" ("The Farmer's Enemy," *Collier's* 97 [1936]: 12–13, 43, 44; 12). Despite his cordial personal relationship with Roosevelt, Borah was a strict constructionist who believed that the president had abused the Constitution by seizing too much power for the executive branch. A severe critic of Roosevelt's ill-fated plan to enlarge the Supreme Court by adding justices sympathetic to New Deal legislation, Borah also opposed Roosevelt over the National Recovery Administration and the Federal Emergency Relief Administration. In 1936, he launched a bid for the presidency but failed to win the Republican nomination (Marian C. McKenna, *Borah* [Ann Arbor, 1961], 306–44).

going to provide it. The first Roosevelt has come down in fame as the president with a big stick;[11] the second may be associated with a yardstick.

Farmers are bad medicine for Marxians. Business men are a little easier; they cannot have quite such a freedom as that of farmers. But those in the South are obstinate small fry, according to Mr. Calverton, which means that a good deal of work will have to be done with them.

Petit Bourgeois. The term is literary and slightly ridiculous, especially where the bourgeoisie is unacquainted with it. It may be expelled through the teeth with the sound of hissing and an effect of moral indignation; in Russia, I believe, good comrades take their conditioning exercises every morning when they get up by reciting, "No petit bourgeois business today." But to be one, as I understand it, is simply to be the sole owner of a small business and to operate it accordingly. A petit bourgeois society is one with a wide distribution of tangible capital properties. That is the sort of society which the South understands.

Now the laws of special function and maximum efficiency do operate in the business world; that is, in business whose capitalization is the act of man and not God—if Mr. Calverton will overlook my nomenclature. These laws determine the form of our modern societies and produce our quick wealth. In the name of maximum efficiency the original little businesses are steadily replaced by much fewer but much bigger corporate businesses, and often with unquestionable economic advantage.

Not always, of course. Economists increasingly find that we have overestimated the savings of big business. However that may be, we know that big business gives us a very speculative and dangerous economic system; it gives us precisely the system that we have today; the system that leads many admirable persons to lean towards Mr. Calverton's program in preference. If we must have the extreme benefits of large-scale production we shall find ourselves at last in Mr. Calverton's net; probably before very long. From big business into collectivism: the Marxians know their formula. But if we are willing to enjoy these benefits in moderation, and leave a great deal of business on the small, personal, moral, and manageable basis, Mr. Calverton cannot get us. We shall remain economically free.

The goose-step of collectivism differs only in degree from the progressive disfranchisement of men as economic agents under big business. A big

---

11. Theodore Roosevelt's 1900 endorsement of the adage "Speak softly and carry a big stick" came to be associated with the interventionist foreign policies he put into effect as president.

business operates an army of men, and organizes and regiments them like an army. Each rank receives its orders from above; they are explicit and peremptory. The personnel likes the arrangement to the extent that it has the army temperament. Responsibility is limited in the army, except at the top, and there are certainly many men in the world who like to reduce their responsibility; who like to carry out orders if they suppose that the orders are intelligent with respect to promoting efficiency. It seems that in a modern efficient society like America the best brains discoverable are behind the patterns of conduct which are imposed upon business men at all points. But it becomes increasingly hard to find work for all the good brains that apply. A few brains go a long way. It is an ignominious situation for the many men with economic initiative and intelligence who find nothing to do but go into employment and take orders; and it takes fantastic ingenuity, almost, to found a new business and make a place of power. There is no less of property to own in the age of big business, but it is owned in a new and peculiar manner. Its ownership for the most part does not carry any responsibility; it is paper ownership. A business may be owned, conceivably, by a hundred thousand admirable widows and orphans, and yet its operation need not reflect either the moral scruple or the business judgment of its tender proprietors; for it may be run by executives who have only a salaried interest. Usually, of course, a business has a few owners with large holdings and a multitude of owners with tiny holdings; the big owners pick the right executives, the little owners concur cheerfully, and are much pleased if the earnings are high.

It is painful to think of adding to the difficulties of widows and orphans, and also to those of the administrators of colleges, insurance companies, and organized charities, whose income is derived from paper property. But it is all but terrifying to reflect upon the extent to which the capital owners in America have delegated their economic agency. Ownership used to be a much sterner affair. Usury was in low repute, though it meant no more than the lending out of money for hire to enterprises in which the lenders did not participate.

In the new group-book I find an agrarian sort of term used to describe those gentry who may well be distinguished in birth, fortune, and education, but whose whole economic vocation consists of watching their "investments." They are called the geldings of the economic society. They exist in great numbers, and the implication is that the economic society could not afford to employ them in their natural potency. But the modern breed of American citizen submits very pleasantly to being gelded. The citizen with large investments is quite an imposing figure. When something happens to the value of some bloc of his shares, he makes a Napoleonic decision, but it is not by way of pitching in to see what is wrong with the business, and then doing something about it; it consists in ordering his broker to sell.

Non-responsibility attaches to the small owners, irresponsibility to the big owners. Determined by these qualities, American business cannot be saved by all the technical efficiency in the world. It will be economically unstable. Morally it will have no status at all beyond that of keeping free of the toils of the law; and the surplus of brains in American corporate business devoted to outwitting the law is larger than the supply of professional legislative and judicial brains engaged in making it stick.

It is not likely that the small Distributist-Agrarian group will cause a vast reversal in American economic practice. Mr. Calverton informs me that Agrarianism is dead, and I think he would have said the same for Distributism, except for the fact that there is a stubborn petty-bourgeois survival which he notes in the South. He may be perfectly right. I can easily suppose, as he supposes, that we will put up with big business until the time when it fails too flagrantly to promote, not health and happiness, but life; and that we will then turn the thing disgustedly over to his well-organized group.

But I must suggest to Mr. Calverton what is a distinct possibility. A great spontaneous political movement may form now, or at any moment, which will press for Agrarian and Distributist reforms without using these terms or even knowing them. Recently we have seen the re-alignment of the West and South, so long separated. A few years ago Mr. [Franklin] Roosevelt appealed against the spirit of sectionalism, but what chance has the New Deal unless the West and the South unite against the East? If Mr. Calverton should travel among the inner areas of this country, he would discover a very strong impression that the ills of the present economy are due to the domination of big business, whose center is in the East. The farm populations and the petty bourgeois who are the West and the South have a great deal of force if they will realize it; they have ballots. Suppose the West realizes what the South has painfully known for a long time: that it betrays credulity if it affiliates with a party whose interests are all Eastern?

There is no telling about all this. If I try, I can imagine legislatures and Congresses for years to come whittling away at that special instrument of big business, the corporation; working some destruction inevitably while they are about it; but trying however clumsily to secure America again to its former proprietors. That, I feel, will be going Southern and remaining American.

Allen Tate

The Problem of the Unemployed: A Modest Proposal

With the onset of the Great Depression, Allen Tate's friendship with New Republic *editors Malcolm Cowley and Edmund Wilson suffered. Annoyed by their Marxist vocabulary, he came to believe that leftist intellectuals treated the vast number of unemployed Americans as economic abstractions, rather than as Jeffersonian individuals. Yet because they remained friends, albeit estranged, he sometimes found it difficult to attack them directly. In late 1930, an opportunity to launch an unusual salvo at them came when the* New Republic *published an editorial questioning inflation as a solution to unemployment. The editorial, which appropriated the title of Jonathan Swift's 1729 satire, "A Modest Proposal," motivated Tate (who was then experimenting with the style of the eighteenth-century satirist) to write his own version.*[1] *In "The Problem of the Unemployed: A Modest Proposal," Tate transformed Swift's idea of feeding poor Irish babies to British gentlemen into a plan to execute millions of unemployed Americans and to use their remains as "raw material" for manufacturing products.*

The essay, which also endorsed large-scale prostitution, was twice rejected for publication, first by the New Republic *and then by the* Virginia Quarterly Review. *Concluding that it would never be published, Tate abandoned it. In 1933, however, he revised the article with the view of publishing it in the* American Review. *Seward Collins liked the essay so much that he made additions to it. "I soon found myself racing along sticking in stray thoughts of my own," the editor wrote Tate, "and having*

---

1. "A Modest Proposal," unsigned editorial, *NR* 65 (1930): 124–25. Tate originally entitled his reply "Relief for the Unemployed."

quite a bit of fun about it." When the article finally came out in May 1933, Tate learned that leftists in New York found it shocking. Their reaction, Tate told Collins, "proves what we've known all along, that they really wish to preserve the moral atmosphere and assumptions of capitalism — that they are not, in short, as radical as they think they are."[2]

Reprinted from *American Review* 1 (1933): 129–49,
with the permission of Mrs. Helen Tate.

Unemployment in the United States is variously estimated at some round figure between ten and fifteen millions. Possibly the larger figure would represent an increase of approximately one hundred percent since January 1, 1931. But it is not within the province of this discussion to set exact figures, nor to suggest a method by which a proportion of these idle men may be returned to work. It is not likely that all the fifteen millions, if there be that many, will be permanently useless to industry. It is just as unlikely that all will be absorbed back into the industrial system in a reasonable balance of labor and capital. We who are seeking for ways to recover prosperity must face an unpleasant fact: there will remain, even after some degree of economic recovery, a staggered residue of the permanently unemployed. We are not prophets; but we need fear no excess of divination if we expect this residue to settle at the bottom of our system with the weight of about eight millions of men. Let us call this residue, whatever it may prove to be, the letter x. It is probable that the total number of Americans left without livelihood will reach four times x. For it cannot be doubted that one great cause of suffering among this class is the anachronism of the family, an institution that survives from the property or land system of society, in which the family was the unit of production. Thus it still regrettably happens that when a laborer falls into indigence, he drags with him a family of three or four.

Since October, 1929, when the industrial system received in symbolic form, over the ticker-tape, evidence that its cogs had temporarily jammed, there have been innumerable solutions to the problem of unemployment. These solutions fall into three classes. I allude now only to those that received official recognition, and thus had a bare chance of being tried. It is not necessary to give their history but merely to describe them briefly. One of the solutions was tried; it failed. Call it Solution Number One. Solution Number Two — a most dangerous proposal — was not tried; we may dispose

---

2. Collins to Tate, 18 April 1933 [carbon copy]; Tate to Collins, 16 May 1933, Beinecke Library, Yale University. On Tate and the leftists, see also Daniel Aaron, *Writers on the Left: Episodes in American Literary History* (New York, 1961), 352–53, 442n, 458n.

of it by reminding the reader that the Dole, in all systematic forms that it may take, was officially rejected. Solution Number Three is now about to be put to the test.

Solution Number One is, of course, that of the Hoover Administration. It is the Religious Solution, for it looked for its success to that kind of religion which is the fine flower of our enlightened spirit—the religion of salesmanship. There was, the reader will remember, a brief period set aside by President Hoover, who called round him the faithful for the celebration of what he designated Confidence Week.[3] I saw none of these festivities, being at the time hid in the savage isolation of a farm in Tennessee;[4] but I heard that they were most impressive. Men marched in parades, lit up bonfires, and carried large gonfalons upon which were inscribed sundry inspiring mottoes and devotional texts, all proclaiming the faith of the marchers in American business. I was struck with the soundness of this method of economic recovery; but there remains dispersed over our population an inert minority still lost in the mists of ancient superstition; and the campaign of Confidence Week failed for lack of universal faith. Among the illiterate farmers of my neighborhood skepticism and heresy, at a time when we had thought these vermin exterminated by public education, once more showed their heads. Certain men asserted that they cared nothing for business; that they were being *hoodooed* into buying what they did not want or need, when the whole trouble was due to their having already bought themselves into penury. The most dangerous doctrine that they uncovered from the Past was the undesirability of being in debt: when they were told that patriotism enjoined them to buy on credit to set the wheels going again, they answered

---

3. Since "confidence" was a Herbert Hoover buzzword, "Confidence Week" might describe any number of weeks during his administration. Tate may, however, be referring to the excitement generated by the U.S. Chamber of Commerce during the National Business Survey Conference, launched by Hoover in late 1929 in Washington, D.C. One of Hoover's principal strategies during the Depression was to rebuild the nation's economic morale by sponsoring highly publicized business symposia. Instead of giving the unemployed direct monetary aid, he celebrated voluntarism and convened optimistic but inadequate coordinating committees—including the President's Emergency Committee for Employment, formed October 1930. Even his Reconstruction Finance Corporation and his Emergency Relief and Construction Act, both passed in 1932, merely loaned federal money. See Albert U. Romasco, *The Poverty of Abundance: Hoover, the Nation, the Depression* (New York, 1965), 30, 34–35, 48–50, 69, 128–30, 143–48, 172, 222–27, 232. See also Craig Lloyd, *Aggressive Introvert: A Study of Herbert Hoover and Public Relations Management 1912–1932* (Columbus, 1972), 156–61.

4. In early 1930, Tate and his wife, Caroline Gordon, moved into a farmhouse outside Clarksville, Tennessee. They named the antebellum home "Benfolly" after Tate's brother Ben, a coal magnate who purchased the property for them.

that they did not wish to mortgage their *labor* to industry for a generation. If these people had co-operated with the President I have no doubt that our crisis would be long past. For the very word mortgage, in the sense of burden or misfortune or disgrace, is obsolete; we now know that the greatest incentive to consumption is debt, for we consume before we have to worry about paying, and thus we are compelled to work, and the world's work gets done. In the end the banks and insurance companies relieve us of the foolish responsibility of property, so that we enjoy the mild routine of labor and consumption, without even needing to decide what we wish to consume.

It was a crisis of religious faith, and we momentarily failed. We have dismissed Solution Number Two—that of the Dole. Number Three is a compromise measure that promises well in the failure of our religion to do the work. I should have no inclination, however, to publish this article if Number Three were a total solution to the problem of unemployment. President Roosevelt makes no extravagant claims for his Reforestation and Public Works projects.[5] He knows that these great undertakings, because they contemplate reclaiming our lands, contain reactionary concessions to those superstitious forces that I have described. They are temporary expedients to relieve some of the unemployed, but they will not absorb that entire suffering class. There will still remain the residue x. It will be a distinct problem, but like a wise man the President proposes to solve one problem at a time. My own solution to the problem of the "residue," which I will describe in the following pages, may never be necessary. *But it will be absolutely necessary unless our people and their leaders are willing to abandon the American system.* Mr. Roosevelt's preliminary grappling with the problem of unemployment is—with the slight concession to reaction that I have noted—all in the logical direction of the American system. For he plans to have them work land that they will not have to suffer the degradation of living on; though of course it is reactionary to put them in contact with the land at all. Leaving out this element of reaction, my suggestion as to the right way to handle the permanent residue follows from the President's position. I offer the suggestion a little early, perhaps, but it is well to cast it upon the waters of opinion— whence it may return to us after many days.

The American system is that method of production, borrowed from England and improved, which in the last seventy years has made us the most powerful and the happiest people in the world, as well as the most humane and

---

5. Founded in 1933, the Civilian Conservation Corps hired workers for forestry and soil projects. The National Industrial Recovery Act launched relief agencies such as the Public Works Administration, which created jobs rebuilding the infrastructure.

cultivated. We have bought up the art treasures of the world. (Of course, the French, a nation of peasants, in refusing to make the last payment on the Debt, showed their envy of us by trying to cripple us: they pretend to their own people that this repudiation is a way of inciting hatred of American institutions which, they say, will wreck the world and which they are trying to make unpopular in France.)[6] The American system has almost annihilated the cumbersome institution of private property, especially property in land. It has put nearly the whole means of production into the hands of an enlightened minority (every industrial magnate collects paintings) who are much better able to distribute material goods to the masses than the masses are able to acquire them for themselves. The richer the capitalist becomes, the more benefits he is able to pass on to the ranks below him. This is, in brief, the American system. As a system it is beyond dispute the most efficient that has ever been achieved by mankind. But it has latterly encountered an obstacle, the obstacle of unemployment.

Unemployment grows out of the wholly unforeseen and perhaps uncontrollable invention of what was once called the labor-saving device, but which we must now see definitely as the labor-eliminating device. Can we call a halt upon its further perfection and spread throughout the world? Surely not; for our whole technological equipment is obviously unalterable, and proceeds upon its own momentum—a process that men as mere trustees and wardens participate in, a process the benefits of which are immune to the instability and weakness of man. But the machine has made unemployment, and the unemployed are thus unable to buy the products of the machine. It has happened all over the world; there is unemployment to some extent in all the buying nations; the markets for manufactured goods are shrinking. It is a temporary course, no indictment of the system itself. *There must be progress.* My solution to the problem of the unemployed residue is in the spirit of American progress.

If our enlightened capitalism does not accept my solution, which is merely one of readjustment, it will have to face one of two alternative proposals that are totally subversive of the American system. These alternatives go by different names, the first usually as Socialism or Communism, the second as Agrarianism or perhaps the Property System. If the residue of the idle, the permanently idle, is allowed to go on as it is, possibly increasing every year, there will be a revolution. The Communists will seize our industrial

---

6. Shortly before Hoover left office in December 1932, several European nations stopped honoring their World War I debts. Legislators in the U.S. urged sanctions and eventually passed the Johnson Act (1934), which the Europeans ignored. See Wayne S. Cole, *Roosevelt and the Isolationists, 1932–1945* (Lincoln, Neb., 1983), 81–94.

organization and distribute its products to both employed and unemployed; by eliminating the price-system and the creation of surplus value for the five percent of the population who own the means of production, they will put everyone to work like robots, and the material welfare of each man will be enormously decreased. Our admirable mild paternalism will disappear; our highly cultivated class of rulers, who give tone and culture to society as a whole, will be destroyed; and we shall lose that zeal for the welfare of the common man that has made our civilization envied throughout the world.

The Agrarian idea I merely touch upon in order to show an example of the kind of irresponsibility with which certain Americans are meeting this grave crisis. They have even criticized President Roosevelt's Reforestation and Public Works projects; they argue that the Public Works cannot go on forever (they are not productive of economic goods, they hold), and they ask: Who will live on the reclaimed land? They demand that these men who are to receive a dollar a day and board, for improving land which will then stand idle, be put upon the land themselves. And this is the argument that exposes their fallacy, and the reactionary character of their views: they are willing to deprive the worker of the great blessings that sift down to him from industry, and to reduce him to the degraded status of the European peasant. They think that our great mechanical progress is negligible. They cry for a restoration of small property, which would lower the American standard of living; they would bring back that unplanned economy in which small owners fought with one another over small matters, leaving the Good of Society out of account. They say, moreover, that the good of society is an abstraction, that the only good that men know is personal. They would repudiate most of the achievements of social research, which teaches men how to be good patriotic consumers, on the ground that the data thus accumulated merely puts an instrument of oppression into the hands of the ruling class.

By an absurd paradox they argue that there is no difference between Capitalism and Communism, that under either system the labor is slave labor, that the only way to remove from Capitalism what they call a fundamental contradiction is to make all men slaves of the owning class, or to make the masses their own owners in a Communist order. They denounce the Communists no less bitterly than they denounce us, as men who with sham heroism are really following the line of least resistance. Under the preposterous notion that men lack "freedom"—when, obviously, until 1929, when our unfortunate maladjustment occurred, there was never a people freer to consume more commodities—for freedom's sake they would make men, or enough men to color society, go back and be free to resume the bestial labor of the farm. And they would ask the business man to resume small business—as if the great business men of our age had not spread, by means of quantity production and modern selling methods, a uniform blessing over the whole country at cheap rates. The Agrarians argue that man does not need the modern industrial commodities to the extent that he has had them; and what he does have of them must be made near home, in moderate-sized factories, so that wealth will not be concentrated in a few places, and in a few hands.

But they are blind to the vital question, what is man to do with himself when he is not consuming? It is the great discovery of our age that man is chiefly a consumer—that he cannot consume too much. Low consumption is the source of many evils; it leaves men idle for anti-social pursuits like the cobweb of philosophy, in which foolish opinions rise, and like the arts, which compel men to question the destiny of man. The Agrarians argue that the Communists have simply taken our great idea from us: that man is nothing but a consumer. To crown all, they—all Agrarians—have the impudence to proclaim that unless we return to small property—or rather, as we believe, to a stupid peasantry—all civilization will collapse. As if civilization did not begin with the American system!

Yet it is certain that unless we dispose of the residue x—the exact figures must await the outcome of President Roosevelt's preliminary program— unless we deal with the permanently unemployed, we shall have trouble. The masses of the unemployed are not consuming. They are beginning to en- gage in anti-social pursuits. A peasantry of course is impossible; it is not in the Spirit of the Age. And besides, Economic Laws forbid it, as well as the civilized sense of man. But Communism is more of a menace. Even apart from that danger, the unemployed are an uncertain quantity in industry, and upset its nicest calculations. Their support is a constant drain on productive enterprise. And in twenty years, as the Technocrats have shown, this class may increase to fifty million men.

Modern man is healthier than his ancestors of the early nineteenth century. After the enclosure laws of England in the eighteenth century went to force, a horde of bestial peasants flocked to the towns, but many of them came to this country. To a large extent they remain, those who crossed the Atlantic, in the Southern States in their original bestial condition. But nearly every- where the industrial laborer has profited as a consumer. He has been well fed. Our improved sanitation and hygiene have also had a beneficent effect. The longevity of the American people has increased enormously. As to the laboring portion, this must be admitted to be, at present, an embarrassment; for it only increases the residue x. But I do think, on the whole, that the su- perior type of manhood and womanhood that our free institutions have cre- ated actually points to the method of disposing of a fraction of that manhood and that womanhood, now that they are a mortal drag upon our efficiency economically and a menace to us politically. They, we know well, would agree that the prime consideration is the Social Good, and not individuals.

Modern Americans have more energy than any other men, and this means that their bodies are more richly stored with the substantial fats and chemicals than any other men. Modern science has made them superior, and because modern science has also made the labor-eliminating device that has rendered them useless, we must face the criticism that we sometimes hear — that it is inconsistent to continue this process, and to let our idle citizens rot in their perfect health. We must be consistent. Our idle men have long been schooled in the true doctrine that we all exist for use. Now what might be mere waste will, through my solution, find utility, and bring back that nice adjustment of labor and capital that we greatly need.

At this point I must pause to glance at a remedy for the evil that was advanced by the *New Republic* about two years ago.[7] It attracted far too little attention. Inflate the currency, the editors said, for the sole benefit of the unemployed; give them the money and they will buy up the goods decaying in our warehouses. Thus would labor be fed, for the factories would have to refill the warehouses. Manufacturers of tinned foods would not alone profit. We have made it clear to the public that patented cigarette-lighters and green bathroom fixtures are also overwhelming necessities. Capital would be relieved of some of its surplus goods. It would be a splendid temporary remedy, but realism compels me to regard its consequences. The money thus distributed and spent would shortly, as it should, return to the Capitalist: more of this extraordinary money would have to be printed, which would also go to the Capitalist. It is a repetitive system, but I am convinced that it is one of the most sensible temporary schemes that have been devised.

There is another method that deserves notice before I come to my own proposal. It has the merit of being but a further extension of that beneficent tendency of our great system to enlist the female portion of the community in productive pursuits, thus freeing women from the bondage of the home and relieving men of part of their burden. Yet the work would be light. Prostitution is considerably easier than bending over a loom. And it would be more profitable in the long run; especially since a woman's span of life is

---

7. "If we want to try a really bold experiment in inflation," the *NR* opined (somewhat hyperbolically), "we ought to do something far more radical than is suggested. We might better print $5,000,000,000 in paper money, and give it outright to the unemployed, to the drought-ridden and impoverished farmers, to all heads of families whose incomes are below, say, $2,500 a year. They would have no difficulty in knowing how to spend the money" ("Modest Proposal," 125).

longer under the modern conditions that permit her to keep till fifty the luster and bloom that faded at twenty-five in the cotton-spinner or street-walker of a century ago. It is obvious that the productive possibilities of prostitution conducted on lines of modern efficiency have been sadly neg-lected. It is equally obvious that the existence of several million unemployed women of all ages and attributes provides a perfect occasion for remedying this defect.

Where all the other great businesses have been so profitably rationalized, we have allowed this, the oldest of all and, until recently, the equal of any in popularity, to remain positively medieval. We are still content to let it be hemmed about by archaic laws and customs handed down from a barbarous age, laws and customs that clearly operate in restraint of trade and would not stand the test of constitutionality. Everyone knows that it has been through a reasoned rejection of superstitious taboos that modern progress has been made possible. For instance, as long as the medieval notion of "usury" pre-vailed, which forbade (by labeling it a "sin") charging interest on loans made for non-productive purposes, the institution of banking, the backbone of the modern world, was rendered impossible except at a very low level. Again, the ancient prejudice against enterprise and ambition (which the Dark Ages damned by calling "the sin of avarice") kept business at a deplorably primi-tive stage for centuries, forcing the populace to waste their time in tending what they called their "souls" and thinking about an imaginary next world.

But these and other equally obstructive delusions have yielded to the light of reason. There is ground for thinking that the restraints which still hamper prostitution would quickly melt away when the benefits to industry of an ef-fectively organized super-corporation of prostitutes were recognized. The main deterrent, of course, is the atmosphere of unrespectability that hangs around the profession. Much has been done to alleviate this situation by our modern social scientists, sexologists, and anthropologists, by the theater and the motion pictures, by the whole process of modern enlightenment and freedom. But the final word that would end all the old prejudice has not been spoken.

The benefits to business of giving legal status to several million prosti-tutes would vastly exceed the benefits of 3.2 beer.[8] Real estate values would

---

8. In the spring of 1933, with the encouragement of Roosevelt, Congress legalized beer that contained a lower than customary percentage of alcohol. Some 20,000 work-ers were thus put to work in breweries, and "tens of thousands of related jobs" were generated (David E. Kyvig, *Repealing National Prohibition* [Chicago, 1979], 177–78; 178). The Twenty-first Amendment, which overturned Prohibition, was ratified later that year.

receive an immediate healthy impetus throughout the nation, as the he-taerae moved into quarters suitable to their trade. They would relieve the furniture industry by buying, on the installment plan, artistic furniture from Grand Rapids. The *Ladies' Home Journal* or the *Woman's Home Companion* [1873–1957] would instruct them in the art of arranging furniture in the best taste. (What great improvements we have made over Europe! Our art is manufactured and distributed, so that the people don't have to bother about it. We now buy up and appreciate the art made by the European peasant-societies without at the same time having to live like peasant-hogs; we reproduce this art by machinery with great saving of time, which is money.) The garment trades, the telephone companies, and numerous other lines of endeavor would share in the proceeds. A simply collected tax on premises or licenses would go far toward balancing the national budget.

Moreover, under the dispensations of this industry, the men, once common laborers, would advance a step socially and become salesmen. Because our great spirit of social improvement has found new names for old occupations, no salesman would ever again be called a pimp—just as no one thinks of applying to a banker, who has mastered the art of making money out of money, the archaic name of pirate. But this would not be the only direct benefit that the male portion of the unemployed would receive, as the public mind progressed in understanding of the industry's merits. There is no need to enlarge on the opportunities for growth under efficient management of male prostitution, always a backward branch of the calling. Women and men alike would have time to improve their minds—another sign of emancipation from the peasant-system. The subscribers to the book clubs would be tripled, our authors would flourish, and the great service rendered by the press to civilization would be appreciated by larger numbers. Altogether the advantages for both culture and business under this system should not be overlooked. As the "ladder industry" for the next boom it would seem far more promising than pre-fabricated houses.

Is there a general market for the commodity? Such a question becomes superfluous as soon as we examine the facts in a businesslike manner. It should be obvious that the economic possibilities of man's passional nature have scarcely begun to be tapped. We have hitherto been content to let ourselves be limited by notions of monogamy and of continence. There is no doubt that once freed of these notions and given the facilities here proposed, man's capacity for sensual indulgence would expand immeasurably. Through a large-scale system of prostitution organized along thoroughly up-to-date lines this great force could be set to productive uses, and the wheels of industry would resume their profitable revolutions. Here again it is simply a matter of clearing away the outworn prejudices; and here again the work has already been largely done. Just as the medieval conception of "avarice," when it was subjected to the light of emancipated reason, turned out to be business enterprise and laudable ambition, so that medieval notion of "lust" has been seen more and more clearly to be nothing but man's natural and harmless desire to be himself and enjoy life; we have come to realize that there is no real reason why the simple desires of the flesh should be curbed and mortified after the model of pathological ascetics. In our present emergency, an emphatic word from a high source—from the United States Chamber of Commerce, from the American Bankers' Association, from the House of Morgan, from Henry Ford, from our Leader—would suffice to bring all public-spirited citizens, who compose the vast majority of the commonwealth, to the support of so salutary an enterprise.

It is true that even when the inhibitions and prejudices still lingering from the past had thus been finally cleared away, there might be a certain measure of reluctance on the part of many to alter the peasant ideas of life, to break with the old ties and superstitions, and give full support to the new dispensation. But here would come to our aid Mr. Roger Babson's method called advertising.[9] Could not our prostitutes having formed a vast merger, advertise so effectively that the rest of the community would be persuaded to buy what it does not feel a need for? After all, not necessity but salesmanship and maximum consumption are the spirit of the age.[10] Take our taste in cigarettes. This taste, to use a Behavioristic phrase, which is always useful, is now largely sexually "conditioned." We buy the cigarettes because the girl in the picture is "alluring." A bathroom scene in the advertising section of the *Saturday Evening Post* succeeds in making a throat gargle appear to have the virtues of an aphrodisiac. The new industry would have an unsurpassed advertising technique ready to hand. Of course, since we understand so well the use of the Conditioned Reflex, the new industry might be compelled to make its commodity attractive through cigarettes, reversing the process now in use.

---

9. Roger Ward Babson (1875–1967) was born in Massachusetts and educated at the Massachusetts Institute of Technology. A prolific author, he wrote advice manuals and how-to-succeed books devoted to economic, investment, and business subjects. "Although advertising has its abuses," Babson wrote, "it certainly has its uses" (*Fighting Business Depressions: Money-Making Methods for These Times* [New York, 1932], 241).

10. Tate echoed the introduction to *ITMS*: "So the rise of modern advertising—along with its twin, personal salesmanship—is the most significant development of our industrialism. Advertising means to persuade the consumers to want exactly what the applied sciences are able to furnish them. It consults the happiness of the consumer no more than it consulted the happiness of the laborer" (xlvi).

I mention this solution of the unemployment problem for what it is worth; but I cannot believe completely in its restorative efficacy, since it has the same defect as the proposal of the *New Republic:* its benefits would be temporary. Prostitution is tied up inevitably with a particular social system: the family. Only while marriage and the family were still popular would this supplementary institution be feasible. Our American system has given us a perfectly machine-like and impersonal corporation that runs so well of itself that it requires no social system for its successful operation. The old-fashioned system of well distributed property required the family for its preservation (and *vice versa*), but industrial capitalism is capable of preserving itself without the family. The archaic peasant-family is disappearing: we are coming more and more to enjoy that self-expression through sex which was impossible under the old regime. The rationalization of prostitution would quickly carry this process to completion. The old attractions of monogamy and the home fade from men's minds, and sexual unions would tend to become wholly based on free choice—a moral system best described by the phrase Regular Irregularity. Thus a regular class of prostitutes would come to have no social function: there would be a reversion, in this sphere, to a universal system of barter. Those citizens who do not see the full implications of our improved condition, retaining some of the muddled intransigence of the old order, may sigh sentimentally at the disappearance of the harlot. We can only remind them, these men of halting vision, that the past is quite completely dead, or rapidly becoming so.

So that while this proposal might well solve our immediate problems and at last allow the current slump to make way for the inevitable boom, it would not be a permanent solution for the awkward problem of trade cycles. After all, our forefathers in clearing the forests, in carrying railroads and highways over mountains and prairie and river, in erecting our towering skyscrapers, in contriving the whole vast intricate network of corporate structure and finance which has made our civilization almost perfect, were building for the future, for eternity. We, too, owe something to posterity. If we can we must solve the unemployment problem for good and all. Since it is unthinkable that we should go off the American system into Communism or peasantry, there is only one solution to the problem of the residue x, the class of the permanently unemployed, and that method I will now completely describe. The exact figures pending President Roosevelt's Reforestation and Public Works must be in hand, however, before we shall know the value of x and shall be able to carry out the plan.

The American capitalist class is the most responsible class of rulers that the world has seen, and although it in no sense *owns* the labor that supports it,

282 / Allen Tate

it is nevertheless *responsible* for it. In this present crisis the only way of making effective that responsibility is to accept all the burdens of *ownership*—though, it must be emphasized, there is no legal compulsion upon the Capitalists to do so. They will accept the burden for the *good of humanity*. The specific responsibility in the crisis would be to dispose of their useless property, in the most economical, the most humane, and the most efficient manner possible. Our age is aware that industrial economy, efficiency, and humanity are all the same thing. The permanently unemployed must be disposed of with the greatest benefit to that property—considered in one aspect as human beings—and to the buying public at large. I propose this in the immediate interest of labor and in the eventual interest of owners.

There is a certain number of useless persons. If that number increases or is even allowed to remain constant, it will, as we have seen, constitute a dire menace to order. It is the fate of labor—and who will question the logic of history?—to be placed as it is placed now. Society would suffer the least rupture, and be spared that violence to its *sympathy*—a peculiarly modern refinement of feeling—if it quietly, and in the ordinary routine of industrial technology, *killed off about eight million workers and their families.*

It should be done, all things considered, gradually, but completed in a year lest there should be an abnormal increase of that class of persons, with the attendant perils. By looking at this scrapped property as raw material, not as productive machinery as we usually do, industry could put it to use. Economy and expediency alike suggest this course. Merely to administer to twenty-five millions of souls some kind of euthanasia would shock the public with its hideous spectacle of waste. To lay them out, even in our handsomest "burial parks," would be a serious abuse of the concept of property-in-labor—the temporary assumption upon which the whole procedure here suggested would be based. To grant to mere possessions all the rites historically allowed at the demise of sentient creatures would of course invalidate the entire program.

The unemployed head of a family, say a family of five, would report to his last owner—or, rather, I should say employer, for ownership has been invoked merely for legal sanction in the emergency. The employer would draw up a schedule of extinction, beginning with the mother in order to cut off first the reproducer. The older daughters would come next. Since extermination, as I plan it, must be gradual if we are to avoid severe economic losses, those whose turn came last, the little boys and the little girls, would have to be fed. They could be fed without loss to the employer in excess of what he would normally pay for raw material. The body of the mother first, then the body of the father, could be valued at the current price of the carbon, nitrogen, chlorine, sodium, potassium, silicon, that each yielded, and a fund deposited to the credit of the remaining family. When the children had eaten through this fund, or when, to be exact, the last child had exhausted the total credit established by the gross weight of his kin, his time would have come.

I need not suggest any precise method of putting away these good people. I need not suggest that the method be painless. We are too humane for the ax, guillotine, rope, or firing-squad. I should personally prefer some kind of lethal gas, but not being a chemist, I leave that proposal to the specialists. There should be some kind of brief ceremony before each demise—a sort of half-ceremony, to remind us that these people are half-human. Perhaps the rite could be conveniently administered to groups, or put upon the air. It would be appropriate if a distinguished pastor of the church—whose Protestant branches have marched in the vanguard of progress—could be appointed to receive the herds at the pens. Our American Christianity has never failed us in our onslaughts upon the errors of the past.

It may be argued against this scheme that twenty-five million people would yield less raw material than the same number of hogs. The objection is sound but short-sighted. I have pointed out one of the great features of the modern age: the physical superiority of our people over their ancestors. We should expect a fifteen percent larger yield than a similar enterprise could have got fifty years ago. The refining process would be expensive and it would render exorbitant the price of the finished commodity. But this criticism that I foresee takes no account of the unique and unreplaceable nature of the material. We should be eliminating the unemployed class forever— a fact that would make the material precious, and marketable, under high-pressure salesmanship, at any price.

For example, that "deep inward satisfaction" that the public gets out of a fine, animal-skin glove would deepen further could men and women wear the whole skin of a hand meticulously removed and tanned into a soft, seamless glove. The "fine art of cookery" would get a richer base for oleomargarine and the shortening oils. The potash and sodium chloride would revise the slogan, "25¢ is enough to pay for toothpaste," to: "This toothpaste is cheap at any price: Human dentifrice for humanity."

I have said that this method of disposing of the residue *x* would relieve us of the whole problem of unemployment. That is not strictly true. It assumes as accomplished a long moratorium on the invention of labor-eliminating devices; it requires for its success a stabilization of our technology. Yet should our technical equipment still further improve, the method is still workable. There would merely be a certain number of newly unemployed to kill off every year. At last machinery would take the place of hands altogether. There would be no workers left. There is no life worth living for men who cannot work and consume manufactured goods. It is this article of faith that makes imperative the acceptance of some such proposal as mine for the perpetuation of the American System.

Allen Tate

A View of the Whole South

As often as progressives and conservatives battled in the South, they found common ground as Southerners preoccupied by the future of their region. The complex relationship between the two groups is revealed in Culture in the South, the 1934 anthology that emerged from the University of North Carolina partly in response to the Agrarian movement. In the preface to Culture in the South, William Terry Couch, editor of the university press at Chapel Hill, grudgingly admitted that I'll Take My Stand was "one of the most thoughtful books on the South published in recent years." Yet it wrongly cast "Southern life in terms of industrialism vs. agrarianism." The Agrarians, he concluded, were oblivious to "the misery, the long drawn-out misery, of over-work and undernourishment, of poverty and isolation, of ignorance and hopelessness."[1]

Yet the presence of three Agrarians—Herman Clarence Nixon, Donald Davidson, and Donald Wade—in Couch's anthology is evidence that the Chapel Hill social scientists and the Agrarians found collaboration worthwhile. This did not mean they agreed with the results. Hoping to show the North Carolinians the error of their ways, the Vanderbilt faction of the Agrarian movement planned a long review of Couch's new anthology. Davidson and John Crowe Ransom, especially, were insistent that Allen Tate should speak for the group. "You will undoubtedly be read by every contributor to the volume," Ransom told Tate, "and that's a crowd of important people; add to it the other important Southerners who'll read the book and hear about your remarks, and

---

1. Couch, ed., *Culture in the South* (Chapel Hill, 1934), vii–xi, vii, viii.

you get the crowd that's run the South. Nobody can talk to them as you can."All things considered, Ransom added, *"the enemy is coming reluctantly over to our side."*[2] Similarly, Davidson, urging Tate to *"smite the wicked and reward the faithful,"* believed that the book's contributors could be alienated from their liberal leader, Couch. *"It is obvious that the majority of his contributors agree with us rather than with him,"* Davidson argued. *"Did you notice that about half of the essays make positive and favorable references to* I'll Take My Stand? *Our policy should be calculated to enlarge this circle of supporters."*[3] But the Agrarians hoped in vain for new converts. The review Tate wrote came under fire for its endorsement of racial segregation and signaled the decline of the Agrarian movement.

Reprinted from *American Review* 2 (1934): 411–32,

with the permission of Mrs. Helen Tate.

To the question: What is the South? it were better not to wait for an answer. For unless one asks it in a soliloquy that can dictate its own reply, one is likely to hear: The South is Uncle Sam's other province. That is the answer that one gets, by and large, out of the enormous symposium edited by Professor W. T. Couch,[4] of the University of North Carolina, and published under the misleading title, *Culture in the South.* I say misleading because culture is nowhere clearly understood in all the thirty-one extremely interesting and valuable essays by as many authors; unless culture be the purchasing-power to buy the latest manufactured articles. It must be remembered that the writers herein on social and economic subjects are mostly sociologists and economists, for whom culture is likely to be the table and the chart. Be that as it may, what picture of the South do we get out of their composite labors? What picture do they wish to turn it into? These questions come down to the critical one: What kind of society do these men of the New South want?

In this long but all-too-brief discussion of the points of view set forth in *Culture in the South,* the reader will observe one underlying contention: when men say that we have no choice in the kind of social system that we shall get, it being quite "determined" beforehand by history, facts, forces, conditions,

---

2. Ransom to Tate, undated correspondence, in *Selected Letters of John Crowe Ransom,* ed. Thomas Daniel Young and George Core (Baton Rouge, 1985), 212–13.

3. Davidson to Tate, 12 Jan. 1934, in *LC,* 288–89. See also the preceding letter, Tate to Davidson, 9 Jan. 1934.

4. William Terry Couch (1901–88) was the Virginia-born director of the University of North Carolina Press. According to Daniel Singal, Couch turned the press into "the single most influential institution in launching Modernist thought in the South." An illuminating discussion of Couch's career (including his editing of *Culture in the South*) appears in Singal's *The War Within: From Victorian to Modernist Thought in the South, 1919– 1945* (Chapel Hill, 1982), 265–301 (268).

we know that what they are really saying is that *they* are determined to give us the kind of system that *they* want. When the ante-bellum planter said that God had ordained slavery, he was saying what Mr. Broadus Mitchell (whom we shall hear again) says when he affirms that industrialism is determined by forces of the immediate past, and is thus inevitable. This kind of determinism, both of the planter and of Mr. Mitchell, must be taken seriously; only we must be careful to keep strictly in mind just what it is they are telling us. Not all the writers in this book say what Mr. Mitchell says, and in order to get a notion of what they think or have found out, I will at once try to summarize the articles, not in order of appearance but by subject-groups:

1. *Preface*. Professor Couch, the editor, gives his contributors a free hand. Yet he offers in his Preface his own point of view on Southern civilization in an interesting commentary on the recent Agrarian symposium, *I'll Take My Stand: The South and the Agrarian Tradition*. Having been a contributor to that book, I feel that I am able to point out that Professor Couch's criticism of it is based on a misreading of the text. Consider, he says, "the doctrine that the agrarian way of life is essentially different from the industrial, that it is better—or, at least, better for the South, and that it is worthy of being preserved even at the price of economic obscurantism" [viii]. If economic obscurantism means self-sufficiency for the farmer, a state in which his "purchasing power" is of interest only to those who have something, usually useless, to sell him, we plead guilty. But it was nowhere said that Southern agriculture at this moment affords an ideal society to set off against the depravity of industrialism: we said that Southern agriculture might be made into a system in which security and stability could be won in a measure impossible so long as the farmer, fixed in the commercial scheme, remains in economic vassalage to his local merchants and bankers and, in so far as these are vassals to the big bankers and industrialists, to the whole financial system. *Item:* This sensitiveness of the Southern pro-industrialist to the disappearance of purchasing-power on the farm, or, put the other way, their dislike of independent agriculture, is symptomatic of the general capitalist imperialism towards the Market. The expanding Market—and here the Marxists, for instance John Strachey in *The Coming Struggle for Power*,[5] are right—is the cornerstone of industrial capitalism; it must expand not only towards greater consumption of commodities, but towards an unlimited supply of labor that it can buy at its own price; therefore the Southern industrialist is

---

5. Evelyn John St. Loe Strachey (1901–63) was a British Labor Party parliamentarian (1929–31) and author whose political writings included *The Coming Struggle for Power* (London, 1932).

greatly concerned for the farmer's purchasing-power if indeed he cannot persuade him to leave the farm for the factory, where he will play the double role of consumer and cheap laborer. There is, in this process, the concealed joker that may wreck capitalism—destruction of the consumer in the act of cheapening labor. *Item:* It must be said that neither the editor nor his contributors, even when the latter are critical of industrialization of the South, are aware of the plight of world capitalism; nor is there any critical perception of its possible alternatives. These men are still catching up with the North, nor do they ask whether there is now anything in the North to catch up with. The reader will judge whether, and in what sense, the South may be a backward region.

2. *Literature, education, journalism, folk-lore.* Ten essays cover these subjects; they exhibit a high quality of learning and judgment, and they are indispensable to future study of these fields in the South. John D. Allen's[6] analysis of Southern journalism [126−58] divides newspaper opinion into three camps—the New South Toryism of industry; the Old South Toryism of the Confederacy, in which sentiment on the one hand has no connection, on the other, with economic interests which easily merge with those of rising industry; and Liberalism. Mr. Allen is both fearless and astute, but like the majority of the authors of this book, he fails to see that Liberalism has no program and that, however brave and pious its criticism may be, it is ultimately futile. Professor Edgar W. Knight[7] contributes an informative article on education problems and "progress" [211−28]; but here progress means bigger and better schools. H. Clarence Nixon, of Tulane University, surveys the colleges and universities [229−47], to the conclusion that a great Southern University is necessary, most of the existing institutions being timid and subservient to the new industrial money of which they have felt considerable need: this is one of the best essays in the book. Yet none of the writers in this field attempts a thorough criticism of the New Education. Arthur Palmer Hudson[8] writes about white folk-songs [519−46]; Guy B. Johnson[9] about

---

6. The South Carolina–born journalism professor John D. Allen (1898−1972) taught at Mercer University. On Allen and the other contributors to *Culture in the South,* see also the biographical sketches, 693−98.

7. Edgar Wallace Knight (1886−1953) was a professor of education at the University of North Carolina and wrote prolifically about Southern education.

8. Arthur Palmer Hudson (1892−1978), born in Mississippi, was a professor of English at the University of North Carolina.

9. Guy Benton Johnson (1901−91) was a University of North Carolina folklorist associated with Howard Odum (Singal, *War Within,* 317−27).

the folk-songs of the Negro [547–69]; and B. A. Botkin writes a more general essay on "Folk and Folklore" [570–93]. These articles, based on the latest results of research, are of capital interest and importance: yet again the relation of this material to the meaning of "culture" is nowhere suspected except at moments by Mr. Botkin: culture presumably remains something that you buy with money, possibly from Europe. Mr. John Donald Wade offers us, under the title "Southern Humor" [616–28], the most distinguished piece of writing in the volume. His thesis that Southern humor rises in the inability of the Southerner, since Appomattox, to take any abstractions or programs seriously, may indeed be seriously disputed, unless Mr. Wade means ideas that are not related to his immediate life. William Cabell Greet[10] has written the first systematic study of Southern speech [594–615] that I have seen—another essay of importance. One of the ablest and most discriminating essays on the general culture of the South is Professor Jay B. Hubbell's[11] "Southern Magazines" [159–82]; he is just and detached throughout; and his conclusions will be the starting-point of future study in this field, as well as advice and warning to the aspiring founder of magazines in the South. In "The Trend in Literature" [subtitled "A Partisan View," 183–210] Mr. Donald Davidson (ill at ease among his Liberal neighbors) puts his finger on a fundamental *malaise* of the modern Southern writer—his inability, for various reasons, to look upon his society as a normal manifestation of human life, with the consequent confusion of purpose that keeps his style and point of view on the defensive or satirical plane. Mr. Davidson, justly I think, makes exception in favor of the poets, who, however, standing outside this *Zeitgeist,* are unread. His essay brings to a head the whole cultural problem of the South, a problem that few of the other contributors seem aware of: that the basis of culture is a dignified local life resting upon the common people, who take all the props from under a genuine culture as soon as they are deprived of independence; hence the complete industrialization of the South, even if the perfect bungalow and kitchen sink of the industrial apologists were possible, would destroy the last stronghold of culture in the United States.

3. *Manners and Society.* Miss Josephine Pinckney examines the social changes of the last generation ["Bulwarks Against Change," 40–51], as these

---

10. William Cabell Greet (1901–72), an English professor and linguist at Barnard College, was born in Texas.

11. Virginian Jay Broadus Hubbell (1885–1979) taught American literature at Duke University and was editorial chairman of the journal *American Literature.*

changes have affected domestic manners and customs; she concludes that the South will not be quickly transformed; for the deep-rooted leisureliness of Southern life is a concrete reality against which abstract benefits like quick wealth and power will break at last in vain. Miss Pinckney's essay is full of shrewd and sensitive observation, not the least interesting of which is her remark that Prohibition with its corn liquor did more than any other thing to lower the social tone of the upper class of the South. Mr. Clarence E. Cason,[12] in "Middle Class and Bourbon" [478–500], tries to discover in the Old South a middle-class, but I think with not very much success, since his notion of a middle-class is a number of people with a "middling" amount of money and power. Again the most advanced Southern "iconoclasm," i.e., the brave explosion of the mythical Colonel, commits itself to that least desirable form of provincialism which consists in seeing itself in isolation both historical and economic. For a middle-class is that class which, producing nothing, buys cheap and sells dear, getting a rake-off from both producer and consumer; the Morgans, for example, being middle-class, regardless of their wealth and power. (This provincial failure to see the South as the last battleground of a conflict that began in Europe with the economic changes growing out of the Reformation, the conflict between producer and *entrepreneur,* between the land and manipulating capital, not only blinds Mr. Cason to the social realities of the South; it confuses the outlook of the larger number of the authors of economic articles in the book.) Mr. J. Wesley Hatcher's[13] article, "Appalachian America" [374–402], presents the entire social, religious, domestic, and economic life of the "mountaineer"; it is the best thing ever written on this subject and it ought to be expanded into a book. Two factors have prevented a proper understanding of the highlander: the old prejudice of the low-country Southern gentry, and modern industrial exploitation. Industry has advertised the mountaineer as a debased creature whose life deserves no respect but to whom, for some mysteriously humanitarian reason, should be given the improvements of the bathroom and the kitchen sink. As far as the highlands are concerned, says Mr. Hatcher, "the

---

12. The University of Alabama journalism professor Clarence E. Cason (1896–1935) accused the Agrarian group of emotionalism in his book *90° in the Shade* (Chapel Hill, 1935). W. J. Cash wrote of "poor Clarence Cason, who . . . felt compelled to commit suicide, in part at least because of his fear of the fiercely hostile attitude which he knew that both the school authorities and his fellow faculty members would take toward his criticisms of the South" (*Mind of the South* [New York, 1941], 334). See also Wayne Flynt's introduction (v–x) to the 1983 reprint of *90° in the Shade.*

13. The Ohio-born J. Wesley Hatcher (1876–?) taught sociology at Berea College in Kentucky.

solution to the economic and social problems of the people is not to be found in coercing them into the slums and bread lines of our industrial centers [as has been advocated by some of our social philosophers], but rather in the adjustment of the educational program and methods to the task of developing the remaining resources in a manner that will give the richest and fullest life possible" [381]. Given the all-pervasive faith in "education," Mr. Hatcher is not to be blamed for missing the key to the difficulty: economic autonomy. And this problem is political, not "educational," as we shall see when we come to the essay on Southern politics.

4. *Business and Industry.* This is a depressing exhibit. Professor Claudius Murchison[14] [in "Depression and the Future of Business," 93–114] hymns the courage of the Southern business man who broke away from "inertia" and "old habits"—to do what? The real answer is: to wreck the South and Southern agriculture, as his *confrere* in the North has wrecked the whole country. Again there is no inkling of the world condition of business; it is assumed that everything is going to get better. This is a perfect example of academic timidity before the industrial masters; for the bankers and industrialists, the real if temporary masters of the South, keep the college, and the professors keep the peace. Let us pass on. "The Industrial Worker," by Harriet L. Herring[15] [344–60], is a competent analysis of the position of the industrial worker, a position that is in urgent need of reform; but there is no hint of the real source of reform, which apparently is to proceed from the sheer charity of the money power. This article has the negative defect of the book as a whole—lack of historical and political sense, and this is a lack of realism. Mr. George Sinclair Mitchell[16] analyzes the relation of Southern industrial labor to organization [629–45]: until the Southern worker is organized he will not get a fair hearing in the courts. This is good sense: the labor movement in the South should be supported, but it must not be supposed that it can achieve the solution to the real labor problem, which is wage-slavery. The hard plight of labor becomes manifest in Mr. Bruce Crawford's[17] article, "The Coal Miner" [361–73], a plain tale of corruption, ruthless

---

14. Claudius Temple Murchison (1889–1968) was an economics professor at the University of North Carolina and a cotton expert.

15. Harriet L. Herring (1892–?), a historian of the textile industry, was affiliated with the University of North Carolina's Institute for Research in Social Science.

16. The Columbia University economist George Sinclair Mitchell (1902–?) was Broadus Mitchell's brother.

17. The Virginia-born labor activist Bruce Crawford (1893–?) edited *Crawford's Weekly.*

exploitation, and insane competition. Mr. Crawford offers a brief review of the Harlan war, and if to this review we add the historical background of the mountaineer already sketched by Mr. Hatcher, we begin to understand the causes of the miner's plight. Mr. Crawford sees the solution to the problem in socialist reform; Mr. Hatcher, in local independence. I think the latter solution is the correct one; for labor legislation is never radical but only ameliorative, the worker remaining, for all his improved condition, a wage-slave. (It may be remarked that in this country, North and South, where there is enough land to support a huge population, wage-slavery could be easily avoided, as it cannot so easily be in England where there is no land this side the colonies for the worker to fall back upon.) On the question of labor legislation Professor Charles W. Pipkin[18] [646−77] tells a story that may well astonish the optimist of Southern industry: the concessions to labor, in the form of child-labor laws, old-age pensions, and workman's compensation, though numerically considerable, are actually so slight as to cripple the operator little if at all. And these concessions will continue to be made, in partial and ineffective form, as a propagandist sop to the worker and the humanitarian public: the operator knows the procedure to be harmless, for he alone holds the *political power*. In the face of this circumstance, Mr. Broadus Mitchell's panegyric of Southern industrialism [80−92] rings out like the cry of blind Pew in the night.[19] I have tried for years to understand what is wrong with Mr. Mitchell. There being, he says, no Old Southern culture that he "can see," it would be well to get more factories in the South. Industrialism is not only the superior economic structure for society; it is also "determined" economically. It is beautiful to observe the forces of history at the service of Mr. Mitchell's desires; I envy him. Now the commentators on Southern agriculture agree that from two-thirds to three-fourths of the thirty-five million inhabitants of the Southern States live on the land. The farmers are in wretched condition; but this does not concern Mr. Mitchell; he can do nothing for them. Although labor troubles in the South have been grievous,

---

18. Charles Wooten Pipkin (1899−1941), dean of the graduate school at Louisiana State University and founder of the *Southern Review,* earned advanced degrees from Vanderbilt and from Oxford (on a Rhodes scholarship). See Thomas W. Cutrer, *Parnassus on the Mississippi: The Southern Review and the Baton Rouge Literary Community, 1935−1942* (Baton Rouge, 1984), 29−33 and ff.

19. "Down went Pew," wrote Robert Louis Stevenson of the pirate, "with a cry that rang high in the night; and the four hoofs trampled and spurned him and passed by. He fell on his side, then gently collapsed upon his face, and moved no more" (*Treasure Island* [London, 1923], 31).

they have not been grievous enough. We must catch up with the world; we must completely industrialize the South so that we shall have a problem that must be solved in socialist terms. There is a moral imperative upon us to do this. This point of view, I gather from certain intimations *passim* in Mr. Mitchell's essay, is "realistic"; that of the Agrarians, backward-looking and sentimental.

5. "Also There Is Politics" [115–25], by George Fort Milton, author of a brilliant life of Andrew Johnson,[20] is the sole essay on that subject. It is very nearly the sole mention of it in the entire book. The trouble with Southern politics, says Mr. Milton, is the Solid South; there is no respectable opposition party. What is Mr. Milton's own view of the State? We do not know. The parties do not have to stand for any view of the State, for Mr. Milton knows, as we know, that the real political masters are the bankers and industrialists. (This knowledge I attribute to Mr. Milton; he does not authorize me to do so.) So we get opposition opposing opposition, while the money power rules. This I understand to be the perfect formula of Southern Liberalism, if we add thereto the tiger's chaudron of pious zeal for reform and progress. The State governments, says Mr. Milton, have of late years been greatly reformed in economy and efficiency; yet, alas, "progress" in public works and highways has provided opportunities for graft and corruption of the direst sort. There is this, of course, on the one hand; there is that unfortunately on the other. The donkey, political thought, starves to death between the bales of hay, doing justice to them both, and hoping for the best.

6. *Agriculture.* This is by far the ablest group of essays in the book. Professor Rupert B. Vance writes a geographical survey of Southern soil, climate, and natural resources [24–39]; he recommends regional planning—an excellent recommendation that ought to be the basis of restoring Southern life. Who will do the planning? It is a political question; it is not probable that a committee of high-minded professors will be appointed to the task. Professor A. E. Parkins[21] offers us a valuable descriptive and statistical account of farming in the South [52–79]; it is a chaos that apparently requires chiefly more efficient machinery to bring it to order—in "harmony with modern commercial agriculture." Here, again, there is no broad critical sense of the

---

20. Milton, *Age of Hate.*
21. Almon Ernest Parkins (1879–1940) was a professor of geography at George Peabody College.

relation of farming to industry; commercial farming, in the face of its collapse, is taken as an inevitable good. The best of these articles, the best article on economics in the whole book, is Mr. Clarence Poe's "The Farmer
and His Future" [319–43]. Mr. Poe clearly and concisely urges two reforms
that contain the solution not only to the farm problem in the South but to
the problem of labor in the city: he urges, first, diversification of crops, particularly towards clovers and grasses for cattle raising, a "crop" that will not
only keep farm labor employed and paid in the winter off-season, but will
enrich the soil for plant-crops; and he urges, secondly, as an indispensable
basis for this reform, a program of self-sufficiency for the farm, in which the
farmer's own living comes off the land first of all. It is perfect in its simplicity; it is not urged by the other contributors for a reason that I have already
pointed out: industrial capitalism wants to sell the farmer *everything he uses,*
subsistence agriculture signaling a shrinkage of the Market; and the farmer's
independence represents also a shrinkage of the market where cheap labor
may be bought. Until recently we were undergoing the same process that
England suffered a hundred years ago—dispossession of the farmer who
must necessarily go to the city to supply cheap labor for industry. (The probable effect of Mr. Poe's "agrarian" program upon industrial labor I shall indicate in a moment.) With this group of essays I have placed Professor Den
Hollander's[22] "The Tradition of 'Poor Whites'" [403–31], a revolutionary
study of the history of Southern social classes. Den Hollander shows that the
fiction of a small number of great planters set above a vast horde of miserable peckerwoods and clayeaters was the invention of Northern prejudice,
one more way of discrediting the South before the Civil War: the great majority of slaveless men were yeomen subsistence farmers, whom the up-
heaval of the war threw as tenants upon the big plantations. Yet the fiction
has been taken over by the modern Liberal and industrialist in the South; it
rationalizes his rejection of the "past"; and it gives moral color to his "uplift"
program for the poor-white coming into his factory. Here the familiar process has been at work: industry crushes agriculture, dispossesses the small
farmer, and then works itself into a moral fervor over his plight; it then res-
cues the miserable victim of wicked plantation exploitation by enticing him
into the factory village (bathroom and kitchen sink), where, as a wage-slave,
he receives the finishing touches of the servitude that tenantry began. It is
worth remarking here that, able as these essays are, none of them offers a
program for the evils of the tenant system, though these evils all through the
book are acutely pointed out and analyzed. Why is this? Simply because it is

---

22. Arie Nicolaas Jan Den Hollander (1906–?) was a Dutch social scientist.

a dangerous political question: it would involve a program to make agriculture independent and prosperous at the expense of industry's monopoly of the commodity and labor markets.[23]

7. *The Negro.* Another dangerous question ably discussed in a long article ["The Negro in the South," 432—77] by the editor, Professor Couch. Although Professor Couch sets forth accurately and fearlessly the economic, political, and social condition of the Negro, he too has no program for the improvement of this race. His zeal is noble, at times lachrymose, but it is not precisely responsible to shed tears unless one is prepared to do something for the pitiable object. Professor Couch is aware that the Negro problem overlaps the white-tenant problem; that both problems are economic problems; but not that the economic problem is a political problem. There is the other problem of the reformers who are anxious to have Negroes sit by them on street-cars, but are loath to devise a program whereby they may purchase land; nor have I any sympathy with reformers who are agitated about social equality, for there has never been social equality anywhere, there never will be, nor ought there to be. Every class and race should get what it earns by contributing to civilized life. (For that reason the American capitalist class, having added nothing to civilization, is an inferior class.) There will be no practical solution to the race question (as a problem it is inherently insoluble and ought to be, like all social problems in ultimate terms) until Southern agriculture, by means of politico-economic action, recovers its independence; that alone will destroy the lynching-tension between the races by putting both races on an independent footing. Liberals like Professor Couch, who find no "justice" in Anglo-Saxon domination, have no precise picture of what should take its place: let us have "justice" and the devil take the hindmost. It is not a question of sentimental justice. I argue it this way: the white race seems determined to rule the Negro race in its midst; I belong to the white race; therefore I intend to support white rule. Lynching is a symptom of weak, inefficient rule; but you can't destroy lynching by *fiat* or social agitation; lynching will disappear when the white race is satisfied that its supremacy will not be questioned in social crises. To tempt the Negro to question this supremacy without first of all giving him an economic basis is sentimental and irresponsible. Since a majority of the Negroes are in the South, and a majority of these on the land, it is a matter of simple realism to begin

---

23. As a result of this charge, Couch wrote "An Agrarian Programme for the South," *AR* 3 (1934): 313—26, an appeasing essay that called for large-scale federal action to create utopian communities for Southern farm families.

the improvement of their condition as farmers. Improvement here depends upon the general improvement of agriculture, upon the rediscovery of the agrarian economy (which the Negro has never quite forgotten), the ground of a prosperity that should lead to his purchase of land. If abstract agitation against white supremacy would give way to concrete programs for the Negro, a great deal could be done for him; but not until then.[24]

8. *Lawlessness.* Professor H. C. Brearley,[25] in "The Pattern of Violence" [678–92], has written an invaluable study of crime in the Southern States. Mob violence and homicide are, of course, the two types of crime chiefly under discussion. Professor Brearley rightly places the origin of quick shooting in the South in the feudal spirit that the plantation system perpetuated in America. This spirit to a large extent survives, but the code of honor that once gave it dignity, prescribing the kinds of grievance that justify killing and setting limits to the modes, has disappeared; we get plain murder in place of the duel.[26] Once may conclude, on the basis of Professor Brearley's argument, that the feudal conception of personal integrity, while it remains, has been overlaid with a middle-class social pattern. In 1878 *The Code of Honor,* an astonishingly late defense of the formal duel, published in Charleston, asserted that "the leading and most rancorous enemies of the Code of Honor are the materialistic Puritan sceptics" [686]. The code of honor set little value upon mere human life; it tended to dignify life with a rigid conception of its ideal integrity, without which it is worthless. (It may be remarked that the modern business man is not sensitive to attacks upon his ethical methods if they are profitable.) Of lynching Professor Brearley has no "explanation,"[27] but it has steadily declined since 1889, that is until 1930.[28] The

---

24. Of these and other racist remarks made by Davidson, Tate, and Owsley in their *American Review* articles, Sterling A. Brown (1901–89), the African-American poet who first achieved fame during the 1930s, has observed, "It is to be expected that the die-hards should interpret Negro aspirations to democracy as incendiarism" ("Count Us In," in Rayford W. Logan, ed., *What the Negro Wants* [Chapel Hill, 1944], 323–24, 324).

25. H. C. Brearley (1893–?) was a sociology and psychology professor at Clemson Agricultural College.

26. On the idea of honor see Bertram Wyatt-Brown, *Southern Honor: Ethics and Behavior in the Old South* (New York, 1982).

27. Tate missed Brearley's explanation: the absence of equitable law and order and the presence of white racism toward African Americans. After the Civil War, Brearley wrote, "social and governmental disorganization combined with race prejudice to justify and greatly extend the custom" ("Pattern of Violence," in Couch, ed., *Culture in the South,* 679).

28. Brearley, "Pattern of Violence," 691–92. W. Fitzhugh Brundage, author of *Lynching in the New South,* has confirmed that "the general outlines of his [Brearley's]

recent outburst of lynching in the South, which is not noticed in this article, is probably due to three factors: Communist agitation, which deludes the Negro into believing that he can better his condition by crime; general economic fear and instability taking the form of mob violence; and outside interference in the trials of accused Negroes. Professor Brearley points out that were it not for the new violence of industrial warfare, the end of which cannot yet be seen, there would be a sound hope for the disappearance of mob violence in the South.

9. *Miscellaneous*. Five articles remain; they round out the comprehensive scope of an invaluable and fascinating book. Dr. Edwin McNeill Poteat, Jr.,[29] writes a brief history of religion in the South [48–69], forecasting towards the end of his paper its future. Southern religion, he says, is still on the whole deeply conservative, adhering, in spite of developments elsewhere of liberal Protestantism, to the strict separation of the natural and supernatural realms. There are, for example, in the South only seven percent of the American Unitarian Churches and thirteen percent of the two thousand Christian Science Churches. Fundamentalism, fortunately (this is not Dr. Poteat's view) still reigns.[30] The South as a whole remains stolidly skeptical of the social mission of the church, putting its emphasis upon individual salvation. There is indeed a great need of religious rejuvenation in the South. Dr. Poteat hopes that it will take a Liberal direction: the historical background of his discussion is unexceptional, but his plea for the future savors slightly of rotarian Protestantism. Mrs. Ula Milner Gregory's[31] essay on "The Fine Arts" [270–98] has the hopeful spirit and a little more than the usual vulgarity of female missionary zeal: "Evidence of a country's love of painting is generally found in the number and size and quality of the country's museums" [279]. Again: "The art schools of the South constitute another important factor in the improvement of the art situation" [283]. On the whole this essay is

---

argument still stand the test of time." If his "specific numbers may be open to question, the pattern he describes is not. During the 1890s lynchings peaked both in the nation and in the South and then declined fitfully until the late 1910s when the number rose again. During the 1920s lynchings either became exceptionally rare, as in most Upper South states, or else became infrequent, as in Georgia and Mississippi" (Brundage to T. A. Underwood, 2 Sept. 1993, letter in possession of editors). See also Edward L. Ayers, *The Promise of the New South: Life after Reconstruction* (New York, 1992), 155–59, 495–97.

29. Poteat headed the Southern Commission on Interracial Cooperation.

30. Tate's own views appear in "Remarks on the Southern Religion," his contribution to *ITMS*.

31. Ula Milner Gregory (1902–84?) was a Radcliffe-trained art critic.

evidence of the disorder of modern society that permits well-meaning persons to convert art into a "cause" and to devote their lives to something that they do not understand. Mr. Allen H. Eaton,[32] however, discussing "The Handicrafts" [299–318], brings to that subject a distinctly superior insight; he is aware that the "higher" arts historically stem from the home-crafts; he pleads for the preservation of the remains of these arts in the South. Foundations, money, museums will exterminate them; their sole hope of survival lies in the restoration of the agricultural, rural society and the dignity of local life. (The Bayeux tapestry was not produced for a museum or subsidized by a foundation.) In one of the best descriptive essays in the volume, Mr. Edd Winfield Parks[33] outlines the rise and position of the city in Southern life [501–18]. He warns us that generalizations are difficult, that urbanization may be only skin-deep; yet the commercial and banking city has come to occupy, in Southern life and economy, a place similar to that occupied by the North before 1860. In "The Southern Heritage" [1–23], Professor Charles W. Ramsdell[34] reviews the entire history of the South; the discussion is intelligent and informed; but his conclusion has some of the facile characteristics of Charles A. Beard's tripod: there is the mechanical prophecy of more and better machine civilization, but not much effort at historical insight.

This brings to a close my summary of a book that is epoch-making in its field: it will doubtless remain for a generation a point of departure for future discussion. Although Uncle Sam's other province is amenable to no definition as a living fact, it remains by will or inertia outside the essence of Americanism. The question of the South for the future can be put into simple terms: Since the great industrial system of the North has been checked in its "progress" and must retrench for a new start, or even face a permanent stabilization at some point short of infinite profit and efficiency, what is left for the Liberal generation of the South to imitate? It can no longer imitate the North of the last decade which has ceased to exist: catching up with the North no longer means unlimited expansion of industry. Mr. Broadus Mitchell, I believe, stands alone in wishing to bring the Southern factory and financial system to the chaos that has overtaken the North; this moral heroism, which finds a good-in-itself in solving the appalling difficulties of

---

32. The former Oregon legislator Allen H. Eaton (1878–1962) joined the Russell Sage Foundation.

33. The English professor Edd Winfield Parks (1906–68) received his training at Vanderbilt.

34. Charles William Ramsdell (1877–1942) taught history at the University of Texas.

industrialism, will leave Mr. Mitchell's weaker contemporaries cold. But the writing is plain on the wall: catching up with the North has come definitely to mean restriction of industrial competition and a resulting stabilization of the system. If the Southern industrial system were stabilized at this moment, the South would remain a predominantly agricultural region.

Now what is the obvious, common-sense moral of this situation? It is that the sixty percent of the population on the land must receive the first attention, not because, being noble farmers, they deserve it, but because the well-being of the State requires that its foundation, which is production on the land, must be sound. Our "realistic" friends, the Liberals, get history to tell them what it is possible to do; it is invariably what they themselves want done. And what they want done is precisely what the drift of events will bring them. The morality of economic determinism is a kind of Pecksniffery that is at last intolerable: it is a rationalization of industrial power that has killed the political impulse.

The weakest discussion in "Culture in the South" is the essay on politics, but it is not Mr. Milton's weakness alone; his temerity in accepting that subject merely exposed him to an attack which the book as a whole equally deserves. Professor Couch in his Preface likewise betrays the general paralysis of the political sense. Without the new industrial wealth, says he, we could not have the universities; without the universities we could not study the problems of industrial wealth. I leave that syllogism without comment. Southern industrialism is the tin can rattling on the tail of the academic dog. And what shall we do about this magnificent piece of historical commentary: "This position [of the modern Agrarians] is a long step backward from that of the agrarians of the nineties who held, in general, that both industry and agriculture could be and must be organized to serve legitimate human purposes" [vii]. The Populists held it very much "in general"; and many Englishmen held "in general" that Mary of Scotland's head should not be cut off, but it is a sad fact that it was. The Southern Liberal can *hold* almost anything for *legitimate human purposes* which presumably will be announced some day after the social scientists have *studied* society long enough to find out what they are.

Meanwhile the legitimate human purpose of the Southern farmer, tenant and landlord, is to get enough to eat in the first place, and in the second, having been fed, to dictate the political terms of his well-being. It is a simple matter of fact that the social-science approach to the farm is actuated by the desire, however unconscious, to teach the farmer how to be a good consumer of industrial commodities; this is called improving him and getting him into the stream of progress. Although Professor Couch weeps for the poor-white, he proposes, so far as I can see, to do nothing but study him.

There is a plain program for the South, and it is a program for all regions of western culture where the majority of the people are on the land and where there is enough common patriotism left to grapple with the future of orderly civilization. Either by legislation or by revolution, in those regions where the land supports most of the people, the power must pass to those people. The basis of this program for the South is contained in Mr. Clarence Poe's article in this book ["The Farmer and His Future," 319–43]. To Mr. Poe's suggestions should be added the regional program of Professor Vance: future Southern industries should rise where the raw materials are most easily available. It is an absurd criticism of the Agrarians to suppose that they would destroy the factories; it is rather that the people must be allowed to dictate what they want to have made in the factory. Moreover, if primary subsistence were the basis of the farm, the land would not only be able to dictate its factory needs, it would be in a position to thwart the factory-migration to the places of cheap labor. If in the South there were—as there is in France—a sound subsistence-farming, the cheap labor market of the capitalist would tend to narrow; his profits would decrease, his political power diminish; and the factory worker, hard to lure from the land, and threatening momently to return to it, could dictate his own terms. Whatever the solution to the problem of wage-slavery may be in the North, or in hopelessly industrialized nations like England, the agrarian solution most easily presents itself to the South. It is a single solution for the farm and the factory worker: prosperity on the land—which does not mean a big dole from industry (i.e., government) to be collected into the pocket of industry again. It means the technique of making a living on the land.

The enormous difficulties of such a program are apparent in every essay in "Culture in the South"; yet eventually the program cannot be so difficult as none at all. That is the dilemma of the South: shall we drift Liberally or shall we take the present situation in hand? With notable exceptions, this notable symposium proposes to study and drift. As far as "culture" is concerned, few of the contributors suspect the existence of anything better than the culture of the foundation, the classroom, and the museum: to this extent, perhaps, culture in the South has been middle-westernized. To possess a concrete image of a living society in which certain civilized qualities may be enjoyed by all classes is to be cultivated; without this, abstract improvements and benefits reduce a people to the barbarism of learning a new technique of living day by day. Agriculture in the past has supplied us with our civilization, and the civilized qualities that survive come remotely from the land. This sense of the history of America, and distantly of Europe, has almost disappeared; the parochialism of the industrial era has taken its place. This latest voice from the South shows, I fear, that she is backward with a vengeance.

Index

THE PUBLICATIONS OF THE

SOUTHERN TEXTS SOCIETY

An Evening When Alone: Four Journals of Single Women in the South, 1827–67
Edited by Michael O'Brien

Louisa S. McCord: Political and Social Essays
Edited by Richard C. Lounsbury

Civilization and Black Progress:
Selected Writings of Alexander Crummell on the South
Edited by J. R. Oldfield

Louisa S. McCord: Poems, Drama, Biography, Letters
Edited by Richard C. Lounsbury

Soldier and Scholar: Basil Lanneau Gildersleeve and the Civil War
Edited by Ward W. Briggs Jr.

Louisa S. McCord: Selected Writings
Edited by Richard C. Lounsbury

A Southern Practice: The Diary and Autobiography of Charles A. Hentz, M.D.
Edited by Steven M. Stowe

The Simms Reader: Selections from the Writings of William Gilmore Simms
Edited by John Caldwell Guilds

The Southern Agrarians and the New Deal: Essays after "I'll Take My Stand"
Edited by Emily S. Bingham and Thomas A. Underwood